WORKS WONDERS

To the two Douggies and Tommy, who helped me to find the right road.

WORKS WONDERS

Rallying and Racing with
BMC, Rootes and Chrysler

MARCUS CHAMBERS

MOTOR RACING PUBLICATIONS LTD
Unit 6, The Pilton Estate, 46 Pitlake, Croydon CR0 3RY, England

First published 1995

British Library Cataloguing in Publication Data
A catalogue record card for this book is available from the British Library

ISBN 0 947981 94 2

Printed in Great Britain by
Hartnolls Limited, Bodmin, Cornwall

Contents

Foreword

I first met Marcus Chambers when I joined the fringe of the BMC works team as a navigator with John Sprinzel and I got to know him as a warm, avuncular figure, both astute in his thinking and warm in his appreciation of the civilized things in life – like starred restaurants in the *Guide Michelin*.

His qualities became even more evident when I took over from him at BMC because I found he had honed a marvellous group of mechanics into a team which was the foundation on which we built during the Sixties. Marcus' ability to choose people is perhaps best reflected in the fact that I can't remember any significant staff changes during the whole time I spent at Abingdon.

When Marcus won the London-to-Sydney Marathon with the Hunter, I was on the event as an official and was glad to see the old magic at work once again. I know that his Rootes-Chrysler days were less happy than those at Abingdon, but I'm glad that he has included them in this major expansion of his earlier book because they complete the story of his competition career. The period that career covered now enjoys historic status among enthusiasts who seem attracted to it in increasing numbers. I hope and believe they will enjoy reading Marcus' book because it will give them some sense of the unique atmosphere of those times, when a measure of professionalism had been brought to bear on what until then had been an essentially amateur sport but had not been allowed to corrupt it.

The sport has changed dramatically since then, not always for the better, and whilst we may stand in awe at the technology and the levels of performance achieved today, there seems to be a growing disenchantment with some of the sleazier side-effects. Not surprising, perhaps, that there is considerable longing for the simpler and less costly forms of motorsport of the Fifties and Sixties.

Like Marcus, I'm grateful that (largely due to him) I was able to experience those days at first hand. I'd like to thank him for the memories of those times that his book has sharpened for me.

STUART TURNER

Preface

We are glad to be allowed this opportunity of expressing our gratitude to the men (and women) behind-the-scenes who have done so much to make our successes in International rallying possible.

It has been said of the RAF in the last war that for every man who flew the 'planes, at least 10 men and women toiled devotedly for long hours on the ground without any hope of glory and with little reward, except the satisfaction which comes from doing a good job and the knowledge that 'their' pilot had the best backing humanly possible.

This same comment can be made with equal truth about International rallying today. When a team wins a big 'classic' rally outright, the press makes much of the drivers, but sheds little or no limelight on the mechanics who built the cars, the men who shrewdly planned the operation and the tireless support party, whose hard work under difficult conditions has often brought back the possibility of success when failure seemed inevitable.

We are sure that this book will do much to place in its true light the vital contribution to the BMC rally team's successes made by Douggie Watts, Tommy Wellman, Douggie Hamblin and the other wonderful boys in the competitions department down at Abingdon, but we suspect that it does not throw enough light upon Marcus Chambers himself, the principal architect of those successes.

A short biographical note on Marcus might read something like this:

CHAMBERS, Marcus Mordaunt Bertrand.
Born August 8, 1910. Married, two sons, two daughters. Educated Stowe School and France. Engaged in motor trade, 1931-39. Served with Coastal Forces, RNVR, 1939-46. Senior maintenance engineer with Overseas Food Corporation, Tanganyika, 1949-52. Estate manager with Colonial Development Corporation, British Honduras, 1952-54. Competition Manager, British Motor Corporation, 1954-61. Service manager with Appleyard Group from 1961. Member of BRDC (10th at Le Mans, 1938) and BMRMC (chief mechanic in the HRG racing team, 1947-48).

Such a note briefly shows that Marcus had a flair for organization, was a first-class driver and a good engineer. It cannot, however, give a complete picture of the man himself. Marcus was affectionately known to us as 'Chubby', alias the 'Poor Man's Neubauer'. Both had been successful racing drivers in their youth; both inclined to 'tubbiness' in later years owing to their liking for good food and better wine, upon which they were great experts; both were genial men with a sense of humour, with whom, however, it was dangerous to trifle upon professional matters. Finally, both were great Competition Managers in their various fields.

Each team driver will certainly have his own impressions of Marcus. To us, he was like a favourite uncle – the man who did everything possible to make our path easy, who was happy in victory and sympathetic in defeat but, above all, the man to whom we could turn in a crisis, knowing that it would be dealt with swiftly and efficiently.

To Marcus and to everyone down at Abingdon we would like to say yet again – "Thank you for all your help. We have only tried to drive the cars as well as you have built, prepared and supported them."

PAT MOSS and **ANN RILEY** (*née* WISDOM)
Ladies' European Rally Champions, 1958 and 1960

John Aidan Hastings Gott, MBE GM

an appreciation

In 1955, when John was appointed BMC Rally Team Captain, he brought with him a wealth of experience that was learnt the hard way. Driving his own HRG on the Alpines, and O'Hara Moore's Frazer Nashes on the Liège-Rome-Liège and other European events, he knew what it meant to have his car break down or run out of petrol when well-placed, to fall asleep at the wheel and crash when exhausted beyond measure. He also savoured the rewards of perseverance in winning two Alpine *Coupes* for penalty-free runs.

Born in 1913, John made the police force his career and, at the time of his appointment (part-time) to BMC, was Chief Police Superintendant at Hatfield. After 13 years there, he was appointed Chief Constable of Northamptonshire, in 1960.

Rally drivers, like most people who indulge in dangerous pastimes, will never admit that courage is part of their character. John was no exception, but incidents in his war career showed that he had courage of a rather special sort.

During the London Blitz in 1941, he was awarded the George Medal when, as a junior Inspector, he and two other men tunnelled into the debris of a bombed house to rescue the occupants. The citation in the *London Gazette* describes how John burrowed into the shattered bricks and timber, found a man and: "...took on his shoulders the weight of the debris." He and his colleague tunnelled to rescue a second man despite being surrounded by falling rubble and exposed to leaking gas.

This episode may well have encouraged him to join the Royal Air Force and become a navigator in Bomber Command. It was not long before his consideration and sheer courage were once again demonstrated. In April 1945, aircraft on the airfield at East Kirkby were being bombed when one exploded. Several men were killed or injured and the fire spread rapidly to three other bombers. John was quickly on the scene with other men as bombs on all four aircraft started to explode.

There were further casualties, including John's fellow officer, but he proceeded to remove the injured to safety and to extinguish the fires burning on the tyres of the loaded bomb trollies. He was the last to leave the scene of the carnage. Six men were decorated for their gallantry, including John, who was awarded the MBE.

He had nothing to prove and everything to give. He shared his rally experiences with anyone who would listen, and if you were sensible you listened very carefully. He knew about the pounding of a rally car over the unmade roads of the Alps and its effect on every component. He knew only too well the insidious effect of fatigue on the crew. John's advice in the early days of the team set the standards which were to produce the most successful rally organization in the world.

Before each event, he produced copious notes for the benefit of each crew member. These were based firstly on his own experiences on the roads of the Alps and later on, as more budget became available, on the results of recces. Each section of the rally was graded and colour-coded to give an idea of its severity, together with warnings of level-crossings, obscure turns and other hazards. On the rare occasions when a car was damaged because the crew had ignored his warnings, the wrath of John and Marcus was awesome, and sometimes terminal for that driver's association with BMC.

John's advice was sought by everyone, and there were times during a rally when I wondered how he could concentrate on his own effort whilst dispensing help and encouragement to so many people. He had numerous friends. Many a time at a control there would be a happy reunion with an official or an ex-competitor who would slap him on the back and launch into a delighted chat. However, when the pressure was on, John's greeting was brief and afterwards his disappointment would show.

He was a stickler for important detail and had an incredible memory. These were really the only places where the policeman showed through the rally driver. For rough and desperate sections like the Gavia or the Croce Domini, John's pace notes were in his head, and apart from being reminded of the hazards spelt out in his own notes, he preferred to judge the corners himself. He would arrive at high speed in a village square in the middle of the night and unerringly take the obscure turn which I had been trying to spot. After each event he would painstakingly type out a detailed narrative report, which described every incident and any piece of knowledge which could be useful on the next event. There were comments on the car, the route, the weather – everything. Where criticism could be constructive, there was plenty, and this included himself and the co-driver! For the 1958 Alpine, his report ran to 36,000 words. No wonder his articles in *Autosport and Safety Fast* were both the most factual and eagerly read.

John was a kind and thoughtful man who understood rally drivers and mechanics. On the occasions when we met up with the team there would be concern and advice for those with problems, real happiness for the crews who were going well, always a tactical talk with Marcus, and a cheerful, encouraging chat with the mechanics. A delightful example of John's thoughtfulness was on the 1958 Monte when we were leaving the Vosges village where we had been given shelter after ditching the Wolseley 1500. Thick snow had fallen and a lady with her shopping basket was standing at the roadside. John stopped to give her a lift. She sat on the back seat and John was soon throwing the car about on the hard-packed snow. As we slid to a stop in the next village, she slowly clambered out, gave us a weak smile and a very quiet "Merci". "I hope she enjoyed that" I said. "She'll remember it" said John.

On the road his concentration was absolute and he talked very little. On the tight sections he expected to be told every kilometre how many seconds he was ahead or behind schedule. On really rough sections on loose surfaces – and there were plenty of those in the Fifties – John was in his element, and very fast. His technique was fierce rather than smooth, with arms crossing on the wheel, fast and hard gearchanges and heavy braking. He was a physically powerful man and he used his strength. But such forceful driving was only used when necessary as he was mechanically sensitive and felt for the car when it had to be caned. When the sweat began to run down his face, our supply of boiled sweets would be readied and fed to him at frequent intervals. His only remarks would be "That's where an Alfa went over the edge" or "There was a Porsche blazing there in '47", as if I was finding the whole thing short of drama!

He would become very impatient with drivers of rally cars who would not pull over when he came up behind them, and his technique was to make them drive faster and faster. We would be right up to the limit and the car ahead eventually way beyond it.

Victims of this treatment included a Ford Taunus which finally burst a tyre on a rock in Yugoslavia, and Tak's works Mercedes, which went much faster on the Croce Domini than it really wanted to – and consequently split its fuel tank. After passing his adversary, the red mist would clear, John would give a broad smile and it was business as usual.

He was generous in handing over the wheel, and most of the driver changes were planned in advance. However, I was reminded on one occasion that a certain responsibility went with the job. On the third night of the '56 Liège-Rome-Liège I drove out of Grenoble with John on the maps. After about half-an-hour, I became worried and slowed. "What's wrong?" he asked. "I think we're on the wrong road" I replied. "Look!" said John, "If we're on the wrong road, that's my problem. If we're late at the next control, that's your problem!" That was a typical JG remark: brief, not unkind and to the point. (It was the right road and we were on time at the next control.)

He loved driving sportscars. Saloons were tolerated, but if Marcus wanted him to drive a Morris Minor or a Wolseley 1500, John did his best. The former was our mount in the '57 Tulip and John was so dispirited at his times on the special tests that he asked me to take the wheel for the Berchesgarten hill-climb. When I was unable to do any better, he relaxed and we enjoyed the scenery for the rest of the rally. When the wheels became loose, he lost patience and tightened them so hard that on one occasion the mechanics pointed out that every one was cracked. Maybe a wheel had come off in earlier rally days; he was often giving the MGA and Healey nuts a good thump with the hammer.

He did a great deal of racing at Club level. HRG, Twin-Cam MGA and his famous Healey, SMO 746, were meticulously prepared and driven in a smooth style completely different from his rally technique. John also took part in light-hearted night navigation rallies and could be seen searching for hidden marshals with typical thoroughness. By tramping through the undergrowth at high speed he could make them reveal their presence just before they were crushed!

If you add to all these activities his place on the RAC Competitions Committee, his work as a senior RAC Steward and his efforts to improve the whole status of motorsport, you will begin to realize that he was a dedicated all-round enthusiast.

When he died, at the wheel of his Healey at Lydden in 1972, we all lost a good friend, and the sport one of its true champions.

CHRIS TOOLEY

Introduction

More than 40 years have passed since the day I took up my position as the Competition Manager of the MG Car Company, and it is almost 33 years since the publication of *Seven Year Twitch*, the book in which I recalled my BMC years from 1954 to 1961. When I wrote it I thought it was a complete story because when I left to pursue a new career path I had no idea that within three years I would once again become involved in competition management.

In recent years the growth of interest in what are now referred to as Historic racing and rally cars, and the events in which they competed, has been both spectacular and, to me, especially gratifying, and I am sure that it explains why so many people have been keen to acquire a copy of my book, which has long been out of print.

When I approached my new publisher about a possible reprint I was told that something more than a straight reprint was called for. Certainly, '*Twitch*' could form the basis of a new book, provided that suitable amendments were made to the text appropriate to the passage of time, but it was also important to add the story of my return to competition management for Rootes and Chrysler, as well as to add certain material relevant to my BMC years which had been excluded from my earlier book.

This, therefore, is a considerably expanded story, and this time it really is a complete one as far as my experiences of competition management are concerned – and I leave it to the reader to decide which of my two spells in the metaphorical driving seat I found the more enjoyable (it will not be a difficult task!). As well as preparing the new material and amending where necessary the old, I have taken the liberty of including the introductory words which Pat Moss and Ann Riley (*née* Wisdom) kindly provided for my earlier book, not because of the nice things they said about me, but because of the tribute which they so rightly paid to my hard-working and loyal staff at BMC, who were such a magnificent team.

One item which has been omitted is the Preface by John Gott, MBE GM, that wonderful man who contrived to be Captain of the BMC rally team from 1955 to 1961 at the same time as bearing the responsibilities of a senior 'copper', ultimately as Chief Constable of Northamptonshire. John's untimely death whilst racing in 1972 was a tragic loss both to motorsport, where his wisdom was in such demand, and to law and order, where his policy of firmness with fairness set the highest standards and must have been an inspiration to his contemporaries. I am more than pleased, therefore, to have included a tribute to him, for which I am grateful to Chris Tooley, who spent so many hours alongside John as they tamed the rally routes of Europe.

I am also delighted that Stuart Turner, who succeeded me at BMC and guided the Corporation to its greatest successes during the years which followed, was happy to provide the Foreword to my book of recollections. Finally, an explanation of the title, *Works Wonders*. Those two words, I think, sum up very neatly what it was all about: working with a wonderful bunch of people – drivers, navigators, mechanics and others – comprising a works team and through whose combined efforts we really did contrive from time to time to work wonders!

I hope through this book the reader will recapture some of the unique atmosphere of a long-gone but never-to-be-forgotten era of motorsport.

Charlton, Oxon, 1995   **MARCUS CHAMBERS**

CHAPTER 1

What's it all about?

"Many people ask why grown men and women wander about the mountains in the middle of the night when the sane ones are in bed."

Four o'clock in the morning. The place? The entrance to a small village called Ste Vallier, in France's Alpes Maritimes. Some mechanics, a pressman, a couple of enthusiasts and a competition department manager stand waiting and cocking an ear in the direction of the dark mountain mass which looms above them.

They are waiting for the first sight or sound of the car which, barring a slip, is about to win the 22nd International Alpine Rally outright for Great Britain. Suddenly headlights shine out on the road above and start their rapid descent of the lower lacets, sweeping the hairpins as they turn. The cars are just completing the final and decisive test on the famous Quatre Chemins circuit. "Wrong headlights" one of the mechanics comments. Another car comes in sight over the flank of the mountain. "That's a Healey" several people shout at once. The well-known roar of a works Austin-Healey 3000 being driven with the usual Morley precision can be heard coming down through the gears for the hairpins. Rounding the last left-hand sweep onto the main road there is no doubt, and the car is flagged into the space allotted on the right-hand side of the road.

"Did you do it clean?" is the first question. "Yes, with 57 seconds to spare" says the navigator. The tension leaves everyone straightaway and they all get to work with a will, checking the car's equipment.

"Headlights? OK. Side and tail? OK. Indicators? OK. Stoplights? OK. Horn? OK. Screenwiper? OK. Foglights? OK." As each item is checked, the navigator methodically ticks them off in his own log. The foreman mechanic, having made a quick inspection of the car's running gear, slams the navigator's door and gives the hardtop a slam with a final "OK". The big Healey bursts into song and the Morley twins are off to the final control at Cannes. The support crew know that their main job is finished and that their efforts have helped to get a car through to the highest honour – an 'outright' in a great classic.

Many people ask why grown men and women wander about the mountains in the middle of the night when the sane ones are in bed. Why drive for hours on end without rest or meals? Why take risks with impossible averages on roads which most tourists shun? Because it's a challenge; it's adventure, with the unexpected just round the corner; and it furnishes the ingredients which so many young men and women are looking for in life.

Some sportsmen battle against the elements; others against the mountain peaks; yet others try to outwit game. The rally driver competes against the organizers who dictate the time and the place, but he also has to contend with the elements in every form, from tropical heat to arctic blizzards. It pays to be fit; endurance is at a premium on these events.

From its early days as pure sport, International motorsport has become Big Money; as the industry has grown, so has the sport. Participation therein is vital to the leading manufacturers and the nations of Europe. Competitive motorsport furthers national prestige, and makers' reputations internationally and at home. If a manufacturer is continually successful, not only do the models with which it competes derive favourable publicity, but the marque as a whole benefits – provided the publicity departments concerned use their opportunities to the full. Back in the Fifties this was shown to be true in the case of Jaguar at Le Mans, Mercedes-Benz in Grand Prix racing, and MG in record-breaking and sportscar racing.

The field was immense and no manufacturer could afford to participate in all the available events, so a choice had to be made with a view to getting the best return for the money spent and in the field which was most likely to influence sales.

Technical developments which have been stimulated by participation in motoring competitions are widespread, and Grand Prix racing has contributed a great deal in that sphere, but over the years, developments derived from rallying have tended to influence not so much design as the improvement of existing models. The weak links are found more quickly when machines are driven past the limit of the ordinary driver and even past anything that can be expected of the works test driver within the normal line of his work. International competition is like the refining of precious metal; the best is tested in the fire and becomes pure metal.

[Publisher's note – The remainder of this Chapter has been reproduced in the words as the author wrote them in 1962, even though many aspects of the government and structure of motorsport have since changed quite considerably, as have some of the categories of car for which major events are staged. For example, the CSI in due course gave way to the FISA, which in turn has ceased to exist as a body within the framework of the FIA itself, while many changes have been made to the rules covering the categorization of production cars in motorsport. What follows, therefore, is a reminder of the organizational structure as it existed at the time of the author's period with BMC, and of the regulations under which he and his contemporaries in competitions management went about their business at that time.]

Some misunderstanding exists as to the differences between the duties of such bodies as the Royal Automobile Club, the *Federation Internationale de l'Automobile* and the *Commission Sportive Internationale*, afterwards referred to by their initials. These are the bodies which control the sport. Any nation intending to participate in motorsport internationally must belong to the *FIA*. Each nation must appoint one of its own automobile clubs to represent it and to supervize the conduct of the sport in its own territories. As a result of this system, the RAC represents Great Britain and many of the Commonwealth countries, but unfortunately that representation is not proportional to the number of Commonwealth countries promoting events. Each nation has the right to send a representative to sit on the *CSI* provided that nation is actively engaged in motorsport. Various sub-committees exist which make recommendations as to the conduct of different branches of the sport. The regulations which govern International Record attempts for speed and distance are also controlled by these bodies.

The events for which international participation is approved appear on the International Sporting Calendar. National clubs must apply for suitable dates on the calendar in respect of those events that they intend to promote and for which they desire International status. This system tends to prevent the clashing of major events but in practice some adjustment is often made after the calendar is published.

As the rules which govern motorsport were first drawn up at the beginning of the century to regulate a sport for which there was then no precedent, much of the phrasing was copied from the already established horse-racing rules. The titles of the officials and the names of the enclosures bear witness to this fact as we find expressions such as Clerk of the Course, Stewards of the Meeting, Judges and Paddocks are still in the regulations at the present day. However, if the rules for racing and record-breaking have changed little since their inception, those for the rally crews have been drastically revised in the last few years.

The object of a rally of the International Rally Championship variety is to try both the car and the driver to the limit and to demonstrate their performance against other competing cars. Every part of the car is tested under the severest conditions, which will vary in difficulty from rally to rally. The minimum distance for the course is fixed at 1,500km (930 miles), although many are much longer and some exceed 3,000 miles. The course may be over any class of road from trunk roads to tracks hardly suitable for cars at all. The schedule speed is set to make it difficult to have time either to repair the cars or for the crews to rest. Those sections which run through populated areas are usually the easiest and their speed is deliberately controlled so that other road users suffer little inconvenience. Once the rally reaches the more desolate parts of Europe and the roads thread their way over the highest of the lesser-known mountain passes, the average speeds, which had been set at 37mph (60km/h) on the approach sections, become very nearly impossible, and in order to make it still more difficult to recapture lost time, the controls which regulate the passage of competitors are placed very much closer together. If several competitors find that they can maintain the average speeds which have been imposed without loss of marks for lateness, they will still be confronted with Special Sections, where the authorities have permitted the closing of the road to the public. These sections are then the subject of increased averages or may become speed hill-climbs.

In order to equalize the chances between cars of different size and type there is usually some inter-class formula, although the organizers may consider that the terrain offers equal opportunities to all by incorporating many fast downhill sections. The Alps, of course, are the happy playground of the rallyman.

The part of the International Sporting Code which deals with cars used in the International rallies is contained in Appendix J, and is headed General Regulations for Touring and Grand Touring Cars. It is of the greatest importance that entrants, designers and organizers should read and understand this section as so many bitter words have been used by people who have not taken the trouble to do this. It is in the interest of the entrant to know exactly what he is allowed to modify in his vehicle and as a result decide as to the category he will enter. He may also see a loophole in the regulations which he may use to his advantage in the event in question. He must, however, consider himself bound by the regulations and always ask himself if he has done all in his power to see that his car complies with them. Finally, a thorough knowledge of them will enable him to argue his case if the scrutineer appointed for the event is not enforcing the regulations correctly.

The designer should know these regulations so that he may produce cars which comply with their basic requirements to the best advantage. For example, it may sometimes be convenient to produce a car with an engine capacity which falls within a class which is not so keenly contested, just as it is sensible to make cars with the prescribed windscreen and fuel tank sizes. A recent regulation permits certain improvements in brakes. Changes such as this should encourage manufacturers to consider the adoption of the improvements as a standard fitting as they may well find that it has become compulsory within a year or so.

The organizers must study Appendix J from their own angle in so far as they are compelled by the *CSI* to organize their event according to the rules. Whilst most of the classic Touring Championship events retain their own character, they must have the observance of Appendix J in common with other events, even if only for its minimum requirements. Certain organizers have in the past attempted to ride roughshod over these regulations by putting their own interpretation upon them, but they have been overruled by the *CSI* in the end and have risked their right to promote a Championship event in the future.

The Touring car, as the series production saloon is called, must first be registered as to its specification with the National club, which in turn forwards the form on to the *FIA* in Paris. In order to qualify, the makers must certify that they have made over 1,000 cars of a similar type. If the cars have an engine larger than 1,000cc capacity the body must have four seats. The coachwork may be of a convertible type, but nothing makeshift or temporary is allowed and the windows must be of the wind-up or sliding type and not removable. Various cubic capacity classes are laid down, and the most popular are usually 850cc, 1,000cc, 1,600cc, 2,000cc, 3,000cc and above.

In addition to Touring cars we have Grand Touring cars for which I will quote the definition given in paragraph 264 of *Chapter IV – Group 3: Grand Touring cars:*

"Grand Touring cars are vehicles built in small series for customers who are looking for a better performance and/or a maximum comfort and are not particularly concerned about economy.

Such cars shall conform to a model defined in a catalogue and be offered to the customers by the regular sales department of the manufacturer. They must be recognized by the *FIA* according to the provisions of Article 265 below."

Art 265 states that to qualify as such, Grand Touring cars must have been produced at the minimum rate of 100 identical units as far as mechanical parts and coachwork are concerned in 12 consecutive months. Various sections deal with such things as steering lock, ground clearance, starting devices, capacity of fuel tanks, special coachwork, extra or alternative carburettors, size of windshield, mudguards, hoods, doors, rear windows and luggage trunk, and minimum weight. Most of these items are for safety or to prevent freakish cars being made which may have a good performance but little practical use.

As the Grand Touring car is eligible for long-distance races, such as Le Mans, and is having a greatly increased following, there is some sense in the regulations. The Grand Tourer of today is, in fact, the modern equivalent of the sportscar of 20 years ago. Its appearance is often greatly enhanced by the use of special coachwork which has a lower drag factor than the production model, but the total weight-saving is limited to a tolerance of not more than 5 per cent below the original.

If the maker of either the Touring car or the Grand Touring car should market a modification which improves the performance of the vehicle in question, such as raising the compression or changing the camshaft, he must make the qualifying number of cars all over again and re-register the model. This is the latest move by the *FIA* to stop makers listing extra items which they have no intention of selling and intend to use only on their competition cars. A few alternative items of equipment are allowed for Grand Touring cars and some extra items which do not help the performance are allowed for Touring cars. These include the following for Group 1 – Series Production cars: changes for comfort in the shape of better seats, lighting, alternative radiators and fuel tanks (if listed in advance), air filters, carburettors, battery, coil and distributor, plugs, petrol pump, silencer, gearbox (if the makers offer an alternative), shock absorbers, stronger wheels and size of tyre (provided it fits the same wheel), whilst certain improvements to the braking system may also be carried out.

This may sound a great deal more for a car which purports to remain in the standard class, but it is not so radical as might be supposed. Personally, I would like to see this Group define the cars as being 'exactly as delivered by the sales department of the manufacturer concerned to the customer'. The public would then feel that the cars which won classes in Group 1 were really comparable with their own. It would also give the Competition Manager some real basis for complaint when he presented the development department with the broken bits. However, whether any drivers could be found who would be brave enough to compete in some models as they came off the production line is a moot point! Brake-lining manufacturers would certainly have to develop a lining which would be equally effective when stone cold or red hot, and at present they show no inclination to do so.

The second Group, for Improved Touring cars, is for cars derived from Group 1, and in addition to the 18 items dealt with in Group 1 there are another seven permitted modifications, the most important being springs and 'finishing off'.

Any spring, whether in the valve mechanism, clutch or suspension, may be changed, but their number may not be increased and they must fit in the same place as the original without changing the spring mounting. This means that the performance of the engine, clutch and chassis may be improved to a marked extent by fitting stronger springs. In finishing off the parts the regulation allows machining and polishing and this can include lightening of parts and raising the compression by machining the head or the cylinder block. As it is not permitted to add any metal to any part, changing the basic shape of the parts is ruled out, but nevertheless, the astute tuner can make a Group 2 engine give nearly twice as much power as the original. As this is an expensive process it is usual to find most of the private entries in Group 1 and the factory entries in Group 2, but of late the two Groups have been amalgamated by the organizers and the private owner now finds himself at a disadvantage. From the foregoing it will be seen that in rallying it is as well to know the regulations and the Competition Manager must make a profound study of them.

In an average competition year there are 12 events which count toward the Touring Championship in which any driver can score points. At the same time, lady drivers may compete in this Championship for the Ladies' Cup which, by implication, gives the winner(s) the title of Ladies' European Rally Champion. Points for the Ladies' Championship are scored on a basis of competition between feminine crews, of which at least three must start in the event. As both the crew members in each car obtain equal points for their placing in General Classification and for their class, it is possible to have two male or female Champions at the end of the year. Each of the Championship events also has a separate *Coupe des Dames*, or ladies' prize, but this is nowadays secondary to the ambitions of the best ladies crews, who are after an outright win or at the worst a class place.

I have often been asked whether lady drivers are worth the trouble. The short answer is that they are no more trouble than male crews and quite often very much nicer to have around the place. There is no doubt that a couple of first-class lady drivers keep the team on its toes. The men feel they have a reputation to keep up and are perhaps a bit more chivalrous as a result. Please don't imagine that any of the girls take advantage of this situation, for any lady who is good enough to drive in a works team is quite capable of looking after herself before, during and after a rally!

Why have lady drivers? Because all top lady drivers at their best are as good as the best male crews, and at their worst they attract better publicity. Fortunately, I seem to have had the best and rather more than most of them at that. For the record, the combined efforts of the ladies who have driven for the British Motor Corporation during the time I was the Competition Manager produced four Ladies' European Rally Championships and one outright win in a Championship event, a share in five manufacturer's team prizes, nine class wins and 24 ladies' cups. The ladies, bless them – I wish I had had a lot more of them in the team.

Many of the 'mere males' ask me how they are to set about getting a place in a works team. The odds are very long, even if the driver shows considerable promise, for the simple reason that many come but few can be chosen. There are at the moment four British works teams which compete in Championship events and they field an average of three male crews and one ladies crew. A simple sum shows that there will be a maximum of just over 30 works drivers representing this country in an International rally. As the number of club members who have these aspirations runs into thousands, the odds are long against the individual enthusiast.

We, the Competition Managers, look at the National rally results in this country and remember the names of any crews who seem to be consistently successful. Experience has shown that pairs who always compete together produce the best results. This is not, however, the only requirement. The crew must have had continental experience, and they must be able to get enough time off to make reconnaissance runs, or 'recces' as they are called in the rally parlance. If the factory has a programme of six such events per year, the total time out of England may amount to as much as 10 weeks and sometimes more.

The best way to get continental rally experience is to crew on the Tulip Rally, which caters for the true amateur because it is an event which does not give prize money and so many of the best continentals stay away. Follow this up with one of the smaller French Internationals, which are short and inexpensive; also, the private owner is handicapped by the knowledge that it will be costly and inconvenient if he bends his own car. The unique atmosphere of a continental event has lost very little in the last few years, and in spite of increased hostility on the part of the French police there is much more freedom for enterprising driving than is wise in this country.

It is not good policy for the factory to change its crews very often, for they tend to improve as they get more experience of the model they drive, and it is unfair to import new blood at the same time as the factory cars get better. If the crews fall in with the team's policy the prospects of a good team spirit are excellent, but if they are frequently changed, that spirit, which is a secret of success, is noticeably absent.

Some years do not seem to produce the desired result: either the ascendance of the marque coincides with that of others, or the drivers are off-form due to inability to concentrate. Continental rally driving requires the undiluted effort of the drivers, the mechanics and the Competition Manager, and the total of their combined efforts must be enough to overcome that put in by another factory at the same time. This simple formula for success is not at all easy to attain, as so many varying factors are entailed.

CHAPTER 2

The organization

"I felt that we were now entitled to call the department by its proper title, the British Motor Corporation Competition Department..."

Before attempting to describe some of the more interesting events in which the British Motor Corporation's new competition department took part under my management, it will be as well to discuss its early history and to explain the organization which came into being after our rather faltering start.

During 1954, John Thornley, who was then the General Manager of the MG Car Company at Abingdon, received permission from his directors to re-open the competitions department which had been closed for many years. It is said that the closing of this and of the Austin Motor Company's racing department had stemmed from an agreement made between Lord Nuffield and the late Lord Austin to cease competing against each other in motorsport. After the Hitler war, however, the Austin Motor Company had sponsored participation in rallies and various long-distance endurance runs for the publicity value which these events were providing, whilst MG had assisted Major Goldie Gardner in his extremely successful International record attempts. So in effect the new policy gave official status to what was already the existing situation as well as permitting participation in races. A committee – originally known as the Nuffield Competition Committee – was formed, with John Thornley as its Chairman, to administer the funds made available and to draw up a programme.

By complete chance, in August 1954, after five years in East Africa and British Honduras, I had decided to resume my connection with motorsport and had written to my friend Jack Emmott at British Automotive Products to ask him if he could recommend any particular manufacturers I might approach. Jack was most helpful and sent me a list of companies which he thought might be useful; although few of them had much association with motorsport, I wrote to them all, and it was not long before I had a reply from John Thornley. He said: "By all means come along and see me so that we can have a talk, but there is really very little prospect of my having anything to offer you."

However, when I met John, he told me that the MG Car Company was about to resume racing and was also starting on a fairly ambitious programme of rallies. There would be a vacancy for a Competition Manager and I could be considered for the job, but he warned me that there were several other aspirants, some of whom were more experienced in team management than myself. The final decision would apparently be with the Board and S C H 'Sammy' Davis, who for some years had been acting as adviser on motorsport matters to the Austin Motor Company. I was very pleased to hear this as I had known Sammy before the war, when he had put Peter Clark and myself through our pit drill in one of the back streets of Le Mans. Sammy was a great believer in discipline, both in the pit and on the track, and had shown us how to do the job to such good effect that we managed to bring our privately-entered HRG into 10th place in General Classification at our first attempt. I didn't see Sammy for some time after meeting John Thornley, but when we did see each other again he knew all about the job and it was not long afterwards that my appointment was confirmed.

The next step was to find somewhere to live, so my wife Pat and I started house-hunting that very day. At the time I was working at Connaught's, near Guildford, where Rodney Clark had given me a job to tide me over, so to speak. I don't think Rodney felt I would be content with the rather insecure atmosphere which pervaded the place at that time, but I was grateful to him and his partner Ken MacAlpine for giving me time to find my feet in motorsport circles after so long an absence. My main duties at Connaught were to supervise the repair of a few obsolete privately-owned cars and to look out items belonging to the MacAlpine family's cars which had somehow become mislaid in the stores. I had not been there long enough to take root, so I left without regret, and Pat and I continued our house-hunting.

Luck was with us, and after inspecting some interesting derelicts and King John's Hunting Lodge, we found a very pleasant old brick cottage with a tile roof, and some fine beams within, at Drayton. The 'domestic offices' had been built on at the back in 1948, but the main part of the house was at least 160 years old. We clinched the deal on the spot, subject to the surveyor's report, and went off to chase the solicitors and the bank manager. Within a month we had moved into the new house, which was only two and a half miles from the MG factory. Unfortunately, the previous owners were waiting for their bungalow to be completed, so we had to move their furniture out of the back door while ours came in at the front. They were to be our neighbours for the next seven years, but this early crisis never spoilt a very happy relationship, and we were indeed blessed with pleasant neighbours in that village.

I had been working at MG's for some time before we moved into *Magpie Cottage* and had been allocated an office which was up a long flight of stairs at the top of the main office building. This was an advantage in some ways as my visitors usually arrived so out of breath as to be speechless for a while, which enabled me to take stock and remember their name! At best, I have a poor memory for names and at that time I had so many new ones to memorize that this 'breathing space' was most helpful.

The workshop for the competition cars was then in the old development shop, which later became MG's tool room. This shop had to house both the existing development work and the competition preparation until such time as the new block was completed at the north-west end of the factory. The old dynamometer test-bed was in the same place, this historical instrument having tested such engines as those used in the blown K3 Magnettes and in the Goldie Gardner record-breaking car in its various forms. The walls and the ceiling were marked with little craters and chips caused by flying connecting rods which had ventilated crankcases in those early days. This evidence brought home to me the wisdom of standing well clear of the side of an engine when it was turning at maximum revs on the test-bed!

On going to the 'factory in the orchard', as someone called it, one could not help being impressed with the enthusiasm and team spirit which animated everyone. Of course, John Thornley was the mainspring and his energy was infectious. When he first showed me round the works, we strode along with such speed that I had almost to trot to keep up with him, and I was treated to a running commentary as we went which amounted to a potted MG history. During the quick tour I was introduced to nearly all the key people, but at such a rate that I couldn't possibly remember all their names; in any case, most of them were known just by their christian name.

Amongst the most notable figures was Cecil Cousins, later to become Works Manager and at one time MG's Competition Manager. Cecil, a Berkshire man, knew his men so well that until 1961 there was never a strike in the factory. I was also introduced to Reg Jackson, subsequently chief inspector, and as such responsible for the appearance and performance of the product and all its components; Reg's staff road-tested every MG that was produced. Reg, too, had been in the old competition department with Cecil Cousins and Syd Enever, the designer, and both had many stories to tell of the old days when enthusiasm and improvization had so often to take the place of money. Syd's, of course, was a name which immediately brought to mind the astonishing string of records which the factory held in the International field.

The combined development and competition workshops were controlled by Alec Hounslow who, apart from a short spell with Squire Cars at Henley, had spent most of his working days at Abingdon. Alec had always been a close friend of Syd Enever's and they continued to work together on new projects. It was a rather delicate position in which I was placed as Alec had to serve two masters for the time being, and development work to his mind took precedence over competition work. To add to this complication, Alec was a racing man who had no time for rallies, and he disliked the complicated rules which at that time were very much in the melting pot.

On the credit side, the MG factory was isolated from the other factories of the newly formed British Motor Corporation, the creation of which had sparked off jealousy and petty criticisms between the Austin and Morris factions. Many of the staff were in positions which they had held for years, and naturally they resented having to take orders from the heads of newly formed departments who might have come from the previously rival factory. In time, of course, there would be a much closer integration, and the letters BMC subsequently made a considerable imprint on the motoring world.

The MG staff, meanwhile, had been almost unconscious of this strife and set about the job of building ever more cars with a dedicated fervour. The whole place was overcrowded, and a new block of buildings, which would add nearly a third to the floor area of the factory, was under construction. In this building would be located the new drawing office, the development and competition departments, the rectification shop, the paint shop, the despatch department and some stores. The service department was due for a move as well.

At this time the MG TD was just reaching the end of production, and its immediate replacement, the TF, was just starting. There was also talk concerning a new MG but, as yet, it had no announcement date, or even a name. The MG Magnette saloon was then in its primary form as the ZA, and the big four-cylinder Riley Pathfinder was also in production, the last of the RM-series 1½-litre Rileys having been built during the month in which I joined the firm; Riley cars had been made at Abingdon since the war.

On December 13, 1954, BMC's Deputy Managing Director, George Harriman, issued a directive to his publicity chief, Reg Bishop, to the effect that BMC were to get to the top in competitions and that the necessary money to achieve this end would be made available. The directive also stated that the present Nuffield Competition Committee would be dissolved and a new one formed, to be based at Abingdon and be chaired by John Thornley, the General Manager of MG. The new committee would include Reg Bishop, plus a suitable person from each of the Austin and Nuffield sides of the organization. The committee would be empowered to enter any BMC car, including Austin-Healeys, in any competition which they thought fit, or to assist private owners of such products to do so; they would not, however, deal with: (a) the MG programme already agreed, or (b) the racing activities of the Donald Healey Motor Company. Austin cars would be prepared at the experimental shop at Longbridge and all the others at Abingdon. The chief designer expressed a wish that the Longbridge shop should not be overburdened and that anything which was inconvenient to handle there should be passed on to Abingdon. A tentative ceiling figure was given for the budget, and the chief accountant was asked to institute a method of accounting.

On January 4, 1955, on John Thornley's suggestion, Mr Harriman nominated me as a member of the newly formed committee. I felt that we were now entitled to call the department by its proper title, the British Motor Corporation Competition Department, and I received permission to use this title on our new notepaper and inscribe it on the sides of our new racing-car transporter, which was being built to our design by Appleyard's of Leeds.

Before I took over, the Corporation had entered six cars for the 1955 Monte Carlo Rally; three of these were Magnettes, for which the crews had already been chosen, and three were Austin A90s from Longbridge. As far as racing was concerned, four MGs of a completely new type were being built, of which three had been accepted for Le Mans.

This plan was already in action, and whether it was a good one or not, there was very little I could do about it. The racing programme was sound, as it was based on the great experience which existed at the factory, but the rally programme was not backed up by the same experience, and to a certain extent was being influenced by drivers who were taking the opportunity to get into the team from the start. Rallies at this time were changing their pattern; sometimes the winner would be found by means of eliminating tests on the road and sometimes by the medium of speed and manoeuvring tests held at the finish. Organizers of the great classics, such as the Alpine and the Liège-Rome-Liège, scorned this type of elimination and relied instead upon an ultra-high speed schedule over difficult country to wear out both the car and its crew.

I did not feel that we had enough data to enter a full team in the Monte Carlo Rally with any real chance of success; it would have been wiser to have entered just one example of our various types in order to assess their potential. Although it would have been bad publicity to withdraw from the Monte Carlo Rally at this stage, if I had been able to forecast the form and the results I would certainly have urged that we scratched the team. None of our cars obtained even a class place and we came back to do some severe heart-searching. The Austin team had fared a little better than the Magnettes, but the best placed car was only 68th in General Classification, driven by Mrs 'Bill' Wisdom, whose daughter Ann was to make rally history a few years later.

To be fair to the drivers of the Magnettes in the 1955 Monte, the rear suspension was too hard and the power-to-weight ratio was poor. The rear springs had been stiffened and bound with cord in order to cope with the extra weight of the crews and spares; the crews consisted of three persons per car and we had carried too many spare parts, plus two spare wheels. The binding was removed at Ashford before the cars left England, but the roadholding was far from ideal. The power output of the ZA-type Magnette was about 60bhp and the cars weighed 21cwt without the extras. In addition to struggling with unsuitable cars, our drivers were not exactly in the top flight.

The blunt fact was that we had no cars capable of winning the Monte, or any other International rally. This had been suspected before the rally was run, and was discussed at a meeting held early in January. The suggestion of running cars in the Special Touring class received approval, and it was agreed that certain models were worthy of consideration for extensive development. I urged that an ideal specification be drawn up, using parts which were either available or about to be so. To this end, I suggested an improved MG Magnette fitted with the new twin-cam engine, disc brakes, 'knock-off' wheels, a close-ratio gearbox and a fuel tank for a range of 300 miles. As at that time it was necessary to manufacture 600 of a particular model in order to qualify for recognition by the *FIA*, as far as I know my suggestion never received any serious consideration, and the twin-cam engine took so long to develop for production that the problem of finding a suitable car was solved in other ways.

The best cars tend to attract the best drivers and we had little to attract the better British crews. Also, at this time there were very few first-class British rally crews available because the best of them were already with Sunbeam, Daimler, Triumph or Ford. My problem, therefore, was first to develop the right cars and then to recruit suitable drivers, at the same time ensuring that they would be backed-up by an efficient organization, capable of preparing the cars to suit the particular regulations for each event in which they were to compete.

The organization would also have to deal with travel bookings, exchange control regulations, passports and visas, hotels, and establishing contacts with our overseas agents. At that time these were few and far between and they carried little or nothing in the way of spare parts. Therefore it was necessary to take nearly all of our spares with us and we became accustomed to coping with every Customs form and regulation which officialdom could devise. But by degree we built up an office organization which could handle all these problems fairly competently. We started files and indexes for our vehicles, the drivers, the agents and likely hotels, in fact any scraps of useful information pertaining to continental touring which came our way were recorded. None of the data which we required was of the type usually made available by the touring club offices, but I think it would have enlightened some of them!

About this time I enlisted the services of a secretary, who rejoiced in the name of Miss Jinks. She ran a very elderly MG, which was nearly always in some sort of trouble, and she got the job because she was mad about motoring competition in any form and had some secretarial training, plus a little French. Her enthusiasm helped the department along at a difficult time, but unfortunately she was not strong enough to stand the pace and had to give up the job about a year later. At that time we were dealing not only with arrangements for our own cars, but also with inquiries from would-be drivers from all over the world, demands for tuning information, and requests for financial help to compete with various BMC cars, so the paperwork was formidable. For years afterwards we continued to receive hundreds of inquiries of this type, but by then, of course, the organization was geared to deal with them and cope with our own problems at the same time.

In spite of the shortcomings of our cars and the disappointments of the 1955 Le Mans and Tourist Trophy races (about which, more later), we began to get inquiries from some of the better drivers who were not satisfied with their present situation. For instance, we recruited Joan and Douglas Johns, and then Ken Wharton, who had been the captain of the Daimler team, indicated that he would like to join us for some events in 1956.

In the autumn of 1954, John Thornley had approached Alfred Moss to see if Pat, his daughter, would drive for us, and it was arranged that she would use an MG TF in some smaller British events. Not long afterwards, Pat came to see me, and looking back on that meeting I only remember that she struck me as being both very shy and very attractive. We went for a short run in a Magnette so that I could get some idea as to her capabilities, and she drove both quickly and smoothly and never took any form of risk. Whilst I never anticipated the heights to which she would rise, I was very happy about the possibilities of recruiting her, and in any case, with a name such as Moss we couldn't go far wrong. Of course, Pat had already made a name for herself as a showjumper and, curiously enough, had jumped against Ann Wisdom in the ring.

Her first important solo appearance for BMC was not a brilliant success, for in the 1956 RAC Rally, when leading the Ladies' class, she made a mistake in the final test at Blackpool which cost her the Ladies' Cup. I was surprised that a person who had ridden horses over much more complicated courses could make such a mistake until I discovered the reason; there had been so much publicity in the press concerning Pat's "certain win" in the Ladies' class at her first attempt, and so much gratuitous advice given to her before she started the test, that she became unnerved and harrassed. Given more experience, some breathing space and less publicity, she would have done the test with ease. But perhaps it was a good thing as it turned out, for she never failed a test during the next six years that she drove for me. As it transpired, the Ladies' Cup fell into our hands after all as it was won by Miss Angela Palfrey in an Austin A40 at the last moment.

The press, of course, wanted to know about our further plans for Pat, and these had to be completed as a matter of urgency because other factories were also trying to secure her services. We decided that she should have a car to run in all suitable British events and that we would review the position when she had more experience and, above all, had found herself a suitable permanent navigator. To keep the motoring press in the picture, I asked them to play the story down until such time as we were ready to launch her in the International field.

After a chapter of accidents, for which Pat was blameless, she told me that she had, so to speak, 'rediscovered' Ann Wisdom and that they were about to start on a series of trial events together. Ann had some difficulty in getting time off from her job in London, so she managed to find alternative employment on a farm which enabled her to take sufficient time off to compete in events. Thus the great partnership was formed, and it was not long before the two girls developed into a real crew, probably the greatest ladies crew that we have seen in this sport.

In those days the press could not help referring to Pat as "Stirling's sister", whereas Ann's only claim to fame was as the daughter of the brilliant motoring pair, Tommy Wisdom and his wife Bill, but as time went on they became just Pat and Ann, celebrities in their own right.

In April 1955 the department moved from its exceedingly cramped quarters into the new shop at the northern end of the works, and at about that time I was approached by John Gott concerning the formation of the new rally team. John had considerable knowledge of the requirements of a serious entry in the great continental events. He had shared the wheel of a famous Frazer Nash with O'Hara-Moore, and before that had competed with distinction in his own HRG during the period when I had been connected with the Peter Clark/Jack Scott team of racing HRGs during 1947 and 1948. With the possible exception of Ian Appleyard, of Jaguar fame, John had more experience of events such as the Alpine Rally than anyone who was not already driving for a works team. He also knew of some likely ex-HRG owners who might be free to drive for BMC, amongst them Nancy Mitchell, who had been the number one lady driver for the Daimler team, which was just being dissolved, and had also driven for Ford.

As we needed an experienced ladies crew, we arranged that she should join us for 1956. At that time she had nobody in mind as a co-driver, so she set about finding a likely navigator. This was not such an easy task as might be imagined, for Nancy was a strict disciplinarian and liked to use well-trained navigators, who would leave her free to think about the driving and not bother her with details which she regarded as elementary.

Having secured the services of some drivers, the next thing was to keep them happy, without actually spoiling them, by seeing that they were given enough driving to prevent them from wanting to join another factory. This was not easy, for the 1955 Alpine Rally was cancelled as a result of the Le Mans disaster, and there was some doubt as to whether the Liège-Rome-Liège Rally would be held. We therefore spent the money allocated for the Alpine on a test run, taking along some of the drivers with Alpine experience. We used one of the Le Mans MGs, which was in effect a prototype MGA, an Austin A50 with a Le Mans engine and an Austin A90 as the principal test cars. We visited Nürburgring, some of the higher Alpine passes and Montlhéry, and came back with quite a lot of information. Apart from the technical data, I began to learn something about rally drivers and what makes them tick.

During 1956 and 1957 there was a more regular pattern of success, and the individual crews began to identify themselves as members of the BMC team. Towards the end we usually had two ladies crews, as Pat and Ann were now appearing on the Continent, and Nancy readily admitted that it would be only a matter of time before they caught and passed her in ability. Nancy herself won the Ladies' Cup in the European Championship in 1956, and again the following year, driving almost exclusively for MG.

After an unsuccessful period with a Magnette, Pat and Ann started their

International rally career together in the Morris Minor 1000 in 1957. Joan Johns sometimes drove with her husband and later with Nancy. It was not easy to hold the balance between two ladies crews, for minor irritations arose and there were sometimes little complaints, although nothing which ever upset team discipline. Ladies crews, I found, were always willing to make the best of a bad car without complaining, or to nurse a sick car to the finish without much chance of even a class place, but they were less likely to allow a team rival to have a room with a bath when they themselves were without one.

In May 1957 we were lucky to secure the services of Margaret Hall as my secretary. Margaret was Canadian by birth, and had met and married an RAF officer when he was an instructor in Canada. In due course they had come to England and had set up homes at various RAF stations until March 1947, when the blow fell, Wing-Commander Hall being killed when the cockpit canopy of his aircraft blew off over Cowley. Margaret thus found herself with two boys to keep at boarding school with only a widow's pension. Fortunately, the RAF Benevolent Fund came to the rescue and took care of most of the boys' schooling, but Margaret had to get a job. Previously she had held a fairly responsible post with a firm of millers in Canada, and was therefore fully qualified as a private secretary, so I was delighted to take her on in that capacity when one of the MG staff heard of her predicament and recommended her to us.

Margaret Hall got to grips with the job of secretary to the Competition Manager with efficiency, coupled with a great deal of charm. Her soft Canadian accent was most attractive, and people both inside and outside the organization would say to me, "When Mrs Hall makes a request, it's hard to refuse. You see she has such a charming way of asking, and that delightful Canadian accent!" Not only charming on the 'phone, Margaret was a great personality to meet. She was not strong, being slightly built, but her tremendous energy covered her frailty. During the school holidays she worked twice as hard, having to go home to look after her boys and keep the house as neatly as possible so as to make them feel that they had a real home. The question of returning to Canada had been considered, but the boys were getting the best possible education in England, so there was not much point in returning to a country where she had few friends.

It was not very long before Margaret began to take a special interest in the private owners who called at the department. She made a point of understanding their problems and often persuaded me to reconsider my decisions and give a little more help here and there; she went to most of the club race meetings and made many friends, who came from all parts of the country and even from abroad. She was a terrific asset to the department and took a great deal of routine work off my hands, so enabling me to start to think more objectively about our problems.

Like so many people from across the Atlantic, she had a good eye and ear for the publicity slant, and it was Margaret who started the News Letter which we sent out to the motoring correspondents, radio commentators and many others to whom our efforts were news. These were confined to facts, not fiction; they gave the event in which we were about to compete, the car, the class in which it was running and the names of the crews. If an event such as the Monte Carlo Rally was likely to be covered by the national press, we tried to give the rally number of the cars and the colour of the coachwork for quick identification. Our own publicity department amplified the information with their press releases, giving biographies and addresses of the crews so that the local papers could print the story or interview them.

From the very inception of the department, we always issued invitations to the motoring and daily press to view the cars through the central publicity department of the Corporation. This side of the work was handled by the Nuffield Organization, who employed 'Goody' Goodchild, an independent photographer of considerable skill, to take the publicity pictures. Pictures which show drivers collecting their rally cars, or inspecting the latest fittings, tend to be very much of a type, but invariably Goody managed to get the best out of everyone and certainly got the co-operation of the crews. His pictures invariably found their way to the right places, in the right quantities, and with commendable speed.

It is only fitting at this point to mention the men in the workshop. In the spring of 1957 it was decided that the development department must have more room, and it was also evident that Alec Hounslow's dual role was not a happy one. How he stood the ever-changing problems with which we were faced I don't know, but he certainly must have thought it would be a relief to have to deal with straight development work only. We therefore moved into the old service department's workshop at the other end of the building. During the war, this had been used to complete tanks and was graced with a 20-ton overhead crane, which ran the length of it. One of my first jobs, therefore, was to get someone on our staff trained to operate the monster, which conveniently was fitted with a one-ton hook as well.

Douggie Watts, who had been running the competition section of the combined departments in the other workshop, became my shop foreman. Douggie was a typical Berkshire native, hard-working but enjoying his play as well, and like all the others in the department, he had a good sense of humour. This is an essential for anyone who decides to make competition motoring his career, for cars can change from exasperating brutes to little darlings and *vice versa* at the drop of a hat. Douggie also had the quality of endless patience, which all first-class mechanics should have. He always kept in close touch with his men and was quick to notice a cause for dissatisfaction before it developed into a really serious grouse. Of course, all mechanics grumble, which is the working man's right; it lets off a bit of steam without doing any harm, provided it's spasmodic. Douggie was also very popular with the drivers, and his ability to see their point of view, without pandering too readily to their wants, enabled him to keep the balance between the practical and the impossible with the skill of a tightrope walker. Our competition department mechanics had to display considerable stamina, for the service cars were regularly set a programme of over 400 miles per day, a target which often had to be accomplished between two or three service stops. Douggie would drive these long distances and yet still arrive fresh enough to deal ably with the problems with which the mechanics might be confronted when the cars came in with mechanical troubles.

It took us several years to develop a service system which met all the needs of a rally team going abroad, needs which were in themselves contradictory. All the parts and tools which might be required needed to be available at the maximum number of places from start to finish. The service crews had to be very mobile and might even need to average higher speeds – admittedly using better roads – than the competitors. Inevitably, there were never enough mechanics or cars to cover an event in its entirety to the satisfaction of everyone. Even with the most careful pairing of individuals, service crews varied in ability, and a journey which might be considered safe for one crew might be inadvisable for another. Over the years there have been fatal accidents in factory-supported organizations because the people responsible did not take the fatigue factor into account or remember that the sheer enthusiasm of mechanics often makes them push themselves until they are near to dropping. I have never met a more loyal body of people than racing and rally mechanics; they will put the success of the marque for which they work before anything.

A typical rally sortie for us would be planned in detail some months before the event took place. Most of the classic rallies took place between April and November, the peak transit season, so the British factories came up against a problem which did not apply to our continental rivals: reservation of travel space across the Channel. The air and sea ferries were apt to be booked up well in advance, so details had to be submitted to the travel agency as soon as they were completed. This meant that the Competition Manager had to decide the events in which to compete, the number of entries to be made and the service and publicity cars to be sent, as early as possible in the year. If the plan was added to, or a driver found that he or she could not cross by the route planned, or wished to return by another, a great deal of extra work was entailed. George Holmes, who used to run the Nuffield Organization's travel bureau, must have said to me a hundred times, "Why don't you people make your minds up?" The short answer was that it was impossible to be definite until the last moment.

Once across that narrow strip of water which caused so much trouble, it usually took between one and two days to reach the starting point of the rally. The local agent was sometimes able to put his premises at our disposal for last-minute adjustments, fixing the rally plates and placing the stick-on numbers on the sides of the cars. Sometimes cars were involved in minor accidents on the way, and some late work would be required to make the start on time, but fortunately, incidents like this were rare, and in every case during my time with BMC they were not the fault of the driver concerned; nevertheless, they caused a lot of worry to everyone at the time.

Of course, if the rally did not start and finish at the same place, all the tools and spares had to be taken to the finish, for the mechanics had to be sure that the cars were roadworthy for the trip back to England. If any of them had been seriously damaged they were usually railed home, which sometimes could mean that they were not available again for as long as two months; it was always advisable, therefore, to have spare cars at the factory if the same type were to be needed again soon. Sometimes the department's transporter would be taken to the start and finish points if the workshop facilities there were poor, this vehicle then becoming useful as a combined baggage lorry, spare parts depot and reserve sleeping quarters, while in an emergency it could bring a damaged car back to England. Its chief limitation was its bulk, for it could not go by air ferry, so had to be booked well ahead by sea as most of the available space was reserved for motor coaches. Moreover, the cost of transport for vehicles weighing 7 tons was high, and then the Benelux countries began to tax visiting commercial vehicles very highly to add to our problems. We found that the best route for vehicles of this size was by night ferry from Dover to Dunkirk or from Tilbury to Antwerp.

While the team was assembling at the starting point, other service crews might have crossed by a different route and be on their way to take up station in some strategically important Alpine village, where sometimes a service car could be left in one place to pick up the cars a second time, later in the rally. But unfortunately such opportunities were all too rare, and it was more usual to have to race over an Alpine pass to the next service point, crossing a frontier on the way.

Our service crews even embarked upon elementary catering, and we would pack a small field kitchen with a butane gas cooker, kettle, frying pan, thermos flasks and plastic cups, and carry self-heating soups and instant tea and coffee. The bread, butter, ham and tomatoes, which seemed to be the staple diet, were bought on the road. Given the time we could even manage a sausage or bacon-and-egg snack, but this was mainly for the mechanics because rally drivers tended to eat very little during the actual event. However, the knowledge that these things were available undoubtedly helped the crews, who knew they would not have to search for eating places during the easy stages. Sometimes, however, it was the other way round: we would organize a tempting spread only to be told that the crews had stopped and had had an omelette before reaching us. Even then there was usually a demand for tea or coffee, but on those occasions the service party had to eat ham sandwiches all the way to the next stop, and the diet could become a bit monotonous.

Often these stopping points were worked out with the competition managers of the accessory firms covering the rally, whose service facilities showed a marked improvement over the years. When we started rallying, service from accessory firms was either conspicuous by its absence or their representatives attended only at the start and finish of the event. It was George Williams of Castrol, later replaced by Jimmy Hill, who was one of the first to appreciate the need for service during the event and to do something about it. Syd Henson of Ferodo, himself a rally driver, obtained his management's permission to set up a rally service and was soon to be seen with his men changing hot drums and brake shoes in some remote village street. There were other 'accessory reps' who followed the rally with varying degrees of efficiency, but I think all drivers and mechanics at that time would have given pride of place to David Hiam of Dunlop, who in a very short time set the highest standard for rally service which had been seen to date. David was in stature a little man and, like so many little men, his energy was inversely proportional to his size. He was appointed to the newly formed rally section of the Dunlop competition department in 1959, as successor to Austin George, and worked to the Mountbatten formula: "The difficult we can do now, the impossible will take a little longer."

Planning was the key to David's success. He usually came to have lunch with me, at the *Dog House* at Frilford Heath, about four weeks before the event, probably having already seen my contemporaries Norman Garrad of Sunbeam, Ken Richardson of Triumph, and 'Edgy' Fabris of Ford, who all had similar problems; thus he had a good idea of the probable total tyre requirements. These, of course, varied from rally to rally, and new types of tyre were always in the course of development. David and I, often aided by one of the rally crews, would talk over the problem and decide where we wanted the tyres, of what type and in what quantity. During the rally David used to drive a souped-up Morris Minor 1000 with considerable verve and would visit all his service points and most of ours as well. His vans would usually carry the crews' baggage to the finish and, before he shamed us into doing the job ourselves, he could often contrive to lay on some refreshments for the rally crews. If anyone forgot a duster, a leather or even a tyre gauge, invariably David produced one! This very happy state of affairs went on until the spring of 1961, when David decided to leave Dunlop and start his own business. He was succeeded by Oliver Speight, a tall, fair, good-looking young man, who set out to carry on in the Hiam tradition, although he was the first to realize how difficult a task he had been set.

As a rally progressed, the pattern became apparent and the skilled crews soon knew how good were their chances; morale could rise or fall accordingly and the service crews were affected by this. The organizers liked to see the best 'names' do well, especially if they were girls, for they were good publicity for the event. The officials also felt sorry when a crack crew had some bad luck before they could show their form, and would wax full of enthusiasm when a favourite was doing well.

In the course of time the organizers got to know the service crews, but at one time there was outright war between them and us because most regulations then expressly forbade any 'organized assistance'. This was an unfair regulation as far as the British factories were concerned: we then had very few garages to represent us on the Continent, whereas the continental factories had agents in every town who were prepared to remain open at all hours if instructed to do so by the factory. That, however, was apparently not 'organized assistance'! Our solution to this state of affairs was to move into a suitable garage on the route and consider them as our agents for that day, having taken care to see that the garage was not already an agent for one of the continental factories. Of course, all the best garages were already agents for French or German factories, so we often had to take second or even third choice. When no suitable garage was available, we were forced out into the road and then a sort of cloak-and-dagger war started. If an official found us, we pretended to be tourists until it was obvious who we were and why we were there. If one of our cars came along while we were being observed, the rally crew had to carry out their work, under our instruction, until the officious official departed. Once we were photographed by a French competition manager on every possible occasion; the situation became ridiculous, so we found a friend to chase him and photograph the French mechanics working on his own cars. There were no protests from either side, and this turned out to be the last great rally in which 'organized assistance' was forbidden.

The situation became more sensible later, with major components on the competing cars being marked with special paint so that they could not be exchanged during the event, and adjustments being permissible anywhere, although they had to be done in running time. If there was a rest halt in the itinerary cars were usually impounded and placed in a *parc fermé*, where no work was allowed.

During our evolutionary period it became apparent that the continental drivers had a great deal more experience than our own of the actual timed climbs, for many of the famous passes were being used time and time again, so it was necessary for our crews to get plenty of practice on these climbs. At first these practice trips were made *en masse* by the whole team, but this method proved unsatisfactory for a number of reasons. It was not easy to produce a quantity of suitable cars, plus a tender car to take care of baggage and transport a mechanic and sometimes the team manager, nor was it easy for everyone to get away at the same time. Progress across country was slow, and the best drivers were believers in 'he who travels fastest, travels alone'. Daily starts tended to be late and robbed us of most of the daylight if it was winter, and of the empty roads if in spring or summer.

On the credit side, if something went wrong there was someone to help, some development work could be carried out at the same time and the actual rally cars could be compared with each other. Crews could also compare notes on difficulties and write up their comments together. However, we decided to abandon the mass recce and to send crews out on their own to practise over and write up the route. The notes concerning the route were pooled and produced as a route card by John Gott, who already had a great fund of information concerning Alpine roads. John also assessed each section so that crews could know its difficulty in advance, sections being colour-coded red, blue or green, according to difficulty.

This specialized information was of particular benefit to crews who had been unable to do a recce. When the crews made their recces, they also wrote up their own Speed Section notes, although these were not really suitable for common team use as they tended to reflect the individual skill and requirements of the driver and navigator. For example, some crews revelled in detail whereas others merely listed the most dangerous points on the climb. These notes, of course, later became universally known as pace notes, the term having originally been coined, I think, by Peter Riley and Tony Ambrose. If a crew lacked pace notes for a hill, these would sometimes be borrowed from another team member, for information on the hill, even if in different form from that habitually used, was far better than having to drive it 'blind'. Nevertheless, someone else's notes had to be handled with great caution. If the navigator became out of step with his notes, he could slow his driver down on an easy part of the climb or, more seriously, take him too fast into a dangerous corner.

Some teams made their notes with a portable tape recorder, whilst others just scribbled; whichever method was used, the odometer or mileage recorder on the car had be accurate and easily read by the navigator. At first we used average speed meters, but these seemed to lose favour, the ideal times and distances being calculated and recorded either in the notes or on the organizers' route card. The driver, of course, is principally concerned with the rev-counter, and to this end we placed the speedometers nearer to the navigators. The hand of the speedometer was most frequently moving between 10 and 2 o'clock and therefore tended to sweep across the odometer at inconvenient times. To overcome this we made up a separate odometer, driven by a dual drive from the gearbox through a separate cable, and sited on the left of the instrument panel in front of the navigator. Separate controls were then fitted for the lights which illuminated the odometer, the time-of-day clock and the split-second clock which was used to time sections of the route.

We used right-hand-drive cars on the Continent because they were more popular with the crews, who liked to see where the wheels were in relation to the edge of the drop when going over the high passes. If one pulled out early enough to have a look at a vehicle ahead, passing was not so difficult as it might have seemed when driving on the right with a right-hand-drive car. One could often see round the nearside of the vehicle as well because the navigator was usually awake and working on the twisty sections, so could prompt the driver. Personally, I still prefer a right-hand-drive car on the Continent, even when driving alone. It is also convenient for the driver to get out on the pavement side in towns when a quick stop is made.

Comfort improved as we gained more experience; as people went faster we found that they needed better seats which held them more firmly, and as they went further they needed more padding. Complicated reclining seats tended to be both heavy and expensive, so we made our own, finally getting them to weigh less than the standard seat supplied with the car.

The worst hazard for the rally driver to meet in the Alps was the motor coach or lorry towing a trailer. These vehicles could load about 10 tons, and tow another 10, while their drivers could scarcely hear anything behind them unless it was making a lot of noise. British wind horns were too civilized for the job, so we had to do as the Romans do and fit Italian ones. They were shrill, penetrating and inspiring, and to me they conjured up the very spirit of rallying. They could be made to talk in many ways, to be polite or imperious, or even imploring, and the Italians understood them perfectly.

I feel certain that our plaintive cries to the management for more power and less weight in order to make it possible to comply with George Harriman's directive were heard, but changes in specification take time. Parts are programmed and ordered in thousands before a car goes into production, and when a number of cars have been built, a sanction is given for a continuation of the programme and further orders are placed for material and parts; as a result, no major changes can be made for months to come. Alterations were made, however, in due course, and we were delighted to see cars going into production with more power, better brakes and improved roadholding. To quote examples: the Austin A90 was developed to become the A95 and later the A105, the MG Magnette became much improved in its ZB form, and the Riley 1.5 appeared with an excellent power-to-weight ratio. The Austin-Healey 100-Six, for which I had great plans, was another much improved car, finally blossoming out with a 3-litre engine.

Competitions have never been won in the International field unless both car and crew were outstanding, but given that all works teams enjoyed factory support, there was a limit to which one could go with preparations and assistance. First and foremost, the regulations had to be observed, for not only were the penalties of adverse publicity too great to be risked, but the first-class driver who had his heart in the interest of the sport would neither cheat nor connive at it. Factories have sometimes sailed too near to the wind in this respect, but this has been brought about either by excessive keenness in preparation of the vehicles, or by failure to interpret the over-complicated regulations correctly. I have myself been guilty of the latter, and the resulting commotion taught me to question any regulation which I did not completely understand, either with the organizer of the event or with the *FIA* itself. I made such a point of this that later I was able to put the knowledge to good use against two organizing clubs in events which were of considerable importance to us.

Whatever the cars, nothing could be achieved without the best drivers. Like their counterparts in the Grand Prix teams, they were mostly extroverts, who could not be permitted to get their own way too often, but who equally had not to be made depressed by constant refusals. A balance had to be held between what could be done with the people and money available and the programme which the drivers would prefer the factory to follow. If the cars were going well it was easy to keep the team happy; nothing succeeds like success. If the factory was experiencing a streak of bad luck, particularly towards the end of the season, around motor show time, then the manager could well find his team lunching with his rivals! Fortunately, at such times, the rival's own crews were probably also taking good care to see that they, too, had a drive for the next season.

At show time it was usual to come to some form of agreement with the drivers, which normally covered a commitment to a specified number of events, for the coming season. If the team was off-colour and dissatisfied with the current cars, one's only hope was that better cars would be available, and a few inspired leaks of information could be made to keep up the crews' spirits. Loyalty also comes into the picture; in this respect I was more than fortunate, for it often tipped the scales in my favour against some very hard currency on the other side. Yes, loyalty is even more precious than gold. It was a remarkable thing that we never had a written agreement with any driver during the seven years in which I had the honour to run the department. We sent them all a set of suggested lines of action and left it at that.

CHAPTER 3

The people who made it all happen

"Each in his or her way I rated quite a special person."

In my original book, I offered a large collection of potted portraits of the people with whom I had been associated in one way or another during my years of competition management, and inevitably a lot of what I wrote at that time has been overtaken by events. But fond memories tend to linger, and so what follows – apart from changes in tense here and there – are extracts from my earlier comments which I think remain relevant, in the hope that they will enable the reader to get to know a little better some of the people who were centre-stage in my particular sphere of motorsport. Each in his or her way I rated quite a special person.

The Morley Twins: Donald and Erle Morley were dissimilar twins who, with their younger brother, farmed in Suffolk. Donald was the shorter, in fact so short that the driving seat had to be raised for him so that Erle, who was well over six feet tall, could barely manage to drive in the same seat. Both tended to be a bit thin on top and had a rather studious air; by their neat dress they could be taken for businessmen rather than farmers. Their slow East Anglian speech, however, brought a tang of the farm, and they took time to think over a proposition; I always imagined them leaning over a farm gate and appraising the wheat at the same time as they discussed the next rally. They would rather not drive at all than enter an unsuitable car. The Morleys worked very much as a team, aided by the extra sympathy that twins are reputed to have. Their planning was meticulous and they left nothing to chance; they retired to bed early before an event, showed no signs of nerves and were non-smokers. Erle was not so strong as the compact, wiry Donald, whose slightly saturnine appearance earned him the nickname of 'The Little Devil', which was given to him by Pat Moss. Donald in his prime was probably Britain's best rally driver.

Pat Moss: From the amazing Moss family, she used to live at *White Cloud Farm*, Tring, along with a great number of assorted animals. Pat was in her mid-twenties when she drove for us, was amazingly energetic and just didn't know how to relax. Almost as soon as she got out of a car after a tough rally she would probably be on water skis, then immediately she got home she would hitch up the horse-box and be away to a horse show. The worst thing that could happen to Pat was boredom; if she got too bored, she would be off to Bond Street to buy some new dresses. She didn't go for the expensive ones, but rather for change and variety; the colours, therefore, tended to be adventurous. She usually wore tight slacks and a tight shirt when driving and she changed them several times in a rally if she had the chance.

She smoked a lot when driving, but never touched alcohol before or during a competition. She would take 'wakey-wakey' pills if the event was a really long one and, as these tended to take away the appetite, she would eat little until after the event. I remember she liked her steak almost raw. "Hold it near a candle", she would tell the waiter. She accumulated a good knowledge of continental food and wines, especially red wine. One of her hobbies was collecting popular jazz records, and like her famous brother she was a keen collector of gadgets of every description.

Pat was immensely strong and very broad in the shoulders, and of course she was a brilliant horsewoman. I used to suspect that she loved horses more than men, but of course that was before she met and married Erik Carlsson. She was very kind and never forgot a favour; the mechanics were always remembered by her, in success or failure, and of course the whole team adored her.

Ann Wisdom: An astonishing counterpart to Pat. As John Gott once said, "Together, the girls form a team, but apart each is less than half a team." Whilst Pat was an extrovert, Ann was much more the novelist's heroine – emotional, temperamental and fastidious. Her dress sense was excellent and she planned each stage of her wardrobe with the greatest care. She would save for a long time to buy something really nice and the completed ensemble would be good enough to make a grand entrance on some special occasion. She changed her hair styles frequently and liked to experiment with tints.

Ann's home was near Ferring, and she knew how to relax by retiring to the country and living her own separate existence; she was an expert at doing nothing when she wanted to. I recall that she tended to spend her money wisely and thought a lot about the future. She liked the Continent, not just because of the rallies, and would usually spend her holidays there, particularly for winter sports. Like Pat, she learnt much about continental food and wine during her rallying years, but her preference was for white wine. However, I remember she had a disappointing habit of losing her appetite quite suddenly in the best eating places.

Ann had been brought up since the cradle in a world of cars and car topics, as her father, Tommy Wisdom, had driven with marked success in every sort of motoring event, and her mother had had a great career in races and rallies. She was nearly always car sick on a rally, but invariably would overcome this and carry on. She was an expert navigator who collected a lot of information by just keeping her ears open, but she would give very little away. Gradually she developed into a very reasonable driver, too, and would take a greater share of the wheel than she had previously. Pat and Ann were England's most experienced team; no other had enjoyed such an unbroken run of success together and they were most popular on the Continent. Ann was the first of them to marry; she chose Peter Riley, who was another BMC driver at that time.

John Gott: He had served with Bomber Command in the RAF, then became a policeman and had risen to Chief Constable of Northamptonshire by the time he announced his retirement from works driving. As a private owner he won two Alpine Cups with an HRG and a Frazer Nash, but was less lucky with BMC. John was the captain of the BMC team for six years and his store of knowledge on the subject was put to very good use by the drivers. Being a policeman, he had a pretty good memory and wrote it all down, the result being a monumental collection of information on roads, times from A to B in all sorts of cars, and who did what and when. He was referred to as the 'Gauleiter' by Pat, and regarded as a Cassandra by some.

John had some very bad luck in rallies, and from time to time drove some very lame cars home because he believed in the old tradition of 'finish at all costs'. He was a great team man who would put his own interests aside to see that a better-placed crew got home. He made his navigators work pretty hard taking notes, and one of his many assets was that he spoke French well and was known and liked by the organizers of many events. It was John who suggested our plan of action from the early days, for which I was always very grateful. He became a member of the Competition Committee of the Royal Automobile Club. An impressive looking man, over six feet tall, he liked to wear green overalls with a Union Jack on the pocket, and he always had something painted in British Racing Green on his team car.

David Seigle-Morris: David joined the BMC team after a successful season with his Triumph TR3, having had one works drive for that factory. Triumph cut down their competition programme in the autumn of 1960 and David drove his first rally for BMC in the 1960 Liège-Rome-Liège. Dark, swarthy and very strongly built, David might be mistaken for a Swiss or a German. He had good taste in clothes and furniture and by profession was an architect. He kept himself very fit and was a judo blue belt. He, too, was a member of the Competition Committee of the RAC. He made a particular study of driving methods and techniques, but I recall that he did not always put them into practice himself.

Tony Ambrose: Tall and thin with untidy fair hair, Tony was the 'boffin type'. He had considerable experience as a navigator with Lyndon Sims and later with Peter Riley and was fired with a driving ambition to get to the top of the Championship at any cost. He made a great contribution to the team with his recce notes. Used to being in command, he was sometimes misunderstood for taking charge of a situation when everyone else was still deciding what to do about it. He ran an interior decorating and Do-It-Yourself business in Basingstoke, but contrived to get enough time off for rallying.

Vic Elford: At one time navigator to David Seigle-Morris, Vic was slim and dark and could have been mistaken for an Italian. He liked to cut a dash with his wardrobe and used to get ragged about it by the team. He took up saloon car racing while he was with us and also drove his own car in British rallies, both with great success, and of course later he became a fine endurance racer and occasional Formula 1 driver. At the time of our association he had forsaken civil engineering in favour of selling life assurance, at which I recall he seemed to do very well.

Peter Riley: Until his marriage to Ann Wisdom, Peter was one of those very rare animals, a bachelor of independent means who raced and rallied for the fun of it. He was known by everyone in the team as 'Bear', due to his resemblance to the nursery variety. His close-cropped fair hair and rotund figure became as well-known in Grand Touring car racing as in rallies. At one time a member of the Ford team, he joined BMC at the end of 1959 and took a flat at Abingdon in order to be really close to the job. Peter had a degree in mechanical engineering and had had a variety of interesting jobs in various parts of the world. Artistic, he painted reasonably well in oils for his own amusement and could write a good account of his driving experiences. He was interested in analyzing the technique of driving and used to put it to good use. I remember that he was very fussy about the controls in the cars he drove and was not happy until they were made and adjusted precisely to suit him. I also recall his good sense of humour.

Gerry Burgess: He joined BMC in 1955 and drove for us on various occasions, particularly on the Liège-Rome-Liège, when not required by Ford, for whom he drove regularly. Large and red-faced, Gerry could have been mistaken for a farmer, but actually owned a company which manufactured cycle brakes and restaurant chairs. Gerry used to compete successfully on cycles himself, but he must have had a better power-to-weight ratio in those days. He used to tell the best hard-luck story of any driver I knew and he invariably suspected that his car was the slowest. He was known in the team as 'Why can't I have...?', but he was generous and full of fun, except in moments of crisis. He would drive to finish at all costs and was well supported for many years by his loyal co-driver.

Sam Croft-Pearson: Tall and slim by comparison with Gerry, and always ready to smile. He ran a garage in Kensington which specialized in repairs and tuning for Austin-Healeys.

Joan Johns: For several years she and her husband Douglas had been the Joint Secretaries of the Hants and Berks Motor Club. Very vivacious, she drove with considerable success with Douglas in British Nationals and with various ladies crews on the Continent, and when she retired from active participation in rallies she continued to follow the sport closely.

Douglas Johns: After Joan's retirement he continued to take an active part in rallies and was one of the best British navigators of his era. He and Joan ran a garage and agricultural business near Reading, and this prevented him from getting away to as many events as he wished, but nevertheless he navigated for BMC off and on for seven years. Douglas was also no mean driver, as he proved in winning the 1,600 Sports class in the 1960 RAC Rally in a Wolseley saloon.

Derrick Astle: Was one of the northern group of drivers and navigators who called themselves the 'Knowldale Boys'. Their headquarters were at Rochdale and they produced some excellent crews, being represented in several works teams. They were a wild lot, full of practical jokes and nonsense collectively, but I considered them to be comparatively harmless singly. Living in Lancashire, Derrick naturally had something to do with cotton; he had taken a chance with the purchase of a mill after the war and it had come off. I recall he was the proud owner of an ex-works Austin-Healey 3000, which carried his personal number DA 3.

Mike Sutcliffe: Another Knowldale member, who usually crewed with Derrick, Mike also drove for Ford when not engaged with BMC. He had a rather acid wit, which from time to time was apt to be misunderstood. Tall and dark, whereas Derrick was short and fair, they made quite a contrast. Sometimes Mike would drive and Derrick navigate and sometimes it was the other way round, then there were occasions when each would take his own navigator, but whatever the arrangements, they could always be relied upon to have a real 'go'.

Rev Rupert Jones: His first contact with BMC was with the Cambridge University team which took the seven-day endurance records with the Austin A35 in 1957. Rupert, even then, had made up his mind that he was going to be a priest, but he intended to continue participating in motorsport for as long as he could. Short and dark, Rupert was a great sportsman with a fine sense of humour, and he showed great aptitude for rallying. Universally known as 'the Bishop', he often made us remember that Christianity is with us all the time, whatever we may be attempting and wherever we are. Ann Wisdom once told me that Rupert took the team to church in Oslo before the start of the Monte Carlo Rally and when someone spoke of praying to win, 'the Bishop' said "No, you must pray that you will be worthy of winning!" Rupert liked sailing and deerstalking and, I was told, was the idol of the younger members of his parish.

Gyde Horrocks: The mind behind the Cambridge University Automobile Club's record attempts in 1957 and 1958, Gyde was not strong, having had polio when young, but he overcame all handicaps and made a speciality of motor racing management. Slight, freckled and studious-looking in his glasses, he worked in his family's heat engineering business in Northampton, and introduced several Cambridge men to racing and rallying.

David Hiam: When working for Dick Jeffrey in the rally section of Dunlop's competition department, David showed that the youngest can bring new light to the subject of rally service, and nothing was ever too much trouble for him. He left Dunlop to run a garage at Minworth, Warwickshire.

Ken Wharton: A man of original ideas who loved variety, Ken had driven just about every type of car in the 10 years before he joined BMC in 1956. Besides being a great driver, Ken was an excellent host who could choose a meal with skill, and he was one of the few members of the motoring fraternity I have met who could talk about almost any subject. He had travelled extensively and took an interest in everything he saw. If he had been content to specialize, particularly in saloon car racing, of which he was a brilliant exponent, I think he would have gained even greater fame, and I doubt if he would have met with the tragic accident in which he lost his life in New Zealand. Ken's drive in the modified Austin A90 at the May 1956 Silverstone race meeting has gone down in history, and he can be said to have founded the line of Touring Car successes which BMC was to experience during the next six years. Ken used to manage his father's motor business at Smethwick.

Nancy Mitchell: One of Britain's greatest lady drivers, following her retirement she became motoring editor of *Vogue* in Britain. Noted for her clothes sense and a great believer in protocol, Nancy liked things done the right way and was inclined to get petulant if there was a hitch in the organization. We had some good squabbles and very often I felt that all was lost, but we contrived to remain good friends. Someone once described her as 'the Mean, Moody and Magnificent Mitchell', but she was never mean. She never managed to hit it off with a regular co-driver for any length of time, otherwise I think she would have won the Ladies' Touring Car Championship for the third time. In 1948 and 1949 she had made a great name for herself while running her own HRG in Internationals, and she also drove for Alvis, HRG, Daimler, Ford, Sunbeam, Triumph and BMC works teams with distinction.

Bill Shepherd: Another of the ex-RAF pilots who took up rallying after the war, Bill, who stood over six feet tall, ran a garage at Leven, in Fife. He often went with John Gott as navigator and when they drove together in the Alpine they were a unique crew in that each had won a *Coupe des Alpes*. Bill knew enough about machinery to be able to argue the advisability of a line of action, and he had a dry wit and lots of Scots logic, which could be very disconcerting at times. He was another of those intrepid HRG drivers.

John Williamson: Known to everyone as 'John Willy' and of part-Belgian extraction, John spoke fluent French and could usually find his way about the Continent without needing many maps as his business in flax and other continental products often took him there. He had a habit of rushing up to 'phone boxes in the middle of nowhere to ring his office or to buy a consignment of this or that; only John Willy could buy 10 tons of cork before the start of a 'Monte' and sell it, at a profit, at the next control! In fact I think he could have managed to do without an office altogether. He was the only man I knew who haggled about rates of exchange at frontiers and he could confound the clerks with his sliderule; he once told me that the haggling paid for his cigarettes.

John Milne: The youngest of the three rallying Scots who had driven for the team, John was at Worcester College, Oxford, when he started with BMC. After taking his degree in law he was called to the Bar in Glasgow and practised there; he had a fine legal repertoire of case histories. He also managed the family business, which had something to do with catering and whisky blending, and as a result he developed a prosperous frontage which was ornamented with a fine gold watch chain. This side of John seemed completely out of keeping with making the fastest lap in his class at Charterhall or stalking the deer.

Anne Hall: Like Nancy Mitchell, Anne had driven for various British factories as well as being a visitor to BMC on several occasions. Anne, of course, first made a name for herself as the navigator to Sheila Van Damm, who gave up rallying to manage the famous *Windmill Theatre* in London. In the North, anyone will tell you that Anne, who came from Huddersfield, was the equal of Pat Moss, and she was certainly the only woman driver who could get anywhere near Pat's performances on similar cars. Unfortunately, though, she had more than her share of bad luck, and on several occasions was unable to temper her dashing driving with prudence so that she failed to finish when occupying a commanding position. Always ready to smile and offer her congratulations to rivals, Anne was universally popular and did much to cement the friendship which later existed between British works drivers linked to rival teams. At one time team managers virtually forbade their drivers to fraternize with the opposition, but I am happy to say that this tradition gradually changed and I had some very convivial evenings with the opposition (after the event).

'Tish' Ozanne: Patricia Ozanne, who lived in Suffolk, was introduced to us in 1959 and drove Minis, both for the works and as a factory-assisted entry. Tish had family connections with the Channel Island of Guernsey and spoke French, which is a useful language for rallying. She, too, had to endure more than her share of bad luck, helped along by some inexperience, but when everything was going well for her she could excel. A kind and thoughtful person, who really appreciated anything that was done for her, she was small, so she was a considerable asset in a Mini. She worked up a good crew partnership with Pat Allison, who was also a lightweight.

Tommy Gold: Used to refer to himself as a haberdasher from Stoke, where he ran a soft furnishing business. Tommy would grace any palace as the official jester; his wit always surprised me for it was all-embracing and covered so many subjects. June, his wife, at one time acted as his navigator, but Tommy made a miscalculation whilst driving a works Triumph and ended up in a tree; after that, he decided that June should stay at home. Tommy became typed as a small-car driver after he had shown great ability, first in a Sprite and then with an MG Midget, and some people even thought him as good as John Sprinzel as a Sprite driver. He was also one of England's leading driving test exponents, which perhaps explained why he liked to use his brakes to the limit. He would always take his misfortunes with great sportsmanship, and indeed was an all-round sport, his hobbies including caravanning, sailing, water ski-ing and shooting.

Stuart Turner: As a navigator Stuart came to the top very quickly. I always thought that as gamesmanship was to Stephen Potter, so rallymanship was to Stuart. Some of his critics at the time decried his methods, which could be pretty ruthless, on the grounds that they were unsporting; perhaps they would have been judged so, 20 years earlier, but methods had changed and Stuart was one of the new generation of professional rally drivers. His book on the subject let a lot out of the bag. I don't feel that Stuart really thought that his methods would bring him into prominence so quickly, and he paraded a somewhat bewildered air, rather like a professor who found himself being publicized on the discovery of a new process. Stuart navigated for many famous drivers with marked success and was popular amongst the people who knew him well, but he was liable to be misunderstood by others who did not appreciate his dry wit. I was sure that he would make a success of his job as my successor at BMC, and I wished him lots of luck, little realizing what a tremendous impact his tenure in my old chair was to have on the whole rallying scene.

John Sprinzel: One of the most controversial figures in the sport, John had a mixed personality which tended to fight within itself. He was born in Germany, near the Polish frontier, and was a mixture of German, French and Portuguese by descent, although he had spent most of his life in England. He spoke several languages fluently and had been trained in his father's business of silk screen printing and transfer manufacturing. John's strong point was publicity, and his critics would claim that anything he did was aimed at the publicity slant. This might have been true later in his career, but it was not when he drove in his first International in an Austin A30 with his father and sister as the crew. His only claim to fame on that occasion was the fact that the organizers gave him the rally number 1. John was to show his skill in his Austin-Healey Sprite over many years, as well as demonstrate his flair for publicity, firstly with the Speedwell organization which he founded, later with the Speed Equipment Division of the Donald Healey Motor Company, and finally with his own company.

John was tall, thin, and at times nervous, and when I first met him he lived in Chelsea, liked good food and seemed to enjoy being a bachelor. He became the author of a number of books on the sport, and although he was not a brilliant mechanic, he knew enough to help himself in an emergency. As well as driving for BMC for a while, John also drove on his own account to publicize his company and later joined the reformed Triumph works team. He could therefore be classed as a professional driver, but he had to work on a budget and make the best terms he could at the beginning of the season. John could be a charming and amusing companion on occasions, but I found that his boyish enthusiasm would sometimes take him past the prudent point; only John could manage to capsize a go-kart on a concrete track when dressed in sub-tropical clothes.

Jack Sears: Known as 'Gentleman Jack' by the mechanics, for he never had a hair out of place in the midst of the most arduous event, Jack gave up rallying because he disliked the rules and regulations and the uncertainty which prevailed at that time. Racing was for him a more precise sport in which the results were apparent as soon as the race was over. I felt that the last straw for Jack was to be eliminated from the 1959 Liège-Rome-Liège with Peter Garnier because they were outside the time limit. Let no-one think that Jack was not a true sportsman, for he raced only for the love of the game. He used to farm with the same planning and energy that he put into his racing, and we all missed him in the rally world for it was always a tonic to see Jack step out of a car looking immaculate, even at six in the morning – a boost for morale, rather like dressing for dinner in the tropical bush. Jack had a considerable sense of humour and a well developed habit of pulling the legs of the Continentals during rallies.

Peter Garnier: At that time sports editor of *The Autocar*, Peter often acted as Jack Sears' navigator and, himself liking a leg-pull, usually aided Jack in his tricks. Peter was another of those large men who so often frequented the rally world. His hobby? Making ship models. He also navigated for Stirling Moss in the *Tour de France Automobile*, and later became the Secretary of the Grand Prix Drivers' Association.

Sam Moore: He was Jack's other navigator, and was nearly as smart as Jack himself; he sported a large moustache, which fortunately did not interfere with his ability to read a map. For a time he was one of the best southern competitors, as proved by the large collection of hardware he had won with two successive MGs. He was Douglas Johns' partner in their agricultural business.

Dick Bensted-Smith: A great humorist on paper, who wrote some excellent accounts of his adventures as a navigator. His best was perhaps Blues in the Night, written about his first Liège-Rome-Liège when he and John Milne won the novices' prize in 1956. Some of his judgments were first-class, and it was he who suggested that we should specialize more. His advice was taken and the victorious Austin-Healey run resulted.

Tommy Wisdom: A regular competitor with the Donald Healey Motor Company's cars in both record-breaking and rallies. In his time one of the most experienced motoring journalists in the business, he drove in most of the European rallies, the Mille Miglia, the Targa Florio, many times at Le Mans and in more places than I can remember. For years he was the motoring correspondent of the *Daily Herald*, and he had a reputation for saying what he thought, even if it was unpopular, and he seemed to thrive on it.

Jack Hay: Co-driver to Tommy, Jack was motoring correspondent of the *Birmingham Post* and became Chairman of the Guild of Motoring Writers for 1961. He was always complaining about someone or something, but he never really meant it. This tended to lead to recriminations until you realized that Jack was not really serious. Had been known to swear that "this is my last rally" or "I don't know why I do it", but he went on just the same; he must have seen quite a lot of Europe in the course of these last appearances. Wrote a very good column and was lucky enough to be given more space than did some of the national press motoring correspondents.

Willy Cave: Another excellent navigator who found his work with the BBC prevented him from continuing rallying. Used to be on the credit titles of Cliff Michelmore's television programme *Tonight*. Slightly temperamental about things before the rally started, but became unflappable after the 'off'. Latterly navigated with John Sprinzel. Willy went to Monaco with Peter Dimmock and Tony Brooks in that famous taxi during the 1961 Monte Carlo Rally, an expedition which didn't do anybody any good except, perhaps, the owner of the taxi, who probably got a new engine.

Ken Best: At one time commentator for motoring events and later something important in the PRO line. A noted wit with a great repertoire of stories who was always welcome during any rally. When employed as the public relations officer of one of the petroleum companies, Ken managed to get away fairly often. He christened the writer 'The Poor Man's Neubauer', in return for which compliment I can only dub Ken 'The Poor Man's Bob Hope'. Ken crewed latterly with Jack Sears in an MGA. He was a competent navigator and a reasonable driver who was universally popular.

Archie Scott-Brown: Only rallied once with BMC before he took up serious racing. Archie was loved and admired by everyone for, although physically handicapped since birth, he had made such strides in overcoming his disadvantages that no-one gave it a thought after first meeting him. A very great driver, he was full of fun, and his death at Spa was a severe blow to both Jack Sears and Peter Riley, who were closely associated with him. We lost a great gentleman when Archie went.

Pat Faichney: Pat deserves a special mention for she navigated for Nancy Mitchell on a number of rallies and sat alongside her, in an open MGA, in appalling weather conditions when Nancy won the Ladies' Cup in the 1956 Mille Miglia. Pat never said much about this trip, but she always seemed to me to be quietly efficient, without shouting about it.

Erik Carlsson: Probably the most colourful personality in the rally scene. Erik is Swedish, drove and worked for Saab and used to live at Trolhattan before marrying Pat Moss and moving to England. Known by the Scandinavians as Petaket, which means 'On the roof', he was an intrepid driver of great skill who drove on the limit in all tests and as a result often inverted the car. Erik's English used to be picturesque, but it improved at each rally. He would not tolerate fools gladly, but was very generous. He often helped the BMC crews and, when forced to retire himself, usually repaired his car and set out after the rally to provide food and comfort to our crews. Erik was so pro-British that he always rallied with a small Union Jack on the front wing of his car, and we were delighted to have him with us so often.

Ray Brookes: He won the 1956 Tulip Rally outright in an Austin A30 with his father Ted as co-driver, having prepared the car himself with some advice from the factory. He rallied extensively with BMC, competing in most of the major rallies, co-driving with John Gott on several occasions, and he ran a garage on the Kent-Surrey border. He was an enthusiastic member of Territorial Army, in which he held a commission, while his father was a great enthusiast for motoring and rifle shooting, having won the King's Cup at Bisley.

The men behind the cars
Douggie Watts: Foreman of the competition shop at Abingdon, he was liked and respected in many parts of the world. A great judge of men, he had the loyal backing of all in his shop. He was also a sound judge of a car, although he didn't have the opportunity to get out in them as much as he would have liked. He hated paperwork and would really have preferred to have been back at the bench using a spanner instead of a pen.

Tommy Wellman: Second in command of the competition shop and a great man for finding things out and improvizing. He made a speciality of helping people at Club meetings. He ran a vintage pushbike and another vivid memory of him is that I recall he liked his beer.

Douggie Hamblin: Also second in command, au pair so to speak, with Tommy Wellman, so that they could get away on alternate events. He had an excellent nose for the right mixture – carburettor, I mean! – and specialized in the development of the Austin-Healey 3000 to good effect; he loved fast cars.

A G 'Nobby' Hall: Nobby was forced to specialize in tuning the smaller BMC engines, although he professed not to like them. Nevertheless, he did a meticulous job and contributed a lot to Pat Moss' successes. He used to restore vintage cars and he would build beautiful exhaust systems.

Den Green: A first-class mechanic, who trained himself to become a first-class navigator. In the latter capacity he went on both the Portuguese and the Viking Rallies with his boss, helping to notch up a class place in one and a fourth in the other. By a remarkable coincidence, his hair turned white afterwards, for which I later apologized to both Mrs Green and Den.

Gerald Wiffen: Had been with the shop, man and boy, and thought there was enough future in the job to risk marriage. A good engine man who was trained under Alec Hounslow in the old development department. Like many of the team, he pulled more than his weight and showed great ability in an emergency. His younger brother followed in his footsteps.

Johnny Organ: A good mechanic who was haunted by bad luck but took it all in his stride. He wrote books on horticulture and liked to experiment with the rarer items of a foreign menu.

Johnny Lay: Another of the boys who grew into men during the seven years of my tenure. He liked to show his dexterity in an emergency and would do a neat job when there was no rush. He was as keen as the rest and had some good cars to his credit.

Brian Moylan: One of the more thoughtful members of the team who liked to ask intelligent questions at the post mortems.

Ernie Giles: The eldest in the shop, a real family man and a good craftsman. I shall never forget the little kindnesses he showed me on one of the early rallies when he came in my car. I always thought he was lucky to live in a lovely little Berkshire village not very far from some of the others in the glorious district called the Vale of the White Horse.

Peter Bartram: He came to us as an apprentice after the usual tour of the factory, fell in love with the competition shop and elected to stay there, where he learnt to be a real craftsman.

Cliff Humphries: He came back from working in California and settled down again without anyone really noticing that he had been away until he started to prepare cars. It was then evident that he was one of the most painstaking mechanics that it has ever been my lot to meet. Cliff was a perfectionist. He was also very quiet, and he preferred home to the bright lights of the Continent.

Ted Eales: Another of the boys, he served to support the faith that Douggie Watts placed in the young men whom he chose when the venture started.

Roy Brown: He took life seriously and devoted his spare time to helping the Church. Quiet and thoughtful, he put the same amount of energy into his work as his play.

Bob ('Dick') Whittington: He started as a shop boy and worked his way up, loved 'going foreign', and enjoyed experimenting with continental cooking.

Neville Challis: Without Neville's determination the whole effort would have been wasted for it was he who ferreted out the much-prized spare parts from central stores and who could tell a part with a common identity a mile away and smell out the reserved-for-special-customers-in-an-emergency bins. He was ably assisted by Messrs Carnegie and Edwards.

Bill Price: A one-time apprentice at Morris Commercial, in Coventry, he joined the department as my assistant after his military service and took over a lot of the routine work on tuning and homologation. This all took a great deal more time in research than was realized, but the work was essential to the efficient running of the department. There was unfortunately little thanks or glamour to it, and I was grateful to Bill for all he did for me.

The feminine influence

Jane Derrington: A young lady who found herself, due to a tragic accident, occupying the post of private secretary to the Competition Manager before she was expecting to do so, but who made a remarkable success of it. She came from a family who all seemed to have brains and initiative, so perhaps it was not to be wondered at. Her father raced outboard-engined boats of his own make, with marked success.

Jean Stoter: She joined the department as a junior typist and survived the wolf whistles in the workshop to such good effect that both she and Jane were respected and admired by the boys in the shop. The boys were lucky indeed to have two such charming young ladies in the department!

CHAPTER 4

The Le Mans 24-Hours race

"At last the magic hour arrived and at 4pm there was complete silence followed by the patter of feet running to the cars."

In this expansion of my earlier book I am including recollections of major racing events in which we entered cars bearing a close resemblance to the types which we had used so successfully in International rallies. In some of the races, rally drivers were employed to demonstrate that their stamina and judgment over long distances could be used to good effect in the longer sportscar races.

The MG Car Company, the Donald Healey Motor Company and, later, the British Motor Corporation all entered cars in races between 1955 and 1961, although restrictions were imposed upon the competition department at Abingdon, for reasons which will become all too apparent during the course of this story.

Soon after I joined MG in 1954 I was told that the factory had entered three 1,500cc cars of a new type for the 1955 Le Mans 24-Hour race. There had been no MG factory entries in races since 1935, but publicity obtained by taking International class records for various cubic capacities and distances, using specially built cars, had been almost continuous from 1934 to 1952. The chassis which was used throughout, fitted with a low-drag body and a variety of MG engines, became known as EX 135. It took records at Montlhéry, driven by George Eyston, in 1934; at Frankfurt, with Goldie Gardner, in 1938; and again at Dessau in 1939. It was then stored for the duration of the war before reappearing in 1948 to take further records in Belgium, and finally it was sent over to Utah to claim records on the Salt Lake in 1951 and 1952, again with Goldie Gardner driving. The variations in the size and performance of the engines used were considerable, and I think I can best demonstrate the amazing versatility of the development department of the MG Car Company by listing the laurels of EX 135:

The first car with a 1,100cc engine to exceed 120mph
The first car with a 1,100cc engine to exceed 150mph
The first car with a 1,100cc engine to exceed 200mph
The first car with a 1,500cc engine to exceed 200mph
The first car with a   750cc engine to exceed 150mph
The first car with a   350cc engine to exceed 120mph

However, record-breaking did not stop in 1952, and a new breed of cars appeared to push the speeds even higher. I mention this because it has a connection with the evolution of the race and rally cars which subsequently came out of Abingdon.

It sometimes happens that the enthusiastic amateur who has a firm belief in his own efforts to improve the breed does, in the end, have an influence on the powers that be at the factory which is out of all proportion to logical expectations. George Phillips was one of those enthusiasts: setbacks never discouraged him and he always pressed on with his main aims, regardless of the difficulties, which were often intensified by lack of funds.

George's background had made him into a tough character. In his earlier days he had been a Fleet Street despatch-rider who had learnt to cover the ground fast in any weather and take his opportunities where he found them. Later he became the chief photographer for *Autosport,* a calling which must have honed-up his reactions. He formed a team of TCs and later TD MGs, with Dick Jacobs and Ted Lund in the other two cars, which had won a string of home events, and this had led to some factory assistance. He campaigned a 1,250cc MG TC with his own design of racing body in many home events, and eventually his entry was accepted for the 1949 Le Mans race. Unfortunately, the car was eliminated on a technicality at the 19th hour when it was still going well, but he was not deterred by this setback and re-entered the following year to finish second in class and 18th in General Classification, thereby securing an entry for 1951.

The factory was so impressed by this valiant effort that they offered George a car for the 1951 race. This was to be a well-prepared 1,250cc TD with a special body of most attractive style and a much lower drag factor, which had been designed by Syd Enever using some of the data gained from EX 135. This put the speed up to nearly 120mph with only a small increase in power. The new car was registered as UMG 400. Unfortunately, it was eliminated by some obscure mechanical trouble during the race. The cause was not explained, but some thought it to be due to inferior fuel.

The car's performance was encouraging, but Enever was unhappy with the driving position, the seat being too high because it was unavoidably placed over the chassisframe. He decided that this was an appropriate moment to approach the management with a replacement for the TD, which was not doing at all well on the export market. Syd ordered two chassisframes to be made with more space between the sidemembers in the passenger area. One of them was made up with a similar body to UMG 400 and fitted out with full road equipment including bumpers, windscreen, sidescreens and hood. The result was a saleable product, but the project was killed by the arrival of the new Austin-Healey 100 at the 1952 London motor show; the Chairman of BMC, Sir Leonard Lord, did not want two new sportscars to arrive on the market at the same time.

After sales of the TD had fallen even further, the model was replaced by a 'facelift' called the TF, which did little to help matters; it was damned by the motoring press and disdained by the public. Worse still was the fact that American enthusiasts who had been loyal to MG over the years were not to be fooled and began to look enviously at the new Austin-Healey with its beautiful lines and excellent performance, even though it cost more. The new Triumph TR was also lurking in the background – and selling for just £5 more than the

TF; although it was soon to earn notoriety with clubmen for its rather dicey roadholding in the wet, it claimed to be the cheapest 100mph sportscar in the world.

Fortunately for MG, George Eyston stepped onto the scene. He knew all the old hands at the factory, his links with them going back to 1934 when he had taken EX 135 to Montlhéry to capture a string of Class G International records at over 120mph. He felt that it was time to take some more long-distance records and, being aware of the state of the market in America, suggested that success over there might give the ailing T-Type a shot in the arm until something better came along.

George knew better than anybody how to make the arrangements for record-breaking at Salt Lake, Utah. As the prototype sportscar EX 175 was not suitable for the purpose, it was decided to use the second frame that Syd Enever had had the foresight to order when he was thinking about the successor to the TF. A similar body to the Gardner MG's was built, but it had to be designed from scratch as the chassis was so different. The stretched XPAG engine was now the 1,466cc XPEG, which was to go into the American-market TF 1500 after the foundry had overcome some casting problems.

The new record car, EX 179, was duly despatched to Utah, where it was to be driven by George Eyston and Ken Miles in an attempt to take the 12-hour records. They were entirely successful in this, taking the 12-hour International record for 1,500cc engines at over 120mph. They then changed the engine to a more highly tuned sprint version and took the 10-mile record at 153.69mph, which was not too bad for an out-of-date, unsupercharged, pushrod, 1½-litre. You may ask what all this has to do with racing? Well, it is all part of what John Thornley so rightly called 'Maintaining the Breed', a phrase which became the title of his book.

In June 1954, Syd was promoted to chief designer at MG and given the go-ahead to turn EX 175 into a production car which would carry on the tradition of 'Safety Fast', using many of the components of the car that had just averaged 120mph for 12 hours. He was given a drawing office at the top of the new development department building where he was to be ably assisted by Terry Mitchell – the chassis and steering specialist – and Roy Brocklehurst – transmissions – both of whom were young and keen, with excellent qualifications for their work.

Sir Leonard Lord was a great admirer of George Eyston and no doubt listened to what he had to say concerning the market in the USA, and it was certainly down to George's influence that things went ahead at such a pace. George was a director of Wakefield Castrol, and it was only a matter of time before he called to see me with an agreement which was of considerable assistance to my budget. This led in turn to a long association with Castrol's very efficient and knowledgeable Competition Managers, Jimmy Hill and, later, Ray Simpson.

John Thornley had entered the three works cars for the Le Mans 24-Hours race as production models, and had planned the introduction date for the new car to coincide with the race.

The pedigree of the new model would serve to promote the car. The chassis was similar to that which had exceeded 150mph the year before, the body style had been influenced by the 1951 Le Mans car and to some extent by the Gardner MG, and the engine was a tuned version of the new B-Series which was performing so well in the Magnette ZA. A rumour was allowed to spread that there would be a more powerful engine later.

Unfortunately, a delay with the body pressings caused the announcement date to be put back by three months, but the *Automobile Club de l'Ouest* was co-operative and allowed us to change the entry from the Production to the Prototype category. I suspect that dear old Sammy Davis, the influential motoring journalist, may have put in a good word at that point.

There were plenty of sets of running gear and the new chassisframes were coming through on schedule. The race cars were panelled in aluminium instead of steel, and built in the development department workshop where Alec Hounslow was in charge. Syd had his office by the drawing office, which was situated over the workshop. My temporary office was underneath them, so I could watch the arrival of EX 182 in the greatest detail.

John Thornley had selected the drivers when making the entries, and in view of their performance with the TD team, Dick Jacobs and Ted Lund were chosen for two of the cars. Dick lived in Woodford, Essex, so it was convenient for him to come over for the test run of the first car at Silverstone on April 28, 1955, the other test driver that day being Ken Wharton. Of course, John Thornley and the development department team were also present, and they heard two or three criticisms from both drivers concerning the handling and the driving position, but nothing that could not be rectified quite easily.

It is interesting to look back at some of the personalities who were present that day. Ken Wharton, who was a great character, had been engaged by John Thornley to do the testing during the shakedown period as he had such a vast experience of all sorts of racing cars. I had met him in the early postwar days when we both ran home-made specials in sprints and hill-climbs. It was a sad loss to the fraternity when he was killed whilst racing 'down under' a few years later.

One of the mechanics who worked under Alec Hounslow was Dickie Green. When I was the manager of Nordec Superchargers, in Caterham, immediately after the war, I needed to find some mechanics who were interested in special tuning, so I advertised in *Motor Sport*. Dickie had just been demobilized and he had the right qualifications. He stayed on at Caterham for some time after I left there, then went to work for John Wyer at Aston Martin, in Feltham. He joined MG in 1955, was with us at Le Mans and stayed for a while until he married Doreen, John Wyer's secretary, after which he went off to America to become the West Coast representative for Rover. Now retired, after being the Service Director of Jaguar's West Coast Division for many years, he carries with him a string of reminiscences that would fill a book.

In May 1955 three MG Magnette saloons were entered in the *Daily Express*-sponsored BRDC International Production Touring Car race, one of those running in the 1,500cc class being driven by Dick Jacobs, who had driven a 1,250cc MG YB the previous year. The 1955 event was over-subscribed and the 1,500cc class was the largest with 10 cars entered: Simca, Ford, Borgward, two Volkswagens, two Peugeots and three Magnettes. Jacobs won the class (at an average speed of 71.45mph) without much difficulty, and confirmed his belief that the Le Mans car, using the same type of engine but in a more highly tuned state, would be very good.

The week after Silverstone, I asked Dick Jacobs to meet us at Silverstone to try out the modified Le Mans cars. We had also invited Johnny Lockett, the well-known motorcycle racer, to come along as he was due to drive at Le Mans as well. Between them they covered about 250 miles and pronounced themselves well satisfied with the car, which they were able to lap at over 81mph. The driving position had been improved and the handling was much better, but there were also other important improvements: since the cars were now entered as Prototypes, we could use the Weslake dual-entry ported cylinder heads, which gave more power, but had been ruled out for the production models on the grounds of increased machining costs and incompatability with the B-Series heads being produced for the rest of the range. Undershields and oil coolers were fitted, and the filler for the 20-gallon fuel tank was to be seen protruding through the middle of the boot panel. The high gear ratios were expected to bring a lap speed of around 85mph well within the scope of the engine, thus giving the cars the chance to qualify for the Biennial Cup entry at just under 80mph. However, there was slight apprehension that the cars might find it difficult to get away from the pits on the 1-in-30 slope with a 9:1 bottom gear and a sick engine.

Two entries had been accepted and the third was placed on the reserve list, with the almost certain knowledge that it would be allowed to start when the time came. There was also a spare car, which had borne the brunt of the testing, but would come in useful if there was any calamity at the last moment such as a crash during practice.

John Thornley, who had a great deal of experience in supervising racing teams and knew exactly what would be required in the way of back-up facilities, had been in consultation with Sammy Davis, for many years 'Casque' of *The Autocar*, and a famous Le Mans campaigner from the Bentley days, who probably knew more about the race than its organizers! Sammy was highly regarded by the *Automobile Club de l'Ouest*, who towards the end of his long and remarkable life would present him with a gold medal to mark his long association with them. A street in Le Mans was also to be named after him; Sammy died in 1981.

George Eyston, too, had considerable experience of Le Mans and was able to help John Thornley find suitable accommodation for the large number of team members – drivers, timekeepers, mechanics and back-up crew – who eventually were all housed under one roof at the *Chateau Chêne du Coeur*, which also provided ample stable accommodation for use as workshops.

John was also able to introduce us to Stan Nicholls, an accredited Auto-Cycle Union timekeeper, who had long experience of timing races in the Isle of Man. Aided by a team of spotters and supported by a stand-in timekeeper for such a long race, Stan was to come with me to a number of races in the following years and it was always a pleasure to have him by me and to know that our time and lap charts were as good as – and sometimes better than – those of the organizers.

All was ready by Sunday, June 5. It had been decided that the race cars should be driven to Le Mans accompanied by the competition department's mobile workshop, which had recently been completed by Appleyard's of Leeds. I was responsible for the slower convoy comprising the lorry, four race cars and a Riley Pathfinder. The rest of the party were told they could go at the same time, but travel at their own pace. I was glad to see them go at Boulogne as there is nothing worse than a convoy composed of cars of differing performance being driven by drivers of different temperaments and abilities.

I knew that my mechanics would be well controlled by Alec Hounslow and so set a pace that would keep the whole convoy together. We stopped for lunch at the *Chateaubriant*, in the newly rebuilt centre of Abbeville, and arrived without incident at the *Chateau Chêne du Coeur* that evening.

Appalled at the number of people who had arrived, I realized that I would have to institute a chain of command in short time to prevent the dissipation of all the willing hands that I had at my disposal. There were 36 of us in the team, and personnel had to be allocated into departments to deal with our relations with the organizers of the event; the control and running of the cars from scrutineering, through practice, to the race itself; and control of the pit crew and drivers. There had to be one man responsible for seeing that transport was available when required, not squandered by people going off on a minor errand and wasting time sitting in a cafe and gossiping. Some of the ladies – wives of various members of the management – had to deal with refreshments for the off-duty drivers and mechanics in the pit while the others could nip off for a snack. Dr M King, ably assisted by his wife and brother, were present to look after our medical needs, and my wife, being a qualified physiotherapist, could take instructions from Dr King if needed. Initially there would be problems with the accommodation, the beds being varied in quality, while the plumbing could best be described as unmodified late 19th century of Latin temperament. Fortunately, there was a bond in the shape of loyalty to the MG marque and a long association with the factory or the MG Car Club, which kept the whole unit working together.

I found a large blackboard and easel somewhere on the premises, which we placed in the hall, and we were soon able to show everyone where they stood in the scheme and to whom they might go if they needed help. Conversely, it showed the bosses who they had at their command. We arranged a large arrow, which could be moved around to indicate if something important was happening so that people didn't just walk past, thinking that they had seen it all before. It would all have been much easier with modern materials, but in those days blackboards were still in use.

I had 'Babe' Learoyd, VC with me as my transport officer and never had to worry about that section for the whole week. The cars and mechanics had all the space they needed in the stables, and the ramps of the lorry could be raised to form an inspection ramp.

We took our meals at *Les Rosiers*, whose patron, M. Menard, fed us for the whole stay in a convivial atmosphere only a few minutes away, near the river Sarthe. The large salon in the chateau served as a conference room for the many meetings between the management and the various sections. There could thus be instant decisions, for example after practice at night, over such things as ability to read pit signals.

Scrutineering went off well, the really beautiful finish of the British Racing Green cars causing admiration from the motoring press and the locals. They were attended by mechanics in overalls to match, with MG badges on the pocket, which put the finishing touch to the team's smart turnout, in contrast with some of our competitors, whose cars looked as if they had been cobbled together with difficulty the night before.

Cars 41 (Ken Miles and Johnny Lockett) and 42 (Dick Jacobs and Joe Flynn) went safely through scrutineering, and the third car, No 64, to be driven by Ted Lund and Hans Waeffler from Switzerland, was at the top of the reserve list and went through scrutineering as well.

The weather was fine, and Sammy Davis and I decided that the moment of truth was to be applied to the drivers in the form of pit-stop drill after lunch in the yard of the chateau. Some of the drivers seemed to think that this would be quite easy and approached the whole exercise with some flippancy, but they were soon taken down a peg or two when, for example, Sammy asked them in a quiet voice why they had left a chock under a wheel when the car was supposed to leave the pit, or a cautionary finger might be raised if a bonnet strap had been left undone. Sammy didn't miss a thing, and he showed infinite patience in correcting the transgressors. He would explain how it should be done and – equally important – why it was done that way. I knew his advice was sound as he had helped Peter Clark and myself to cut our stationary time at the pit by half from our 1938 to our 1939 class-winning time in the HRG; time saved in the pits is as good as a bonus on the track.

Russell Lowry kept an excellent log of the week's events in his capacity of General Secretary of the MG Car Club, and several who have subsequently written about the event owe him a great deal. I for one was fully occupied for about 16 hours a day during that week, and many of the amusing incidents which cropped up must have escaped me, but life was not all too serious, especially as some of the party were enjoying their first visit to France, let alone the Le Mans 24-Hours. Ted Lund, who was a prolific postcard writer, put several of his daily outputs into the letterbox placed in the wall of a local bank and no doubt enlivened things for their staff the following morning. Johnny Lockett had trouble with a local caricaturist and journalist who printed his name one day as Sockett and then as Kickett!

Previously missing members started arriving on the Wednesday, but some, having to earn their living elsewhere, could not get away until the last minute. The Kings turned up in a pair of TR2s and were made to park them round the back. Stan Nicholls arrived by air from England, bringing a set of bearing shells for a sick Riley Pathfinder which had played up on the way down. This was the result of protracted telephone calls which were not helped by the chateau's instrument, which bore the inscription '*Modèle de 1910*'.

Sammy took the drivers round the circuit in a touring car and explained the finer points to them before practice that night. This started before dark, so the drivers were able to play themselves in gently before beginning to lap in the 80s. When darkness fell the Lucas experts were available to set the lamps correctly.

The Mercedes were running with an air brake, which popped up like a huge desk lid when the car was braked hard, such as before the tight corner at the end of the long Mulsanne straight. Dick Jacobs complained about this, as did other drivers, as they were completely unsighted if the Mercedes passed them going into the corner. Johnny Lockett (41) became overdue due to a stretched waterpump drive belt, which caused overheating, but the head was lifted the following day and no damage was discovered.

Thursday found the helpers shopping for aluminium sheet and steel tubing to construct a better pit signal board, which the drivers said they couldn't see.....and Sammy said they had to! The drivers of car No 41 went out to practise to make sure all was well, but the other crews stayed behind; then the Arnott crashed and the driver was attended to by our Dr King, one result being that we gained a pit for timekeeping and lap scoring as it was next to our own.

On Friday it was confirmed that the Lund/Waeffler car (No 64) was in the final entry list, and everyone was fully occupied in packing the gear and provisions needed for the race. During the afternoon we had another driver practice for the traditional Le Mans start, in which drivers sprinted to their cars from positions on the other side of the track. Dick Jacobs was told by Sammy to wake his ideas up, but Dick had had experience of these starts and bet Sammy that his would be first of the MGs away on the day. Those Le Mans starts were not as easy as they looked, but Stirling Moss was a master of the technique and was nearly always first away.

Saturday dawned fine and, after photographs had been taken, the convoy left soon after 10 o'clock to begin what is always a real marathon for the mechanics and pit personnel. The cars had to be in place by midday for the tanks to be drained and refilled with the official fuel, then sealed. This took place between 12.00 and 2.30pm. The service vehicle was parked at the rear of the pits and all the parts and tools carried on the cars had to be paraded on the pit counter. As usual, a running battle would ensue to keep unwanted people out of the pits, whether friend or foe; things tended to get pilfered as souvenirs if minders were not posted. I lost a Leica camera from the pit on one occasion. During the race, and particularly until the novelty of things had worn off, there were invariably too many people in the pits. We painted a broad white line across the floor in each of our pits and furnished Sammy with a referee's whistle. Even our own personnel who were not directly concerned with the pit-stop had to keep behind the line as soon as the whistle went.

The drivers arrived a little later under the supervision of Babe Learoyd, a big man, who I knew would get them to the circuit on time whatever happened! At last the magic hour arrived and at 4pm there was complete silence followed by the patter of feet running to the cars. Jacobs made good his boast and his was first of the MGs to start. However, Fangio's Mercedes was starting from in front of our pit, and the great man jumped in and put his foot through the steering wheel and wasted a few valuable seconds in disentangling himself!

About six minutes later our cars went by without incident and were soon lapping at 5min 45sec (87.28mph), well within the schedule we had set for them. After six laps they were given a 'Slower' signal to settle them down and they continued to pass steadily in the order 64, 41 and 42. Dick had allowed his two team-mates to pass him on the straight as he was determined not to over-rev in the excitement of the opening laps. Meanwhile, a big fight was going on amongst the race leaders between Jaguar, Mercedes and Ferrari, as well as the usual class struggles, but our job was to get three cars to the finish at the qualifying speed.

A little later, as Dick Jacobs was to write in his book, *An M.G. Experience*: "At this stage everything was fine and I was thoroughly enjoying some of the best motor racing I can ever remember. On two occasions the leading drivers in the race, Fangio (Mercedes), Castellotti (Ferrari) and Mike Hawthorn (Jaguar D-Type) lapped the MG just as I was approaching the 400 metre braking point at the end of the Mulsanne Straight. Up went the air brake on the Mercedes, on went the brake lights of the Ferrari, and Mike with his disc brakes sailed past them round the corner and away in the lead. It was a wonderful sight."

At about 6.30pm, cars were being called in for refuelling, one of these being Lance Macklin's Austin-Healey, which occupied the next pit to our left. Due to a misunderstanding by Pierre Levegh (Mercedes), he did not appreciate

Macklin's intentions and hit the Austin-Healey with his right front wheel when travelling at high speed. The sloping back to the Austin-Healey acted as a launching ramp and the Mercedes flew over the crash barrier into the crowded spectator area in front of the grandstand, causing terrible carnage as it burst into flames and, being partly composed of magnesium castings, burnt fiercely. The accident happened about 150 yards to our left, so we didn't realize what had occurred at the time, but everyone in the pit heard the bang and the cries from the crowd. The Austin-Healey carried on for some yards and Macklin scrambled out and ran to his pit, actually climbing over our pit counter.

Dick Jacobs was passing the pit area and later wrote: "Just after about two hours' driving I came through the pit area as Lance Macklin was picking himself up. The notorious Mercedes crash into the crowd had happened. I had no idea of the extent of the accident and carried on. Coming up the hill on the approach to White House Corner I could see the smoke rising from the grandstand area and I think this must have distracted me and I lost concentration. Anyway I lost control, hit the embankment protecting the crowd and got thrown out, skating along the road for some distance. I don't remember much after that. When I came round in hospital I was very upset and sent a message to John Thornley apologising for breaking the car."

It has been suggested that Dick had lost his rhythm after having had a 'Slow-down' signal, but I do not think this was at all likely as he was a very experienced driver and had already had several laps to adjust to the slower pace. I am inclined to support his own theory that the huge column of smoke straight ahead distracted him. Poor Dick had complications in the hospital at Coulaines, which was terribly overcrowded. He was visited by Dr King, John Thornley and his friend Fred Crossley and later, when they thought it wise, by his wife. He became worse and contracted pneumonia and was then flown back to the Churchill Hospital at Oxford on Sir Leonard Lord's instructions. He was in hospital for four months and never raced again.

Back at the circuit the remaining two MGs continued to run very well. The public address system did not say anything about Dick's accident until 8pm, when he was reported to be slightly hurt and in hospital. The race had become a sad occasion, the music had stopped and people spoke in hushed voices. Our intention was to continue just as we had started until circumstances changed. There was talk that the race might be abandoned after 12 hours. At 71 laps our two number-one drivers got back into Nos 41 and 64 and continued to lap with incredible regularity. Lockett was the most regular, turning a whole series of consecutive laps at 5min 37sec and sometimes with just a one-second difference. Miles and Lund had put in the fastest laps at 5min 22sec and 5min 23sec, or about 94mph, and a speed of 117.69mph was recorded on the flying-kilometre on the Mulsanne straight, with the drivers actually having to lift off.

Just before 2am we heard from Stirling Moss' father that Stuttgart had authorized the withdrawal of the rest of the Mercedes team and the public address system made the announcement shortly afterwards in the most solemn tones. The night dragged on with everyone sticking to their allotted jobs, whether it was spotting, timekeeping, or catering to supply endless cups of tea or soup. Sammy Davis was still on his stool on the pit counter, looking rather like a bedraggled old eagle, with Alec Hounslow and Dickie Green always in attendance. As the enthusiasm had gone from the whole exercise, fatigue was more difficult to combat.

At dawn it began to rain, at first imperceptibly and then more intensely, to increase the depression. To make matters worse the *toilettes* at the rear of our pit overflowed and we had to move our transporter and service cars to a nicer pitch and make room for the pumping wagon which came to alleviate matters.

Soon after 6am Lund took over and ran steadily, but then overdid it in trying to reduce the gap between his car and Lockett's, which had increased during the night when Waeffler was driving. There was a Jaguar in the sand at Arnage with its tail sticking out a little into the roadway, and Ted took a slightly wider line and clipped the left front of the MG. The result was a six-minute pit-stop at 9am with some intense work by Hounslow and Green which entailed some panel-bashing and a quick track-rod adjustment as well as a change of driver.

We were now lying 15th and 19th, the weather improved, Waeffler reported that he had successfully avoided a spinning Porsche, and both drivers commented on the apparent lack of traffic. Our Belgian member, John Valentyn, who was our bilingual interpreter, diplomat and public relations man, had had a hard night coping with officials, the hospital and public announcements, as well as acting as our filter for unwanted guests – either drunk or sober – who seemed now to have become more numerous. One of our cars moved up to 12th place, but the British announcer ignored us.

By 3pm both cars had covered the minimum distance necessary to qualify for the 1956 race, then No 41 came in for a final pit-stop, and Alec and Dickie checked it over in the rain.

Just before 4pm the police started to line the track, barriers appeared and seconds after the chequered flag came out, Ted Lund crossed the finishing line in No 64. We could show 248 laps at 86.17mph and 230 laps at 81.97mph.

That night the dinner at *Les Rosiers* dawdled to a somnolent conclusion and we all staggered back to the chateau for sleep, knowing that we had many problems to solve on the morrow. John Thornley had to attend to the diplomatic side of things, flowers had to be sent to the cathedral, Dr King had spent the night at the hospital with Dick Jacobs, by now critically ill. The wrecked cars had to be sent home through the good offices of M. Hallard, the local Austin agent. The MGs were to be checked over for the drive home, the transporter had to be packed, and the international travel documents put in the hands of the right people. Some of the visitors and helpers had gone, and my own little convoy left early on the Tuesday morning.

When I got back to Abingdon I sat down to write my report to the directors with a heavy heart as I knew that we had only been partly successful and that the fault was not entirely our own.

The French Government panicked; motorsport of any sort was banned from then on. Perhaps it was to give time for thought, but it spread to other countries and things looked grim for a while. The 'yellow press' gloated over the 80 dead and many more injured, poor Macklin came in for much criticism, and Levegh – being both dead and French – was a martyr.

I sent a memorandum to the management by which I hoped to persuade them to use their influence to further Production Sports Car racing at the expense of Prototypes. Of all the other entrants, our cars and those of the Triumph company were closest to the models which, at an economic price, were available on sale to the public. Production cars could be exciting and give the public an interest in the makes they supported. Our quickest car had finished the race at a higher speed than the winning Ferrari driven by Luigi Chinetti in 1949. In 1960 a privately-entered MGA Twin-Cam Coupe was to win the 2-litre class at 91.92mph and put in a lap at 99.46mph.

As the Alpine Rally had been cancelled, John Thornley decided that we could spend the money in a little sortie to the Continent. Members of the design department and some test drivers and mechanics were to take an MGA pre-production model, an Austin Cambridge fitted with an MGA Le Mans engine and improved suspension, a ZA Magnette with the Le Mans engine, a moderately tuned Austin Westminster and an EX 182 prepared for the Alpine Rally.

The drivers included John Gott, Bill Shepherd, John Milne and John Williamson and two Swiss drivers, J Keller and H Zweifel. We went to the Nürburgring, the Savoy Alps and Montlhéry and came back with a lot of data which we could use for racing and rallies, as well as staying at some excellent hotels, having covered over 2,300 miles and demonstrated that improvements were needed to the brakes, the roadholding, the oil coolers, the gear ratios and the ventilation. The factory engineers were being educated by the rally drivers, who were prepared to give the cars a lot more 'stick' than the factory testers.

In September 1955 the factory ran three MGAs in the Ulster Tourist Trophy race, one being fitted with a twin-cam engine and the other two with pushrod units. The Twin-Cam retired having been fitted with Weber carburettors at the last moment as the Solex carburettors originally fitted were unsatisfactory. The revised inlet manifold had a fault in the welding, which caused an air leak which in its turn induced piston failure. One of the pushrod-engined cars went out with a leaking experimental aluminium fuel tank. This was one of the tanks used at Le Mans, but the Ulster course was much rougher than the French surface. Jack Fairman drove the finishing car into fourth place in the class behind three Porsches at 71.07mph. Both of the above failures were brought about by the late arrival of the twin-cam engines at Abingdon, one of these being from Longbridge and the other from Morris Engines at Coventry. There was no time to test the cars at Silverstone before taking them to Ulster, and the Longbridge engine was discarded at the last moment on Syd Enever's instructions. The race was a disaster as there was a seven-car accident, resulting in the death of two drivers. The press reports did little to help our 'Safety Fast' image, and the BMC directors decided to discontinue our racing programme for the time being, although a modicum of assistance was to be allowed for private entrants due to John Thornley's belief in that policy.

Early the following year I received a proposal from John Thornley for an entry of two MGAs in the Mille Miglia, in response to which I wrote a strongly worded memorandum outlining my reasons against the entries. I pointed out that this would interfere with our rally programme and, in any case, it had not been budgeted for. Also, and more importantly, if the crews, of which two were feminine, became involved in an accident it might do the Company even more harm. I also pointed out that we had no recent experience in service assistance on that event and could not give the two cars as much support as we should like. I was overruled.

The crews were to be Nancy Mitchell and Pat Faichney, and Peter Scott-Russell and Tom Haig. The cars were prepared in the new competition department and I took Alec Hounslow and Douggie Watts with me in a Morris Oxford Traveller, which would act as the only support car, while I went in my

A90 Austin Westminster.

The race was run in terrible weather; it rained very hard and it was cold for the time of the year. The rivers were in flood and rose so much towards the end of the race that when the road was re-opened for traffic the debris was building up so high against the parapets of the bridges that I feared they might collapse before we passed over them. I can't imagine why we fitted the cars with aeroscreens as the Italians, realizing that April was a wet month in those parts, fitted their cars with wraparound Perspex screens which deflected the rain very efficiently.

We had stood by to give service in Rome and Florence, but the drivers could not afford any time other than that needed for petrol and oil and a drink. There was an interesting scrap between the two MGAs, Nos 228 and 229, and the Sheila Van Damm/Peter Harper Sunbeam Rapier, No 254, which had started 25 minutes after the MGs; and the Scott-Russell MGA finished with a time of 15hr 2min 15sec, just 2min 22sec ahead of the Sunbeam Rapier, whose occupants must have had a much more comfortable run with a roof over their heads. Nancy Mitchell was 2min 51sec behind them, and Tommy Wisdom, in the Warwick-prepared Austin-Healey, was just 1min 40sec further behind. The organizers did not present a Ladies' Cup, but the local MG agent very gallantly took Nancy to a silversmith in Brescia the day after and let her choose a very beautiful hand-made silver flower bowl. It was undoubtedly one of the finest performances which Nancy Mitchell put up in any motoring event; to average over 65mph for over 990 miles in such appalling conditions was a highly creditable performance, nor must one overlook her navigator, Pat Faichney, who must have felt a lot colder and wetter than the driver. Peter Scott-Russell described the event and the weather in general to the British motoring press in his own inimitable manner, while Gregor Grant, who drove an MG Magnette, wrote an excellent first-hand report of his experiences in the race, which was published in the May 11 issue of his magazine *Autosport*.

There was an interesting sequel to the participation of the MGAs in the Mille Miglia. Peter Scott-Russell noticed that the level-crossing keepers would lift the barriers for the red-painted Italian cars, but kept them down until the train passed for other competitors. As we were to pass through Italy in both the Alpine and Liège-Rome-Liège rallies I decided that we would paint all our cars red, with white roofs in the case of hardtops. This became the BMC Ecurie Safety Fast colour for many years.

The factory supported private entrants in Touring Car races and in the RAC Touring Car Championship during the following years, with occasional sorties into the more popular events with Riley Pathfinders or Austin A105s. The event which gave me the most satisfaction was winning the team prize with the Pathfinders against the Jaguar team at the 1958 *Daily Express* Silverstone meeting.

Eventually we presented a trophy to the RAC to be awarded as a challenge trophy each year for the driver who won the Touring Car Championship run by the BRSCC (British Racing and Sports Car Club). I suggested that we called it the Bonneville Trophy, to commemorate the many British successes at the Salt Lake, and we were particularly glad to see Jack Sears win it with an Austin A105 in 1958.

CHAPTER 5

The Monte Carlo Rally

"People got out of their cars and immediately fell over, surprised that they had had the temerity to drive so fast under such conditions."

The 'Monte', as most enthusiasts call it, is probably still the best-known of the International rallies, and it certainly was during my time with BMC, as well as the least understood, the most popular for the true amateur and the most disliked by the ace works drivers. For the team managers it meant nothing but worry from the time the entries were sent in until the wrecked cars were safely back in the home country and the works accountant had presented them with the bill, which in my experience was always about three times as much as for any other event.

On the credit side, the factory obtained an enormous amount of free publicity, though not necessarily all of it favourable, for its cars and drivers. As for the argument as to the extent to which this or that car bore any resemblance to the one the public could buy, this is so old as to need no further comment here.

There was also a time when the Monte attracted the most bizarre collection of crews, and I was not at all sorry when things were tightened up and the authorities quite rightly insisted that any competitor had to be in possession of a proper International Competition Licence. Prior to that, we used to be inundated with applications for the loan of a car for the Monte by people who had no qualifications whatsoever as competition drivers; usually, the reason for their request was because they happened to be triplets, or a member of the House of Lords, or perhaps just nice people who wanted a cheap winter holiday on the Riviera.

Mike Couper, in his very instructive book *Rallying to Monte Carlo*, went into the question of the cost to the private owner in some detail, and I seem to remember he quoted a figure of over £500 per car as long ago as 1955, which was quite a lot of money is those days, though less than half what it cost to prepare a works entry properly and provide it with the technical and human support necessary to give it a realistic chance of success.

The Monte has always been a rally in which chance plays as great a part as it does at the famous Monte Carlo tables, and one of our first gambles was to select the most favourable starting point from the several on offer from which competitors would converge on a concentration point in the foothills of the French Alps. The mileages were adjusted for approximate equality, but this couldn't compensate for variations in the weather conditions. Also, as the entry in those days could well exceed 350 crews, it could take the field about six hours to pass any given point, during which time daylight could turn to darkness and the state of the roads could alter dramatically. This meant that a competitor's chance of success rested as much on his or her place in the long convoy as on their skill in the cockpit.

Why, then, has the event been such an attraction for so many years, especially as it has never been considered a particularly severe one as far as the car is concerned? The answer, I think, lies in history and goes back to the days when to journey across Europe in mid-winter was in itself something of an achievement. The very idea of setting out to battle with the elements when most people were sitting at home by a fire or in centrally heated comfort, finally to arrive in warm sunshine at a place where many of us would like to be, kindled the imagination. The Monte, therefore, was always well covered by the daily press, who would send journalists to Monte Carlo to watch the finish on the quayside when these very publications hardly ever mentioned a great British victory in the Alpine Rally, or even gave as many as five lines to Le Mans – unless, of course, someone was killed there!

Nor did the regulations help to even out the chances; quite the reverse, in fact. The organizers were noted for framing these in such a way as to encourage protests and recriminations, and in some years they put such a bias on them that it was a foregone conclusion as to the make of car that would win. This state of affairs, of course, encouraged factories to enter cars which were not representative of their normally successful touring cars.

Yet in spite of all these annoying circumstances it was very hard to find the courage to refrain from entering and just stand by and watch without competing, as one might the play in the Casino. The attendant publicity of an outright win in the Monte was always too much of a temptation, so time and again the factories would have yet another try.

It was usual to graft a great weight of winter equipment onto a Monte car. In the distant past this consisted of chains for two spare wheels, shovels, wire ropes, Swedish unditching gear, spare parts in abundance and a great many small items which people thought might come in handy. The total added weight, including the crew, might come to more than half the weight of the car, and then the crews used to wonder where the power had gone when they reached the mountains. Moreover, French petrol was not of the best in those days and, of course, snow tyres also caused some drag.

During one event I looked into the boot of Wolfgang Levy's DKW and realized that it was time to think along new lines. I think he carried a nylon tow rope, a can of fuel and one spare wheel; the tool roll was of the minimum and there were a few small electrical spares. After that we started to cut down on our own spare parts.

The Monte invariably served as a good test for dynamos, foglamps, batteries and heaters. The nights were so long that the electrical equipment was tested to the full. Snow tyres were used a great deal until they were gradually displaced by the studded tyre, the tungsten carbide tips of which were mounted in a rigid breaker carcase. Dunlop made great advances in the development of these tyres, which were the only solution to fast driving on sheet ice, but at that time they were still too expensive for general commercial application.

The 1956 Monte Carlo Rally can be said to be the first serious attempt by BMC to win the event. Perhaps we rather overstepped the numbers, but then the money went further in those days. The entries were as follows:

Cars	Crews
3 Austin A90s from Lisbon	John Gott, Bill Shepherd and John Williamson
	Gerry Burgess, Sam Croft-Pearson and Ian Walker
	Joan Johns, Pat Moss and Doreen Rich
2 Austin A90s from Stockholm	Ken Wharton and Gordon Shanley
	Raymond Baxter and Reg Phillips
1 Austin A90 from Glasgow	Mike Couper, Pat Fillingham and Nevil Lloyd
2 Riley Pathfinders from Lisbon	John Bremner and Tom Oldworth
1 Riley Pathfinder from Glasgow	Lyndon Sims, Reg Stokes and Tom Bounds
1 MG Magnette from Stockholm	Nancy Mitchell, Doreen Reece and Sue Hindmarsh
1 MG Magnette from Rome	Gregor Grant, Norman Davis and Cliff Davis
1 A50 (modified) from Lisbon	Jack Sears, Archie Scott-Brown and Ken Best

The 12 cars were ready in good time to reach their various starting points, those from Stockholm and Lisbon being sent by sea with their crews following by air. Then about a week before the crews were due to leave, and the day before the cars were to be taken to the docks, there was a fire at Cowley. The Lisbon cars were away, but the Stockholm cars were in the export despatch block, which was burnt to the ground. Fortuitously, the car for Ken Wharton had been delayed, so it was not damaged, but Raymond Baxter's was reduced to ashes.

The service car I had intended to take to France was the only one available with any of the right equipment on it, so I decided to prepare that for Baxter to use. Another Brooks average speed meter was made up quickly by Harold Brooks and sent down from Manchester, various other special items were obtained at short notice and within 36 hours we had a replica of the Baxter car ready to send to Sweden. But by that time the last boat had gone, so we had to decide whether to drive the car to Stockholm or find another route. The former plan was considered too risky as the weather was not promising, so we hired a Bristol Freighter from Silver City Airways and the car was flown to Stockholm. This was very expensive, but we were determined to get Raymond to the start at any cost, feeling that it was an honour to be able to supply a car for a BBC commentator, quite apart from its publicity value. Unfortunately, the car was dogged with electrical trouble and was put out of the rally in Germany, but Raymond turned up at Monte Carlo in time to cover the finish. He was the most knowledgeable of the radio commentators on motoring matters at the time and he gave everyone a fair share of the story when covering an event. He was also very popular with the mechanics at Abingdon and would often give them a credit line during a commentary.

With my own car actually in the rally, I took a very standard Austin A90 to France and set off in it for Reims, where we had decided to service the cars.

The common route began at Paris that year, but Reims seemed a better service point as the cars would have more time in hand there. This proved a wise choice for the arrival of the cars in Paris coincided with the evening rush hour and some crews were late at the control, despite not having stopped for service.

The weather was very cold and there was a lot of fog in northern France, but we arrived in Reims on the morning of Wednesday, January 18. Throughout our journey we had kept tuned-in to the BBC commentaries, so we had some news of our cars, and were glad to hear that they were all still on their routes, though alarmed to learn that Gerry Burgess had left San Sebastian without obtaining the necessary official stamp on his road book. He had handed the book in at the control, but somehow it was not stamped. Unfortunately, Gerry and Sam had not verified this at the time and their attention was not drawn to the omission until they arrived at the next control at Auch, by which time it was too late to return. Frantic telegrams were sent to Monte Carlo confirming that the car had passed through the San Sebastian control, and when Gerry arrived at Reims we told him not to worry and to proceed as if nothing was wrong. However, it must have been a worrying drive for him, and to make things worse he got caught in a secret time control just after he left us!

The garage we had chosen for our service point was small but hospitable, and with the aid of the patron's wife, both my wife and Mrs Bob Porter managed to feed the crews and see that they had a wash. Lucas and Castrol also had service stations at this point.

As the cars had all gone through by soon after tea, we had time for a meal and some sleep ourselves before setting out early for the run to Monte. The fog was thick and it froze on the windscreen, so that even with the heater bar on and the full heat of the blower directed onto the screen there was only a small clear space through which I could look. Needless to say we made slow progress and got well behind schedule, so it was midnight by the time we reached Monte Carlo.

Our other support car was at Chambéry, at the start of the difficult section. It was bitterly cold there, with thick fog over the Col du Granier and the Col du Rousset. As a result of these weather conditions only 35 of the 308 starters reached Monte Carlo without losing time, and our only 'clean' cars were those captained by John Gott and John Bremner. Gregor Grant in the Magnette had had a bad time with dynamo trouble, and in spite of laying in a stock of batteries had had to retire at Chambéry. Mike Couper had to complete the road section in order to qualify for the *Concours de Confort* (the 'comfort' competition), but as he had to get there without damaging the car he took things easily and didn't mind if he was a bit late here and there, though not so late as to risk disqualification.

On arrival our hopes ran high for we had eight out of our 12 cars in the first 90 placings. Only the first 90 were allowed to compete in the final elimination test, known as the Mountain Circuit, on the Saturday, which was an exceptionally high percentage for our teams. Meanwhile, the cars were impounded and placed in the *parc fermé* for the night. Adjustments were allowed to be made to the brakes between the braking test held outside Monte Carlo and arrival at the *parc fermé,* and due to fatigue Bill Shepherd slacked off John Gott's brakes instead of tightening them up, an error which could have been fatal. Our girls had done well, for Nancy Mitchell was then third in the Ladies' class and Joan Johns had set a very good time in the downhill brake test just before the arrival control. We had a good chance of the team prize with the Austins, which were then third out of 89 teams, and the press were tending to play up our position for more than it was worth. John Gott had been worried about his brakes over the Alps, but he was to be a lot more worried when he got out on the Mountain Circuit and found he had practically none!

The day dawned fine, and so did BMC's hopes as we went out on the circuit to lend any help we could. Ken Wharton had asked me to arrange to have a couple of buckets of water handy as he came down the Col de Braus. There was just time to throw them onto his front brakes as he came round a tight hairpin. His brakes were very hot and clouds of steam came away from the car, but further down the route a front wheel collapsed and he lost valuable time changing it. The Austin team went past at speed and we were rather surprised to see Joan Johns up with John Gott for we had no idea that John was almost without brakes.

One of the works Citroens which were leading for the team prize crashed at a hairpin, fortunately not seriously, and our hopes of the team award rose yet higher. All our cars being accounted for, we started down the hill to l'Escarene and had hardly covered more than three kilometres when we saw a car upside-down on the apex of a hairpin bend. Joan Johns waved us to stop and with intense relief we saw that Pat and Doreen were with her and apparently unhurt.

They told us that the brakes had failed as they were going into the hairpin. Joan had placed the car up a bank on the right-hand side of the road with the object of slowing it down as much as possible. The car rolled over to the left and stopped on its roof a few feet short of a very steep drop which ended about two lacets further down. The girls were shaken, but pleased to be alive. I think Pat had been smoking at the time and had been sitting in the back, so she had a fright when she smelt the petrol.

This was the first and last time that Pat ever participated in a rally just as a member of the crew as distinct from being the first driver; she said that she preferred to be responsible for her own accidents in future! The only casualty was Doreen, who had sprained her ankle after she had got out of the car. We returned to Monte Carlo with the girls and then found that most of our cars were missing. Archie Scott-Brown had put a wheel over the edge and the A50 had rolled down a gulley onto its roof. Jack and Ken got to work and slid the car, still on its roof, for the length of the gulley and finally got it back onto its wheels, and they completed the course, but by then they were hopelessly late. The three of them actually drove the car to the prize presentation the next day, although it was not a very beautiful sight.

Nancy had hit something hard higher up in the snow and had laboured for some time with the jack to get the front bumper clear of the wheels. Gerry Burgess came to grief somewhere else, and thus John Gott's car was the only Austin to complete the course without incident, in spite of some very frightening moments, but with time lost due to stopping at each Austin crash. John Bremner also crashed at about 60mph after avoiding a Frenchman in a 4CV Renault who was out on the course when he should not have been; the Riley had to be driven to the left to avoid a head-on collision and the left-hand wheels dropped into a gutter which held the car against a very jagged rock face. The whole of the left-hand side of the car was battered beyond recognition and the Riley was so well wedged in that it took us a lot of time to get it out.

Our chances for the team prize thus vanished into thin air and the Sunbeams were waiting to step in without delay. However, there were some small consolations for us as Mike Couper won the comfort competition, and the intrepid Scots, Archie and Ian Sutherland, won the *Autosport* Trophy for the best performance by a British crew driving their own car, in their case a Riley Pathfinder.

There were 233 finishers in the rally, and our best car, the one captained by John Gott, finished 55th, while Nancy retained third place in the Ladies' class. We hadn't much to show for the money we had spent except a lot of hard-won experience. Tired crews were not permitted to adjust their own brakes on later occasions; thereafter we took care to have a good service crew in the right place at the right time. Moreover, next time we decided to concentrate on a quality entry with fewer cars and better attention, whilst the brake troubles were cured by using fluid with a higher boiling point.

We could not grudge the winners their laurels, for Ronnie Adams, assisted by Frank Bigger and Derek Johnson, brought their large 3½-litre Jaguar saloon home with great skill. It was not a very snowy event that year but, even so, such a large car must have taken a great deal of handling on the twisty mountain roads. The speed of the car on some of the downhill sections in the mountains impressed the organizers greatly, and Jacques Taffe talked for years afterwards about Ronnie Adams' ability.

This was one of the few occasions when a British car had won the Monte. Of the first 30 events (the first one took place in 1911), the rally had been won by British crews driving British cars only four times, although a foreign crew driving a British car had managed to win twice. It was hard to understand at that time why we hadn't done better as a nation in this event, for it seemed to have no bearing on a lack of snow-driving experience because the Scandinavians had only won the event twice. How things would change in the future!

There was no 1957 Monte Carlo Rally as, owing to the Suez situation, the French and British Governments restricted the use of fuel to essential purposes in both countries. So instead we made a small-scale sortie to Italy in February to participate in the Sestriere Rally and tried to contain our patience until things returned to normal. In view of the fact that the Austin A90 had been developed into the A105 and was capable of dealing with anything in its class, the Suez crisis could not have come at a more unfortunate time for us. We had a car that could have won the Monte, and the 1957 regulations were sufficiently straightforward to preclude the chances of the outsiders.

So we waited until 1958 and set out with high hopes as our entry was well-prepared. For the first time we fitted rooflights operated by the passenger, as well as Halda average-speed meters, whilst the cars were shod with Dunlop Weathermaster tyres all round. By now the Riley 1.5 was in production, but the company had fallen behind in their manufacture and the necessary 1,000 qualifying cars would not be made before the rally, so the rally cars had to run as Special Series entries. Nancy had been entered in one of these, but the organizers agreed to change her entry to a Magnette at the last moment. The final line-up, therefore, was:

From Paris

Wolseley 1500	John Gott and Chris Tooley
MG Magnette	Nancy Mitchell and Joan Johns
Riley 1.5	Ray Brookes and Edward Brookes
Riley 1.5	John Bremner and Tony Oldworth
Austin A105	Jack Sears, Sam Croft-Pearson and Ken Best
Austin A105	Mike Couper and Pat Fillingham
Morris Minor 1000	Pat Moss and Ann Wisdom
Austin A35	John Sprinzel and Willie Cave
Austin-Healey	Tommy Wisdom and Jack Hay

From Glasgow

Austin A105	Bill Shepherd and John Williamson

The Shepherd/Williamson car was fitted with brake performance recording equipment supplied and fitted by Ferodo. This not only measured the temperature of the brakes at the shoes, but also recorded the number of times the brakes were applied during the entire rally.

The Wolseley 1500 was a fully modified car entered in the Special Series class, which had to compete with the Grand Touring cars. It was designed to test the car's components to the maximum, and having a fair degree of comfort we hoped that the crew would arrive at the difficult sections feeling less tired than those of the sportscars against which they were in direct competition.

We started our teams from Paris because we thought that the risks of crossing the Jura mountains were outweighed by the conveniences of an all-French route. These were: a single currency, no frontiers to cross, only one foreign language, excellent service at the starting point, the proximity to England if we wanted any part in a hurry before the start and, most important, our service cars could reach more than one control during the event.

A typical car from our entry that year was fitted with the following equipment:

Lights: Two long-range headlights, two dipping foglamps with yellow bulbs, one remote-controlled long-range rooflamp (used for picking up signposts, acute turnings and reversing) and a navigator's lamp adjustable for brilliance.

Electrical equipment: Two-speed windscreen wipers, screen washer filled with anti-freeze solution, supplementary wiper on rear window, hand-operated strip heater on screen to supplement demister, and twin high-frequency horns.

Navigational equipment: One 24-hour clock and two stopwatches, one stopwatch with a split second hand to take intermediate timings, a Halda average-speed meter, average-speed tables calibrated in seconds per kilometre, marked maps, all with suitable distances and times inserted, shelves and pockets for maps and road book, and clips for pencils.

Crew comforts: Passenger's seat modified to let down for resting, lap strap to prevent crew being thrown out of car in the event of an accident, extra padding on the doors to prevent bruising when sleeping, driving seat of 'bucket' type or altered to prevent the driver sliding from side to side.

Tyres: Six Weathermaster tyres of the snow or mud grip type, and strap-on or clip-on chains (wraparound chains tended to break or run loose at high speeds and were very heavy). Many cars had insufficient wheel-to-mudguard clearance to permit chains.

The two days before the start from Paris were not very cold and the weather reports gave very little indication of impending snow. All the crews got away without incident and the service crews departed to their appointed stations. There were 342 cars and crews entered for the rally that year, of which 91 chose Paris. Conditions were fairly normal until halfway to Chaumont, which was about 150 miles to the east. Ice had formed on the road at this point, and it became difficult to see it in the dark; the first cars had left Paris at 15.15 hours local time, and it was dark by 17.00. We had decided to spend the night at Dijon and pick up the crews at Chambéry, while Douggie Watts and his boys pressed on for Gap.

Just before the start, our crews had begun to get anxious for there had been some rather ominous weather reports posted up in the headquarters of the *AC de l'Isle-de-France*, most of these forecasting snow and warning of icy roads throughout the Jura. We experienced bad weather ourselves to a minor degree on our way to Dijon, but little did we know what had happened to our cars.

Before they reached Chaumont, a Fiat retired and one of the British Army team cars, a Triumph TR3, collided with a Sunbeam, putting both cars out of the rally. All our cars reached Chaumont with time in hand and the crews had a meal, but the bitter wind already bore a few specks of snow. No time could be lost and as soon as the cars were allowed to leave the control at their proper time their crews set about putting as many kilometres into the hours as the roads would allow, for now they knew of the bad conditions ahead. The highest average speed allowed was 80km/h (50mph) and the organizers had the right to put in secret controls on sections where they thought crews might exceed this figure. However, there was no point in being prudent as it would probably mean exclusion later on through lateness. John Gott put his average up to nearly 100km/h as soon as possible and in so doing passed a number of other cars, amongst them being Cuth Harrison, the Ford team leader, who appreciated the urgency of the situation and joined the race with a will. The temperature was now down to 26 degrees F and there was some fog which froze on their windscreens.

John Gott now takes up the story: "The road is also icy and the steering immediately feels dangerously light, so telling me that tyre adhesion is at its minimum. I always recall the instructor at the Hendon Police Driving School dinning into his pupils that to brake, decelerate violently or suddenly twitch the steering wheel on the skidpan will have unpleasant results. Whether at 20mph on a skidpan or at 90mph on an ice-covered road, the advice is sound, but even now I find it hard not to decelerate and I am convinced that an intensive course of skidpan training for all drivers would do much to reduce the toll of winter accidents.

"Just what happens is all too vividly brought home to us by the sight of a Simca which we are about to overtake shooting off the road in a series of pirouettes and overturning in the ditch, the crew climbing out to tell us they are unhurt and waving us on."

John and Chris arrived at Gérardmer, another 100 miles further on, with 26 minutes in hand, as did most of the other members of the team. At the control Pat Moss said that it was a miracle that none of the cars was damaged for the road down into the town was so slippery that cars even slid when stationary and many could not stop at the control. People got out of their cars and immediately fell over, surprised that they had had the temerity to drive so fast under such conditions. It would have been better for them to have remained in their cars, ignorant of this, for then they might have continued to drive with confidence.

The control was in a café where drivers of many nations exchanged news. The Munich starters had experienced a terrible journey on the *autobahnen* and some had seen a lorry with two trailers which skidded across the central verge, just missing their car as it plunged, jack-knifed, into the ditch. Pat Moss had a small incident with a lamp-post in her Morris, and Jack Sears was late.

As the cars restarted it began to snow again and John Gott described the night's run as one of the most hectic he had ever experienced: "The route lay right up a pass, where the snow plough's attentions had been sporadic, for it was not by any means a main road. Throttle control was a problem here as too much induced spin and too little threatened to bring the car to a standstill. We passed a couple of cars and almost immediately came on a Jaguar which had failed to get round the corner and had run violently into the rocks, without any injury to the crew, who were standing forlornly alongside inspecting the damage."

On this section they were passed by a rear-engined Brissonneau, which was going well with so much of the car's weight being on the driving wheels.

"On the descent of the pass the snow got thicker, which was not only worrying to me, but equally worrying to Chris, who could not pick out his landmarks. At these high speeds the driver must be warned of the turnings at least 50 yards before they come up and this he was finding increasingly hard to do. One turn we overshot – not by any means the first car to do so, as the wheel marks showed. At the foot of the pass we were now five minutes down on schedule and as the snow was now lifting I put the cruising speed up into the seventies (mph) once more. We caught and passed the Brissonneau and also the car with the bagpiper, which was sliding all over the road; perhaps he was again playing the lament, for their run finished quite shortly. (The bagpiper, incidentally, had been parading with his pipes before the start, much to the amusement of the Parisians.)

"The Wolseley was absolutely magnificent, answering every demand made upon it, and handling beautifully, so enabling us to pass cars of much higher performance such as Jaguars, Triumphs, Mercedes and Alfa Romeos. Our shares went right up when we passed Louis Chiron, who had started 23 minutes ahead of us, and it was obvious that if we could keep this up we would be well in the lead of the Paris starters. With 100 miles done, we had retrieved the five-minute deficit and had half a minute in hand."

Things were looking rosy and the crew were confident when their hopes were dealt a sad blow. A five-road junction loomed up in the swirling snow; there was little time to decide and as luck would have it Chris selected the wrong road. A string of cars followed them and to stop in the narrow road was out of the question: quick calculations and a return route to the proper road was selected. It meant an extra 10 kilometres and time lost again. They just had to hope that the road back would not be blocked and looked for a chance to let the pack past so that they would not miss the next turning.

In the next village there was a scene of great confusion with crews out of their cars looking at obscured signposts and brushing away the snow. Someone knocked at the door of a cottage and roused a sleepy inhabitant, who must have thought that the place had been invaded by madmen. There were cries of horror when the signs revealed unfamiliar road numbers. John and Chris knew exactly where they were going and lost no time in pleasantries, selecting their route without hesitation. The pack gave chase, but the Wolseley had a start and was well away.

Then they met two enormously deep snow drifts and were nearly brought to a halt. Snow got into the exhaust and the ignition and the engine faltered, but then it picked up and they were off again. They reached the proper route and checked the time – 10 minutes down! The headlights were dim, so they had to stop to scrape the caked snow off the glass, keeping an eye and ear open for the others, who were not far off. Every car that passes you may be a later hazard, either because it is not cruising fast enough or because it may be going too fast for the driver's ability and thus spins off and blocks the road. So many good crews have been put out of the fight by these unexpected incidents.

John and Chris kept going to such good effect that at Besançon they were only eight minutes behind schedule. The average speed which they had to maintain was 60km/h (37mph), which was rather more than most tourists could have managed on those roads in high summer, even in daylight. Most of the works drivers knew this part of the mountains very well, but villages and junctions look unfamiliar when covered in a thick coat of snow.

They picked up the Munich competitors and were now leading all the Paris starters except Edward Harrison, who was in a modified works-entered Ford Zephyr and was driving superbly.

John wrote: "Passing was extremely hazardous; to get up to the overtaken car one had to drive through a spray of snow thrown up by its rear wheels. This spray was about 8ft high and quite obscured any turns on the road ahead. Expert drivers pulled over to let us by. The less expert were less courteous, until Chris gave them a dose of the roof light shone through their rear window. In either case, however, I had to put the left-hand wheels into deep virgin snow and chance hitting either a gulley or a marker stone hidden in the snow. The problem of different grip for the nearside and offside wheels was another complication. However, crews we passed assured us later that it was less terrifying to pass than to be passed by us."

To add to their worries the temperature was now down to 16 degrees F and all their anti-freezing devices could not prevent the screen from becoming obscured. Ice formed on the wiper blades and lifted them off the screen so that the arc they swept became even smaller and the crew had to lower the windows and try to reach round to knock the ice off the screen. They passed a lot of stationary cars, which had come to rest at the most grotesque angles; some were up trees, others were on their sides and one was on its roof in a field; others half blocked the road, but in spite of everything no-one was hurt. The average speed in a rally was most likely to be set at 37mph for the road sections and it therefore follows that accidents, if they occurred, were most likely to happen at around that speed. Snow also has a cushioning effect, which minimizes the damage, but makes it more difficult to release the car from its grip.

John and Chris now had only 20 miles to go to reach the control at Ste Claude when disaster came in the little village of Foncine-le-Bas. They were only 11 minutes late at the time and were going down the hill into the village when they were hit by a Triumph TR3 from Munich which they had just passed. The Triumph had started 35 minutes in front of them so its driver might have been forgiven for hurrying as it was then 46 minutes late and would be excluded if it lost another 14 minutes. John was put off balance and left the road on the left. The Triumph scraped through on the right; the Wolseley rested against a bar. The Germans stopped their Triumph and murmured a few words of regret then shot off into the night. They might as well have helped for they could not have reached Ste Claude in time.

The time was 03.30 hours and snow was falling heavily. John and Chris got out their spades and started to dig, and they made some progress until they glanced up and saw a large saloon bearing down on them; there was a crash and the Wolseley was pushed even further into the ditch. The saloon bounced off and sped on.

A number of cars went past, their crews determined to reach Ste Claude, and they could only shout words of encouragement, but Jack Sears stopped and his crew started to help. They lifted the car almost back onto the road and were just checking it when a convoy swept down the hill; two cars passed but the third, a DKW, made a real job of the shunt and hit the Wolseley fair and square, putting it back further than where it had been before! As the DKW, which was being driven by two doctors from Paris, was by then nearly out of time they need not have been going at the 60mph at which they hit the stationary car.

By a miracle neither of the Frenchmen was more than superficially injured, so they were handed spades and told to do their share of the digging or pushing. The local policemen and the driver of a trade van following the rally also turned up to help, and a telegraph pole was used as a lever, but all in vain; the cars were by now frozen in. The pole snapped and the party fell down on the icy road to the accompaniment of oaths in several languages. It was obvious that they would need mechanical assistance to get the cars unstuck; time for the Wolseley crew had run out. They were taken to a house in the village and given warm drinks and a seat by a stove. Suddenly they were tired and the whole thing seemed pointless; they fell asleep in a row. It was just 15 hours since they had left Paris.

Of the 303 starters, 122 had left from Paris, The Hague and Munich, and of the 59 crews who were officially classified as finishers, only three came from those ill-fated starting points, the car captains being Edward Harrison (Ford) from Paris, Maurice Gatsonides (Triumph TR3) from The Hague and Walter (Mercedes) from Munich. The blizzard in the Jura had eliminated the rest.

Meanwhile, we had been at Dijon without any news, but even if we had been at Ste Claude we could have done very little about it. We heard later that Pat Moss and Ann Wisdom had slid off the road and hit a kilometre-stone under the snow, which damaged their radiator. The girls spent the night in another village nearby and had the car repaired the next morning.

We left Dijon early and soon found the road icy, this being brought home to us by the sight of a car on its roof in a field and another nearby with a white horse looking into the missing rear window. Soon we saw a British car joining our route by way of a side road from the Jura. It turned out to be Peter Dimmock with his camera crew, who had given up the struggle of keeping up with the rally and were bound direct for Monte Carlo. Peter was having a great deal of trouble with wheelspin on the ice and must have been making all of 20mph. We took one of the camera men into Douggie Watts' car so that he could film the BBC car going through its crab-like dance. After a short time we changed over again and put up the cruising speed. Douggie went on ahead to take up his station at Gap, but he had to wait in vain by the control in the cold street.

Some of our crews got past Ste Claude, but Nancy Mitchell, Tommy Wisdom and Mike Couper were eliminated before there. John Bremner failed to make the next control at Villefranche, and Brookes was 40 minutes late, Jack Sears 31 minutes and John Sprinzel 46 minutes adrift. By the next control, at Millau, they were all gone. Brookes crashed and Jack Sears and John Sprinzel were exhausted, their second drivers could go no faster, and so they were eliminated. The Glasgow crews fared no better for if they weathered the Montreuil snowstorm they got caught in a blizzard on the Col de Bayard just before Gap. Douggie Watts and his boys waited in vain and cursed the inhospitability of Gap, which closed its bars and eating places early.

Shortly after Grenoble, I failed to climb the hill out of Vizelle on the N85, then found reversing back down was difficult as the car tended to slide into the ditch. So we let the tyres down and were making another rush at the hill when John Gott and Chris Tooley appeared in the Wolseley which, although bent, was still mobile. We both made the climb and stopped to compare notes at the top. John told us the news, and from what he said we knew that it was unlikely that the Glasgow starters had got through.

At that moment all the works cars were out, but there were two BMC private owners who had enjoyed a good run. The classification test at Monte Carlo was to include Gordon Stratton in his Austin A105 and Constantin Mikas in his MGA, who had started from Oslo and Athens respectively. The service crews transferred their attention to these with a will, but unfortunately Stratton crashed and Mikas had gearbox trouble, so that was the end of our chances in the 1958 Monte. Too many eggs in one basket, but it might have come off.

On reaching Monte Carlo, I wrote some notes on the event which appear to me to be as true today as when they were written. Unfortunately they might also have been written about any Monte Carlo Rally run between 1955 and 1961.

"There has been some criticism about the organization of the rally. The belated unloading at Boulogne must have taken it out of the Glasgow starters, even if they did make up the lost time later; as a result many of them did silly things because they were that much more exhausted. Misdirection by the police occurred in several places and controls often re-routed competitors when the proper route was not actually blocked by snow. In one case, competitors who used the direct route arrived at the next control before the re-routed cars which had left before them. Crews who disregarded the official route and made their way by the shortest route generally came off best and were not penalized. The arrangements at the start of the mountain classification test were the most disorganized I have ever seen at a motoring event in any country, and that is saying something. Chaos reigned and this is supposed to be Europe's most important rally! There is not much doubt that the French residents and some others were better placed as to pre-knowledge of the route than the majority. The location of secret controls was not a secret in some places. It seems a pity that an event should be won by inside knowledge as it does not prove who is the best crew or which is the best car. The Monte Carlo Rally is the most publicized rally in the world and should therefore be run in such a way that no criticism is possible. The organization of the Tulip, Alpine and Liège-Rome-Liège Rallies leaves nothing to be desired except that one feels that the last two are run at a time when tourists are too numerous for safety. (I would like to see either the Alpine, now run in June, or the Liège-Rome-Liège run in October.)"

The delay in unloading the cars at Boulogne had been caused by a miscalculation as to the time required to embark, cross the Channel and disembark the cars. As a result the cars were released in any order from the ship and some of the least lucky people left Boulogne at the time when they should have been clocking in at the first French control at Montreuil, some 37 kilometres further on. This meant that they had lost 37 minutes in penalties before they had even left the boat.

The chaos which prevailed at the exit of the *parc fermé* when the cars were released for the mountain test was caused by the lack of imagination on the part of the organizers, who had permitted the crews to remove their cars only half an hour before they set out on the final test in order to effect minor repairs and refuelling. As the nearest garages were over five minutes away most people were in a hurry and in no frame of mind to be baulked by spectators' cars parked in the same street, which was just wide enough for two cars. The officials also released cars at one-minute intervals for the final test, and as all this took place in the dark, with no thought of one-way traffic, a great many people lost their tempers at the same time.

In those days the officials of the *AC de Monaco* seemed to have very little imagination for they invariably allowed a situation to develop to such an extent that it was hard if not impossible to cure it, when a little foresight would have prevented it from happening in the first place. The staff appointed to deal with questions, protests and arrangements for the programme of cocktail parties and the gala dinner were all placed in the same office which, besides being understaffed, was much too cramped to deal with the largest entry of any International motoring event in Europe. Nearly all the competitors who were forced to retire *en route* made a point of getting to the finish to witness the prizegiving and attend the dance. There were invariably delays in the publication of the results, which would appear with so many errors that the office once more became crammed with irate customers trying to make themselves heard in about 18 different languages.

The secret control virtually disappeared soon afterwards following a barrage of protests in 1958, 1959 and 1960 by competitors and representatives of the national clubs concerning their location. The competitor had no way of checking the validity of the organizers' calculations when he was not told the location of the control at which he was penalized, and there was always the nasty suspicion that their location was 'leaked' to the local competitors.

In fact one year we saw a man holding out a board for the benefit of the French competitors which read *'Controle 200 metres'*, but the board was hidden when a British car came in sight. The regulations as to timing were so complicated in 1959 that the organizers themselves interpreted them incorrectly and Tony Ambrose had to protest about this, the result being that the entire results had to be redrafted and competitors found themselves either promoted or demoted overnight.

As a result of suggestions made by Jack Kemsley of the Monte Carlo Rally British Competitors Club, the organizers subsequently carried out a number of improvements in the organization and character of the rally. But although these tended to eliminate the complaints which had been made after every event for the previous five years, the organizers would then introduce some new factor which would start the trouble all over again. I came to the conclusion that this was an ingredient of the Gallic character which would be with us for all time.

Of course, on the credit side for the competitor in those years was the great sense of achievement on reaching Monte Carlo, which was made all the greater if the weather had been severe. Gone would be the petty squabbles which the cramped quarters of three days had magnified from slight irritation into earnest arguments. With the Mediterranean in sight, all the crews' worries seemed to disappear at the sight of the sparkling blue sea, fringed with white villas and hotels.

The palm trees outside the Casino which shaded the magnificent flower displays; the 14 hours of unbroken sleep; the return of one's appetite as the effect of the 'wakey-wakey' pills wore off. Then, the stroll down to the Casino to pick up the English newspapers at the kiosk and to read that they were having frightful weather at home. The cabaret at the gala dinner, which was always worth the fight for a table, and the solemn prizegiving in the palace forecourt with the appropriate national anthems and the chance to see Princess Grace accompanying Prince Rainier at the ceremony. Finally, the evening dinner that would go on and on at some little restaurant that none of the other competitors knew about. Yes, there were compensations.

As far as BMC were concerned, the results of the 1959 Monte were a great improvement on the year before, but I must admit to having been a little worried before the start. We chose Paris again for half our entries and felt fairly certain that the route would not be so severely penalized as the year before. "Lightning does not strike twice in the same place", someone said, but another wit turned up and told me his house had been struck twice on the same day.

The Channel crossing was uneventful that year and on arrival in Paris we were given the usual crop of hair-raising stories about snow, ice and fog, to be followed by severe flooding. When the Seine rises the French newspapers send out their photographers to get pictures of the statue of the Zouave soldier which ornaments one of the bridges. If the water comes up to his knees it means it's a special sort of flood – but what it proves I have never found out! If it got up to his neck the editors would probably get wet feet on their way to work. Anyway, there were a large number of camera crews at the start and a good many sound recorders. Pat was interviewed by all and sundry and repeatedly asked why she was starting from Paris after the year before. She always replied: "Because I was told to do so", thus neatly absolving herself from the possible consequences. The girls started at the horrible hour of 02.41 and we retired for a few hours' sleep until the buzzer by my bed went off at just before 7am. I hadn't asked for a call, but as I normally did, I had set my alarm clock. My first reaction was that the hotel had made a mistake, but I picked up the 'phone and heard the operator say "Chalons wants you". My heart missed a beat. Ann Wisdom said, "Marcus, what shall we do, our carburettor has broken. What *shall* we do?" "Get a Simca carb if anyone is open. I'll ring you back." I went to sleep again; there was nothing I could do, Chalons was too far off to send help, so they must help themselves. Just after 8am Ann 'phoned again. "We've had it welded, it wasn't the carburettor, it was the manifold just underneath, do you think it will hold up?" "Yes," I said. "The French garages are very good at that sort of repair and it will be stronger than before. Best of luck."

By devious means the BMC agent in Cambrai had a spare manifold that evening. The girls were intercepted at the control and carried the manifold with them for the entire rally. Pat's luck was in, for the organizers had deleted the run through Belfort and allowed the cars to go direct from Chaumont to Gérardmer due to very deep snow in the Vosges mountains. As they could not adjust the time without desynchronizing the Paris starters from the rest of the rally, the girls had extra time at Chalons to get the welding done. The work was perfect and it lasted until the car got back to England.

The weather improved and the floods did not materialize, so in a happier frame of mind we set off for Bourgoin, a small town near Lyons through which most of the rally was to pass. The Paris starters were due to come through some 41 hours after they had left us, by which time they would have covered 2,517 kilometres of their 3,431-kilometre route to Monte Carlo. The other mechanics, who were to cover Blois and Chambéry, left before us, for ours was a comparatively simple journey with ample time in hand in case the weather turned sour on us. Leaving Paris about 10 o'clock, we were well down the N7 before we stopped for a picnic lunch; the lunch baskets were excellent, having been prepared by the de Vries organization, who were the distributors for Austin in France. I suspected that Madame de Vries, who took an active part in the management of the business, had had a hand in the ordering of the contents. The lunches were packed in Air France travel bags and labelled with the car number and the names of the crews, with additional bags for the service cars. This was typical of the *AFIVA* organization, which made it such a pleasure to garage the team cars there.

The team had stayed at the *Hotel Baltimore*, in the Avenue Kléber, for the previous few years, and although it was by no means a luxury hotel it was well situated and the staff were obliging. Almost opposite the hotel there was the restaurant *Sebillion* in the rue Longchamps, which subsequently became a meeting place for rally drivers and press if there was a BMC team starting from Paris. For another diversion, if there was time for a stroll down the Champs Elysées, it was convenient to drop in at the *Collisée*, which was quite near the *Lido*; this restaurant was not much patronized by tourists, and externally it might have been mistaken for a brasserie, but there was an excellent restaurant in the basement and prices were reasonable for the quality of the table.

Returning to the N7, we ran for some distance in company with John Ross, the motoring photographer, who was driving his swift Speedwell Austin A35. Their cruising speed being over 70mph down the long, straight, wet and windy, tree-lined roads, we began to wonder if John would reach Monte without mechanical trouble. That night we reached Lapalisse to stay at the

Galland, a small, unpretentious hotel which took a pride in excellence, the rooms being simple and clean and the food always good. My wife had discovered the hotel in the *Michelin Guide* when we were on a tour in 1954, and the visitors' book made interesting reading.

Diverting from the rally for a moment, there were – and to a certain extent still are – many advantages in travelling on the Continent in mid-winter, when traffic is so light, making high average speeds possible if the weather is reasonable even when avoiding the *autoroutes*; then there is the warm welcome at any hostelry which stays open during the winter; the availability of those dishes which the summer tourist never sees – such things as jugged hare, game pie and roast venison, or occasionally roast boar, washed down with one of the more interesting local Burgundies. I recall that the proprietor of the *Hotel de Paris* at Arbois in the Jura was a great sportsman, and he filled his larder with snipe, woodcock, pheasant, pigeon, hare and rabbit at suitable seasons. Arbois is in the foothills of the Jura mountains and is most conveniently visited on the way to Switzerland from the Channel ports.

Two more of my favourite posting points were the *Renaissance* at Saulieu, which could also be relied upon to offer this traditional form of winter welcome (except when they closed from mid-January until the end of February), and, also in Saulieu, *La Vielle Auberge*, where John Gott, Douggie Watts, Bryan Noyland and I had a fine evening meal one October when returning from a test run to the Stelvio. This was composed of oysters, snails and roast pheasant, followed by a local cheese. The rest of the evening was spent on a conducted tour of the cellar, which was only terminated by the threat from Madame to lock both her husband and us in for the night!

Back on the rally route, we had no difficulty in reaching Bourgoin before lunch the next day, although after Lyons we came across some snow, and as there was a very strong wind, which looked like veering to the north-west, I expected that we might see some more snow later. As our cars would not be due until later in the afternoon we repaired to the *Commanderie de Champarey*, which stood a little below the road to Grenoble in a miniature park. There was an enormous fireplace in the dining room where they burned logs about 4ft long.

The competition manager of Shell-France, M Noaille, and Pierre About of the French sporting daily *l'Equipe* were there with their assistants. They were a little ahead of us with their meal, but we eventually joined forces over the coffee and *digestif*. After a while we felt that we ought to go down to the control to welcome Raymond Baxter and Jack Reece in their Sprite, but were told that we must stay a little longer as there might be some useful news which we should pass on to our crews. "Be patient, we are expecting a 'phone call", they said. After another delay we were handed a sheet of paper to copy; it contained details of the sectors with imposed averages between Chambéry and Monte Carlo. This was a 'leak' of information which actually reached a few more people than was intended, but was part of the Shell rally service, which could be of great help to a tired crew. By giving the information to the crews at Burgoin they ensured that they received it seven hours before they would normally have been handed it, and thus would be able to assess the difficulties well in advance by adding the new figures to their timetable. In all, we typed out 12 copies and handed them to every BMC crew we saw at the control.

Once the rally cars had passed through, we took the road to Monte Carlo, for

I had two mechanics with me in the car and we planned to get to the finish at about the same time as our crews. We turned back to Valence and were soon cruising down the N7 at a steady 75mph. Apart from the heavy lorries which travel at night, the *Route Nationale* was almost empty and it was a simple matter to average 100km/h as far as Aix-en-Provence. Many of the petrol stations remained open all night and there were plenty of places for a quick coffee to keep one awake. We reached the *Hotel du Helder* at Monte Carlo at 05.00 hours and had time for a nap, after which we went down to the arrival control to see how the boys and girls had fared.

Here the difference between the professional or works driver and the amateur was to be most marked. The former could give you facts about the car's performance and an accurate estimate of their chances. Experience tells, and the works crews seemed to arrive in a calmer state, with fewer signs of exhaustion. Pat and Ann were always quite unruffled and even had the energy to put up a good front for the hosts of cameramen and give a couple of TV interviews before taking the car along to the *parc fermé* on the quay. Crews were allowed one hour at a service station for minor adjustments before the cars were put back in the *parc fermé* for the rest of the day, but little serious tuning was possible as many parts, including the valve cover, were sealed before the start of the rally, so that slack tappets had to stay that way.

With one exception, the classification test – consisting of one lap of 460 kilometres in the mountains behind Monte Carlo and Nice – was to be run off that night without any major disasters as far as we were concerned. The exception was John Gott, whose MGA Twin-Cam slid on the ice and shot down a very steep bank, being stopped from destruction by a sapling. John and Ray Brookes scrambled up the bank, removed the boulder which had caused John to swerve on the icy road, and set off to the nearest village. A real party was in full swing, and after joining the festivities they were given a bed for the night and told not to worry about the car. The next day the MGA was retrieved with a crane, which needed two trucks to anchor it. There was no major damage, and it was driven back to Monte Carlo and later to England without any trouble.

I was in the *Hotel du Helder* when a journalist asked me if we intended to go and fetch John and Ray back. "No," I said, "it is a point of honour with BMC crews that they always bring the car back if it's humanly possible. They realize that we usually have important things to do, and diverting mechanics to salve a car which is out of the running is not one of them. If they are in a bad way they will 'phone for help." Just as I said this, in walked John and Ray, so I was able to illustrate my point.

Scrutineering was carried out at the Auto Riviera garage, the biggest in Monaco. It surprised us that the Moss/Wisdom Austin A40 which had won the *Coupe des Dames* was the only one of the prizewinners to be stripped on the first day. Apparently the technical scrutineers wanted to see the marvellous Shell film *Coupe des Alpes*, which featured the 1958 Alpine Rally, and so I think the others were not dismantled until the next day! Pat's car passed the scrutineers and so their three Cups were 'in the bag'; they were also second in their class for Touring cars up to 1,000cc. Also, at first they were classified 20th out of an entry of 361, but the next day, when the calculations were revised, they found themselves 10th. Monsieur About said "Stay another day, Pat, and you'll be first!"

There was nothing quite like the judging for the safety and comfort competition which used to take place on the terrace in front of the Casino. There were usually about a dozen entries and the cars had to have qualified as finishers in the rally. Gone were all the travel stains, the cars and their crews looking their very best, and the equipment which had been carried in the cars laid out alongside them, all brightly polished. I had been given a good tip by Mike Couper about this. He told me to have lists of the equipment with notes pointing out any particularly interesting item typed in as many European languages as possible so that they might be handed to the judges when they inspected the cars.

The girls' performance in the rally had attracted the press and TV from seemingly everywhere and they spent nearly two hours being photographed and interviewed. Huw Thomas took a great deal of trouble, and I think the girls enjoyed their interview with him more than any of the others. It is always a pleasure to see someone who really knows what he is about putting it into practice.

Again we were in luck. The A40 won the RAC Challenge Trophy for the best equipped and best placed car in the rally, while John Sprinzel and Willy Cave were 15th in General Classification and third in the class for Grand Touring cars up to 1,000cc. So we went home next day feeling that it had been a pretty good event...thanks especially to the ladies.

CHAPTER 6

The Tulip Rally

"...there was nothing to prevent a team or group of drivers getting together and artificially weighting the marking."

The 'Tulip' was the most popular of the continental rallies as far as the British private owners were concerned. Traditionally the rally started and finished at Noordwijk-aan-Zee, near The Hague, the route usually taking crews through Belgium, Luxembourg and France, then returning the same way, but on one occasion an excursion was made into Germany as far as the Czechoslovak frontier. The contents of the road book were kept secret until the last moment, so no practising was possible, and although it was usual for some of the famous hill-climbs to be included in the tests, it was not unknown for the organizing club to discover some new hill and incorporate it in the route. The entire proceedings were usually confined to six days, which made it very much less expensive than some of the other International rallies in both money and time.

The organization of the event was first-class, and I found that the organizing club – the RAC West – always made a point of interpreting its own and the International regulations with strict impartiality. The winning car was stripped down to the major engine, gearbox and axle components and the parts were then compared with those held in stock by the local distributor for the make in question.

The organizers always encouraged the entry of Group 1 Series Production Touring cars, which had to be virtually unmodified and were thus of the type which the private entrant was most likely to enter. Although there were no money prizes, the handmade silver tulips awarded as class prizes down to fourth place in the bigger classes were very highly prized. The normal first prize was a set of three tulips, two were offered for second and one for third and fourth places. The other prizes were also made of silver and most attractive, being in most cases something really useful.

For many years the rally ended with a series of races run class by class at the former Grand Prix circuit in Zandvoort, which took place in the reverse to normal direction so as not to favour Dutch competitors familiar with the track. The placings in these races could have a very marked effect on the results of the rally and as a result they tended to be extremely exciting; they were well patronized by local enthusiasts, many of whom would also attend the prizegiving and ball afterwards.

I well remember the prizegiving as an impressive but rather lengthy affair held in an upstairs lounge of the *Huis ter Duin* hotel at Noordwijk; as there was most likely to be a strong south-westerly wind blowing all the time, all the windows had to be kept closed and it usually became unbearably warm. The Clerk of the Course, Piet Nortier, would make his opening speech in Dutch, English, French and German, and he always had something amusing and original to say. The national anthem of the winning crew would be played, and if they were British, the success took on new meaning and one felt extremely proud, even if the winners had not been driving one of our team's cars.

After the prizegiving there would be a buffet supper, which could be rather a scramble, but the dishes were lavishly displayed with the most beautiful set pieces. The ball was unique in so far as there were at least three dance floors with bands playing entirely different styles of music, so that in those days one could, for example, 'jive' on one floor, 'swing' on another and dance Latin American in the next room. In addition to the dance bands there was the town's brass band, which paraded throughout the hotel lounges making a tremendous noise, followed by a procession of merrymakers in a conga train. There was also a miniature street fair, with stalls at which one could win very good prizes, and a traditional Dutch street barrel organ of the windpipe, drum and cymbal type, which customers could wind for their own amusement. All proceeds from this fair went to maintain a children's home in Switzerland. It was traditional to stay to the very end of the dance if one had the stamina, then go down to the sands to bathe one's tired feet in the cold water of the North Sea. For me, it was undoubtedly the greatest after-rally party of them all, and quite typical of our Dutch hosts, who loved to work and play with equal zest. So much for the celebrations.

The 1959 Tulip was not of the usual pattern as regards the start, for the RAC West decided to start from Paris by way of a change. Whether this was done to try to encourage more French entries I do not know, but it did not seem to have that effect, and a few of the Dutch stayed at home as well. Some people said that the wives of the Dutch crews would not let them go to Paris on their own! We felt that it was all a waste of time in so far as we couldn't stay up very late to see the sights before the event started.

The team was made up as follows:

Austin-Healey 100-Six	Pat Moss and Ann Wisdom
Austin-Healey 100-Six	Jack Sears and Peter Garnier
MGA Twin-Cam	John Gott and Chris Tooley
MGA Twin-Cam	John Sprinzel and Stuart Turner

Tish Ozanne took Anne Hall as her co-driver in the Riley 1.5 which she owned, and we helped to prepare the car. Eric Judge and C M Seward took another Austin-Healey 100-Six so we made up a team with them. In addition there were four privately owned and entered MGA Twin-Cams.

I had decided that the main party should cross by air from Ferryfield on the morning of Friday, April 24, so we went down to the *Royal Oak*, near Hythe, which was sometimes known as 'No 1 Motel', the night before. I had Lucien Gillen, the racing cyclist from Luxembourg, and Margaret Hall with me. Margaret, my secretary, had recently been promoted to the position of my assistant and had been promised a trip to one of the continental rallies as a reward for the excellent work she had been doing. The mechanics, who were crossing by the same route, were in the Morris Oxford Traveller, which was fitted with a twin-carburettor engine to MG specification to enable them to keep up with the faster cars. The girls were not coming over until the Saturday as Pat was due to jump at the Ascot Horse Show and Ann had accompanied her to help with the horses. The girls used to sleep in the horsebox in those days, and cook their own meals, although Pat later bought a caravan to give them a little more comfort.

John Gott had to go to some conference in connection with his work, so Chris Tooley brought the MGA Twin-Cam down by himself. John Sprinzel and Stuart Turner were in the other Twin-Cam, Jack Sears and Peter Garnier in the Austin-Healey 100-Six, and the party was completed by Ken James and Mike Hughes, who took a Riley 1.5. We had a convivial evening at the *Royal Oak* and crossed over the next morning without any trouble. We all stopped for lunch at the *Chateaubriant* at Beauvais, but I recall that on that occasion it failed to live up to its reputation, presenting us with poor service and mediocre cooking.

On the way we tuned Jack's Healey and tried some new plugs as the 100-Six engines had all suffered from a peculiar misfire after running slowly. At first we thought this was due to the cold weather as it became better when we raised the running temperature, but after a while it was shown to be due to the fouling of the sparking plug because we were frightened of 'cooking' them at high speeds on the open roads and on the hill-climbs. To overcome the trouble the plug company had produced a special plug which they wanted us to try in this event.

We had also endeavoured to improve the handling of these cars, but the front end was still too soft and they oversteered a bit. At this time the roadholding was not up to the performance of the engine, which we had improved a great deal that winter.

We arrived in Paris in good time for dinner and put the cars away in the de Vries organization's premises on the Boulevard General Leclerc, then we went to the *Baltimore*. Someone suggested that we should go to the café *Voltaire*, near the Place des Nations, for dinner, but this too was not an outstanding meal, although it was enlivened by the fact that Jack Sears said that he could judge brandy blindfolded and afterwards correctly selected some special Edward VII brandy as against some special Remy Martin; the result of that was that *le patron* stood us all a brandy on the house. The drivers retired to bed early, but the rest of the party went on to the *Crazy Horse* saloon which used to be one of the cheapest and most amusing night spots around the Champs Elyseés and a great favourite with the motoring fraternity.

The extra day which we had allowed for any unexpected troubles and scrutineering formalities proved to be unnecessary and as a result I had time for lunch at the apartment of Monsieur and Madame de Vries on the Bois. They owned the Austin distributorship for France, which was located in the Avenue de Madrid, at Neuilly-sur-Seine, and had invited me to take Margaret Hall along. Margaret made a great hit with Madame, who was inquiring after some special English diet for her pet poodle, which Margaret said she could get for her.

Madame de Vries suggested that we should go and see the *Florallie* that afternoon. This had just been opened at the new exhibition hall at Rond Pointe de las Defence, Puteaux, and was held in the new stressed concrete building which later housed the *Salon de l'Automobile*. I had seen this being built the year before, so I was interested to go, although I had very little idea as to what a *Florallie* would be. When we arrived at the hall we found that it was filled with a very large floral exhibition which was being run on truly international lines. Each nation had its own garden in full bloom, especially designed and installed by the finest horticulturalists of that country and arranged in typical style. There were gardens with lakes and lawns, and more varieties of flowers and shrubs than I had imagined existing. The Rally for Florists, as its name implies, was not an annual event, but took place in various European countries every second year, and Her Majesty Queen Elizabeth the Queen Mother had made a flying visit to the exhibition on the day we were there. For us, therefore, the 1959 Tulip Rally was to begin and end with an exhibition of flowers.

The organizers of the rally had decided to start the event from Montlhéry Autodrome, which is some 25 kilometres outside Paris on the road to Orleans. This race track is a little further on from the centre of the town up a turning to the right off the main road. There was no speed test, but the track was of convenient size to marshal a large number of cars at the same time and the starting point saved the inconvenience of driving out of Paris under rally conditions.

As the starting time for the first car was fixed for 08.01 hours on Monday, April 27, everyone took things very easily on Sunday. To begin with the rally went down N20 to Orleans and afterwards turned off to the left at Salbris to make its way to Bourges and from there to Vichy. From the start the Austin-Healeys were still dogged by the misfiring and we proved to the satisfaction of everybody that the plugs were not suitable for either pottering through towns or fast driving on the long straight roads near the Loire Valley. Although they often cleared themselves after a town there was always a risk that the trouble might occur again before one of the timed climbs.

We left the rally when they turned off on the road to Vichy, continuing on the N7 which goes to Lyons. We stopped at our old friend Madame Galland's hotel for lunch at Lapalisse as the cars were not due to arrive for a rest stop at Valence until 7pm. The weather, which had been fine up to then, began to change and large drops of rain were falling by the time we reached Valence. The rally had also run into the same rain in the Auvergne and the test at La Baraque was spoilt in a shower, which however did not affect the larger cars, which were running first. The fastest time of the day was made by W J Tak in his Mercedes 300SL, and as he was running in the same class as the Austin-Healeys there were signs of depression when we met the crews at the control.

The crews were allowed one hour for a meal at Valence and most of them sat down to eat in the *Hotel Europe*. The night was wet but warm and the heavy rain saturated everything to such a degree that one's headlights seemed duller than usual. After supper the cars went off to the west one by one, to cross the swollen Rhone and climb up into the mountains of the Southern Auvergne in the Massif Central, commencing with a test on the Col du Pin. On this test, just after Valence, the fastest time was made by Wim Poll in a Porsche, but Tak had made the best time in the Austin-Healeys' class again. Peter Riley was driving well in his Ford Zephyr and starting his struggle against the Mercedes 220S driven by Schock and Holder, managing to beat them on this second climb. The Morley brothers, who were in their Jaguar 3.4 with Barry Hercock, were also beginning to show their form and led their class. Then their route lay through Lamastre and Ste Agrève, where it turned south and ran through the extremely twisty mountain roads to recross the Rhone near Avignon before going on to Mont Ventoux and Gap.

With the thinning out of the customers in the *Europe*, we were able to find a table for dinner and then to partake of a small *digestif* before retiring for the night. I had hardly had time for my brandy when the telephone rang and the barman asked for me by name. My heart always fell into my boots on these occasions, particularly when I knew that my crews and the mechanics were the only people who knew where I was to be found. This time it was Pat, who told me that they had crashed near Ste Agrève; she said that they were both safe and asked me to come to fetch them.

Taking Douggie Hamblin and David Hiam with me, we set off on the climb up to Lamastre. We soon caught up the tail end of the rally and with a Mercedes which was being driven by D A Vetch, but we had some difficulty in passing him because his stop and tail-light glasses were defective and allowed so much white light to get through that we were dazzled each time he applied his brakes.

Near Lamastre we made the same mistake as the Twin-Cams had done earlier and took the left-hand fork, but fortunately I remembered that this turning had been in some rally notes, so we only overshot by a few yards. Unfortunately, Chris Tooley had not been feeling well, so when the Twin-Cams had arrived at this fork they went to the left and then lost many valuable minutes before the mistake was realized and the route could be rejoined.

The road was very difficult all the way up to Ste Agrève and one became very tired just winding away at the wheel of a big car; no sooner were we out of one corner than the next one began. But eventually we arrived in Ste Agrève, where we found the girls in a small café. Ann, who had a slight cut on the inside of her mouth but no teeth broken, was having a sleep, while Pat was talking to the driver of a Saab which had crashed at the same place and jumped right over the abandoned Austin-Healey. The co-driver had been a bit shaken up by this and had been put to sleep on the floor wrapped in a rug.

Someone suggested giving him a brandy, but I pointed out that it was dangerous to give a person alcohol when he might be suffering from concussion and that it might be better to give him a warm drink such as tea with plenty of sugar, so this was done and soon the patient seemed a little better. The crew of the Saab had also telephoned for help and someone was coming to collect them, so Douggie and I went down to the wrecked Healey to salvage anything valuable before turning it over to the local garage to rail back to England.

It had stopped raining by now, but everything was still soaking. From the position of the car it was apparent that Pat had been going downhill very quickly when she got onto some loose granite chippings on the right-hand edge of the road approaching a left-hand corner. The car had slid more to the right than intended and the front wheel had fallen into a narrow box-section stone gutter, which gripped the wheel so that Pat could do nothing to pull the car further round the corner and instead was led straight on into the rock cliff where the gutter turned to the left and went under the road. Pat explained that as the starter had become stuck they had had to remove everything that had been stowed behind the seats in order to get at the battery and disconnect it. They also had to get the tools out of the boot to do this, but had been very frightened that someone else would do the same as they had and land on top of them.

The girls didn't have to wait very long before this Saab did that very thing, jumping over the Healey and landing up the bank; fortunately, the girls were no longer in the danger area at the time.

Pat told me that there had been something wrong with the car because it had been handling very badly ever since they had left Valence; the brakes were pulling first one way and then the other, and they had been half off the road three times. Whilst I was full of sympathy for them, I felt that in those circumstances it might have been more prudent if they had abandoned the rally and enabled us to get down to finding the cause of the trouble; as it was, the evidence had been destroyed and we never did find out what had caused the unpredictable swerves under braking.

We then went back to the café, then retraced our steps to Valence with the girls, where Tommy Wellman and young Gerald Wiffin were waiting with the Morris Oxford Traveller in case further help was required. Margaret, of course, had stayed up to make sure that the girls were all right and had shown them to my room while Douggie Hamblin and I slept in the hall with the night porter, the hotel being full to bursting-point and we too tired to look elsewhere for a bed.

It had been a tough night, and a disappointment to many, for there were only eight clean sheets by the time the rally had run through Ste Agrève. After this the route crossed the Midi and climbed Mont Ventoux under such difficult conditions of fog, snow and ice that the test there had to be abandoned; the cars then made their way to Gap for the next eliminating test, which was a timed climb up our old friend the Col de Bayard. By this time Tak's Mercedes 300SL was out of the running with a hole in its sump, and the Ferrari 250GT of Faure and Guyot made the fastest time, the second quickest coming from the extraordinary Chevrolet Impala of Dee and Teding van Berkhout, who used its 5,697cc to such good purpose that it was faster than all the Austin-Healeys and Jaguars.

Starting next morning with two more people in our car, we had to carry the luggage on the roof rack, which I usually took empty for such emergencies. Tommy Wellman bought a canvas sheet and some rope and rubber ties and we soon had everything restowed. The three girls were put in the back of the 'Barge' and Douggie went in the front. David Hiam had his own Morris Minor 1000 and someone travelled with him whilst we sent Tommy Wellman and Gerald Wiffin back to Eindhoven via Liège. We then set off to Uriage, near Grenoble, where we expected to see our cars before lunch time.

Jack Sears duly arrived looking cool and collected with a slightly less svelte Peter Garnier. They had enjoyed their rally very much and felt that they were making a real impression on the opposition in their class. There had been a certain amount of 'rallymanship' going on and Jack had been enjoying himself in exploiting the weakness of the Ferrari, which was in its brakes. He did this to such good effect that the Ferrari went straight on at a T-junction, with fortunately only minor consequences. The Ferrari owner was very sporting about the incident and after the rally was over he congratulated Jack on his good driving and tactics. In order to demonstrate this Jack had to overtake the

Ferrari after a control and run just in front of it, leading it into corners at speeds which were better suited to his disc brakes. But the Ferrari sounded wonderful; I heard it climbing the Chamrousse, which is 17.2km long, and the sound of the exhaust note was most inspiring.

Unfortunately, Eric Judge had come to grief in the Auvergne in his Healey, failing to reach the control at Les Vanels, and one or two others failed to get much further than Uriage, amongst them Jimmy Ray, whose Sunbeam had back axle trouble, and a couple of Peugeot 403s. Tish Ozanne and Anne Hall were doing well in the Ladies' class and leading the fight for the title with four other crews. Jack Sears made a good climb at Chamrousse, making the best time in his class of 15min 12sec against the Ferrari's 15min 31sec.

The next test was at Ste Cergue, in Switzerland, but the weather was again very bad and provided a hailstorm complete with thunder and lightning. Jack was 5.4sec slower than the Ferrari here. I had decided to press on up to Luxembourg, where we planned to meet our cars again, so we left Uriage at about midday and steered due north.

We reached Luxembourg that night and managed to find a good hotel where we could get an evening meal. After we had eaten, Douggie Hamblin and I went out and located the control as well as the road into the city from the direction of the Vosges, for it was getting foggy and we knew that the control would be difficult to find in the early light. We then went back to the hotel and told the management that we wished to go out at about five in the morning, but would be back for breakfast. On these occasions I was always surprised at the trusting nature of hotel managements who let their guests sneak out at the crack of dawn without much certainty that they would ever come back.

When it was time to go we were let out by the night porter into a cold and foggy dawn. We ran down to the filling station we had selected and waited for the first cars to come by. A thick fog blanketed the sound of the cars and, as there were a few people going to work by car at that time, it was hard to tell whether an approaching car belonged to the rally or not.

We waited for half an hour, then I began to get worried for it was going to be touch and go as to whether Jack Sears and Peter Garnier would reach the control on time. At last the Healey arrived and I ran out into the gloom to stop it; a quick word to Jack and we made a dive for our car and were away past the station and up the main boulevard without worrying too much about the speed limits. Jack followed closely and we crossed the bridge which spans the gorge dividing the new town from the old, and the Healey reached the control with a minute or two to spare. Peter Garnier wrote afterwards that they would never have found the control in time if we hadn't been handy.

After leaving them safely we went back to see if there were any other crews who were in trouble, but it was now light and the fog was lifting. There were only five or six crews who remained unpenalized at that point, amongst them being the Morley brothers in their Jaguar 3.4, Peter Riley and Dickie Bensted-Smith in a Ford Zephyr, Keith Ballisat and E Marvin in a Triumph TR3, and Erik Carlsson and K E Svensson in a Saab 93b, which was in Grand Touring trim and very fast.

The route onwards through the Duchy was on secondary roads and not made any easier by the fact that there was still a bit of mist about. The field had been reduced to 110 by the time the survivors reached Luxembourg. The Porsche of Poll and Scorr had been unpenalized as far as the control at Linthal in the

Vosges, where they dropped only a minute, but after this their screenwiper refused to work and the handicap of having to operate the wiper blades by hand was too much and they lost a further six minutes by Luxembourg.

At the border the rally crews were welcomed back into Holland with traditional Dutch hospitality, the cars being wreathed with garlands of tulips in orange and red. At Eindhoven the Phillips organization always placed one of its large recreation halls at the disposal of all rally personnel and furnished the tired crews with an excellent breakfast of bacon and eggs; other comforts were provided in the shape of washing facilities for everyone and the use of electric razors for the men. Prepaid postcards were distributed with various printed messages on them, by which the writer could send news of his success or failure to his home address wherever it might be. Then, after a short rest, the crews were despatched to the final control at Noordwijk. As usual, everything was well organized, and after an impartial scrutineering the cars were placed behind a roped-in enclosure on the promenade.

The following day the races were held at Zandvoort. Jack Sears and his Healey were on the top of their form and Jack made the fastest time of the day in winning his race. Erik Carlsson had a magnificent race with a host of Porsche 1600 Supers and Carreras and, after oiling up a plug on the start line, he was leading by the third lap and went on to win. The regulations did not permit any work to be done to the cars in the paddock, which was, of course, treated as a *parc fermé*, but there was nothing which forbade the changing of a plug between the paddock and the starting line, so Erik was within his rights to change the offending plug there. John Sprinzel overdid things in the same race and left the circuit on the fast corner at the end of the straight, where the speed of the car was considerably reduced by means of a woven wire fence, and it landed in some bushes without damage to itself or the driver; however, John lost his fourth place. Don Morley drove a well-judged race and added to his bonus points to such good effect that he won the rally outright from Keith Ballisat in a works Triumph TR3A, which was also without penalty points.

The Inter-Nations Trophy was won by the RAC's team for Great Britain and we were glad that Jack and Peter were in it. Jack left as soon as his race was over as he had to return to Silverstone, where he was due to compete on the following day in the Grand Touring car race in his own Austin-Healey. It looked as if he would not be back in time to receive the prizes for his class win and his FTD (Fastest Time of the Day) at Zandvoort, but his impeccable timing produced a dramatic moment when Piet Nortier called for the winners of Class J precisely as Jack and his wife, Cecily, came through the doorway, having flown back to Holland that evening.

We were also very happy that Tish Ozanne and Anne Hall managed to finish second in the *Coupe des Dames* and 21st in General Classification with Tish's own Riley 1.5. This was a fine effort as they had finished fourth in a class of 16 which included the works Volvos and Sunbeams. Only five cars finished the rally without loss of road points, and although 154 cars had left the start only 96 of them reached the finish.

I always felt that no-one should fail to visit the *Keukenhof* during Tulip Rally week, or during that fortnight at the end of April and the beginning of May when the tulips are invariably at their best. There in the park the best tulips and hyacinths could be seen growing in profusion in the most beautiful surroundings, and the latest varieties viewed on display in glasshouses. The famous bulb-growing houses of Holland had their offices and displays there, so it was possible to select one's order for the following autumn and pay for it on the spot. When October came the parcel would arrive and one had a pleasant reminder in the garden the following spring of both the Tulip Rally and the charming Dutch people.

For those who enjoyed Indonesian dishes, there were several good restaurants in The Hague, Scheveningen and Amsterdam, my favourite being the *Minangkabau*, on the east side of The Hague. The building, I remember, was a genuine South Sumatra thatched wooden house raised on a superstructure, and the long room was furnished in the authentic style. The dishes were numerous and as in Chinese restaurants one portion was enough for two people. Personally, I used to find Indonesian cooking more interesting than either Indian or Chinese, but maybe that was because I had not sampled the best of either of the latter. I would always recommend starting with a sherry and then to drink beer during the meal itself. I also remember the *Garoeda*, again in The Hague, as worth a visit.

With the exception of Jack Sears' and Peter Garnier's excellent performance, we could hardly call the Tulip Rally a great success that year, but one other good thing came out of it. The Morley brothers, despite winning the event, failed to get any firm offers from other factories, so I approached them soon afterwards about a drive in the 1959 RAC Rally and they accepted. I can't think why I hadn't noticed them before they won the Tulip; perhaps it was because they were such modest fellows.

We returned to the Tulip Rally in 1961 with considerable confidence, for the Austin-Healey 3000 was then at the peak of its development and we had enjoyed a reasonably tranquil spell between the end of the Monte Carlo Rally and our successful expedition with the MGA 1600s to the Sebring 12-Hours race. When the entries were sent in we still had four weeks to complete our preparations and finish the work on the two Mini-Minors and the Sprite.

Our entries were as follows:

Austin-Healey 3000	Pat Moss and Ann Wisdom
Austin-Healey 3000	Donald Morley and Erle Morley
Austin-Healey Sprite	Tommy Gold and Mike Hughes
Morris Mini-Minor	David Seigle-Morris and Vic Elford
Morris Mini-Minor	Peter Riley and Tony Ambrose

The regulations for the rally contained a peculiar clause which was inserted to give every class an equal chance of an outright win in the event. To arrive at the General Classification the average of the times for the first three cars in each class was used as the bogey time for the class in each test. Performances were expressed as a percentage of the average time, thus an outstanding performance would produce a lower percentage relative to the rest of the class; consistently good performances would keep the percentage figures down, and the car with the lowest percentage would thus be the outright winner of the rally.

However, there was a snag in this system which few people, even the organizers, foresaw, namely that there was nothing to prevent a team or group of drivers getting together and artificially weighting the marking. If a team which dominated the performances in their class abandoned the practice of inter-team rivalry and let one of their members make fastest time in each test, they could do much to influence the result in his or her favour. The retirement of a car which was lying second in the class could also reduce the average performance for that class and give the leading car in the class a better percentage than it might otherwise have had, thus putting it higher in the General Classification.

A closely contested class made up of entrants from various sources, therefore, was unlikely to produce the winner of the rally because there would be too many equally matched cars in it. Class A, for instance, comprised an Aston Martin DB4, two Mercedes 300SLRs, a Ferrari 250GT, eight Austin-Healey 3000s, a solitary Austin-Healey 100-Six and one modified Ford Zephyr. But even if they were not going to produce the winner of the rally, they were expected to produce some of the fastest times in the tests, and they did so.

Class F, which contained the Austin-Healey Sprites, could have produced the rally winner, for Tommy Gold or John Sprinzel might have dominated the class by a sufficiently large margin, which would have been greater if either of them had fallen out. A very strong favourite was Hans Walter in his Porsche Carrera, for only Harry Bengtsson in a Porsche 90 was expected give him a run for his money. There were 13 cars in that class.

We felt that we had a very good chance of winning the manufacturer's team prize with our two Austin-Healey 3000s and the Sprite and an excellent chance of a class win with the Minis, which were tuned to the same recipe as we had used in the 1960 RAC Rally. Naturally, we expected the privately owned Austin-Healeys to put up a good fight and act as our reserves if the works cars failed. Young Peter Smith had tuned his own car and was keen to show the works drivers what he could do in his first big foreign event; in fact he promised to do a great deal. Also, Don Grimshaw had had his car prepared at the works and it was going very well.

I did not go to the start at Noordwijk as it seemed pointless to go to Holland only to return to the south to meet the cars in France. Therefore, I sent one mechanic to Holland and I set out with two cars for Champagnole, in the Jura, stopping one night in Paris on the way. We lunched next day at the *Cote d'Or*, at Châtillon-sur-Seine, but although it had a high reputation our meal was expensive and by no means memorable. We had no difficulty in reaching Champagnole before the rally cars, which were not due until about six in the evening, so we decided to spend the afternoon sitting in the sun just outside the town for there was little else to do. Eventually the arrival time drew near and we went down to the Shell garage we had chosen. The cars arrived in good style, having completed three of the timed tests. The first was up the Cote de Fleron, near Liège, which was 1.9km long, and fastest time of the night – a wet one at that – went to Pat Moss, who took 1min 23sec, with Tak in the Mercedes three seconds behind; the Morleys took 1min 27sec, Walter 1min 25sec and Peter Smith was 12 seconds slower than Pat.

The next test, at the Moulin de Bourscheid, was near Luxembourg; here Hans Walter was the fastest with 2min 8sec against Pat's 2min 11sec, and the Sprite crews had their pride dashed to the ground by Bo Ljungfeldt in a fully modified Ford Anglia, with every possible Formula Junior modification, who made the fastest time in their class at 2min 27sec. This battle lasted for the whole rally and must have given the three crews a great deal of fun.

The road sections were easy, for the pattern of the rally was to consist of 15 timed tests and three tests for which there was a target time for each class. This meant that Class A could only expect about an hour and three-quarters of high-speed motoring during the whole event; how different from the Liège or the Alpine rallies! The third test was in the Vosges, over the Col de Charbonnière for a distance of 7,800m (4.9 miles).

The finish of this test was sited on a bend where there was some low cloud obscuring the road, but this did not prevent Walter from going up in 4min 47sec, with Pat at 4min 55sec and the Morleys two seconds slower. Tak's Mercedes was a second slower than Pat, and Grimshaw made the best time for a private Healey at 5min 6sec, Peter Smith doing no better than 5min 50sec. It was shortly after this that Peter began to realize that works drivers were in the team because of their outstanding ability. I saw that he was putting a brave front on things, but looking a little puzzled.

After this they went on to the Chamrousse, which was one of Pat's favourite climbs. This great hill was worth inspecting as it wound its way up through the pine woods for a distance, on this occasion, of 10.3km (about 6.5 miles), climbing 550m (well over 1,700ft) in the process. Donald decided that if he put his mind to it he could show Pat a thing or two here, and he went up two seconds faster than she did, making FTD in 7min 56sec, which was 11 seconds quicker than Tak's Mercedes, and eight seconds quicker than the Porsche Carrera. While the faster cars were showing what they could do, some members of Class H were performing consistently, if somewhat more modestly. In this class were Tiny Lewis and Geoff Mabbs, both in Triumph Heralds, and both were destined to play a curious part in the rally. Mabbs was driving well, but Tiny Lewis was experiencing some trouble with the machinery, which prevented him from producing his usual form.

After Champagnole we had run straight through to Monte Carlo by way of the N7 to reach there early the next morning. We did not have long to wait, for the crews arrived and placed their cars in the care of the Austin agent, The Sporting Garage, owned by M and Mme Jacquin. Pat told us that she had left her handbag with all her money in it on a wall at the start of the Col de Turini hill-climb, but she was not very worried because the control had been manned by members of the London Motor Club. Sure enough, the bag turned up a few hours later with everything intact, but then Pat usually did get her handbags back, even if she did leave them behind fairly often.

The Turini was over a distance of 11.5km and reached a height of 990m from the starting point. The big cars were set a target time of 10min 42sec and the smallest 12min 42sec. Pat and Ann were the only crew to achieve this target and were three seconds faster than the Crone-Rawe Mercedes 300SLR and 10 seconds quicker than the Morley brothers on whom they were revenged for their defeat on the Chamrousse. The organizers were delighted with Pat's performance because they thought that the target time would be very difficult to achieve.

After nearly 24 hours of rest, the rally returned to Holland by very nearly the same route. Tests were held at the Col de Braus, Col de Lecques, Col St Jean, Col de Rousset, Col de la Faucille, Les Trois Épis, Breitenback and Francorchamps; most of them were well-known to the experts, and as the weather was good there were few incidents. In spite of the fact that Pat had made fastest time of the day in most of the tests, she was lying only eighth in General Classification. At Monte Carlo the leader was Skogh in a Saab, with

Hans Walter second in the Porsche, Bohringer third in the Mercedes 220SE, Schottler fourth in an Alfa Giulietta, and Mabbs and Griffiths, in a Triumph Herald, fifth. Tiny Lewis, whose Herald was still down on power, was 20th.

Skogh was later to lose his position as leader by reason of the fact that Monica Kjerstadius was still hoping that something might throw the *Coupe des Dames* her way, so she kept on trying to such good effect that she penalized the other Saab in her class and forced her team-mate down to third place. Tiny Lewis must have had a very good idea concerning the averages in his own class as he found time to put a telephone call through to his boss at Triumph's and ask for instructions. As a result he retired just before the end of the rally, which put the average performance for the first three cars in his class down by so much that Mabbs and Les Griffiths went up into first place.

Was this fair or sporting? Of course it was fair, and well within the regulations, but sporting? Perhaps not by the traditional British interpretation of the word, but internationally no-one thought it had done Tiny any harm. Indeed, some people thought it had been most sporting of him to give up a certain third place in the class, but I suspect that he had his own reward with a surprise entry in the Acropolis Rally the following month.

Hans Walter was second in his Porsche Carrera and, if he could have persuaded Harry Bengtsson in his Porsche 90 to retire, he would have won the event in the same way. The organizers slipped up badly by trying to be too fair, and thus spoilt what otherwise would have been a very good rally.

It is of interest to compare the totals of the test times as given in the official results of the rally. The lowest aggregate was recorded by Hans Walter in 1hr 42min 4sec, followed by Pat Moss in 1hr 42min 22sec and Donald Morley in 1hr 42min 32sec, the latter two cars being first and second in Class A. Tak was third in this class with a total of 1hr 44min 4sec. This well demonstrated the skill and consistency of the ace drivers.

Peter Smith, whom I had classed at the time as a better than average club driver, but who had still to gain experience the hard way, was disappointed in his own performances until he began to realize how brilliant were the works drivers; his envy then turned to admiration and enjoyment of the privilege of having driven so many miles in close company with the great ones. He said to me after the event: "You know, if I could have changed cars with Pat, the result would have been just the same." This, I thought, was the most sporting remark I had heard for a long time. The times for the best two privately owned Austin-Healey 3000s were Don Grimshaw's 1hr 48min 31sec and Peter Smith's 1hr 57min 11sec.

The results, as far as BMC were concerned, could hardly have been better, for we had done what we set out to do, with the exception of winning the event outright. Both Peter Riley and Tony Ambrose, and Tommy Gold and Mike Hughes secured well-merited class wins, and when I looked back on my first Tulip Rally, when we had returned empty-handed, I felt that we had come a very long way since then.

Our results were:

Manufacturers' Team Prize
Austin-Healey

Coupe des Dames
Austin-Healey 3000   Pat Moss and Ann Wisdom

Class A

1st Austin-Healey 3000	Pat Moss and Ann Wisdom
2nd Austin-Healey 3000	Donald Morley and Erle Morley

Class F

1st Austin-Healey Sprite	Tommy Gold and Mike Hughes
2nd Austin-Healey Sprite	John Sprinzel and Mike Wood

Class J

1st Morris Mini-Minor	Peter Riley and Tony Ambrose
3rd Morris Mini-Minor	David Seigle-Morris and Vic Elford

Club Team Prize
London Motor Club

Pat Moss and Ann Wisdom
John Sprinzel and Mike Wood
David Seigle-Morris and Vic Elford

CHAPTER 7

The Acropolis Rally

"Ann's first thought was much more analytical as she wondered how many times the car was going to turn over before it hit the ground."

Early in 1959 I received the prospectus for the Acropolis Rally, an event which already had a reputation as an exacting test for both crew and car, with the added attraction of delightful hospitality by the organizers, the Royal Hellenic Automobile Club. We felt that a sortie in strength would be inadvisable for the first attempt, but that Pat and Ann should go for the Ladies' Cup as they were still trying for the Championship, in spite of the dismal failure in the Tulip Rally. The regulations later came to hand and disclosed that both stamina and speed were essential to success. I therefore decided to send Pat and Ann with the Austin-Healey 100-Six, backed up by John Sprinzel and Dickie Bensted-Smith with an MGA Twin-Cam, which had the same tough chassis as the MGA 1500 which had done quite well in this event when driven by Greeks. I took Pat's ex-Monte Carlo Rally Austin A40 as the service car.

I had a possibly unfounded dislike of sending cars ahead by sea, for ships very rarely sailed at the most convenient time and had been known to take cargoes on to the next port by mistake. If we had gone by sea, we would have had to ship the cars about three weeks before we ourselves were due to depart, and rather more if the crews flew out at the last minute. Furthermore, most rally cars went a great deal better if they had put about a thousand miles on the clock since their last rebuild, though against this had to be measured the extra tyre wear occasioned by the journey out. However, this was not considered to be serious because we were using the improved Dunlop Duraband tyres, which had a redesigned carcass. We therefore arranged to drive across Belgium, Germany and down through Italy as far as Brindisi, where we were to ship the cars to Greece.

We crossed over by air from Southend to Ostend on Tuesday, May 19, Johnny Organ coming with me as mechanic to the team. The crossing was uneventful but, about 20km along the *autoroute* to Brussels, Pat signalled us to stop; she had left her handbag on the aeroplane, and as it contained all her money and traveller's cheques she had to go back whilst the rest of us went on. Incidents like that used to depress me. I knew Pat would probably get her bag back – she always did – but I didn't like having the party split up unless the rendezvous had been fixed and was not too far away. We decided to carry on to our night stop, the *Moderne* at Liège, but the journey wasn't the same with the girls out of my sight. Moreover, I felt that things like this had a habit of happening in threes and even fours, and if the trip started out wrongly it always seemed to require a superhuman effort on my part to prevent things continuing in the same vein. However, as we put the cars away in the garage, the girls arrived safely with Pat's handbag, which the air hostess had left with the RAC man at the airport. So, feeling more cheerful, we had dinner in the restaurant opposite and then went to bed early.

Wednesday went according to plan except for some major road repairs which were being carried out on the *autobahn*, but in spite of these we managed to reach Munich by 7.30pm, despite pausing for a picnic lunch near Frankfurt. Stopping at the *ADAC* office there, as they always had an interpreter, we asked about hotels on the other side of the city on the Salzburg road and were recommended to try the *Rosenheim* motel, but unfortunately it was full. We took a guide to show us the way through the city, and after making inquiries at a petrol station about 25km out, were directed to a charming village inn in a little hamlet just off the main road. The fare was good and the beer, of course, typical of the district. We were entertained during dinner by the village lads and lasses, who were practising their Bavarian folk dances in the old peasant costume of the district, the men wearing leather trousers and braces and the girls in dirndls. We had covered about 740km that day and Pat hadn't lost anything.

The next day we made a reasonably early start, occasioned by the fact that the church bells rang at six and regularly thereafter. I had often thought of the energetic priests who had to rise so early to toll great bells and mentioned the fact to an inn-keeper in France. "Think nothing of it," he said, "they are nearly all automatic and work by electricity"; closer scrutiny of the village church at Fuching proved this to be true.

Our route lay through Kufstein to Innsbruck, but at the frontier it was found that one of the cars had not got 'Austria' endorsed on the insurance Green Card, so it was necessary to pay the premium at the Customs. We crossed the Brenner without incident; this pass was always open in winter and, being only 4,495ft high, was a very easy climb. Unfortunately this was not so on the Alpine Rally on one occasion and the delays during the descent to the control at Vipiteno resulted indirectly in a serious accident involving Wolfgang Levy, at the time a well-known German DKW driver. Most organizers subsequently avoided the Brenner, but it remained a good tourist route for those with no head for heights.

We made Rimini that night, having covered 740km during the day, and stayed at the *Parc Hotel*, which we found was large and externally impressive, but rather pricey. Friday dawned fine and we all felt that we were now in real summer weather. The roads became emptier and the long straights, which formed part of the old Mille Miglia course, conjured up visions of flying Ferraris, Maseratis and Porsches harrying Moss in the Mercedes 300SLR. We lunched at a little restaurant at Francoville, taking care to park the cars where we could see them. We always liked to do this to guard against possible looting; even if the car was locked it could still be broken into. The country after Ancona became more primitive, with people still riding donkeys and mules and the more prosperous farmers having high-wheeled cars which carried no lights after dusk. After Pescara, where the Mille Miglia route turned to the right, the road became even worse.

In Foggia we were held up by a religious procession and, following the example of the locals, took to a side street which ran parallel to the main one; when we judged that we had reached the head of the procession we turned right to regain our route. Unfortunately, though, we had not calculated correctly and arrived at the intersection a little before the leaders. There was nothing to do but go on, as staying where we were would only have obstructed them. I looked up and saw six hooded figures dressed in monks' habits, with ropes as girdles, bearing down upon us. I felt like the Elizabethan sailors must have done when confronted by the Spanish Inquisitors – a chill feeling in spite of the afternoon warmth. Somehow I didn't think this rally was going to be a great success.

We left Foggia at speed and hoped we hadn't offended the locals too much. The countryside was dotted with various ruins which might have been there since Roman times, and the flowering shrubs were very lovely in the evening light as we left Bari for Brindisi, where the *Hotel Jolly* was modern and the service excellent, but unfortunately the swimming pool was empty owing to a shortage of water.

Brindisi, I thought, was an interesting town; situated on the heel of Italy, it has been a port of embarkation for Greece since the earliest days of the Greek and Roman empires. The Appian Way, the oldest and finest of the traditional Roman roads, which had been built in the fourth century BC, ended there and the terminal point was still marked by one graceful column at the top of a flight of stairs; the other column fell in an earthquake. Opposite there was a memorial to the Italian merchant navy, which was a lot less graceful. As the cars were not due to be shipped until the evening, there was time for some sightseeing, although the drivers did not put in an appearance until late in the morning. However, I didn't complain because I attached a great deal of importance to the matter of building up reserves of sleep to make up for the lack of it during the event; however, you can get to the state of having had too much.

The tickets had to be handed in with the passports at the shipping office by midday; this was usual as the agents used to take a very long time to make up the ship's papers and presumably they wanted to know if there were any extra berths for late or chance arrivals.

We embarked on the *MV Miaoulis*, a modern Greek ship, at 7.30pm, the cars being lashed down on deck after a great deal of argument and many shouts of 'Vira', which I think means 'Push' in Greek. A considerable amount of tipping was necessary in order to get everything stowed to our satisfaction, and the services of an interpreter came in very handy to deal with Customs. At 9.15pm we were away on a calm sea, and I recall that the food was good, if plain, but the resinated Greek wine was not appreciated by the majority, so Johnny Organ and I finished the bottle to see if we could acquire the taste for it. We never did.

On Sunday morning we arrived at Corfu, the clocks having been put on an hour to East European time. This made England seem very remote, and there was already a slight smell of the Orient, which was exciting; the Greeks often spoke of "going to Europe", as if they were not part of it.

Corfu has had many owners – the Romans, Venetians, Austrians, French, British, Italians and Germans to name the principal ones – and the winged lion of St Mark, symbol of the Venetians, is still carved over the entrance to one of the fortifications. We were met by the Greek Customs on the ship, and after having our respective cars entered in our passports, we were allowed to land without any formalities. The ship was to stay for about three hours, so everyone except Ann Wisdom decided to see what they could in the time available and we piled into a very elderly American six-seater tourer and were driven to Kanoni (Cannon Point).

I had been prepared to see something of interest, but not one of the most beautiful places upon which I have ever set eyes in any part of the world. The Point was a couple of miles from the town, and after getting out of the car and walking to the edge of the cliff we were confronted with a view of the wooded slopes encircling a bay, in the shallow blue and green waters of which were two small islands. In years to come, following the arrival of an airport nearby, the scene, with Vlacherena supporting a small white-walled nunnery and a few cypress trees, and the adjacent Mouse Island, once the home of a poet, was to become familiar to so many thousands of holidaymakers to Corfu. Just a little further along the coast is the birthplace of Prince Philip; it must have been a marvellous place for a boy to grow up in.

We left Cannon Point reluctantly, but time was running out and our driver wanted to show us something of the town before the ship sailed. On our way back we encountered Ann taking an airing in an elderly horsedrawn cab, looking very decorative reclining in the back. We visited the centre of the town and inspected the outside of the palace, which had been built when Corfu was under British occupation in 1818. According to our guide it housed the Order of St Michael and St George and was still referred to as 'our Palace at Corfu' when proclamations affecting the Order were published in the *Gazette*. We also visited the cathedral, where Mass was being held, but we were reluctant to enter in spite of our guide's assurances that it was in order; I would not dream of going round a church or other holy place while a service was being celebrated in my own country, so I saw no excuse for doing so as a tourist.

We were soon back on board and the ship sailed, punctual to the minute. We ran down the east side of the island, and after a few hours we were off to Ithaca, the birthplace of Ulysses. The town had been destroyed by an earthquake a few years before and the buildings now presented a uniform style – neat and tidy, but uninteresting. Being Sunday, the whole town turned out to see the few passengers embark, all of whom were travelling steerage and therefore had brought their food and wine with them. The ship left after 15 minutes, so we had no chance to go ashore – a pity because I had heard that the other side of the island was attractive. Later that night we put in at Patras, but saw nothing of it in the dark except the quays. We were told that there had been a landslide in the Corinth canal and we were therefore going right round the Peloponnisos, so would be some 12 hours late docking at Piraeus. That night we were entertained by a three-man band, who were travelling to Athens. They had good voices and performed with a will until late in the night.

Next morning we were in rougher seas off Cape Akritas and spent the rest of the morning rounding Cape Tenaron and Cape Maleas. We docked at Piraeus just as it was getting dark, and I was a little apprehensive about our accommodation for the night as the Club had said they would make all the arrangements, but I need not have worried; we were met by an official of the Club who made everything easy. The cars were left at the Austin garage, which was run by the Ducas brothers, and we were taken to the *Semiramis Hotel* at

Kirfissia, about nine miles north of Athens.

Kirfissia is slightly higher than Athens and many people have villas there to which they move in hot weather. Our hosts said that they felt foreigners would find it too hot in the city, so all the foreign competitors were accommodated at Kirfissia. Whilst we appreciated the thought, we were at a disadvantage in being so far from the Club, where all the latest information was available, and we were even further from our garage. However, the Ducas brothers were a great help and put a car and chauffeur at our disposal, which removed this difficulty for us.

The next day, Tuesday, marked the end of our first week away, but it had seemed like a lot more. The car called for us and we went down to the garage, where I left Johnny Organ to service the cars. I went on to the Club and picked up some of the paperwork, rally plates, etc and met some of the organizing committee. It appeared that we were the first British factory to send out a team for this event and as such were made more than welcome. Unknown to us, we were in fact blazing a trail which was to help to make the rally even more popular. Gregor Grant, the founder and editor of *Autosport*, had been out the year before and his report had aroused my curiosity. We met Mr Canellopoulos, the Clerk of the Course, and his very beautiful secretary, Helen Marangos, with whom all the boys fell in love. All the committee spoke English, for they had mostly been to school in England, and some of them had also served with the British forces during the war. This was one of the many things which created such a pleasant atmosphere that we became lulled into a state of false security, believing that we would find the rally easy. Little did we know what was in store for us.

A lunch party was arranged for the drivers and myself by Mr Ducas at Glyfadha, where there were a number of restaurants along the shore. It was a simple meal of seafood and fruit, with white wine or beer according to taste. The fried octopus was excellent, and it was the first time I had tasted it. We also had cockles. Greece at that time was poor in meat, but well provided with the produce of the sea, which was just as well for the standard of living amongst the working class was very low.

That evening Mr Canellopoulos took us down to Turks Bay, on the east side of the Piraeus peninsula. This little crescent-shaped bay was the harbour for the yachts of the Royal Hellenic Yacht Club, which was situated on a rise at the eastern end, with a splendid 'quarter-deck' from which the Acropolis could be seen in the distance. The club also overlooked the anchorage used by visiting naval squadrons. In the little bay were moored some of the finest cruising yachts I had ever seen. Every sort of rig was represented, and the owners and crews were to be seen preparing for the coming season; the Greek owners put off for the islands when the heat became unbearable in Athens.

Around the shore were any number of restaurants where one could dine at the water's edge after selecting the fish in the deepfreeze across the road. However, the customers were given little time to park their cars or select a restaurant before they were surrounded by touts, but at least they proved quite friendly and seemed to make no complaint if we happened to go to the place next door. One sat on a concrete terrace at the water's edge, under a canvas awning. There was a wide selection of seafoods and it was easy to spend most of the afternoon in these pleasant surroundings. Owing to the fact that the Greek 'lunch hour' is an elastic term, it was not considered a sin to spend a couple of hours over lunch, and shops and offices stayed open until about seven in the evening as it was more agreeable to work in the cooler part of the day. Meals in that part of the world, we discovered, were for conversation, and the talk could range from business to politics to history. At these lengthy meals we learnt a lot about the people, the civil war which tortured Greece for so long after the world war was over, and the difficulties in a country which had so little to export.

The next day the cars were ready and, having a little time to spare, I took Johnny Organ to see the Acropolis. It was about 11am and very hot. We drove up to the car park which stood on the slopes of the great rock, and while we were standing there and looking up at the huge, golden blocks of stone a man struck up a conversation with us and asked how long we were staying and what we hoped to see. I am always on my guard when a chance meeting happens in strange places and was a bit off-hand at first. After a while it transpired that our new friend was only waiting to have a puncture repaired on his car, which stood just down the hill, but meanwhile was prepared to point out the landmarks which lay in Athens below.

Talk somehow got round to the war, and our friend, who had spoken lovingly of the Acropolis, suddenly grew sad. "Yes," he said, "that was the saddest day of Greek history, seeing the swastika flying up there." He went on to say that this was a bad blunder by the Germans, as it was such an insult to the Greeks that they were even more bitter than they would otherwise have been. I asked him if he would show us round the Acropolis, but he said that he had never set foot up there since the Germans came.

Before the war he had been the official photographer to the Government for things of historical interest and had published books of photographs. After some time I talked him round and we were privileged to have a unique conducted tour which lasted nearly two hours. Fortunately, I had two cameras and, with the advice of an expert, was able to see things from better angles than I would have chosen myself. The result was that I came away with some very fine pictures and useful potted history, plus some amusing bits of information which I was able to pass on to other visitors in subsequent visits. I never got our friend's name, but he did say that he lived in a house with bow windows near the Royal Palace, and bow windows were rare in Athens.

On Thursday morning we were all up early for the start, which traditionally is staged, with a fine sense of the dramatic, below the Acropolis, with the Parthenon standing out against a pure blue sky in the background. The cars started from a ramp, with thousands of enthusiastic spectators lining the sidewalks, and in a short time they had all gone and we were left to worry about the unseen and unforeseen.

Mr Canellopoulos had very kindly arranged for me to fly with him by Olympic Airways to Thessaloniki, in the extreme north of the country. The flight took about two hours and we were met by the members of the committee of the Automobile Club in Macedonia, who took us to the Club where they had set up the central control point for the rally while it was in the north. Here I could trace the position of our cars fairly quickly, as information was 'phoned in from control points along the route. Meanwhile, someone was detailed to show me the old and new city in a short drive. Although the light was getting a bit dim, I was able to get a picture of the great arch of Galerius, the Roman Emperor; much of the relief work was still intact and it was interesting to note elephants amongst the procession of troops depicted.

As the cars were not due in until the middle of the night, we were later taken to a little country tavern where meat was roasted on a spit and there was a profusion of strange dishes. To cap it all, we finished off with strawberries liberally covered with brandy before returning to the control in the city to find that the first car had just arrived. The cars appeared nearly two hours before their scheduled departure time for the next section and thus the crews could either sleep or eat, according to their choice. Pat Moss, John Sprinzel and Dick Bensted-Smith had been taken off to a meal by Mr Ducas, who also had the Austin agency for that area.

Ann Wisdom was the subject of much curiosity from the locals as she had chosen to sleep in the Healey, which was parked in a side street near the minibus belonging to the Club where they were dispensing hot soup and sandwiches. A policeman was posted to keep people away from Ann and as a result she slept peacefully for an hour. The others came back in good time and we checked over the cars, which were due out at one minute past midnight.

After they had gone I went back to the flat of our agent, which was situated on the top floor of a high block overlooking the bay. It was warm enough for us to sit on the balcony and I had a pleasant conversation in French with Mr Ducas' wife and daughter. The Ducas family had been forced to leave Smyrna in 1920 at the time of the Turkish massacres. They had fled to France and worked in a garage for some years before settling in Greece and founding their own business.

I did not stay long, then returned to the hotel, intending to get some sleep before going up to the control at Serrai, where the competitors who had started at Trieste were due to meet the Athens starters. The telephone rang at a quarter to six. It was Pat, to say that they had crashed about 100 miles east, near Kavalla. She told me that they were both all right, but that Ann was in hospital for observation.

I was not best pleased about this as it had happened before the really competitive part of the rally had started and must have been due to bad driving more than anything else. However, the thing to do immediately was to get the girls to a more comfortable place and see about salvaging the car. I went round to the Automobile Club and set about locating the Ducas flat. Someone came with me and we found the address on a brass plate on his showrooms. I don't think Mr Ducas was too pleased at being woken up at that hour, but he fixed up a car and a couple of mechanics to leave at eight o'clock. We left without much delay and met Tak, the Dutch driver, in his Mercedes 300SL, looking for the control. He seemed to be lost at the time, as he was going the wrong way and took no notice of our shouted directions. Conversation with the mechanics was at a minimum as we had no common language.

We made good time and got to Kavalla in two and a half hours, having inspected the wrecked Healey on the way. Pat was at the *Hotel Astir*, which was modern and comfortable and a contrast with the old town with its Turkish castle and Roman aqueduct. We then went round to the hospital, which was close by in a squalid dusty street. A strong smell of garlic defeated even the disinfectant, and the place was crowded to the extent of having beds in the passages. The doctor told me that they had been turned out of their last premises because of overcrowding; that must have been the end! A small boy with a broken arm had been turned out of his bed to make room for Ann. The X-ray slides showed that she had no broken bones and I felt that she would recover more quickly in the *Astir*. I said that I was prepared to sign a certificate to the effect that I took full responsibility for moving her and, having paid the bill, and added something as a thanks-offering, we thankfully departed. I felt sorry both for the patients who were staying behind, and for the overworked staff who were fighting so hard under such conditions; they said they hoped to get a new hospital in two years.

It transpired that Ann had been driving and Pat was asleep when the crash occurred. The Healey had been running in a high-speed convoy of Greeks, who knew the road and the conditions. They had come to a tightening left-hander which went downhill, Ann had over-corrected and the car had spun and rolled down a steep grassy bank into a cornfield. They had been helped back onto the road by the others, but the timing had slipped and the car was in no fit state to go on.

We found that the bitumen-surfaced roads in Greece were deceptive to a degree: when dry they were nearly as slippery as a wet road in England and when wet they were like an ice-covered road. Nobody seemed to know why this was so, but I suspected that the marble and clay dust which became rubbed into the surface had some effect. There had been a shower that morning and John Sprinzel and Dick Bensted-Smith had also found themselves in a field in the MGA Twin-Cam. They were joined very shortly afterwards by a Porsche and a Chevrolet, which seemed to show that there was more to the Acropolis Rally than we had thought.

The next day we put Ann on an aeroplane from Kavalla to Athens and got the crashed car going well enough to set off for Athens by road, Mr Ducas having fixed up a Perspex screen and knocked out most of the dents. Pat was in no mood to tarry and I had little time for photographs on the way. We tried to take a short cut through Kymina, which was incredibly dusty, and we actually lost some time. I tried to persuade Pat to stop for a bathe near Mount Olympus, but she was all for pressing on. We passed the Spring of Venus, near Tempi, at full speed and made very good time through Larissa and Lamia, stopping once for a wash in a horse-trough and later for some fuel. Finally I persuaded Pat to visit Delphi and we turned off the main road at Brallos; the road was rough and stony, but we swept up to the top of the pass in fine style and finally got to Delphi at dusk. We had a quick look at the superb view over the Gulf of Corinth, bought a couple of goatskin rugs and left for Athens in the usual Moss style – flat-out – arriving in time for a late supper.

The prizegiving was held on a hill opposite the Acropolis, and the Crown Prince of Greece, who was deputizing for his father, presented the awards. He was accompanied by his two sisters, who asked that Pat be presented to them so that they might offer her a few words of consolation. The Ladies' Cup was won by the French crew, Annie Soisbault and Renée Wagner, driving a works Triumph TR3A.

I flew back to England the next day, the crews and cars returning via Austria, where they were to do a reconnaissance for the Alpine Rally. When the Healey finally reached England it was found that both the front engine bearers were broken and the engine was just resting on the frame. The 1959 Acropolis Rally was definitely not a success for us.

On examining the reasons for our failure, I thought that there were two main ones, the first being over-confidence and the second a lack of experience of the event and, as a result, of the conditions to be expected. This underlined my point that you had to know the character of your event before you could expect to do really well in it. I must say, however, that I thoroughly enjoyed the chance of seeing so much new country on the way to the start; for this reason the Acropolis became one of my favourite rallies.

The 1960 Acropolis was a more ambitious event as far as we were concerned for we entered three of the new Austin Sevens, or 850s as they were then called on the Continent, to be driven by Tish Ozanne and Pat Allison, Mike Sutcliffe and Derrick Astle, and John Milne and Bill Bradley, plus two Austin-Healey 3000s, to be driven by Pat Moss and Ann Wisdom, and Peter Riley and Tony Ambrose.

That year I decided to start from Trieste, as time was short between the Acropolis and the Tulip Rally, although if I had known how bad the roads were in southern Yugoslavia I might have had other ideas. We left England on May 14 and stayed that night in Liège. The following morning, Pat's battery was flat, but the car started with a push. She had left the long-range spotlight on all night, but no-one had noticed it because the lamps had padded covers in the daytime to protect them from stray stones, and the car had no ammeter as we had had trouble with these previously. I suppose this was another omen. We finally left at 10 instead of 9am, which did not improve my temper. Pat, of course, was terribly sorry, and I felt much better when she said so.

We lunched at Frankfurt airport, where we were due to meet John Milne and Bill Bradley, who had not been able to leave at the same time as ourselves. Air arrangements like this were all right in the spring, but in those days had a habit of going wrong at other times of the year, so I did not like to rely on that sort of arrangement when there was a tight schedule. This time, however, the boys flew in on time.

We stayed at the *Sonnehof*, at Leonburg-bei-Stuttgart, that night and had time for a look round the Solitude race circuit before supper. Pat had had a most spectacular crash there in the Lyons-Charbonnières Rally in the March. She had been coming down the hill to the pits during the speed test when her Healey went over a wet patch on the track, which was mostly dry. The front wheels lost adhesion and the car went off the course to the left, leaping into the air so high that Ann, who saw it all, was certain that Pat would be killed. The Healey twisted in the air and impaled itself on a fence post so firmly that the post, entering by the bootlid, went through as far as the door pocket on the passenger's side. Pat stepped out unhurt and lit a cigarette.

Having spent the previous night at Villach, we arrived in Trieste on the evening of Tuesday, May 16, and put up at the *Savoy Excelsior-Palace*, a fine, modern hotel which was large and lush enough to please even Miss Moss. As we were only there for two nights, and proper rest was an essential, I felt that the expense was justified. The cars were housed in a rather primitive collection of garages at the back, but against this the proprietor did not mind us working on his premises. Unfortunately BMC at that time had no agent of any sort in Trieste and, although I had written to the firm formerly listed, on the off-chance that they would be able to help, I had received no reply.

Soon after I arrived at the hotel, the telephone rang and I was surprised to hear a charming voice announce that it was Mrs Hall speaking; she introduced herself as the wife of the gentlemen who had formerly held the Nuffield agency in Trieste and said that she would like to come round and see me. We met in the cocktail bar and Mrs Hall, who was half-Chilean and half-Yugoslav by birth and spoke several languages fluently, turned out to be as charming in person as she had sounded on the telephone. She offered to show us the town and introduce us to anyone, if we needed anything. Her husband, who ran a trading agency, had insisted that she did this in his absence on a tour of the American PX stores in the Near East. The rest of the party came down and were as surprised and delighted as I was to find we had such an interesting guide for the evening, which would be our only chance of seeing something of Trieste night life, as the following evening everyone would have to go to bed early. We had already been to the Automobile Club, collected our rally plates and informed them that we would all be starters, so we had nothing in the line of duty left for that evening.

Mrs Hall said she would take us to an interesting restaurant and we set off on foot, in spite of the complaints from the non-walkers in the party. The restaurant in question was called the *Piccolo* and specialized in seafood and dishes of the district. We sat down to table 13 in number, but I don't think any of the more superstitious noticed. The management knew Mrs Hall well and went out of their way to make us all happy; some of the party went back to lunch there the next day as they had enjoyed it so much.

After dinner we went on to a beer cellar; this was a famous place, but I made no note of the name, although I recollect that it was situated under a brewery. There was even more of a party atmosphere here; the cellar, which was gargantuan, was crammed full, but Mrs Hall had influence and we were ushered to a large table near the band. The party was informal and everyone was enjoying themselves immensely. There were several games of bingo in full swing, with large baskets of food and wine as prizes, as well as a talent contest for singing popular songs. Beer of two types, light and dark, was served in large steins, but it could also be ordered in glass boots holding about a litre. Some of us bought these glass boots and managed to get them back to England without breakage; mine, I believe, is still to be seen behind the bar of the *Dog House* at Frilford Heath.

At last the cellar shut and we found ourselves out in the street waiting for a tram back to the *Excelsior*. However, trams were few and far between and all seemed full, so after a long while we decided to use taxis, but they had to be ordered by telephone. When they came, each driver would only take four people, and as four into 13 won't go exactly, the last four wanted either to walk home with the odd man out, or make the driver take five. He would not take five on any account, so the unwanted five decided to walk. The taxi-driver, who had come some way, wanted paying and went off to get the police. There was a certain amount of anti-English feeling in Trieste that night, but the police did not trouble to intervene.

On Thursday, May 18, we left Trieste after the rally cars, at about 8.10am. I was driving one of the faithful A99 Austins with Den Green as my mechanic and co-driver and we had all the spares and luggage with us. Unfortunately, I had miscalculated over fuel and on getting up to the top of the hill leading towards Yugoslavia, found that there were no more filling stations in Italy. We had therefore to come back to the town, fill up and set off again. This delay cost us about 45 minutes and as a result we never caught the rally cars up until after Zagreb.

At Zagreb we located a *putnik*, or tourist bureau, and cashed a traveller's cheque; this turned out to be a wise precaution as the petrol coupons we had with us only applied to commercial spirit and it was necessary to pay a supplement to get leaded fuel. The amount of cash which one was permitted to take into the country was very small, so it was a good thing to get some ready money as soon as possible. The control officials at Zagreb told us that all the rally cars had gone through about an hour before, so we set off after them down the monotonous *autoput* to Belgrade. This motorway, which was marked so imposingly on the map, was really nothing more than a concrete road of modest dimensions with one lane in each direction, and subject to a speed limit of 100km/h, which was not enforced. There were few filling stations on it and, as far as I can remember, only one place at which to eat. It was quite without scenic attractions as it mainly ran through swamps and damp woodlands, although in places the countryside was dotted with little white farms where the peasants were cultivating the more fertile strips of ground.

At length we reached Belgrade and were about to make our way to the Automobile Club where the control was to be when we spotted the Healeys parked outside the *Hotel Metropole*. Pat and Ann had plenty of time in hand, so had taken a room with a bath and ordered some food. Den Green and I found a very helpful hotel manager who directed us to a wash-place and a restaurant with a good menu. We opted for a lager beer while our omelettes were coming and filled up on bread and butter and coffee. Here we were joined by one of the Austin Seven crews, but of Tish and Fanny, as Pat Allison was nicknamed, we heard nothing. Until I made inquiries later, I was not aware that the navigators of both our ladies crews had decided to take the road out of Belgrade to the east, as this was well-defined on the maps which they were using. I knew there were refreshments at the Club and assumed they might be there, so did not worry unduly.

After our meal, we went round to the control and left immediately behind the last car, finding our way out of the city easily enough by following the Acropolis Rally signs, which soon put us on the road to Kragujevac. It was here that our troubles began, for on the way out from the control we saw the Ozanne-Allison Austin Seven going in the wrong direction. It would have been stupid to give chase as we didn't know where they were going.

The map in the regulations showed a more southerly route than the other crews were taking, and my own maps showed that route as being the main road to Sofia. Unfortunately, not all the crews were using the same maps. After about an hour we stopped; none of the baby cars had passed us, so we felt they must be behind us. Some 20 minutes later Mike Sutcliffe passed us, going like the wind, with rather an ashamed look on his face as he knew that we had started behind him. We found out later that Milne and Bradley were on the right road, that the two Healey crews rejoined the route at Kragujevac, and of Tish more anon. This situation developed because we had not had a navigators' conference, not thinking that there were any navigational problems as far as Serrai, in Greece, and had not done a recce, either.

There was no point in waiting any longer; to go back would have made us even later and we could only think that Tish was on a parallel route and hoped that we would contact her later. Our job was to look after the interests of the greatest number, but unfortunately Tish was a member of the Austin team of the three cars and her disappearance broke it up. So we pressed on through the night, and the road, which up to then had been reasonable for some 50 miles, became very bad. It was worse than many East African roads, having been completely neglected in favour of the new *autoput* which was then under construction. Near Nis, we found a German crew whom we had met on the Portuguese Rally the autumn before; they were now in a Saab and were removing the right-hand rear brake drum. We stopped to help them and they were soon away. We were saved from complete dejection by 50 miles of completed *autoput*, but the Saab was again overtaken, stopped this time with some obscure electrical trouble; we couldn't help any more as we too were getting late, so left them to their fate.

On arrival at one of the few open petrol stations, we were just about to fill up when there was a power cut; unlike most Yugoslav pumps, these were electrically operated – so that was our lot. Fortunately we still had enough fuel to get to the next petrol station about 30 miles away. Further on, road construction was in full swing and there were labour camps with all the lights on, rows of sleeping bodies in wooden huts and miles of barbed wire; it looked very much like films I had seen of labour camps during the war and I wondered how many were 'volunteers'.

The road got worse, we felt tired and I decided to have a cat-nap. I woke up feeling that I was about to be run over by a train and one indeed panted past a few yards away, making scarcely 10 miles an hour up the grade. At one point we could not find the road at all; it just disappeared into what looked like a hedge. Finally I blew the horn by mistake and the 'hedge' started to move. It was actually three hay carts side by side across the road; their drivers were all asleep. Perhaps if our headlights had not been smothered in dust we should have been better able to distinguish hedge from hay.

Earlier that evening we had been driving down a village street when I was dazzled by the headlights of another car. I turned out our headlights, which was the normal procedure in that part of the world. The drill was for the other man to put his lights out, then you turned yours on again to have another look, and so on. This method, which seemed to us completely crazy, was practised in Greece and also much used by lorry drivers in East Africa. At the time when I switched my headlights off, Den Green shouted "Look out!", but it was too late. We hit a barrier, hurdled a pile of stones, landed in a deep ditch with the front wheels and then jumped right across it. The take-off was spoilt by the fact that I braked just as I hit the pile of gravel; otherwise we might have used it as a ramp and made a clean job of the thing. Halfway through the air, I had one of those visions of broken sumps and lengthy stays in the wilds. We landed with an appalling crash and there was a shocked silence. The other car, of course, never stopped. We went on a little, found one of those ever-burning street lamps, pulled up and looked underneath. All seemed to be well, so on we went.

Dawn began to come up at about 4am and we got into Skopje to find the control just closing. Three cars had not signed in: a non-starter, the Saab and Tish. I told the official where the Saab was and said that I had last seen Tish on the way into Bulgaria. Whilst this was true in substance, that it was a practical impossibility never seemed to occur either to the journalists who later wrote up the story, or to the officials who inspired it, or to the interested parties who worried. Nobody remembered that the Danube was about two miles wide at the point towards which she was heading and that neither she nor Fanny had Bulgarian visas. We quit the control and immediately the wires began to hum; Reuter, Press Association, Uncle Tom Cobley and all had a real go. The next day the English papers had headlines about two poor little English girls lost behind the Iron Curtain. The Embassies were telephoned, but no-one knew where they were for the simple reason that they hadn't gone into Bulgaria at all.

Afterwards we found out that Tish had left Belgrade by the east road, as we had supposed; this was quite good for about 30km, but when it turned south towards Kragujevac it deteriorated rapidly. Approaching that town she found a level-crossing gate shut and some shunting going on. After a quarter of an hour had been lost, waiting in vain for the gates to open, Pat Allison looked at the map and found a cross-country route to take them back onto the main Sofia road. They got back on route, but in Kragujevac they took the right-hand fork to Kraljevo, which is on a road that does go to Skopje, but by a slightly longer way. About here they realized that one of the front shock absorbers was coming loose but, being late, they knew they could do nothing about it. Continuing with this uncoupled led to more trouble, as on an ADO15 the shock absorber is a vital part of the front suspension. The ball-joint, which acted as a swivel pin, resented the increased angle through which it had to work and finally snapped off.

Tish and Fanny spent the night in the car and a local workshop made up another ball-joint next morning. They slipped up badly here because if they had troubled to look through their spares they would have found one there. We always sent out the cars equipped with tools and spares carefully suited to each event. For instance, a really hard event like the Alpine, in which the controls were close together, did not permit much fitting of spares, but the Acropolis, with long stages on which time could be made up, was a different matter and far more spares could usefully be carried. Knowing this, most crews checked on their tools and spares before leaving England, so that not only did they know exactly what they had, but also where to lay their hands on the various items as quickly as possible.

The Yugoslav mechanic, we knew, was a great improviser, for he had no readily available spare parts service for most of the machinery he looked after. As a result, he improvised, and did so very well and cheaply; the ball-joint, for instance, only cost Tish about 10 shillings (50p) and a packet of English cigarettes. On a previous event, John Sprinzel had broken a stub-axle. He and his co-driver stripped out the other broken parts and took them to a workshop some miles off, using a scooter as transport; within the day they had a usable replacement. Some improvisation was required with the front brakes as one of the brake-shoe assemblies had been demolished, but the repair was good enough to get them back to England.

At length we reached Titov Veles and the road began to show some signs of attention. Gangs of young students, mostly dressed in khaki shorts and very sunburnt, were heading to work and singing as they marched behind the standard bearer who carried the red flag. As we came down a wide, sunny valley, we saw that the road surface was different and at the small frontier post we crossed over into Greece. The Royal Greek Automobile Club had arranged for a Land Rover to meet the rally crews here in order to transport their heavy luggage to Athens. When we arrived, the Land Rover was full up, so we had to take our own crews' baggage on to Athens ourselves.

We caught up with the rally at Serrai where there was a couple of hours' rest for refreshment, which also allowed the starters from Trieste and Athens to join up. The control there was a country inn, much used for outings from Salonika (Thessaloniki). Several streams ran through the garden, which was shaded by large trees, under which were tables and chairs, although one could also sit on the low stone walls. Sometimes they roasted a whole sheep on a spit, but I have never seen it done. Even without the sheep, however, there was plenty to eat and enough to drink, although naturally there was no wine. Even in those days rally drivers in general were careful about intoxicating drinks, and I would say they were a very good risk in respect of drink and its consequences.

Everyone was there except Tish and Pat Allison. Erik Carlsson, who had started from Athens, joined up with our party there and added to the general air of gaiety which the changed conditions encouraged. Den Green and I had come over two of the Special Stages on the road up to Serrai and I was thus able to describe the conditions. These had to be covered at speeds which varied according to the class and theoretically were closed to the public traffic. However, in practice this was impossible so one was likely to meet a large lorry, and perhaps a trailer, coming the other way just when the car had been set up for a fast corner at, maybe, 80mph. To add to the fun, the already slippery surface might suddenly have become wet, as light showers would sweep across the country without warning at that time of the year. If the surface did get wet, it became like a skating rink and competitors who did not treat it with respect tended to fly off the road in all directions.

I spent some time telling the newcomers that they should treat the roads, and above all the Special Stages, with respect, but they had heard it all before. It was quite astonishing to me how good drivers would not believe that you were quite right until it was too late. I waited until all the cars were away and then tailed on behind as, although we had press plates on the car, we were not allowed to do the Special Stages until the roads were opened. It was most interesting to look at the black marks on the corners and notice that most drivers followed the same line. Some of the more enterprising, however, took such a tight line that they had ripped the tarmac off the edge of the road and cut up the edge, scattering stones all over the place. We came on a couple of wrecked cars, but neither was ours. Later the stages were rougher and not on tarmac; variety has always been the spice of rallies.

Our plan was to go to Lamia, where we would intercept the cars. I took the new coast road which I had been over the year before with Pat, but now the bridges were intact and we did not have to make diversions across the fields. We reached the new roadhouse, the *Xenia*, at Larissa, where we had supper. As there was no hotel of any size at Lamia, we decided to return to Larissa after we had serviced the cars. This was a silly thing to do as we should have telephoned on to Delphi and booked in there.

We arrived just on time at Lamia, in fact at almost exactly the same time as Pat and Ann. The girls were exhausted. They had taken a wrong turning somewhere up near the north-west frontier and had entered a military zone without knowing it. They had not stopped when challenged, so had been fired on and, to cap it all, had done about 60 miles up a road which resembled a dried-up river bed. They had been told by the crew of the Volvo service van that the Healey's chassis was broken. We had a look and confirmed this, finding also that a rock had carried away the hydraulic pipe to the clutch. It would take about an hour to get the car right, perhaps more, but it could be done in two 'bites', as the control was near, which meant that the car could be taken to clock in and then returned to us.

Pat said she was prepared to retire if I told her to do so. I looked at the girls, who were very tired, and considered our chances of making a decent job of the car with the help of Volvo's welding gear. I thought what might happen if the steering or front suspension went on a mountain section and felt the risk was not warranted. I told the girls to retire. Pat heaved a sigh of relief, but Ann continued to sleep, exhausted, in the car.

The Riley/Ambrose Healey had also crashed on one of the Special Stages. It had thrown a tyre tread at about 100mph and the crew had lost time changing the wheel. Then they tried to make up the lost time within the Special Stage, but not only was this a rash thing to do, it was very nearly impossible; the Healey ran off the road at high speed, both of the crew being thrown out; the car, however, landed on its wheels and travelled a long way down the slope. The ground being rocky, Peter Riley landed with some damage to his back, fortunately not serious. Tony Ambrose got off much more lightly, but both of them suffered torment at the hands of a Greek Army medical orderly, who used a large blunt needle for the anti-tetanus injection.

Being well brought up in these things, Peter and Tony set about salvaging the Healey. With the assistance of the faithful Ducas organization they obtained a large lorry with a crane, which needed no less than 265ft of wire to haul the car back on the road. It could not be driven back to England, and unfortunately the ship which was selected to take it back made an extensive tour of the Black Sea ports before turning towards England. As a result, we did not see the car again until August.

I sent a somewhat caustic telegram to Dunlop's about losing the tread and the result was a much improved type of tyre for the Alpine Rally; Peter and Tony did not therefore suffer in vain. As far as our other runners were concerned, on the very first Special Stage, Sutcliffe disregarded my warnings and soon perched the Austin Seven in the branches of a tree. By a miracle, and with help from the soldiers who manned these sections, Derrick and he were back in the fight with a loss of five minutes. Those five minutes, however, were fatal to any chances of even a class place.

These adventures only confirmed my growing conviction that a complete reconnaissance of the Special Stages was essential, which in turn meant a start from Athens, where the crews would have to arrive about a week before the rally started.

Whilst the two Austin Sevens continued the rally, the girls spent the night in Lamia and returned next morning to Athens with the battered Healey. Den Green and I went back to Larissa and had a few hours' sleep for we had to be in Athens that same day to meet the Austin crews. There was no point in going back for Peter and Tony as we knew Ducas would be looking after them.

On arriving at Athens, I was surprised to hear that no-one knew where Tish Ozanne and Pat Allison had got to. This was worrying as we had a message from England asking for news of them. Fortunately, the next day I had a telegram from Kraljevo saying that they were safe and getting the car repaired. All this anxiety upset me and my temper was not improved by a call from

London at 2am which kept me hanging on for 20 minutes whilst the operator on the *Daily Mirror* sorted out if I was making or answering it. Consequently I was not feeling too helpful when the operator eventually put me through to the sub-editor who had originated the call.

On Sunday morning the intermediate results showed that John Milne and Bill Bradley were lying seventh in General Classification and second in their class. This was very promising, but John had used up most of his brakes during the rally and it would be touch and go whether he had enough left to do the race at Tatoi airfield. When he went to take the car out of the *parc fermé*, John discovered that he had no footbrake at all; we later found that one of the seals had been so burnt up by the heat that it had let all the brake fluid run out. As one of the brake cables had also broken, John's car was virtually brakeless, so I told him to retire from the test. Mike Sutcliffe, although badly placed, made a fine showing in this race and was warmly applauded by the large crowd when he overtook many larger and faster cars on the corners.

So, once again, we had to return from Greece defeated by the Acropolis. We at least had the consolation of having done a little better than the year before, and Tish Ozanne had unwittingly given the Austin Seven a great deal of publicity by getting mislaid for 72 hours. Whilst I flew back to England to brood over the reasons for our failures, those of the party whose cars were still runners crossed by sea to Italy and set off to do a quick return trip to England, as the Rally of the Midnight Sun was not far distant.

My last attempt at the Acropolis, in 1961, was most carefully planned to take full advantage of the lessons which we had learnt the hard way during the previous two sorties. Firstly, I arranged for Peter Riley and Tony Ambrose to do a recce of the common route from Serrai, with particular emphasis on the Special Stages. They flew to Athens on May 10, just after the Tulip Rally, and were to use an Austin A55 supplied by the Athens agents. Tony and Peter did an excellent job of this and there is no doubt that much of their later success was due to this recce. Secondly, we started from Athens; I had had more than enough of crews losing their way and smashing up their cars before the rally even started in earnest. Thirdly, the team was made up mostly of drivers with previous experience of this somewhat specialized event. Peter and Tony were to drive an Austin-Healey 3000, which was to be taken to the start by Douggie Hamblin, who was to act as chief mechanic to the team. The Healey was our main hope for a major success but, to encourage interest in cars more likely to be bought by Greeks, I also entered two Austin Sevens and a Morris Mini-Minor. David Seigle-Morris and Vic Elford drove the Mini and Mike Sutcliffe and Derrick Astle drove one of the Austin Sevens. The other was to be driven by Donald Morley and Ann Wisdom.

Pat Moss had decided to cry off the Acropolis this year on the grounds of poor safety arrangements. With some justification, Pat contended that the Special Stages were not really closed to traffic and said that she didn't see any future in trying to make fast times when she didn't know what to expect around the next corner. Ann Wisdom, however, was undaunted by all this (or perhaps she did not realize how 'near' had been the near-misses of the year before), and agreed to go as Donald's co-driver. As Donald had never before done either the Acropolis or, indeed, any rally with a lady as co-driver, they looked like having an interesting ride. It turned out to be more interesting than either of them had thought.

The party was made up by the works-assisted Mini-Minor of David Hiam and Mike Hughes, with Douggie Hamblin and myself acting as 'support' in our Wolseley 6/99. Those of the main party who did not fly out crossed over to France via Boulogne on May 9 and travelled down to Lyon that night on the train ferry. We shipped the cars out to Piraeus on the *SS Izmir* from Venice, where we arrived on May 12 after spending the previous nights at Turin and Verona. Darkness had fallen, but the view from the large dining-saloon windows brought us all to our feet as the *Izmir* steamed past the entrance of the Grand Canal. The Campanile San Marco and the Palace of the Doges were floodlit and flanked by magnificent buildings which, with their illuminated windows and lighted landing places, made a beautiful setting. The sky was lit by a few stars and the whole scene was reflected in the tumbled waters in which plied the gondolas, water taxis and other craft.

Although the dinner was not elaborate, it was good, whilst the price of the wines astonished everyone. Whether the Turkish Government provided a subsidy I do not know, but it was possible to buy a reasonable white wine for about four shillings a bottle. At these prices, it was as well that most rally drivers were normally abstemious people.

The *Izmir* was an interesting ship with a chequered history. Completed about three years before, she had been designed for passengers (in three classes) and freight traffic around the Mediterranean, and was well fitted out although, unlike others in her fleet, she lacked a swimming pool; this deficiency was made up for by no less than three bars. She carried an efficient lady public relations officer, who seemed to represent the Government rather than the owners, and I always felt that she might be keeping an eye on the crew as well as on the passengers. There was an extraordinary lack of small change in Turkish money, and as the bars would accept nothing else, we lived on a rather complicated system of IOUs to the barman, who, however, seemed to keep track of the situation. I took care not to cash a large traveller's cheque, as I was not certain if the Greeks would change Turkish money and knew from previous experience that the Greeks like to discount most things of Turkish origin very heavily – it's traditional.

When on the top deck, I noticed signs of teredo worm in the planks, and could not reconcile this with the information that the ship was new, so asked the lady PRO about it. She said that the ship had been built in Germany and on completion had been taken over by her Turkish crew for delivery to Istanbul. On entering the Sea of Marmora, or thereabouts, the captain had allowed her to run aground and she had sunk in shallow water. I expect he was celebrating their arrival back in Turkish waters. The ship was salvaged and towed back to Germany, where she was refitted and recommissioned in the middle of 1960. At the time of our trip, her bottom needed cleaning and she was due for her first docking.

Her present captain was apparently a martinet and ruled everyone with a rod of iron. None of the crew had a drink for the entire voyage and the captain did a round of inspection each evening in which he had a good look at everything and anything that took his fancy. On one evening when they were watching he even removed the caps from the fire branches to see if they turned easily on their threads. The chief evening recreation seemed to be chess and both Vic Elford and David Seigle-Morris showed that they were not beginners. While I was having a game with Ann Wisdom, the chief engineer came along and started to help her. I was rather annoyed at this until I saw an opening to take her Queen; after this the gallant engineer departed and left Ann in the lurch.

The men of the party who were so minded had a long tour of the engine room on Sunday morning. It was very well maintained and the chief spared no pains to explain everything in his halting English, which was more than any of us could have attempted in Turkish. The eight-cylinder diesel engine was turning over at 130rpm and each cylinder was developing 520bhp. The engineer showed us the indicator diagrams which he took at regular intervals on each cylinder. If the readings fell below about 510bhp he knew there was something amiss and had a look inside that particular 'pot' at the next port of call.

On the morning of Monday, May 15, two and a half days after leaving Venice, I woke up sensing that the ship had slowed down; on looking out of the porthole I realized that she was steaming very slowly through the Corinth Canal. Although it was only six o'clock by local time, it was getting light and so I dressed and hurried on deck with my camera as I had always wanted to see this canal with its steep sides running up very nearly vertical for, I should think, about 250ft. When I got on deck I found the usual gaggle of German tourists who never miss either a view or a historic building on these occasions. The British appeared not to be so interested in curiosities or culture, rally drivers in the main being more interested in their beds. The small tug which had pulled us through soon cast off and we were now in the Gulf of Aegina and virtually within sight of our destination.

Soon after breakfast, Pireaus came into view and the ship's PA system could not refrain from producing *Never on a Sunday* – and how well it suited the atmosphere. The Customs men remained aloof on the jetty while the cars were slung ashore, but the Immigration and Exchange Control people were reasonably helpful and we had high hopes of getting the entire team to Glyfadha, where we were staying, well before lunch. However, it would appear that the system was not geared for the arrival of more than one car from abroad per day, and that to inflict the officials with as many as six was not in accordance with the rules. The result was that the paperwork took nearly two hours.

Finally we got to the *Astir Beach* just on lunchtime. After lunch I was feeling revived, which was as well for the management were being particularly obtuse about the methods of payment and charging accounts, which made it necessary for me to argue the point. About now, Peter Riley and Tony Ambrose returned from the recce in the very tired A55, which they had borrowed from the Austin agents. The A55 started with good tyres all round and with everything more or less in place, but after three days the tyres were bald, and the shine had gone off everything else. The only item which did not suffer from the bumps and dust was the Smiths radio. Peter said it kept them awake at night by reproducing the wails of some oriental female who was presumably the current favourite singer. They had been on the move for three days, almost non-stop and practically without food, for hotels on the minor roads were non-existent and the restaurants were mostly soup kitchens serving a very thick and greasy mixture which did not appeal unless you were both acclimatized to it and desperately hungry.

In spite of their hardships the recce was complete and Tony set about getting his notes into readable form. The next day we collected the plates from the

Club, met our old friends and checked the cars over. My own work being negligible from now until the start, I did a small conducted tour of the Acropolis.

The next day, Wednesday, May 17, scrutineering took place in one of the large garages on the road to Kirfissia. 'Alfa Harry', one of Pat's friends, who lived in either Athens or the United States as he had rich parents, asked me where Pat was. I told him that she wasn't coming because she didn't think the Special Stages were really closed to traffic. Harry, who looked like a very fair imitation of Hercules, said quite solemnly: "You know, I think she's got something there."

The International 'rally circus' was well represented at scrutineering, prominent being Erik Carlsson, Saab; Bohringer, Mercedes-Benz; Peter Harper, Sunbeam; and Gunnar Andersson, Volvo, with his amusing co-driver Charlie Lohmander, who had travelled extensively in the Balkans and lived with the gipsies. Charlie picked up foreign languages as a dog does fleas – a more useful acquisition for the man than for the animal. John Sprinzel was there as a private owner, and co-driver for Bobby Parkes, who had an ex-works Austin-Healey. As Bobby made brake linings, they had at least to win their class if they were to have anything to advertise, but to do so they had first to beat Peter Riley and Tony Ambrose.

Peter was not at all happy about the throttle on the Healey, which he said opened too quickly for the delicate control required on the slippery roads. This was investigated at scrutineering while we were waiting our turn, and we decided to give the centre carburettor a 'lead' over the others, which cured the sudden rush of power to the back wheels. The accessory boys were also around at scrutineering. Oliver Speight was there with one of his Dunlop rally service fitters. Oliver had not been able to bring his own transport with him, so had had to take the tyres round in a one-ton lorry which he had hired, but unfortunately the man who drove it had no language in common with them. Despite this language trouble, he undertook to see that we had tyres in the north, in the centre and in the south of Greece. Castrol, too, had sent along Ray Simpson, who would give the drivers oil when they needed it.

The rally was due to start on the following evening, but Douggie Hamblin and I left in the Wolseley 6/99 at 3pm that afternoon as we had to get to Larissa in time for a little sleep. We had a pleasant run of just over 200km up to Lamia, an important town on the road to Thessaloniki; despite this, we found neither a good hotel nor a decent eating house there. We stopped in the main street and bought some food and a few crates of minerals for the crews, and just as we had completed these purchases, Oliver Speight appeared with his lorry so the locals were entertained by a rather noisy English reunion in the middle of the road. The old man who had sold me the fruit said "*Auf wiedersehen*," to which I replied "*Nicht auf wiedersehen*. Goodbye." He then asked if I were American, and I said "No", so with some diffidence he tried English and, when I said "Yes", he gave me some more fruit free. This kindness was typical everywhere: as soon as the locals found out we were British, they were generosity itself.

That night we put up at the *Xenia* motel at Larissa (which can be spelt with one 's' or two, according to taste), and had dinner on the terrace whilst observing a coach load of tourists who were on a conducted tour. They had their national flags planted on the table in front of them and never have I seen a party who appeared to be taking their pleasures more sadly.

To bed early, for we had to be up to meet the first car at 4am. I always took an alarm clock for those early starts, but usually woke automatically just before it went off. If the rally was tough and I worried about the crews, I slept very lightly and got into the habit of picking up the telephone and becoming fully awake as soon as it rang; all too often it would be a driver on the line telling me the worst and giving the name of some outlandish place where he or she was stranded. It was so easy to get cut off on some lines that this vital information had to be taken in instantly, even before one had time to write it down. That night nothing dramatic happened; the drama was to come later.

When we arrived at the control, which I had located the night before, it was still dark, but I could hear a Healey coming down the main street. This was Peter and Tony, who were running second in numerical order. They said that the car was misfiring and complained that the starter wouldn't work. As we had had similar trouble before, which we had traced to battery posts vibrating loose on rough roads, I thought this might be the cause, but it turned out to be a defective dynamo. Fortunately, we had a spare one with us and Douggie changed them with commendable speed. We had to start the Healey by pushing, but we knew that they would be all right as soon as the new dynamo started to charge.

Parkes and Sprinzel came in with a broken accelerator pedal, having driven the last few miles by rigging up a piece of wire with which to pull on the throttle. We couldn't help them much, for this was a welding job and we were not carrying welding gear in our car, which was already overloaded, so I advised them to get the repair done in Salonika. Not long after, Donald and Ann arrived complaining of lack of acceleration and incipient misfiring. As they had plenty of time in hand, we did everything we could to cure it, changing the carburettor, the coil and the condenser in turn, but without much success; not until the car was rebuilt in England did we finally fix it by changing the cylinder head.

When David Hiam reached the control he brought the bad news that Vic Elford had run out of road in the Seigle-Morris Mini some 20km away. David said that this had bent the front suspension, so it sounded like a welding job and the time was just before 6pm, when everything shut down. We tore all round the town looking for a garage which was still open, but had no luck, so I decided to give up the idea of locating a welding plant and drove out to fetch the Mini in. On the way I noticed that a workshop where Caterpillar tractors were repaired was not quite shut, so I rushed into it. By dint of using a mixture of English, French, German and Italian I managed to persuade the owner to bring his welding plant to the scene of the accident, but the main problem was to get his oxy-acetylene cylinders into the Wolseley. They were the largest I have ever seen, but by letting down the back of the passenger's seat they just fitted into the length of the car. The Greek and Douggie Hamblin sat in the back with the cylinders and I fear they had an uncomfortable trip. It was necessary to hurry, as David would be excluded if more than an hour late at the control, where I think he had to clock in at about 07.20 hours, and when we hit one hole in the road the gas cylinders and the back-seat passengers hit the roof.

When we arrived at the scene of the crime, our new-found friend and Douggie set to work with a will. The front torque stay-bracket had been torn off the subframe. This was welded on again and the rod straightened. Unfortunately, the welder was almost too much of an artist and, although he made a very good job of the repair, he took longer than I liked. If we could have explained, I would have asked him just to patch the car up and we then could have brought it back to him, after David had clocked in at the control. As it was, after nearly 40 minutes' work the car was going again, and David and Vic tore off at full speed. We followed at a more leisurely pace when we had collected our tools. On entering the town we found that the Mini had failed to make it by about five minutes, as a lorry had refused to let them pass. This was very annoying after all our efforts but, quite honestly, there had been no need for Vic to run the car off the road for he had had ample time in hand to drive at a more reasonable speed.

We returned to our hotel with the disappointed Mini crew and had a wash and breakfast before setting out for Salonika by way of the new coastal toll road; this had been recently opened and the saving in time made it well worth the amount charged. David went on to Serrai to check that our other cars had passed through. This support was the normal procedure when a member of the BMC team was forced to retire, as they could encourage the others at points not covered by our 'umbrella', supply them with food and drink and, if need be, spare parts from their own car. If anyone thinks this was not sporting, I must stress that this was a recognized procedure practised by all the continental teams, who often fielded more cars than were required to win the team prizes for just such an eventuality.

We lunched at the restaurant next to the *Hotel Mediterranean*, where we took a room for the afternoon's rest against the labours of the evening. In due course David Seigle-Morris piloted the cars in from the control to the Austin garage, which I had arranged should stay open. Two of the baby cars had trouble with their front shock absorber brackets and the Morley/Wisdom car was still dogged by the flat-spot and misfiring. We did what we could for them, but the position was not very satisfactory.

Peter Riley, on the other hand, was pretty happy about things for the big Austin-Healey was going well now and he was about to begin his great duel with Walter in the Porsche Carrera for supremacy in the Grand Touring category. This duel, of course, was being closely watched by Parkes and Sprinzel, who knew that if either of the leaders made a mistake, it would be their turn to step in. The German driver Hans Joachim Walter set out to win the 1961 Rally Championship – which he duly did – and spared no expense to do it. His car was prepared by the factory and carefully adapted to the requirements of each event, whilst his own great driving ability was strengthened by his taking a local co-driver whenever possible, particularly if the Special Stages were of a type requiring local knowledge and technique.

It appeared that both the Healeys had made good times in the first test and that David Hiam was also starting a private duel with a BMW 700 driven by the German, Block. Unfortunately for David, the rally leader, Erik Carlsson, was in his class.

As soon as we had finished work on our cars we returned to Lamia, which we reached soon after daylight by dint of stopping only for a snack near the Fountain of Venus at the end of the toll road. The town was looking very untidy as there had been some sort of a market and most of the stalls were packing up. We could not get into a decent hotel and our movements were restricted by the throng, but eventually we found a little café which served a very odd imitation of an omelette, the only thing which it had in common with that dish being the eggs. The coffee was of the Turkish variety, with about one-third fine grounds, so that only the first two mouthfuls were drinkable. At many of the more sophisticated hotels it was usual for the waiter to ask the customer if he preferred Nescafé to Turkish, but in this place they had never heard of instant coffee in any form.

After our primitive meal, we left the town and stationed ourselves on the road in from Volos on the forecourt of another little café, where they sold tepid beer. The proprietor had just killed a goat and now proceeded to skin and clean it at the side of the terrace, oblivious to whether his patrons minded or not. Some colourful gipsies rode by in a high-wheeled cart drawn by the thinnest white horse I have ever seen, so thin that I forgot to spit and wish. The dusty road stretched away across the parched plain to the sea, and we were bored, tired and slightly anxious, for the cars were late.

But eventually we sighted a Healey, heralded by a cloud of dust, and flagged it down. It was Peter and Tony, who had thrown a tread after the last two difficult Special Stages at Volos; they were doing about 90mph when it happened, but had come to no harm. I checked the tyre pressures and was far from sympathetic when my gauge and another showed that they were at only 26lb per square inch. When I remarked caustically on this, Peter's excuse was that they had been checked by Dunlop's at Serrai or Salonika. As it was inclined to be wet up there and the later stages were run in the cool of the night, it was a reasonable pressure to use then. Peter, however, should have rechecked his pressures during the day and, under the conditions now prevailing, I would have liked to see the tyres at 32psi cold, which would have gone up to over 36psi when hot. Luckily he had two spares, and Oliver Speight had returned from the north and was, we thought, at the next control. Peter was sent off to get some more air in his tyres after some minor attention had been given to the throttle.

Soon after this, David Hiam came along with everything very much under control. He was driving to finish, but had not been hanging about, and unfortunately he again brought bad news. Donald and Ann had gone over the edge of a cliff near Volos, as was confirmed by Mike Sutcliffe and Derrick Astle, who limped in later with more shock absorber bracket trouble.

Donald and Ann told us the story later. The Volos Special Stage was very twisty, with a loose surface. Donald was following an Alfa, hoping to pass if a chance occurred. A Mini under these conditions, even when not giving its best, is hard to shake off, especially when being driven by the imperturbable Donald. When in full cry on a tightening bend, the Alfa driver lifted off in the middle of the corner; this put Donald off balance, one wheel went over the edge and the Mini was airborne. Donald's first thought was for Ann and he felt this keenly on the way down. Ann's first thought was much more analytical as she wondered how many times the car was going to turn over before it hit the ground. The Mini shot clear of the cliff and somersaulted two-and-a-half times before hitting a ledge and then bouncing about another 50ft into someone's garden. The total drop was about 125ft. Donald's first question was "Are you all right, Ann?" to which the indignant reply was "Of course I am." I think Donald was the more shocked of the two, and there is no doubt that their safety harness saved them from serious injury.

The cliff was too steep to climb, but they got back to the road by a goat track after salvaging the clocks. Almost the first person they met was an agent for the insurance company covering the car, so that was one worry shifted onto someone else's shoulders. Donald and Ann soon got a lift into Volos and within 10 minutes were the occupants of the last two vacant seats in a small bus bound for Athens. It had been an adventurous afternoon.

We others left for Daphnis, just outside Athens, where we were to change the Healey's brake pads and tyres before the finish. Peter had told us that he was just ahead of Walter, who had dropped a few minutes in a foggy Special Stage, so it was vital that he should do both the half-hour high-speed test at Tatoi and the hill-climb within seconds of Walter's Porsche. Sprinzel had crept up to second place in the class and was now making every effort to overhaul Peter on the next two Special Stages.

We arrived at Daphnis on schedule, having had time to get back to base for a clean-up. The filling station there had been adopted by most of the service crews, and I was glad to see Oliver Speight who had completed his historic lorry ride without a hitch, but who still did not know any Greek. Our Healey rolled in and we changed five wheels to racing covers and put in new brake pads in under 15 minutes; as there was still time in hand we then washed the car. David Hiam did most of his own work and appeared satisfied with things. He was still having a tussle with the BMW 700, but now at least seemed to have got the upper hand. Sutcliffe and Astle unfortunately failed to make the last 100 miles, having been defeated by assorted troubles. After retiring, they took a ferry across the Gulf of Corinth to get onto better roads, but could not keep going even so.

John Sprinzel and Bobby Parkes came sadly unstuck on the final Special Stage when John clipped a corner, hitting a rock hidden in the grass, which broke a kingpin and the front brake disc. This was a great disappointment to me, for we had looked like getting first and second in the class, but the crew, of course, were even more disappointed. Ann and Bill Wisdom both turned up at Daphnis and we were delighted to see that Ann seemed none the worse for her unplanned flight.

The next morning we got out to Tatoi bright and early. The circuit was laid out on the aerodrome, to the north of Athens, on which it was not possible to practise properly as it was part of the Royal Hellenic Air Force base. Before the test started, all the cars were allowed to do a few warming-up laps and they were then split up into two heats, the larger and faster cars running first.

The first heat was a duel between Peter and Walter. The German built up a lead of about 10 seconds in the first four laps, after which Peter got the hang of the circuit and started to hold him. Peter, who was driving at his best, would gain nearly 100 yards on the twisty part of the circuit owing to the great urge of the Healey out of corners, but the Porsche was faster on the long straight, so that Peter could not pull back the time he had lost on the opening laps. Walter said afterwards that Peter might have beaten him if we had used a different type of tyre, and I think he was right.

David Hiam drove a fine race in the next heat, taking many cars on the inside of the hairpin and having a magnificent dice with the BMW, which was passed and in turn repassed on nearly every lap.

The final results showed that Peter and Tony had finished third in General Classification, winning their class and the Grand Touring category in the

Austin-Healey 3000. David Hiam and Mike Hughes were second in class to Erik Carlsson, who won the rally outright. This was the 12th time that an Austin-Healey had won its class in an International rally. Unfortunately for the local distributors, neither of the Austin Sevens finished and the Mini-Minor was only second in its class. Thus, whilst we had something useful to advertise outside Greece, there was nothing of much value to the locals, for the import duty on a big Healey was over £1,000, so it did not exactly fall within the popular price-range.

The rally dance was held that night at the open-air pavilion at Daphnis. The Knowldale boys were in good form and I had been warned that anything might happen that night. Phil Crabtree, who had driven in the Ford team, and Mike Sutcliffe joined in the Greek traditional dances which were being presented by a troupe in peasant costume, and received more applause than the professionals. Shortly afterwards the lights went out, and when they went on again, there was an Austin Seven in the middle of the dance floor. Within seconds, Mike and his wife were placed on its roof and the band were playing the Wedding March, for this was their honeymoon.

I noted some of our party sneaking away after this, but was told that they were off to a party at Piraeus. This was not really true, for the evening was to end with another little surprise for the honeymoon couple. When Mike and his wife returned, they saw no beds in their chalet, but a jacked-up Mini, the wheels of which had been removed and used as chocks. They could not find their beds anywhere, but seeing that Derrick Astle and his wife were not yet home, they took over their chalet. Derrick, I believe, finished up with the Hiams.

In the morning the management were very annoyed and rang all and sundry to locate Mike. When they did, they said quite bluntly, "You do not put beds on the roofs of the chalets." Mike is noted for asking difficult questions and asked simply, "Why not?" To this the management could only repeat, "You do not put beds on the roofs of chalets." The conversation continued along these lines until Mike paid his bill and left. I myself had to fly back to see about the preparations for the Alpine, and David and Margaret Seigle-Morris were booked on the same plane. This meant that the team had to organize themselves for a change, so I gave the tickets to Tony Ambrose with instructions to see that the team got their cars back to England. The tickets stated that the ship sailed from Piraeus to Brindisi on the afternoon of Thursday, May 25, so Tony told the team that they should get to the dock at midday as a precaution.

Vic Elford, who was ferrying the Seigle-Morris Mini, had some last-minute shopping in Athens and was in any case noted for cutting things fine. The rest of the party, being more prudent, got to the dock a few minutes before noon. To everyone's surprise the gangway was up, but the ship was being held by the last pair of wires on the off-chance that those mad English would finally arrive. The cars were whisked up into the air and were lashed down in a wink, the lines were cast off and the *MV Miaoulis* was away. Her sailing time was midday, but she actually sailed a few minutes late that day. Just as the gap was too big to jump, but not too great to shout across, Vic arrived in a cloud of dust. He wore only a pair of shorts and a beach shirt and had no more money and no petrol in the car. He was advised to try to catch the ship at Patras, which is 220km to the west at the narrow entrance to the Gulf of Corinth, being its last port of call on the mainland. I don't think anyone really worried about Vic, who was never short of enterprise.

Fortunately for him, the shipping agent lent him enough money for petrol and so he set off literally not knowing where his next meal would come from. He stopped on the steel bridge high above the Corinth Canal and sadly watched the ship creep past below; the other drivers looked up, recognized the Mini and waved to him. Fortunately for Vic, the ship was not due at Patras until late in the evening, for his troubles were not yet over. He ran out of petrol and, having no money, decided to risk barter. He asked for a gallon of petrol at a filling station which happened to be where he had run out. After the fuel was in, he explained to the attendant by signs that he had no money, but offered to let him have two small tins of Castrol. Vic still doesn't know if the offer was accepted, for he was away before he heard the answer. At Patras it was dark and getting chilly, but again his luck was in for the shipping agent took him to a soup kitchen and did what he could to make him seem at home until the ship arrived. Vic was very glad to get on board and I suspect was vowing to be the first person to arrive at the quay in future.

The results which follow show that the Acropolis Rally at that time was an event which offered a real test for both crew and car; that experience was essential to achieve success; and that the difficulties were such that even the best of the experienced crews sometimes fell by the wayside.

Results obtained by the BMC teams in the Acropolis Rally, 1959-1961

1959

Austin-Healey 100-Six	Pat Moss and Ann Wisdom	Crashed
MGA Twin-Cam	John Sprinzel and Dick Bensted-Smith	Crashed

1960

Austin Seven	John Milne and Bill Bradley	16th in General Classification; 4th in Class A5
Austin Seven	Mike Sutcliffe and Derrick Astle	31st in General Classification; 5th in Class A5
Austin-Healey 3000	Pat Moss and Ann Wisdom	Retired with broken chassis
Austin-Healey 3000	Peter Riley and Tony Ambrose	Crashed
Austin Seven	Tish Ozanne and Pat Allison	Retired with suspension trouble

1961

Austin-Healey 3000	Peter Riley and Tony Ambrose	3rd in General Classification; 1st in GT category
Austin Seven	Donald Morley and Ann Wisdom	Crashed
Austin Seven	Mike Sutcliffe and Derrick Astle	Retired
Morris Mini-Minor	David Seigle-Morris and Vic Elford	Retired after accident

CHAPTER 8

The Alpine Rally

"The petrol was of shockingly poor quality and the engines detonated so badly that the crews almost cried at having to torture them so."

At one time the *Rallye Internationale des Alpes* had no outright winner. A *Coupe des Alpes* was awarded to any competitor who succeeded in completing the course and time tests with no penalties, and the prizemoney was shared amongst the *Coupe* winners. Subsequently there was an outright winner, a General Classification for Touring and Grand Touring cars, but the Alpine Cup remained the coveted award, a sort of Blue Riband for the competition driver. Any driver who won three successive Alpine Cups was awarded a *Coupe d'Or*, which was indeed the supreme accolade of the rally world. Only two *Coupes d'Or* had ever been awarded: the first went to Ian Appleyard for three drives on a Jaguar XK120 in 1950, 1951 and 1952, the second to Stirling Moss for three drives on Sunbeams – a Sunbeam-Talbot in 1952 and Sunbeam Alpines in 1953 and 1954. Of the two I think Ian Appleyard's was the more remarkable because he used the same XK120 (the famous NUB 120) and was driving as a 'lone wolf' with only his own organizing ability to see him through, whereas Stirling was driving as a member of a crack works team, with all that implied.

The Alpine was a great test of endurance for both car and crew, but I think the crew suffered less than the car. The course was mostly over secondary roads and featured as many mountain passes as the organizers could find open during the last week in June or the first in July.

The controls were placed so close together that there was little time between them for repairs, refuelling or refreshment. The event used to have up to five night stops during which the cars were impounded, and only spare wheels could be removed from the *parc fermé* for repairs or replacement or worn tyres. Later, the night stops were reduced to just one, with a little longer rest period, and the stages before and after the night stop were lengthened to compensate. The 1961 event, for instance, was made up of 1,142km (709 miles) for the first leg and 1,893km (1,180 miles) for the second leg, with a night stop at Chamonix.

Not only were there uphill speed tests, but the cars had to cover three laps on the Monza race circuit at a high speed, extra penalties being incurred if they were more than a certain percentage slower than the fastest car in their respective category or class. Some of the higher passes tended to be still covered with rocks and mud brought down by the recent winter snows and

117

landslides sometimes made last-minute re-routing necessary. Tyre equipment which was suitable for the rough roads in the remoter valleys of the high Alps was not suitable for speeds of over 120mph on hot concrete at Monza. Engines tended to use a lot more oil under these conditions and gearboxes ran very hot when climbing mountains in the indirect gears for mile after mile.

When the summit was reached it might be necessary to drive even faster to the control in the valley below, and brakes were punished to such an extent that the discs were often glowing a dull red when the navigator swung open his door to dash to the Printogines clock to stamp his card. Timing was to the nearest minute, so if you took the extra 59 seconds you might scrape in without penalization, but should the next section be even tighter, then you had used 59 of the precious seconds before you were even away. These 59 seconds could also be used for getting ahead of another slower competitor, which was valuable tactically if the road was narrow or dusty.

As the 'Alpine' was organized by the *Automobile Club de Marseilles et Provence*, the start was always at Marseilles and the finish often at Cannes, although it had also been at Marseilles or Nice on a few occasions.

Our 1956 Alpine entry consisted of five MG hardtops, a convenient arrangement because we had only to cover one range of spare parts. The competition department transporter accompanied the cars with the necessary equipment and spare parts, and the team was as follows:

Rally number 308   Bill Shepherd and John Williamson
Rally number 314   John Milne and Douglas Johns
Rally number 324   John Gott and Ray Brookes
Rally number 326   Nancy Mitchell and Pat Faichney
Rally number 330   Jack Sears and Ken Best

All the cars were red except John Gott's, which was white, and they went across by road to Marseilles, calling at Lapalisse for the night on the way. Syd Henson of Ferodo travelled down with us and, at this first stop, inspected the new VG95 brake linings which we were using. The cars were also using the Le Mans-type oil coolers for the first time in a rally, and on the run down the flexible pipes connecting them to the oil filter and crankcase began to leak. By the time we reached Meaux from Boulogne it was obvious that the situation was serious, so a telegram was sent to the works requesting that new pipes be flown out to Marseilles as soon as possible. That year we were running on the new type of Castrol R, which had a vegetable-oil base. This had been developed for Mercedes-Benz by Castrol and was used both in their 1955 Le Mans cars and also in the Le Mans MGAs.

Bill Shepherd was very caustic about the whole thing and as good as told me that the factory didn't know what it was doing and that he wished the whole team was back in their faithful HRGs. Bill got more and more aggressive as the evening wore on, and I had to tell him bluntly that the matter was in hand and mechanical problems had nothing to do with the drivers; we were there to solve them and he was there to get on with the driving. John Gott backed me up the next day. The pipes that gave trouble were of a different specification from those used at Le Mans the previous year, but we finally ran without the coolers connected.

As the transporter had left Boulogne before the MGAs, they pressed on at speed in convoy down N7 with John Gott leading. As the team was passing through a long straight village with a 60km/h limit, two gendarmes jumped out in the road and brought the cars behind John Gott's to an abrupt halt. I came down the hill just as the police were getting their notebooks out, so to speak. In practice I've never seen a French policeman use a notebook to begin with; they just fix the victim with a stare and look as if they might reach for the little black pistol in their holsters if he doesn't soften up.

I strolled up to see how the matter would go, as the drivers declined to speak any French. The police put their case concisely; the cars had exceeded the limit and the crews had disobeyed the sign which prohibited overtaking. There were some protests when this sunk in, but the police started to get tough for they just did not believe that no-one in the party spoke French. After being threatened with summary punishment on the spot, we decided that it might be better to co-operate.

The village had experienced a number of accidents, some fatal, during the spring and the law was going to be enforced very strictly. The cars had overtaken a van which was in the act of turning to the right down a side street and must have been proceeding at about 15mph. Admittedly the MGs had been cruising at about 10mph more than the limit, but that was a practice which was condoned in France. The whole affair seemed most unjust and we all said so. "If we were to be fined, could we elect to go before a magistrate?" "No, we could not." We gathered that there was no right of appeal and the police had the same powers as a magistrate. If we refused to pay, we would not be able to leave the country, for the numbers of the cars were now in the possession of the police and the frontiers would be advised. Feeling that we had been done an injustice, we had a 'whip round' and paid up. Meanwhile, John Gott waited down the road as he had got out of the village before the others were halted. I never found out if John had seen it all in the mirror, but he had the last laugh and, being a 'copper', I suppose he thought it indelicate to interfere.

The BMC publicity department had decided to film the event and accordingly we had fitted out a couple of Magnettes for the film crews; they, however, failed to appreciate the fact that camera cars either have to travel faster than the rally or be sufficiently numerous to make this unnecessary. Fortunately, Syd Henson took over driving one of the camera cars and the result was a great deal better than it would otherwise have been.

Scrutineering took place outside the *ACMP* in sub-tropical heat and, as the cars were impounded before the start, we all sweltered in Marseilles until we could leave. After seeing the MGs off, the service cars were to go to Monza, near Milan, where the race track ran through the grounds of what at one time had been a royal palace. In those days there was a choice of a high-speed banked circuit, a road-racing circuit with flat corners, or a combination of the two.

We had two service cars as altogether there were six mechanics. Douggie Watts came with me and Alec Hounslow took the other car. On leaving Marseilles we made our way up to Aix-en-Provence and on to Gap, through Embrun and by way of Briancon to the Col de Montgènevre. This was the easiest of the French-Italian passes, being only 6,100ft high and 11km long, with an easy descent to Susa, after which the road dropped very gradually to Turin. We picked up the *autostrada* to Milan and reached Monza in good time. The MG crews arrived on schedule with nothing very spectacular to report; the cars were serviced at the Esso station at the exit of the *autostrada,* and when this was over we followed them to the track. The fastest MG lapped in 2min 34sec (83.2mph) at Monza, which was very gratifying. The team had lost no points thus far and Jack Sears was lying third to two Porsches in our 'hot' class of 14 cars, in which all our MGs were leading Norman Garrad's Sunbeams.

We hoped to pick up the rally again at Ponte Gardena, a few kilometres north of Bolzano, and travelled there by the direct route through Bergamo and Bolzano. The first part followed the *autostrada* to Brescia and was subsequently converted into double lanes in two tracks, but then it was still the old single-track road which Mussolini had ordered in the early Twenties. Although completely out of date by virtue of the volume of traffic which it was called upon to carry, it had been in its day a very farsighted project which set the fashion in motorways.

Stirling Moss once told me that he had a lot of trouble with the little Fiats on these roads when he was testing his car for the Mille Miglia. Like many owner-drivers, they considered that they had bought the road with the car and never glanced in the driving mirror. Stirling's tactics were to drive alongside and give the door panel of the offender a resounding smack with the flat of his hand as he accelerated away. In most cases, being overtaken at about 120mph had the desired effect. To drive fast in Italy was easy in those days; if you had the right type of car the locals expected it, especially as most of them drove their ordinary cars with the throttle wide open all the time.

After Brescia, the road turned to the north and threaded its way along the side of Lake Garda. Here were the lakeside resorts where the gardens of the villas ran down to the lake; beautiful flowering shrubs were everywhere and stately vistas were framed in cypress. Gardone was a favourite resort for drivers before the Mille Miglia, for here were luxury hotels and water ski-ing and bathing. We stopped for lunch at a small hotel adjoining the lake at Maderno, on the road leading out to Promontario. It was a quiet family hotel, which also catered for the younger set as there was a court for deck tennis and other games. A small jetty boasted a couple of motor boats and there were two instructors giving lessons in water ski-ing as well as some experts who were using the place as a training camp. We were sorry to tear ourselves away, but this was so often the case when one was chasing the rallies; there was just time for a glimpse of a luxury holiday and then it was whisked away as duty called.

For the next few miles the terraces were full of orange trees; these seemed to be protected from the occasional frost by walls which looked as if they were arranged to support some sort of covering stretched over wires. There were also stalls selling rather expensive oranges in clusters. The road itself had been so engineered that it passed through many tunnels cut from the solid rock with windows looking out over the lake. In some places one could park in a small embrasure and admire the view. In one case indeed there was even a restaurant cut out of the cliff just below the road; I had passed it a dozen times but never had a chance to sample its wares, unfortunately. On this fascinating road, however, it was wise to beware of the large motor coaches, which had to be driven some way off the rock face in these tunnels for fear of scraping the edges of their roofs against the tunnel.

At length we reached Riva, at the head of the lake, and started the climb over the hill to Trento; this was the valley of the Adige where plenty of good wine was produced. There were quarries in the hills on the right of the road and one could see the masons making the square blocks of stone used for the pavements on the hairpins of the mountain roads. We reached Ponte Gardena and looked around for a suitable garage, eventually finding a small one just over the railway crossing on the road leading up to the Passo di Gardena and the Passo di Falzarego.

It was not long before we saw our cars, and one by one the crews stopped to give us the news of their adventures. In the last section they had passed over the Giovo and Pennes passes which, although later largely tarred, then exacted much respect from even the best drivers. Nancy Mitchell was in good spirits and had lost no marks. The oil consumption in her gearbox was excessive, but otherwise things were normal. Jack Sears and Ken Best were also satisfied with their performance, being likewise unpenalized. So, too, were Bill Shepherd and John Williamson. Thus we had three cars without penalty, and Cortina and its night stop was not too far off.

The news was not so good where John Milne and Douglas Johns were concerned. John had been following another car in a cloud of dust on a tricky mountain section. He had mistakenly assumed that as he could see the stoplights of the car ahead he was on a straight section of road, but there was actually a bend intervening and John had attempted to jump the gap without success. He saw his mistake at the last minute and had not gone over the edge, but had only been able to get back on the road with Jack Sears' assistance. As a result, he had lost marks for lateness, but the damage to the car was only slight. John Gott had much the same sort of accident, also due to bad visibility in the dust of another car, and had hit a stone road marker with the left-hand rear hubcap. This had shifted the axle back, broken the spring and bent the halfshaft. They had rigged up a temporary 'lash-up' with a block of wood and turned up, still unpenalized and with a little time in hand, although the MG was running in a most peculiar, crab-like fashion.

While we were waiting we were entertained by the antics of the other competitors who were crossing the railway line after the river bridge. The track made a curve here and was super-elevated, but the road crossed it at right-angles. The resulting ramp threw many cars so high into the air as they tore up the hill that one could see their sumps. They came down with a crash that made one shudder, and accelerated fiercely away. John Gott was flagged down and we soon had him into the garage and closed the doors. It took but a few minutes for the experts to remove the spring and fit another, but the axle casing was bent and there was a bit of a struggle to get the centre bolt to fit the casing and bolt it up in its proper place. Douggie Watts was straining at the axle and suddenly let out a yell. I thought he had let the car fall on his leg, but in fact he had put his knee out. This was the same knee that he had damaged playing football in Italy during the war.

Douggie was taken upstairs into the proprietor's flat whilst John's car was finished and sent on its way with something like half an hour to make up. The local doctor was called in, but could do nothing. It was a case for the clinic, he said. Douggie was placed as comfortably as possible in the Austin and we set off for Cortina, where we were booked in at the *Concordia*. On the way my Austin showed a drop in oil pressure; although this was on 10lb, it was a bit worrying and it was not made any better by the fact that Alec Hounslow foretold that the bottom would fall out of the engine at any time!

Fortunately, there was an efficient and charming receptionist at the *Concordia*, who took charge of the situation. A doctor was called and arrangements were made for Douggie to go for the night to the local sanatorium, where they had a specialist. As Cortina was a winter sports resort which had only recently been the site of the Winter Olympic Games, they were fully equipped to deal with all breaks and sprains. Douggie's leg was reset and put in plaster and he returned to the hotel the next day, looking and feeling very much better.

The next morning we had to be up bright and early for the test known as the Circuit of the Dolomites; this was actually shorter than planned as authority to close the full Dolomite Cup circuit had not been obtained. We met the MGs in a mountain village where we borrowed a transport garage for the morning and carried out some much needed repairs to John Milne's car. The Perspex rear window of the hardtop had come out of its rubber seating and so we had to wire it in. John Gott's car managed to keep going on the circuit without losing any marks and the other MGs easily retained their 'clean sheets'.

This, I thought, was one of the finest sections of mountain roads in Europe. The towering red pinnacles and precipices of the Dolomites were quite unlike anything else and the sky was of that vivid Italian blue which seemed to make life worth living. Little wisps of white cloud hung round the mountain peaks in the morning and slowly evaporated as the day became hotter. Later, large clouds crept down from the north and the rumble of thunder was a prelude to the large drops of rain that fell in the afternoon; fortunately, although the storms could be severe they were soon over and the pleasant smell of the damped dust quickly followed.

Cortina is a delightful little town; the older buildings are decorated with frescoes and the town has a tradition for art, having been used to escape the summer heat of the plains by several Italian artists. Cadore, which is not so far away, was indeed the birthplace of Titian. The shops, I recall, were good and the main street, the Corso Italia, was a promenade at all times of the day. It was here that John Gott introduced me to a delightful confection of fried bread and melted cheese which I have never met elsewhere.

The cars were parked for both nights in the Olympic skating stadium car park, from which on the second morning we saw them away on their run to Zagreb. We had decided not to go into Yugoslavia, and awaited their return to Cortina with impatience, whilst Douggie Watts added to the collection of autographs and good wishes on his plaster.

When the drivers returned from Zagreb, they had some good tales to tell, for it was the first time they had ventured into Yugoslavia. The roads were rough and covered with a deep layer of white dust like talcum powder, which pervaded everything. The horse-drawn traffic and the peasants left an assortment of nails and other ironware in the dust, and nearly every competitor had had one or more punctures; those who drove nearest to the edge of the road seemed to have got the most – a point of which we took note. The petrol was of shockingly poor quality and the engines detonated so badly that the crews almost cried at having to torture them so. The hotel at Zagreb was described by Jack Sears as something left over from the Hapsburg era; there was an excess of red velvet upholstery with lace curtains and a stale smell reminiscent of stables. The bars nearby were apparently the promenade of some attractive young ladies, who seemed anxious to acquire some currency harder than their own looks. However, our crews returned to Italy with relief, which even the prospect of the following day's climbs of the Stelvio pass, 9,042ft, the Favia, 8,604ft and the Pordoi, 7,346ft, could not dispel.

As far as the more serious business of the rally was concerned, although five cars had retired and a further 14 were penalized in Yugoslavia, all our MGs got back to Cortina and only Bill Shepherd and John Williamson had lost marks, Williamson having checked out five minutes early at the San Candido control, an error which was to lose them their *Coupe des Alpes*. This mistake was inexcusable in a navigator of Williamson's experience, especially as it was made at the end of an easy section on which there was plenty of time to think clearly.

On a happier note, despite the appalling petrol, Jack Sears had clocked 96.3mph over the flying kilometre in the speed test at Zagreb, and even John Gott's 'lame duck' had managed 92mph. John and Ray had had a very hard trip, however, for the battered rear axle casing was now leaking badly and they had to refill it at every control to keep going at all.

The following day the 45 cars still running left for Megève before it was properly light, and the *parc fermé* was bitterly cold. Having seen the MGs away, we drove straight to the Stelvio, where all the MGs did the speed climb on time, although none of the Sunbeams could manage it. Once they were through, I made for the plains, for it was more than a fair step to Megève.

The weather was superb and this without doubt contributed to the fact that there were still 26 clean sheets amongst the 45 survivors of the 75 starters. After we had reached the flatter country by way of Brescia and Bergamo, we took to the *autostrada*; the high cruising speed which can be maintained there helped us to outflank the rally and we reached Santhia, where we were to contact our crews in the Fiat garage, in good time. The cars themselves had picked up about three-quarters of an hour on schedule by using the *autostrada* and we were thus able to give them a good look over. Some of the drivers went round the corner for a little refreshment and left the boys to get on with the job, but others gave a hand, for we still had five cars to service.

Santhia is in the middle of the rice-growing district and we saw the women walking home from the fields wearing the large straw hats such as many saw for the first time in the film *Bitter Rice*, starring Silvana Mangano. Most of the women were typical middle-aged, hard-working peasants and not the glamorous sort at all, but the newspaper shop proprietors made the best of the myth for all sold postcards which, although really stills from the film, they pretended were typical of the 'local talent'.

When the cars had left us, we packed up our belongings and started off for Ivrea and Aosta. The weather, as it is so often near the mountains in summer, was overcast and menacing. Before we got to Ivrea we ran through a torrent, but we were through it before Aosta and started to climb the St Bernard pass, 8,110ft, as the light was failing. Douggie Watts was travelling in the back of the Austin and we had tried to make him as comfortable as possible. By this time I was very tired and was only kept awake by the knowledge that a mistake on the St Bernard would be fatal to us all; nevertheless, I did doze off at one place but fortunately the car was in second gear going down the steepest part. I woke to hear the engine reach valve-crash at the same time as Douggie Watts, who remarked that I must have gone to sleep. This frightened me more than a little and I stayed awake without any further trouble all the way to Megève, which we reached about midnight. The crews had gone to bed, but we knew they were all there as we had counted the cars in the *parc fermé* as we drove in. Fortunately, I had not got to call them at the ungodly hour of 4am, which had been necessary for the 5.15am start from Cortina, as there was to be a 24-hour halt at Mègève.

When at Cortina we had made inquiries as to the best method of getting Douggie back to England, for the specialist there had said that he should have the knee re-examined and that an operation might be necessary. Douggie was therefore booked to fly home from Geneva and we left soon after breakfast on the 60-mile journey to the airport, where he was soon enjoying the attention of a number of good-looking young ladies who were to see him safely aboard the aircraft. We left Douggie to their care without any regrets, but with considerable envy! At this point we still had two cars which were unpenalized and, as all five MGs were still running, we had high hopes of winning a team prize, the *Coupe des Dames* and a couple of *Coupes des Alpes*. Nancy and Pat were quite confident and Jack Sears and Ken Best felt that they might retain their clean sheets. The day being relatively warm and the front of the *Hotel Résidence* sheltered, the crews relaxed in the swimming pool.

The cars left that evening on the final stage to Marseilles from 19.30 hours onwards. We saw them all away and set off for Briançon by way of the Col du Galibier, 8,399ft, expecting to see them again at about 4am. It was a fine dry night, although a little chilly at that altitude, for Briançon, at 4,496ft up, is the highest city in France. Alas, only three of the MGs reached Briançon. Bill Shepherd passed through with the sad news that Jack Sears had crashed on the very difficult mountain section coming down from the Col de la Croix-de-Fer, which is above, and south of, St Jean-de-Maurienne. On the Galibier Nancy shed all the spokes of a wheel and Bill Shepherd helped her to change it in four minutes; later a throttle spring broke on her car and John Milne changed it in under two minutes. These examples of the penalized crews helping the unpenalized car to get home were all part of the real team spirit which one came to expect in a well-trained works team.

We waited for John and Ray until it was obvious that they were out and it was not until much later that we heard what had happened to them. Apparently the bent halfshaft finally gave up the unequal struggle and snapped off in the differential; inevitably, of course, this happened on a mountain top, miles from anywhere, in the middle of the night. They pushed the car over the crest and free-wheeled down towards a light in the valley, where they hoped to get help. Arriving at the building from which the light came, John knocked at the door. This was cautiously opened on a chain by a forbidding-looking lady, who told him in no uncertain terms where he could go. Startled by such a reception (most unusual in France), John beat a hasty retreat, pausing only to shine his torch on a bronze plate by the door, from which he hoped to find enough information to justify a strong protest to Monsieur Michelin. The building, however, turned out to be a home for unmarried mothers-to-be!

Freewheeling on, John and Ray eventually found a hotel where they borrowed an assortment of kitchen knives with which Ray worried the broken end of the halfshaft out of the differential. These two bits they took into Annecy on a school bus, where they got them welded together; Ray refitted the halfshaft and they got the MG down to Marseilles under its own power without calling on us for assistance. I thought this was a hard-luck ending to a sporting effort, for they had struggled on for nearly 1,500 miles in a car which, as Ray said, "steered like a brick", but had lost no more marks after their first incident.

When the three cars had gone, we set off to climb the Galibier for the second time that night and were rewarded by the sight of the sun tingeing the clouds with pink as the wind swept them away at dawn. We got down into the valley at St Michael-de-Maurienne and were delighted to see Jack and Ken coming slowly toward us in their MGA, which was without its hardtop or windscreen. They were quite unhurt, but still very shaken, so we took them to a café which was just opening for some hot coffee and an omelette. I still rate that breakfast as one of the best I have ever had, and I know Ken and Jack felt the same way. Over breakfast we heard what had happened.

They had been going well round the Croix-de-Fer circuit, which was a difficult one and, according to Ken, had only about four minutes more of the dangerous part to do when Jack misjudged a corner or the surface changed before he had time to correct the skid. The car spun on the edge of the precipice, hit the inside cliff, and then rolled over on to the hardtop. Jack and Ken managed to escape through the doors and the space where the side screens had been, but when they stood up the car was balanced on the edge so precisely that they had to press down on the highest part to stop it from toppling into the depths. Help soon came in the form of other competitors who could not get past, and the car was swung round and turned over on to its wheels. The rally went by whilst Jack and Ken took stock of the situation. The screen was wrecked and the hardtop was only fit to throw over the edge, where it probably still is. They might have gone on, but they were by then very late and one never knew what other unseen damage had been suffered; the steering might break or a strained brake pipe might fail. Wisely, they decided to call it a night and drove down to the valley for some first-aid.

Fortunately, we had with us a spare windscreen, complete with brackets, which I had been carrying for the entire rally; I was glad to be able to use this, although I would have preferred to offer it under happier circumstances. With this in place, and after a wash and some breakfast, Jack and Ken felt much better, so together we started off on my third climb of the Galibier in 12 hours; this made a total of over 16,000ft of climbing and a similar amount of downhill motoring. However, we felt no ill-effects from these frequent changes in altitude.

We now followed the rally route over the dusty Col d'Izoard with its weird eroded rock formations and were soon running down towards Gap and Marseilles. We arrived at Marseilles some time after the finish and were delighted to hear that Nancy had kept her clean sheet and should win the *Coupe des Dames* and a *Coupe des Alpes*, as well as finishing third in a 'hot' class of 14 cars.

The prizegiving took place the next day on the terrace in front of the chateau of the Parc Borely. This open-air prize distribution was one of the features of the Alpine. The unpenalized cars were lined up in front of the rostrum and the crews called forward to receive their prizes from the President of the *ACMP*, Baron d'Huart St Mauris; there was always champagne for the *Coupe* winners and kisses for the ladies. That year there were 17 *Coupes* out of 34 finishers, primarily due to the very good weather and the fact that only half of the

Dolomite circuit was used, and that at much slower speeds than usual. If the weather had been worse, I think Nancy would have finished higher than 15th as the roadholding of the MG was superb in the wet and British crews were often at their best in adverse conditions.

The film crews duly crept in with their battered cars and rather more film than we had once thought possible, which, when cut and edited, made a nice little tribute to Nancy and Pat. This graces the Nuffield film library under the title of *Ladies First*, and Raymond Baxter's commentary does much to enhance it.

The dance which took place after the distribution of prizes was held that year at the *Résidence*. The meal was excellent, but the speeches were too long; fortunately, the evening was livened up by a beauty parade and dress show, the models joining in the dancing afterwards. Some of the more enthusiastic drivers spent the evening collecting souvenirs and the party finally broke up in the early hours when we realized that we had to drive back to Boulogne. There was no train ferry from Lyons in those days. We got as far as the *Hotel Royal* at Chalon-sur-Saone the following night and caught the afternoon boat from Boulogne the day after. The expedition had not been such a brilliant success as we had hoped, but perhaps we had experienced an undue amount of bad luck – or was it bad judgment?

The 1958 Alpine Rally, which was the second Alpine in which the BMC competition department participated, was the most publicized and the most dramatic in the whole history of the event. At one time we had hoped to enter five MGA Twin-Cams, but for a number of reasons this was not possible and at the last minute we decided to enter the same number of Austin-Healey 100-Sixes. Owing to the change in our plans there was little time to carry out much testing or to do any of our own development work, although we had been lent the duo-green demonstrator from the Donald Healey Motor Company. This car had most of the works chassis modifications which had been developed by Geoffrey Healey and was fitted with Dunlop disc brakes on all four wheels. We added the alternative twin-carburettor equipment, larger fuel tanks and twin spare wheels. As we only had three cars of our own in addition to the Healey Company's demonstrator, we had to borrow another demonstrator from the Austin Motor Company. This car was red and black and was normally used by the Vice-Chairman, George Harriman. He very sportingly released it for this event and we allotted it to Nancy Mitchell. The three other cars were bright red, a colour which I considered lucky and which subsequently came to be regarded as the BMC team colour. These were captained by Jack Sears, Pat Moss and Bill Shepherd. The green car naturally went to John Gott, who had a preference for this colour.

Shell, with whom we had a contract for fuel, were to make a film in colour and sound of the entire event. Competitors were asked to co-operate as much as possible with the film unit, and we were given some indication of the size of the project when we were told that the unit would film at night as well as by day. This time the camera cars were to be driven by experts so that the cameramen could concentrate on the job and the cars could keep up with the competitors.

In addition to the five Austin-Healey 100-Sixes, there were three Austin-Healey Sprites, which were making their first appearance in the International rally field. Private entrants had formed a team of three Riley 1.5s, and we had lent one of the works Austin A105s to Frank Grounds and a private Austin-Healey 100 rounded off the list of 14 BMC cars. The mechanics were in for a busy time.

We decided to use the new train ferry service from Boulogne to Lyons and crossed over on the afternoon boat of Thursday, July 3, the transporter having left with a load of spare wheels and other impedimenta on the Dover-Dunkirk boat on Tuesday, July 1. In addition to the normal complement of mechanics, we persuaded Syd Enever to let us take Terry Mitchell of the MG Design and Development department. Terry had been responsible for much of the profile work on the streamlined cars which did so well at Salt Lake, Utah, and we felt that it was time that a designer had some first-hand experience of the problems which cropped up before, during and, indeed, after a rally. The train ferry was a new experience for everyone, and we all stayed up far too late watching the poplars of northern France swing past and congregating in each others' compartments for endless rally talk, as everyone was excited at the prospect of another Alpine after the cancellation of the year before. The cars were unloaded after breakfast and some of the party got away before 9am to do a check on the Mont Ventoux hill-climb, which was to figure in the first part of the route.

I travelled down in company with John Gott, and on one of the new sections of the N7, just before Valence, we came across a crash which involved a British-owned Ford Zephyr containing a family who were going to spend their holiday at Cavalière, on the Cote-d'Azur. A local car had apparently ignored a stop sign and come out into the main road right in the path of the Zephyr. John Gott took charge of the situation and acted as interpreter for the British party and the French police. When everything was under control, we left John, who was going on to Mont Ventoux, and reached the *Hotel Rose Thé* at La Ciotat without any further adventures. The rest of the day was spent fetching the rally plates for the cars and arranging the times of scrutineering, which took place on the Saturday. At the Club we found that there would be 56 starters, of which nearly half – 24 cars, actually – were in our class.

The warm weather was a mixed blessing as some of the crews found it hard to get acclimatized, but after three days, spent mostly on the beach in front of the hotel, they were all in fine form. The mechanics, headed by Douggie Watts, used to get up shortly after 5am and work in the cool of the day and often in the hot part, too, for there never seemed to be enough time to prepare a car to everyone's satisfaction. One of the cars – I think it was the ill-fated green one – had some obscure trouble which was first thought to be ignition and later turned out to be some fluff which had got into a pipeline. The Sprite crews were in great form; Sprinzel and Cave were enjoying the sun and food and Tommy Wisdom and Jack Hay were as usual having their friendly arguments about nothing at all.

With all their troubles finally ironed out, the cars were placed in the enclosure by the old harbour in Marseilles before 11 o'clock on the Monday morning and the crews dutifully attended the reception given by the Mayor of Marseilles at the town hall close by. This was important because any last-minute route alterations were to be given out here. John Gott usually made a speech in French thanking everyone on behalf of the English competitors and then another in English explaining any last-minute instructions. After this, everyone returned to the quayside and tried to find some shade or, as rally drivers always do, just stood about and gossiped. The amusing Kat brothers were there with their white Triumph TR3, which had a witch painted on the side; they wore identical outfits, red overalls and straw hats with bright bands, and their wives kissed them goodbye on the start line, much to the delight of the gallant Gauls. Annie Soisbault, the French lady champion, was nearly late for the start, but again Gallic gallantry prevailed and no-one minded.

Various stars were to be seen about, some serious like Peter Harper and Gunnar Andersson, others happy and lighthearted, like John Sprinzel and Pat Moss. At 14.00 hours an official raised the blue flag of the *ACMP*, the first car mounted the ramp, the announcer poured forth a potted history of the drivers' past rally achievements, the flag was dropped, and the car was off on its 2,360-mile journey, which was to include four timed tests on mountain passes and four speed tests. As soon as all our own cars were away we got into our two Austin A105s and set out for the Italian border at Mongenèvre, where we hoped to contact our cars around midnight.

The rally route up to the Italian frontier ran by a devious path over some nine mountain passes, including the Col d'Allos and the Col d'Izoard. We made our way to Aix and thence to Sisteron and Gap. We then turned east and drove up the valley of the Durance to Embrun, where we had a meal. It was but a step from there to the top of the Col de Montgenèvre and we arrived at the frontier at the same time as Paddy Hopkirk in his Triumph, much to the annoyance of the film director who had just bathed the landscape in millions of foot-candles or whatever film men measured light in. I might add that we had no desire to put Paddy out of the picture, but just hoped to slip over the frontier before him so as to set up our service point on the Italian side. However, all was forgiven as Paddy figured dramatically in the film later on.

Our timetable allowed us some six hours to get to the Monza autodrome, for the rally cars were to make a detour to the north of the *autostrada* in order to avoid Turin and Milan, so we ambled along from coffee bar to coffee bar, consuming one Espresso after another until the last bar closed and we were forced to drive on to Monza. We slept in the cars outside the gates of Monza Park, for the caretakers had not yet opened them. Perhaps they had not expected the rally cars to arrive so early, but the reduced average speed which was imposed by the authorities for the main road sections in Italy had enabled them to make up a lot of time on schedule. The route had also been slightly modified owing to landslides, but out of the 56 starters several had already fallen by the wayside.

Norman Blockley in his Austin-Healey 100-Six had been involved in a minor collision in France, and Harper and Kremp in the Minor 1000 had retired because they had been given a route card for the class above and found they could not manage the speeds imposed for that class. We pointed out that they should have done their best and asked for a proper card at the next stage when the matter would have been corrected. Anne Hall and Tish Ozanne in the modified Ford had suffered from locking disc brakes and they had finally gone off the road, but without serious consequences. Maurice Gatsonides was unlucky enough to break a brake pipe on his Triumph TR3; this not only involved him in a crash, but also deprived him of his chance of an Alpine Gold Cup. Of our cars, Nancy Mitchell's had been late at a control owing to a miscalculation on the part of her navigator, but up to this point we still had four Healeys without penalty.

The bigger cars, such as our own, the works Fords, the Ferrari and the Mercedes 300SL, had to put in three laps of the road circuit at Monza at 86mph. This meant that the Fords had to lap three and a half seconds quicker then they had done in 1956, and the Series II Sunbeams had to improve by eight and a half seconds per lap. Several teams had their hopes dashed to the ground here, but the big Healeys went well, Jack Sears making second FTD to Tak's Mercedes 300SL. Both cars and crews were hot by the time the test was run and the drivers imbibed large draughts of cooling glucose drinks. The tyres were let down to more normal pressures and the team sped away to Brescia. We followed by the *autostrada* and arrived at the *Hotel Moderno Gallo* very shortly afterwards.

This was the hotel at which we had stayed for the Mille Miglia during 1956 and 1957. It was pleasantly cool, like so many of the hotels of its type, unpretentious, but adequate and near the centre of the town and the *parc fermé*. The high ceilings and marble floors made the rooms airy, while the closed shutters kept out the glare of the midday sun. The drivers retired to bed as soon as they had had lunch, but the mechanics went for a stroll round the town. However, the shops were closed until four or five in the afternoon, for the Italians did little work in the hottest part of the day.

Only 44 cars arrived at Brescia and, of these, only 16 were unpenalized and four were ours. We all sat down to dinner feeling very contented, but my contentment was tinged with the apprehension which all competition managers must feel until the event is over. I went round the tables and made out my list for the times at which the drivers wanted to be called. Norman Garrad had impressed on me that one should never trust anyone else to call the crews and that they must be personally escorted to the *parc fermé*. Nancy, who had driven for Rootes, knew of this and was always the first person to ask for a call; the mechanics too were on my calling list. One difficulty was that the bedrooms were not always on the same floor and I had to dash around the hotel looking for unfamiliar numbers, although at the end I usually did a recce the night before.

Most of the crews left the door unlocked as they slept soundly and feared that they would not hear the knock. One had to go in to have a little chat with the drivers to make certain they didn't turn over and go to sleep again. Pat was a marvellous person to wake for she was fully conscious as soon as she was called, but she would then sit up and make unparliamentary remarks about rallies in general and this one in particular. Ann woke up a bit more slowly, but sounded very businesslike straight away. John Gott would probably be up and about already, but Bill Shepherd liked to stay in bed, and John Williamson usually had to go and wake him again. Very often the male crews shared a room, but the ladies preferred each to have her own room, and we always tried to get each a private bathroom as well.

The day dawned fine, all the cars got away without any trouble and we set off for Bolzano. The rally route lay over the Passo di Croce Domini, which was new in this event; it was rough pass with fearsome drops. The Burton brothers, of tailoring fame, hit a rock outcrop in their AC and went over the edge, but rolled down one of the less steep parts before coming to rest without serious injury. On this pass, too, Tak in the big Mercedes 300SL holed his petrol tank and was stranded.

While service cars were running north along the shores of Lake Garda the rally crews were twitching and sliding their cars over the loose rocks of the dusty Passo de Vivione. Frank Grounds and Gordon Shanley, who had been lent a works Austin A105, removed the left-hand rear door on a marker post. Some people said that the drop at this point was 4,000ft, but others disagreed and said it was only 3,500ft. The Austin crew carried on with the panel flapping in the wind until temporary repairs could be executed, and the other rally crews promptly dubbed the place 'Shanley's Corner'. The Vivione was followed in short succession by the Tonale and Mendola passes, which were on the main road from Bergamo to Bolzano, and not so difficult. It was on this section that Jack Sears and Sam Moore had a brush with Ronnie Adams due to a misunderstanding of the correct route; the cars only suffered minor damage, but Jack's steering was put slightly out of track, and he was late at the next control.

We ourselves had earlier set up our first service point at the AGIP Supercortemaggiore filling station at the junction of the Bolzano to Merano and Bergamo roads about 3km east of Bolzano. This was one of the smaller stations belonging to the Supercortemaggiore company, which had set a new standard in European service stations. The larger ones had restaurants, cloakrooms and money-changing facilities as well as a bar for snacks and quick service for the car. Supercorte was particularly attractive to competitors as it had the highest obtainable octane rating anywhere and so these stations were well patronized as soon as the cars left France, where the quality of the fuel was poor. Moreover, the opportunity for a quick snack while the cars were serviced was very convenient.

The smaller stations had no catering facilities, but the staff were housed on the premises and would sometimes provide a cup of coffee or a cold drink if asked. Large or small, the staff of the stations were all very courteous and customers were encouraged to comment to head office if they felt that the facilities were not up to the required standard. For these reasons, the BMC team knew that they could always find us at the nearest Supercorte station before a named control. These support points were chosen so as to be at the end of a long, easy section or, if that was not possible, just after a difficult section and before a long, easy section. The latter practice was not wise unless no other arrangement was possible as time used was hard to make up again and drivers preferred to run near their top average so that they had a margin in hand for the unforeseen, such as a road blocked by an accident, or unexpected delay caused by a puncture or minor mechanical trouble.

We had not been in position for long when the rally cars started to pass; no-one was in need of attention except Jack Sears, who had damaged his steering and needed it retracking. Fortunately, we had altered the outer portions of the track rod so that the ends had left and right-hand threads, which made it possible to compensate for a bent steering arm without losing the centreline position of the arm on the steering box. During 1958 and 1959 we carried out a series of small modifications to the steering and front springing of the Austin-Healeys, which improved the handling to a marked degree. This became necessary as the performance of the cars was being improved on each occasion they appeared. I always made a point of good steering and suspension, for an increase in the output of the engine was wasted if the roadholding was inferior. At this time the maximum speed of the cars was about 112mph, but the following year, with the introduction of the bigger engine, it went up to well over 120mph and finally nearer to 130mph. In my opinion this was about the limit of the development possible for the suspension in question so that any further improvement had to be obtained by better acceleration.

We sent Jack Sears on his way and set out for the Stelvio. Leaving one of our cars at the bottom for the mechanics to check over the Healeys before the test, we set out to climb the 48 hairpin bends which led to the summit. This was a pass which stirred the imagination of those who had never seen it before. The straight frontal attack up the valley, for 28km from Spondigna at 2,903ft to the summit at 9,042ft, followed by the descent of 22km over a more varied type of country to Bormio at 4,019ft, were tests of the first magnitude for both man and machine.

There were large banks of snow on the sides of the road towards the summit and these made the road so narrow when the pass was first opened in the spring that the cars sliced the frozen snow with their wings and hubcaps as they slid round the hairpins. About halfway to the top, the surface deteriorated and the tarmac gave way to stones, with the hairpins made of pavé. The timed climb was taken from Trafoi to the summit and the fastest cars had to cover the 14km to the summit in not more than 18 minutes and not less the 16min 50sec. None of the Healeys had any difficulty in doing this.

The film crews were much in evidence here and we noted a blue Alfa Romeo with the number 212 on it. As this number was not in the programme and was being driven by the test driver for the factory, we assumed rightly that it was part of the 'props'. Denis Jenkinson, the foreign racing correspondent of *Motor Sport*, was also in an open Alfa with a camera mounted in front of the passenger's seat. The Ford Zephyr camera car, driven by Dean Delamont, the Competitions Secretary of the RAC, was there as well.

This test was to put paid to Paddy Hopkirk's chances of a *Coupe*; he had a puncture near the top of the timed section, but pressed on, running only on the back rim and a tyre that was in ribbons. He made the climb inside the allowance, but the resulting vibration was too much for the radiator and he retired with cooling troubles later. Another of the Triumphs also came to grief here, for Annie Soisbault misjudged a corner and hit the rocks with a resounding crunch. The Denzel of Edgar Wadsworth did the same thing in avoiding the Triumph, which was being pushed to one side by the camera crews and Dean Delamont.

As we were watching the end of the climb and spotting for another camera crew, I particularly noticed that one of the French officials was accompanied by a very pretty girl in a Tyrolean hat and green costume to match. When the last car had gone we waited for our sister car and set off together in pursuit of the rally. Down the easy lacets to the Customs where the road forks to the Umbrail pass, which dropped down to the Engadine on the right, we swung to the left and were soon on the straight across the plateau where a few vital seconds could be made up. The respite was short-lived, though, for you came to six hairpins on loose dirt, followed by five rock tunnels which were paved with smooth stones and wet in places with springs which seeped through the roof. It was here that the great pile-up occurred on the 1954 Liège-Rome-Liège, when no less than five cars got jammed in the tunnel. The sudden change from sunlight to apparent darkness was so marked as to make headlights essential. It sometimes helped to wear dark sunglasses on the section before and have the navigator whip them off your nose as you entered the tunnel. We reached Bormio without overtaking any of our cars, so we knew that all was well.

The rally route had swung to the left to cross the Gavia, another narrow, rough, rocky pass which was disliked by many for its great drops, which were marked with unpleasant reminders in the shape of monuments to unlucky travellers who had gone over the edge with fatal consequences. There was also a beautiful Calvary near the summit which was erected at the expense of a family who were overtaken by bad weather while motoring over the pass and thought they would never get down; Providence intervened, and the weather cleared at the last moment, so they got down safely and built the Calvary in thankfulness. Personally, I disliked the descent of the Gavia to Ponte di Legno more than the climb in the opposite direction from Bormio.

We cut out the Gavia pass by running on down the valley to Tresenda, where we turned left and climbed the short twisty pass which led to Aprica and then on down to Edolo. The rally was well ahead of us now and the cars were up on the Vivione for the second time as we sped on to Bergamo by another short cut. Unfortunately, the exact location of the Bergamo control had been left to the local club, who were manning it, and we had failed to keep up with two official Citroens which we had followed as far as Aprica.

We arrived in Bergamo in the evening rush-hour, as did the first rally cars. There were rally cars going frantically in all directions, as this was at the end of a tight section, and no-one knew the exact location of the control, for the local police seemed to have been caught napping. Storez in his Porsche was late here, but his car was sick and he retired, for he knew he was out of the hunt. One or two competitors protested about the location of the control, which we had finally found at the exit of the town on the road to Monza and not at the entrance, as officially stated. Bill Shepherd was a minute late and I told him that he should protest at Megève on finishing the section. We stayed on until everyone had gone through and by our check there were only about 33 cars left in the rally. The Clerk of the Course turned up at this moment and was not at all pleased with the location of the control, producing a copy of the written instructions which the Club had received from the *ACMP*. These confirmed that the control should have been sited at the entrance of the town. Fortunately, I knew enough French and Italian to get the substance of the argument and to understand the endorsement which the official made out on the back of the timekeeper's sheet. This said that the control was wrongly sited and that an extra time allowance should be made for crossing the town.

It was now getting on for seven o'clock and, as we had had very little to eat since the morning, we stopped on the *autostrada* for a meal. After this we made haste to cross the Grand St Bernard pass and the Col de la Forclaz into France, reaching Megève at about 2am after being on the road for 23 hours. The film director at the arrival control mistook us for one of the competitors and asked us if we had had a good rally; I said politely that we had.

On reaching our hotel, *la Résidence*, there was a message to say that Pat Moss had brought two spare wheels out of the *parc fermé* for new tyres to be fitted, and that Jack Sears had had to lend her one of his. Pat was still unpenalized, as were John Gott and Bill Shepherd, so BMC had three cars running for their *Coupes* out of a possible 11; 32 cars were still left in the rally. Dunlops had no tyres on the spot and the situation looked bad. We had to get at least four new tyres during the day and it was already 3am when I went to bed.

The next morning I set off for Geneva, where I was certain we could find some tyres. The MG agents were very helpful and found us some Pirelli Stelvios but they would not match up with the Dunlops we were using; however, they were better than nothing and I got them back to Megève by lunchtime. It was evident that Pat would not complete the course on the tyres she was using, and would have to do a swap round with Jack Sears so that one of the cars was running on four tyres of the same make. We estimated that this would be possible at some point before Gap, where there was to be a short break on the final stage back to Marseilles.

The restart took place at 04.00 hours the following day and, after a day's drive which included no less than 31 passes, the crews were to be permitted nearly three hours' rest at Gap before completing the night section. This was a rally with a sting in its tail!

We had arranged for our first support point at Valdrome, which is a small mountain village some 67km south-east of Die in the Vercors district. Here there were barren slopes with little cultivation except lavender, which had brought a cash crop to an otherwise poor district. The people were shy of strangers and peeped out of their half-shuttered windows if a strange car stopped during the heat of the day. Hot it was, and there seemed to be little local hospitality. We did not even like to drink the water from a stream which obviously came from the village above. The best place for working on the cars was in the shade of an old barn. Pat stopped and told us that she thought the carburettors were lacking air because of dust in the air-cleaners. We told her to take these off if the car did not run better after we had weakened off the mixture.

After the girls had gone there was a pool of oil on the road which indicated either that the gearbox had been overfilled or that the rear main bearing was leaking oil. Douggie Watts and I talked the matter over and came to the conclusion that there might be trouble later. Meanwhile there was little we could do about it; the controls were so close together that it took three controls to get a quart of oil in the sump; first, to get the can out of the boot; second, to get the top loose and the third to get the bonnet up and dash the oil in. A major examination of a gearbox was out of the question. Without much hope we made our way up to the village and went into the only bistro, which was dark and quiet. An old crone came out of the shadows, asked what we wanted and, much to our surprise, put on an excellent scratch lunch of five courses in a few minutes. We enjoyed the meal immensely and were soon on our way to Gap.

The second service car was to meet the crews in the BP garage at Gap, so we went direct to the *Hotel Lombard* to secure the bedrooms which I had previously reserved for our crews. I inspected the rooms, made a note of the numbers and left the keys in the locks. The manager agreed to my arrangements and I went out to welcome the drivers, for the control was opposite the hotel, the cars being placed in the *parc fermé* for the brief rest.

As this was one of the most accessible points in the rally, the press were there in strength, and the camera crews were filming each car as it arrived. Both John Gott and Bill Shepherd were still unpenalized, but Pat came in and announced that she had almost failed to climb the Col de Soubeyrand owing to a slipping clutch and had lost so much time she felt it was useless to continue. Ann could stand the disappointment no longer; after doing so brilliantly their hopes were being dashed to the ground; she ran up to me and burst into tears on my shoulder. After a few moments she felt better and we all sat down on the terrace of the hotel and talked things over. Douggie felt that we might cure the trouble when the car got away, but it seemed doubtful if it would get up the Col Bayard out of Gap in its present state. Pat told us that she had somehow found time to remove the rear air-cleaner, but we didn't attach much importance to this at the time.

At this moment one of the mechanics, I think it was John Organ, came from the BP garage and told me that he had seen the breather pipe from the valve cover bent back away from the carburettor. We asked Pat if she had done this as it might have a direct bearing on the trouble. She said she had not touched it. We told her to drive out of the *parc fermé*, then open the bonnet and straighten out the breather pipe, and arranged to meet the girls at a side turning which we knew of at the top of the Col Bayard. The next thing was to get them to bed.

When I went upstairs things were not as they should have been for the chambermaid had accepted a bribe and let my rooms to other people. At the same time the press were milling around for a statement. Was it true that the girls were retiring? I said that it was not. Could they see the girls? No! And so on. I put Pat and Ann in my own room and locked them in, saying that I would call them when the time came. I then went down to deal with the manager, feeling in no frame of mind to be thwarted in my plans. The others must be fed and given their rooms. The manager was being difficult and could not remember any arrangement that we had made; he was, in fact, in a panic and needed bringing back to his senses quickly. I was extremely angry and, taking hold of his coat lapel across the counter, was about to hit him very hard with my left hand when he capitulated and produced a sheaf of keys. My drivers got their rooms and some well-earned sleep; I suddenly felt very tired.

The position at Gap was still fairly favourable for BMC as we had two cars 'clean' and either Nancy Mitchell or Pat Moss were leading the ladies. The works Alfa team was doing well for the team prize, but no car had achieved the set times for the Col de Soubeyrand, when the rally leader, Consten, in an Alfa, had made FTD with John Gott just behind him. There was talk of excluding this test as no-one got within 30 seconds of their scheduled time. Penalties were eventually 'scrubbed' on the grounds that the timed distance was in excess of that given in the regulations, but the times returned were used to decide ties. Jack Sears was still in the picture, although penalized. All three Austin-Healey Sprites were running and, if they finished, would be placed first, second and third in their class. Frank Grounds was still running and so was the Riley 1.5 of Bill Meredith-Owen and Bill Bradley, who finally finished third in the 1,600 Touring class behind Peter Harper and Tommy Sopwith on two works Sunbeams.

The crews were called in good time and as soon as I was satisfied that everyone was downstairs we left for the top of Col Bayard. Organized assistance was not allowed at this time but there was little risk of being detected as it was already dark. The Healeys were easy to recognize by their distinctive exhaust note – the poor man's Maserati, someone once dubbed them. Pat would be the third of the Healeys up the col and soon we saw the headlights of Jack Sears and John Gott, who went past as if driving for their lives. Pat was due about 10 minutes later, and never have 10 minutes gone more slowly. At last we heard her coming and strange to say the car sounded perfect; we waved her in with a torch and soon had the car jacked up so that Douggie could squirt some fire-extinguisher fluid into the clutch.

Pat told us that the car had come up the col in a perfectly normal manner after she had untied the breather pipe. It afterwards transpired that a technical journalist who should have known better saw the pipe hanging loose and clipped it back over the valve cover at the same time as Pat was finishing off the removal of the air-cleaner. In fact there was nothing wrong with this, but the carburettor level had risen and richened up the mixture. All seemed well now and we had time to go over the car fairly carefully; the two new tyres were put on the rear wheels and Pat was told to get the other two from Jack Sears to make up the set, and to let him have the two we took off her car. These were fairly good and we hoped the exchange would improve the handling of Pat's car.

We afterwards heard that the exchange was effected in the opposite direction, for Pat didn't like the new tyres. They must have been pretty good really, as Jack was to prove in the final test. Pat's car was with us for a little over 10 minutes; the girls were a lot happier when they left and we sent them on their way with a little prayer for success. With climbs over the Cols d'Ornon, Glandon, Croix-de-Fer, Galibier, Izoard, Vars and Cayolle before dawn, it was going to be a very tough night indeed.

When all the cars were gone, we packed up and drove off to Bedoin, a small village at the foot of Mont Ventoux, on which the last timed hill-climb was to take place. Nancy Mitchell's was the first Healey to arrive and she brought bad news; John and Chris were out, having lost a wheel coming down the Col de la Cayolle. This was shattering both for them and for me, as owing to their rapid climb on the Soubeyrand they were our best-placed crew, then possibly just leading the class and lying fourth altogether.

According to what we heard later, the left-hand rear wheel came off owing to a break in the splined flange which carried the knock-off type wheel; the car dropped onto the disc, which bit into the soft surface, and the car spun, coming to rest across the road. John and Chris were naturally shaken, but were even more shaken on seeing the ravine into which they might have gone. After they had pushed the car off the road to let the others through, John set off downhill to get help, whilst Chris stripped out the hub. John walked about six kilometres to the nearest village, from which he got a bus to the nearest town, where he arrived quite exhausted. Apparently, being unable to get a lift, he tried a short-cut across country, but this didn't save him much time, for he had to ford a river and climb a steep gorge.

They got the flange welded together and drove slowly down to La Ciotat where a new one was fitted. Terry Mitchell immediately got to work on the one which had failed, and worked out revised stress calculations which he telephoned back to England for a modification to the production cars. As similar flanges had run through the Mille Miglia without failure, I felt that this incident showed not only how valuable a test these tough Alpine rallies were, but also how the lessons learnt were applied to the production cars.

After all our other cars had gone through, we drove round the foot of the mountain to Malaucène to meet them as they came down from the climb right over the top. The drivers were looking worn out by the time they reached us and fatigue made some of them do some silly things. The French driver of a Citroen, for instance, left his co-driver behind until halted both by the officials and the enraged co-driver.

The first car was due in Marseilles at 14.29 hours at the Parc Borély, where the final test would be held; as if they had not been tested enough already. This was to be five laps of the J P Wimille circuit, a total distance of 13.2km to be covered in 9min 40sec maximum, or 9min minimum, for the big cars and at slightly easier speeds for the smaller cars. The highlight of the afternoon was a couple of spectacular spins by Bill Shepherd which brought our hearts to our mouths, as his Alpine Cup looked like going west; however, he straightened them out and finished within the time limit. Jack Sears made FTD and the others were all within the qualifying times.

The published results showed that Pat and Ann had won the *Coupe des Dames*, followed by Nancy Mitchell and Mrs Wilton Clark. The class for Grand Touring cars over 1,600cc was won by Keith Ballisat and Alain Bertaut in a Triumph TR3 with Bill Shepherd second and Pat fourth in the class to another Triumph. This made me even more determined to put an end to the long line of successes which the Triumphs had achieved in events of this type. Until the last moment, Bill looked like being deprived of his *Coupe* as he had been penalized for his minute lost at Bergamo, but John Gott acted as his advocate to such good effect that the penalties for Bergamo were annulled; I think an extra five minutes were allowed to cross the town. Jack Sears was awarded a cup for the fastest time of the day at the Parc Borély circuit, so we did not return empty-handed.

The rally, however, was marred by the news that one of the two official Citroens which we had seen on the Stelvio had gone over the edge on the descent of the St Bernard. The pretty, vivacious girl in the Tyrolean hat and the green costume, who was one of the secretaries to the Club, had been killed and the driver badly injured. The accident must have happened as we ourselves were actually crossing the pass. I felt thankful that all our crews had come through safely and reflected that the new tunnel would do much to prevent accidents of this type.

The Shell film turned out to be the best rally film that had ever been made or was likely to be made for some time to come, for films of that calibre cost a great deal to produce. The sounds of the cars were authentic, although added later, for the BMC competitions department lent an actual Alpine car for sound recordings, as did some other factories. John Gott viewed thousands of feet of film in his capacity as technical adviser to the producer, and reluctantly pruned it down to a suitable length. It was said that there was enough film discarded to make a second edition, which would have been of even greater interest to the motoring clubs, and I wished this could have been made available to them. This film conveyed the spirit of the sport far better than I could ever hope to do in this book. Its producer was John Armstrong.

I will not dwell on the 1959 event; it was not a good year for us as John Gott and Chris Tooley were the only finishers of our five crews. We estimated that the set averages over some sections were impossible for a big GT car, but I felt it essential to rally-prove the new Austin-Healey 3000, of which I had high hopes. Our estimate and our hopes were shown not to be unfounded.

No GT car over 1,000cc won a *Coupe*, but the Healey was always amongst the fastest cars in the speed tests and, over the crucial section in Austria, John was quicker than the works Mercedes 300SL Roadster. Unfortunately a stone later damaged his radiator and the time lost in repairs finally dropped him to fifth place in the GT category and second place in his class. However, we learnt a great deal from the event and applied the knowledge to such effect that the Austin-Healey 3000 became one of the great rally cars of subsequent years, winning its class no less than 17 times over the next three seasons.

The 1960 Alpine was an enjoyable event both for the crews and for the mechanics; we had very few worries and the results were a lot better than we anticipated. The Austin-Healey 3000 had got over its teething troubles which marred the 1959 rally season; we had started the 1960 season with a good Tulip Rally and so went on to the Alpine full of confidence. The teams were as follows:

Austin-Healey 3000 Pat Moss and Ann Wisdom
Austin-Healey 3000 Don Morley and Erle Morley
Austin-Healey 3000 John Gott and Bill Shepherd
Austin-Healey 3000 Ronnie Adams and John Williamson

Morris Mini-Minor Tommy Gold and Mike Hughes (running modified)
Morris Mini-Minor Rupert Jones and Ken James
Morris Mini-Minor Alec Pitts and Tony Ambrose

The rally was run from June 27-30, and we left England on the 22nd to board the train at Boulogne, as we had done before. We reached Lyons by nine the next morning in glorious weather and, after the usual warning about scrubbing his tyres, John Gott detached himself from the party to do a recce of the parts of the route with which he was not familiar. This turned out to be a rather protracted affair as he didn't present himself at La Ciotat until the following evening. The crews got acclimatized while the mechanics and I got on with the hundreds of little jobs which never do seem to get finished in time. Scrutineering for the Mini-Minors was on the Saturday and for the Austin-Healeys on the Sunday.

We had a slight difference of opinion with the scrutineers about the interpretation of the rule which said that fully modified Grand Touring cars may run with Appendix C Sports cars. The Club wished to enforce the rule about the braking system for Appendix C Sports cars in respect of our modified GT cars, and specified dual master cylinders. I argued that this was not in the spirit or letter of the regulation, which meant that duly modified cars ran with, but not as, Appendix C cars. They compromised and made me sign a declaration that we had done nothing by way of modification to the braking system which would make it less safe than before. I heard afterwards that the *CSI* had already dealt with this point and had interpreted the regulation in the same way as I had done, but the ruling had not at that time reached the *ACMP*.

The usual last-minute rush occurred as I had to meet Ann Clayton of Publicity at the airport on Saturday afternoon and Tommy Wisdom and Jack Hay, who were driving a Sprite, at 3.30am on Monday morning. Tommy and Jack were late in because they had to report the Le Mans 24-Hours race. I did these chores myself because the mechanics needed the maximum amount of sleep before the event. On Monday morning we had to ferry the crews to the start at the *ACMP* and then rush back and pack our cars. The luggage had to be in the hall for the Dunlop van to take to Cannes as David Hiam had laid this service on for all crews; we had not brought the transporter that year as we felt the expense was not justified. I was not very happy about the tender car which I was to drive as it had developed bad clutch slip the day before, so I took the Wolseley 6/99 which Rupert Jones had brought down from the Rally of the Midnight Sun the day before. This car had been driven hard and the tyres were smooth, but we changed over the wheels from the other car.

Amongst other notables at La Ciotat, Erik Carlsson joined the ladies on the beach; the ever popular Erik was always to be found with the BMC team and he was a great man to have about the place, always helpful and polite, invariably full of fun, and sometimes offering good advice in his picturesque English. We left La Ciotat at about 10 o'clock feeling satisfied with our cars and ready for the long trip over the Alps. We reached Bedoin before lunch and found some of the officials typing a list of the times for the first test at St Baume, which was a short one to keep the competitors on their toes until they reached Mont Ventoux. Henri Oreiller in an Alfa had made FTD in 8min 17.6sec, which was unnecessarily fast and probably damaged his engine. Robbie Slotemaker broke a halfshaft on the Triumph, and Pat Moss put in a very commendable 8min 27.6sec to be the fastest in the Healey class; all the Healey drivers did well under 9 minutes, while the fastest Ford did 9min 8sec, so their team looked less menacing.

The crews turned up and a few had time for a snack and to report how they were going before tackling the climb of Ventoux. This was 21.6km long and started in the vineyards and olive groves, finishing at the summit of the extinct volcano, 6,171ft up; it was very fast at the beginning and speeds of over 100mph were reached before the steeper part starts. Few cars could cover the distance in less than 15 minutes in rally trim, although the Formula 2 cars bettered 12 minutes for the climb during the European Hill-Climb Championship.

Five cars climbed the hill on this occasion in under 15 minutes, these being the two Grand Touring Alfa Romeos of Oreiller and de Lageneste, then Spinedi in the 250GT Ferrari, Rey and Burggraf in another Alfa and Pat Moss and Ann Wisdom in the Austin-Healey 3000. The Morley brothers had some bad luck and punctured a front tyre, but continued undismayed until it caught fire and liquid rubber splashed all over the car; when they passed the timing point they stopped and changed it, but it was still smoking when they came down the hill to Malaucène. In spite of this they managed 15min 50.3sec against Oreiller's time of 14min 22.4sec, which was a rally record. The 1,600cc class was developing into a fight between Peter Harper and Gunnar Andersson in the Volvo, the latter getting up in 16min 25.1sec; the Citroens seemed to have the wrong gearing and the best took nearly 17 minutes.

We felt we should be getting away as there was thunder in the air and we had a long way to go, having planned to eat at Embrun before meeting the crews at the top of the Col de Montgenèvre, where the tyre, brake and electrical people had planned to set up their service points. Everything was going to plan until the big Healeys came in and then the picture changed. Ronnie Adams arrived without the intermediate gears and, as inspection seemed to indicate that the constant-mesh gears had sheared, there was nothing for it but to send John

Williamson and him back to La Ciotat for a holiday on the beach. Shortly afterwards the Morleys arrived with a doubtful overdrive and third gear missing, so we wired up the overdrive to operate in second gear and sent them on their way without much hope. It looked as though the gearboxes were to be our Achilles' heel.

David Hiam, of Dunlop, had a secondhand Mini which he had just bought and christened BOJ after its registration number; it had a curious collection of wires which was said to serve as a wiring circuit. The Lucas boys spent all their spare moments trying to sort the muddle out, but without much success. They were still at it when we left for Monza. As usual, on arrival the gates were locked and the service crews had little time to unpack before the rally cars appeared. Tommy Gold had some trouble with his brakes, which Syd Henson soon put right, but otherwise our cars were in good fettle.

At Monza the cars were sent onto the track in groups of 10, setting off behind a pace car to do a warming-up lap, followed by three timed flying laps. Only the fastest lap counted, so the cunning ones held back in order to have a clear run. O'Connor Rorke's Jaguar (which was later alleged to have a D-type engine) surprised everyone by lapping at 97.1mph, which was a lap time of 2min 12.4sec, but the effort caused the exhaust system to disintegrate. Pat put up a very fine 2min 14.5sec, which was the second fastest time of the day and, much to my surprise, the Morley brothers equalled Oreiller's time of 2min 16sec, which showed that they were not very worried about the loss of third gear. Les Leston had failed to reach Italy in the Triumph TR3, which was not to be wondered at as he had just driven in the Le Mans 24-Hours and looked nearly dead when he arrived at Marseilles. Annie Soisbault lost a wheel in Italy and also failed to appear, so the Triumph team were not having a happy rally.

The Vivione, which had been deleted because of landslides or road repairs, was put back in the schedule at Monza, much to some people's disgust. The Vivione was always the subject of some narrow escapes and inevitably produced the most hair-raising stories, and it came up to scratch again with the tale of the Wisdom/Hay Sprite, which slid on the loose surface in a great swerve of understeer, apparently straight into space, but stopped on the brink with the front wheels revolving in the air. The crew abandoned the car with prudent haste as they were not certain if it would stay balanced. They managed to jack it up in the middle, and Tommy actually got back in and engaged reverse, eventually getting all four wheels onto the ground again; they finished the section on time. Three of the ladies also had trouble here: Nancy Mitchell had a puncture in her Sunbeam, as did Claudine Vanson in her Citroen, whilst Mary Handley-Page's Alpine had an argument with a rock wall.

We packed up and set out for Lecco, a pleasant little town on the edge of Lake Como, while the others went to Biella and Aosta. We arrived there well before the rally was due and had plenty of time for a belated breakfast at the little hotel just north of the town. Ann Clayton found it very hot while we were waiting by the Shell station, but eventually our cars arrived and were parked by the side of the lake. Pat then took one look at the water and dashed off to the ladies' room to change into her bathing dress; within a few minutes she was cooling off in Lake Como, but unfortunately I had left my camera behind. Now that the worst of this section was over, we felt that our cars should reach Chamonix intact.

There was, however, one tricky little section after Biella, some 24km from

Graglia Borgofranco, when the road twisted in such a way as to make the 31mph average difficult. It was here that we found Anne Hall sitting on a rock in the middle of a stream bathing her wounds while the Zephyr stood on its nose, in the water. This was very bad luck, for when she was just out of the bad part and had only about 5km to go to the control the brakes seized on at a tricky little bridge, and the car gave a quick twitch to the right, putting one wheel over the edge. There was nothing Anne could do and the Ford plunged into the bed of the stream, which was about 15ft down. Safety belts saved her and Valerie Domleo from more than a few scratches. Valerie had gone off to get some help and Anne sat on a rock to bathe her cut hand and keep an eye on the car. I felt that she should get to a place where she could have a rest and a warm drink until the shock passed. We set about collecting the valuables from the car, left a peasant in charge of it (having instructed him to stop smoking!) and set off down the hill with Anne.

On the way down we met Valerie coming back with an official and a decrepit crash wagon; Anne said she felt better, so we handed her over and set off for Aosta. We met our other service car at the Supercorte station there and were told that all our cars had gone past safely. Jeff Uren, who was the travelling captain of the Ford team that year, stopped and asked after his girls; he had come back over the Grand St Bernard pass to look for them, having heard that they were missing. We told him that they were all right.

Jeff set off towards Borgofranco to pick up the girls, but missed them as they were by that time in one of the official Alfas which was following the rally. When he got to the control he turned back, hoping to overtake the Alfa on the pass, but it reached the top of the St Bernard before he did. Here the official, not liking the fog and remembering the fatal accident of 1958, decided to spend the night in the hospice; he was just putting his car away when Jeff Uren went past on his third ascent of the St Bernard that afternoon. If Jeff had seen the car he would have recognized it by the rally plates which it carried on the back and front.

We decided to get to Chamonix at all costs in order to see how the team was faring and to sleep in the beds which we had booked. The fog was clearing when we reached the top and we got to Chamonix for a late meal to join the mechanics. I had forgotten that there was an intermediate prizegiving at the town hall and none of the crews attended as they were all very tired. I was therefore surprised and annoyed when Ralph Martin of Shell came in with the various cups which BMC had won for the hill-climbs and class placings at half-distance, for as a matter of courtesy either I or the drivers always attended to collect any prizes won.

The next morning the cars were to remain in the *parc fermé*, for the restart was not until after lunch. Of the 68 cars that left Marseilles, 49 had reached Chamonix and 15 of those remained unpenalized; amongst these were the three Austin-Healeys captained by Moss, Morley and Gott. Leading the rally was the Giulietta of Oreiller and Masoero, with Pat Moss second and de Lageneste in another Alfa third. The Giuliettas were the new short-wheelbase SZ types, which were very suitable for the event, but I felt that the most noteworthy performance was Pat's, for the Healey, although tough and powerful, was not such a handy car for the job. It was also interesting to note that the first four cars were all GT models, which the previous year had been too harshly handicapped. Of our other cars, the Morleys were fourth and John

Gott seventh, so we were in a strong position.

The cars left Chamonix with their crews refreshed and ready to deal with the next stage, which comprised 37 passes in little over 24 hours of non-stop motoring. We had a quick service point a little south of Chambéry, where Dunlop planned to check the tyres and Castrol were providing some oil. David Hiam had been joined by Erik Carlsson, who was now out of the rally, and together they decided to follow round to the maximum number of points and provide our crews with some food and drink.

We had been joined at Chamonix by friends of mine who were on their honeymoon and who felt that they would like to follow the last stage of the rally. They were travelling in a Magnette and had offered to help with the various jobs which always cropped up during an event of this sort, such as finding food and drink for the crews and locating places to wash and rest while the cars were serviced. Douggie Watts was driving the Morris Oxford Traveller, which had served us well on many events, and we decided to take the short-cut to Die over the Col de Grimone. Douggie and the Magnette made very good time over the pass, but I felt that more prudence was indicated and took things easily. We had decided to avoid the rougher Col de Menée as our cars were heavily laden.

Die was a very important point for us as the cars were scheduled to pass it twice that night. This was therefore really the most vital service point in the whole event. The fork of N93 and N518, where we set up our base, was the junction of the two roads which led to and from the Vercors, a high plateau of limestone split by deep gorges and covered in forest, which was the stronghold of the Maquis in the Second World War. It also contained the famous St Jean-en-Royans circuit, which was used as a speed test in many rallies because it could be closed to other traffic with little difficulty.

We saw our crews away on the right-hand road and settled down to a meal in the local café, imagining the cars fighting their way in the dark over the 25km of the St Jean circuit during their 185km run over the mountains. The cars should have returned to Die at 00.21 hours and it was possible that the fast cars might have 20 minutes in hand, which would have been enough to fill up with fuel, change the brake pads and check over the cars. No major parts could have been changed, even if required, for they were marked with special paint before the rally started.

After about an hour, there was a commotion outside and we found that a couple of rally cars had arrived back down the wrong road. A little later half of the runners turned up with the news that a Renault Alpine had crashed and turned over, catching fire in the process. It transpired that the forest was on fire and that 20 cars were on the other side of the crash and therefore pressing on, quite unaware of the fire. Meanwhile, the police had closed the road and sent the rest of the rally back to Die, where the officials held a conference at which they decided to 'scrub' the St Jean circuit and restart the rally from Die when the other cars got there.

Aided by John Gott, the organizers put everyone in *parc fermé*, and placed them on their honour not to work on their cars until their proper restarting time from Die. As this took a little time to get organized, Oreiller, one of the Alfa drivers, had already removed his radiator and was getting it repaired while his service crew made frantic telephone calls to his garage, which happened to be in Valence, for a new one. He was promptly told to stop the work by an official until his proper restarting time. This ruling was all very well, but it made no allowance for those who hoped to arrive early and use the time, although most people thought that the organizers did the right thing in cutting out the St Jean circuit.

We managed to get our own crews fixed up; the girls had a bed in a garage, and the Morleys and John Gott had the use of the other cars. Meanwhile, the crews who had got through before the fire had to sweat it out over the mountains and got no rest. We sent a car down the road to see if any of them were early and waiting further off; none was, however, for it was a very tight section for the smaller cars. Eventually, the officials called the cars up to the line and we were permitted to work on them. We changed the pads on the Healeys while they were refuelling, for there was nothing else to do. All of them were unpenalized and the drivers were very confident.

Our next rendezvous was to be at Comps at 09.26 hours, so we set out for Digne where we hope to breakfast at the *Hotel de Paris*, one of my favourites. However, we were too early and couldn't rouse anyone, so we made for Castellane and found a hotel open there. Comps is a little village 28km due south of Castellane; the road was narrow and there was nothing in the way of houses before the control. We sat at the side of the road in the hot sun and listened. Soon the smaller cars arrived and then the 1,600cc class.

We still had the Mini-Minor of Tommy Gold, but John Sprinzel was in trouble with his gearbox and could not make the Col d'Allos. Rupert Jones had hit a rock and wrecked his front suspension, so that the Mini team was broken up. Then the big Austin-Healeys arrived, all of them still unpenalized, but the Morleys now only had top gear. However, despite the difficult section ahead, Don and Erle felt sure they could get to Cannes. Douggie Hamblin wanted a service car to follow the Morleys through the next section. If they made it on time we would probably win the team prize; if they stopped on one of the hairpins, all was lost and if we got caught pushing them they would be disqualified. I agreed that we must follow up.

Everything of any weight was thrown out of the Wolseley 6/99, which had virtually no shock absorbers after its run in Sweden. The Morleys, of course, had no reverse, so they had to make all the corners at one attempt and could not afford to miss a turning. When they had gone, Douggie and myself set out to follow them to St Auban, which was the start of the Quatre Chemins circuit. We knew that we must give the Ford team a clear run for they were the only other cars left in this part of the rally, but we also knew that we must do our best to keep up with the Morleys, or at least not to fall too far behind them. I gave Douggie the map so that he could tell me where we were and how long we had been at it.

At St Auban we dared not wait, even though there were two Fords on the line at the control; we knew that if we stopped the officials might tell us that the road was closed. I kept an eye on the mirror and asked Douggie to tell me if anyone came up behind. I also kept an eye on the sides of the road for any place to pull in as it would have been a crime to have baulked a competitor here. Suddenly a bright yellow Ford came into sight and we were just able to dive into a disused quarry and let it pass. The road was very narrow here, and did everything that a track can do in the mountains; the car leapt about, but there could be no slacking off if we were to be of any use. Suddenly we saw a small blue car behind us which was gaining fast, although we were doing between 60 and 65mph. I pulled over and Erik Carlsson with David Hiam in the Mini-Minor went by as steady as a rock; they must have been doing over 80mph at the time.

This section was very fast in spite of the bends for it dropped from 1,100m at St Auban to about 600m at Sigale in the 32 kilometres before the climb to the Col de Bleine. At the next control we were just in time to see the Mini leaving, having given way to the Ford which had passed us. The official and the police tried to stop us, but we managed to get round the corner before the policeman blew his whistle; I hoped he wouldn't feel strongly enough about it to use his pistol!

The climb up the side of the valley to the little village of Aiglun was hair-raising. The road clung to the side of the cliffs by its eyebrows and roadholding was not improved by the fact that the local authority had thought it fit to spray the corners with new tar, sprinkled liberally with granite chippings. I asked Douggie how we were doing, for the fire had gone out of my driving and I was now getting ragged through trying too hard. We were both thirsty, having drunk nothing since breakfast, and it was now midday and very hot. Douggie informed me that we were a little over halfway round and doing all right.

We passed Vic Preston's Ford undergoing repairs to the brakes high up on a bank. It was here that Pat spun the Healey and the front wheels went over the edge. Ann jumped out and ran back to warn Edward Harrison, who was following, and before much time was lost they all had the car back on the road. The girls were now two and a half minutes down, but Pat responded to the emergency as nobly as only she could and they reached the control with just nine seconds in hand. John Gott was less lucky. Descending the Col de Bleine, and when only a mile from the control, he also spun, but the distance was too short to make up the time lost and he missed his *Coupe* by 24 seconds. You must know where to spin! Oreiller, the rally leader, had a puncture and dropped from first to seventh place on this section, which was disastrous for many hopes.

Meanwhile, Douggie and myself continued our erratic progress over the Col de Bleine, little knowing of the changes of fortune ahead of us, and I wondered what on earth I was doing up on this rocky shelf conducting a barge of a car which would only just go through the rock tunnels with about six inches to spare on each side. We never did see the Morley brothers, for they completed their fantastic drive of the Quatre Chemins circuit with only top gear but a penalty of only four minutes. This was an outstanding performance and an indication of their potential for the following year, for Cuth Harrison, on a fully modified Ford Zephyr with five speeds, was three minutes late, this being the best Ford performance. As a crew I considered the Morleys to be Britain's best.

We finally reached something more like *terra firma* at the Quatre Chemins crossroads and set out on our run down to St Vallier. On the way down we met Erik Carlsson and David Hiam, who had run out of petrol. Our own spare can had been thrown out at Comps when the car was lightened, so we had to go down to the village to get them some more. After the delay this caused, we were glad to make for Cannes to see if everyone was safe. The usual check of the *parc fermé* confirmed this, in fact the crews were still standing about gossiping; such is the stamina of the rallyist when wound up.

The next day showed that the rally had been won by de Lageneste and Greder, who had driven a perfect rally in the Alfa Romeo Giulietta SZ. The highlight of the event, however, was undoubtedly the second place which Pat Moss and Ann Wisdom occupied, for never before had a ladies crew finished so high in an Alpine. They naturally won a coveted *Coupe des Alpes* (of which only six were awarded that year) and the *Coupe des Dames*.

In the over 2,000cc Grand Touring class, the Austin-Healeys finished first, second and third and thus won all the team prizes except that reserved for French entries. I must admit to being delightfully surprised at this as I had been so occupied with the rally itself that I had forgotten to calculate how we were faring. Donald Healey came over to Cannes and showed his gratitude by entertaining the crews and everyone associated with the team to a very enjoyable lunch at the *Eden Roc*. Most of the drivers spent the afternoon water ski-ing and the undoubted highlight of the party was when Pat lost the top half of her bikini whilst proceeding at about 20 knots on the end of the tow-rope. She let go the rope very smartly and a gallant gentleman dived in to retrieve the offending garment.

The Alpine Rally must not be left without a tribute to the magnificent drive of Don and Erle Morley the following year. We set out with great expectations that we would retain the five team prizes which we had won in 1960, and based our hopes on a team of Austin-Healey 3000s for the third time running. Luck was not, however, with us. On the first stage, Pat and Ann turned their car over on some loose gravel descending the Col de Menée, and David Seigle-Morris and Vic Elford had nearly gone over the edge before that; they dug the car out of the soft bank with the aid of a crash lorry and carried on to act as a support car. This left us with Peter Riley and the Morleys, who were unpenalized at half-distance, supported by John Gott and Bill Shepherd, who actually had gone over the edge but had managed to get going again. At Chamonix our chances looked good, but Peter Riley and Tony Ambrose had a bad crash on the descent of the Stelvio through a brake failure. This was not a design fault but one induced by a human error. Still, the Morleys carried on unpenalized and finally, after the Quatre Chemins circuit, they were the only car to remain unpenalized. It was a great honour to arrive at Cannes just in time to see the organizers acclaim them winners of the event and of the only *Coupe* for 1961. Moreover, we did keep two of our team prizes after all.

The Alpine always seemed to end with a good party and lots of fun-and-games. One year I offered Lewis Garrad a lift in my car from the dinner to the cabaret to which we were going. On unlocking the car and pressing the starter, the engine failed to fire, and it was only too evident that some wit had stolen our rotor arm. Lewis was never at a loss in an emergency and returned a few minutes later with a spare rotor arm; even though it was for a four-cylinder engine, it worked quite well in our 'six' and we were soon on our way. I asked him where he found it. "Oh, I just borrowed it from Ken Richardson's car!" he said. I got my own back on the thief in the morning by waking him at some unearthly hour, before his hangover had had time to wear off, and demanding the rotor arm.

The 1961 dinner was held at the Casino and it was a unique occasion for we had the two Morleys, Pat and Ann, John Gott and Bill Shepherd, as well as Ian Appleyard and his wife, all sitting at the same table. Our party thus had a total 'bag' of 10 *Coupes des Alpes* dating from 1948 to 1961. Ian had that day driven the winning car and had said some very nice things about it during his short run. After dinner people started to bet as to whether anyone would jump into the swimming pool to retrieve the balloons which floated in the middle. Someone pushed Tiny Lewis in and, just as I was wondering who would be next, John Gott put three of the opposition in without even getting splashed! One of us (I think it was John Sprinzel) was laughing at the antics of Tommy Gold in the pool when it suddenly occurred to him that the man in the water was wearing his dinner jacket! Still, no-one lost his temper and the French thought we were mad but amusing.

CHAPTER 9

The Liège-Rome-Liège Rally

"For me the 'Liège', whether it went to Rome, Zagreb or Sofia and back, was the greatest adventure of the year..."

It was really John Gott who sold us the idea of the Liège-Rome-Liège Rally in 1955, but if Peter Riley had been available at the time, I'm sure he would have endorsed the plan, for up to then he had been one of the few Englishmen who had finished in the first 10 places in this tremendous event which the organizers so rightly called the marathon of the road, *le Marathon de la Route*. The reasons for its popularity amongst the finest drivers were comparatively simple. The rally covered a distance of approximately 3,000 miles through at least five countries and took place between Wednesday night and the following Sunday afternoon over a period of about 90 hours. No time was allowed for rest or repairs except that which could be saved in the running time. A number of speed hill-climbs and other eliminating sections were held at intervals during the rally and were sited on famous passes in France, Italy or Yugoslavia.

Cars were allowed to run in any form the driver fancied, although the ultra-special had no great advantage as it tended to lose its reliability. There were never any protests and this would be made quite clear to the competitors before the start by Maurice Garot, the Clerk of the Course and architect of the event. The controls were all supervised by members of the organizing club, the Royal Motor Union of Liège, so it followed that misunderstandings were reduced to a minimum. The sense of achievement on finishing the Liège was tremendous and I know of no other event in which crews took such pride in gaining their finishing plaques, even if they had not been very well placed in General Classification. Almost everyone swore that each Liège would be their last, but they always came back if given the chance. The duration of the event, including formalities plus the celebrations, made it possible to include everything in eight days' absence from home, and the fact that one did not need a bed for four of those eight days reduced the cost considerably.

The rally formalities followed the same pattern each year, and for this reason it was easy to plan in advance. Our cars were usually flown to Ostend on the Monday, but on one occasion I booked them back by sea; we discontinued this method, however, after that first experience of using the Belgian steamers, owing to the incredible rudeness and off-handed manners of their staff. I had travelled several times on this line since the war and had always experienced the same trouble, so it was not an isolated incident.

If the air crossing was made from Southend at any time in the afternoon, Liège could be reached in good time for dinner, and if a late start had to be made, then dinner could be taken at one of the many road houses *en route*. The following day, the Tuesday, would be spent rechecking the cars, fixing the rally plates and numbers and dealing with any last-minute route changes which might have been forced upon the organizers by local authorities. The scrutineering of the cars took place on Wednesday morning in the magnificent courtyard of the *Palais des Princes-Évêques* a well-preserved piece of medieval splendour situated in the middle of the city. Many of the drivers of all nations were friends, so the courtyard had a lively social atmosphere about it on these occasions. The atmosphere was informal and the cars were assembled mainly to check the engine and chassis numbers and for the drivers to present their competition licences and insurance certificates, if this had not already been done at the Club. The continental press would be there in force, for most of the drivers were well-known internationally. Such men as Olivier Gendebien, Johnny Claes and Willy Mairesse first made their reputations in this event and there were always others to take their place, so the Liège-Rome-Liège winner of the day could well become the Grand Prix driver of tomorrow.

In addition to the 'stars' who had to guard their reputations in the coming event, there were a number of Liège-Rome-Liège addicts who made a speciality of this event but rarely appeared in other Internationals. Some of these were mixed crews, such as the French pair, M and Mme Schlesser, who were placed second in General Classification in a Mercedes-Benz in the 1957 event. The same sort of enthusiasm pervaded the officials, many of whom manned the same control points year after year. For example, there was a married couple with a Porsche who regarded the Predil frontier control between Italy and Yugoslavia as their own personal preserve.

For me the Liège, whether it went to Rome, Zagreb or Sofia and back, was the greatest adventure of the year because it was nearly as hard on the support crews as on the drivers, and many of the support cars travelled only a few miles less than the actual rally cars. In 1961, for instance, my own faithful Wolseley 6/99 had recorded about 4,000 miles by the time it returned to Abingdon, all in nine days. With an opportunity to drive like this I was full of admiration for the crews who made the finish within the allotted time, even if they were only at the bottom of the list. This was the only event I knew of where the support crews could be driven into the ground and might turn up 24 hours or more after the rally finished. There were no short-cuts for them in the later type of Liège, which went nearly straight to Sofia and back at speeds which would do credit to one of the old transcontinental road races.

Strictly speaking, the rally did not really start from Liège, where the cars assembled, but from Spa, 35km away. On the Wednesday evening at 6pm, the cars were led in convoy to the centre of Spa and placed in the *parc fermé*. At 10pm, under the glare of floodlights and with the blare of canned music, the cars were brought up to the starting line in groups of three at three-minute intervals. The commentator gave the spectators a short history of the successes of the driver and co-driver, the flag fell and they were away, with the crowds cheering madly from the other side of the split-chestnut palings. It always seemed a point of honour with some drivers to reach the top of the long hill to Malmédy first, but the more prudent hung back, realizing that they had 3,000 miles to go before they saw Spa again or slept in a comfortable bed, and appreciating that this initial sprint meant nothing, except possible damage to a cold engine.

The finish was at Spa on the following Sunday evening, when the town band, the civic dignitaries and the Club committee, headed by Maurice Garot, waited with smiling faces, champagne and enormous bouquets to greet the victors, who drove slowly into the finishing enclosure with the stains of travel upon them and most of the crews looking at least 10 years older than when they started. It became a tradition with the BMC team that they found time to have the cars washed and the crews spruced-up on the last easy stage through Belgium. This came at a time when in any case it was difficult to stay awake, so the opportunity to be able to drive a little faster in order to make up some time and then to stop to have the car cleaned, whilst the crews had a wash or a coffee, helped to ensure a finish. Needless to say, any garage was only too willing to wash the cars in double-quick time, for the Belgian radio had given a point-to-point commentary about the surviving cars from the moment they re-entered Belgium, and the garage staff would know with whom they were dealing.

Maurice Garot always looked happy at the finish and made each crew feel that he was particularly delighted that they had finished, whether first or last. Then, when all the stragglers were home, or the time limit was up, the cavalcade formed up, headed by a flight of speed cops on Harley-Davidsons, and proceeded to Liège at a steady 60mph (100km/h), the sirens wailing and the tired but happy crews jockeying for position all the way. The public traffic was diverted and the cheering crowds lined the road. On arrival at Liège the cars were placed in the main street outside the Automobile Club for the admiring crowds to see and touch with inquisitive but never damaging fingers, all the time wondering at the fabulous achievement.

The next morning the official results were posted, but few of the drivers would be there to read them, for they would be catching up on their sleep. By 2pm, the official time for protests had expired and the cars were released from the enclosure. The banquet was due to start at 8.30pm, but it was rare for anyone to sit down until well after nine. There were prizes for everyone who finished and substantial money prizes for the first 20 places. In 1961, for instance, the prize for first place was 150,000 Belgian francs, which was well over £1,000, and bonus money from the petrol, oil and tyre manufacturers would bring this figure up to at least £1,500 – and the victors had earned every penny of it!

Reverting to the first Liège-Rome-Liège in which BMC competed, I am almost ashamed to reveal the part that the servicing crews played in this event. By present standards it was negligible, for I had not at that time appreciated that we should lay on an 'umbrella' which should cover the event in its entirety. One of the reasons which prompted me to do this in later events was the fear that one of my crews might be injured in a crash and end up in some inadequate foreign hospital. This possibility was brought home to me very forcibly by the accident in which Dick Jacobs had been involved at Le Mans in 1955. If it had not been for the way in which John Thornley and James Woodcock organized the air transport for a special medical unit, which flew out to Le Mans and returned with Dick, he would undoubtedly have died. After this, Dr White, the BMC staff doctor at Cowley, used to keep in touch with our department on his weekly visits to Abingdon and was duly informed as to the destination of our next continental expedition. He also made a point of seeing that his staff had their passports in order for any emergency. I am glad to say that their services were never required by the department during the six years which followed the Le Mans accident, but it was reassuring to know that we could have our own medicos on the scene at very short notice.

The 1955 Liège was the last of the series to visit Rome and the 25th to be run. It started on August 17, in the middle of a heatwave, and the field comprised 133 starters, 77 of whom were to fall by the way. The BMC entry was of a purely exploratory nature, the object being for two saloon cars to finish and demonstrate their reliability and an Austin-Healey 100S, making the best use of its superior performance, to finish as high as it could. Our entry was made up as follows:

Modified Austin A90   Gerry Burgess and Sam Croft-Pearson
Modified Austin A50
with Le Mans engine   John Gott and Bill Shepherd
Austin-Healey 100S   Peter Reece and Dennis Scott

We stayed at the *Grand Hotel des Boulevards*, which was not quite so grand as its name sounds, but was nevertheless quite comfortable. The first two days went according to plan and the only excitement was a warning from the Liège police who did not approve of the action of the crews who rode on the roof rack of my Magnette on the way back from the *parc fermé*. As they insisted that seven of us should be within the vehicle, Peter Reece and Dennis Scott compromised by sitting inside but leaving their legs outside. We reached the hotel without further trouble, except that some of the drivers complained that they couldn't see the selection of girls so well from the inside; Liège was reputed to have five females for every male of its population and I could well believe it.

After the rally started, Peter Morrell, the Castrol competition manager, and I moved into the *Hotel Britannique* in Spa. This particular hotel must have seen little change since Edwardian times, although it was reputed to have been the German headquarters for a time during the Second World War. I walked down the long bare corridors of the second floor, feeling like someone in an escape story, a feeling that was heightened by the arrival in a black chauffeur-driven Mercedes of the representatives of the *ADAC* (the German national motor club), dressed in rather sinister black coats. Somehow I felt that we had lost the rally and I had got into someone else's all too exciting adventure!

That evening, Peter and I strolled down the road at the back of the hotel and had a few drinks in a neat little *boîte*, which turned out to be a mixture between a gaming house and call girls' establishment. We managed to avoid both temptations and returned to our mausoleum after we had finished all the Cointreau the *boîte* had in stock. The management's offer to replenish provided an excuse for us to depart on the grounds that we could scarcely wait for any more, and why we chose to specialize on Cointreau I cannot now remember.

The organizers or the rally had a most efficient scoreboard which they kept written up by telephone information so that the position of any car might be seen at a glance. The results so displayed were not completely up to date, for the leading cars might already have reached the next control by the time the list had been telephoned through, but the information was useful and retirements could be located fairly easily. Peter and I went into Liège the next morning to check up; it had been a dirty night, with plenty of fog for the competitors as well. Burgess had got lost near Idar Oberstein and dropped two minutes, and Dennis Scott had crashed the Healey at a corner on the way out of that town; he apparently went straight on instead of turning to the right, and landed in a wood. Dennis and Peter abandoned the car to seek help and on returning found that both the clocks and the spare wheel had been stolen. They returned rather sheepishly to Spa the next day.

The times over the Sella and Pordoi passes showed that the A50 was making heavy weather of it. The axle ratio (4.55:1) might have been right, but the close-ratio gearbox was wrong, although the car was fast downhill and on the level, reaching 6,100rpm (over 100mph) in top. Our cars got over the Dolomite sections with Burgess making the stipulated times by means of greater power and more torque and John Gott losing a minute here and there. The weather was hotter on the Italian plains, and Johnny and Bill, with the Count Metternich, stopped at a small hotel during one of the easier sections. They all stripped off in the bathroom for a shower and wash, when in walked an Italian girl who had the same idea. She was not so embarrassed as the drivers, but perhaps she had more clothes on. Finally, both our crews reached Rome, but not before Gerry had had a scrape with a fruit barrow in the narrow streets of some town.

They did not have time to look at the sights, but they did get some breakfast at the control in the centre of a square. The spectators were most interested to see British cars still running at this point, where 100 cars were left in, 32 of these being unpenalized. Gerry Burgess was still two minutes down and must have cursed the foggy first night, John Gott was three minutes down, and they were both in the first 50. The only British crew which was still 'clean' was Ken Richardson and Kit Heathcote in their Triumph TR2. 'Chippy' Stross, in the Jaguar XK140 which made up the RAC club team with the two Austins, had lost three minutes, so our saloons were far from disgraced.

On the way back from Rome, it was even more evident that the A50 had the wrong axle ratio and gearbox, but Gerry was quite happy with the A90. Some of the 'aces', on the contrary, were not at all happy. Tak (Mercedes 300SL), Jacques Ickx, the 1952 winner, and Les Brooke (TR2) had all lost more marks than our cars with no ace! The works Renault of Redele and Pons and the Nathan and Glockler Porsche had retired. John and Bill tried for some lunch at Arezzo, but the smell in the two cafés they tried was too much for them and they departed, sickened but still hungry.

The route went through the Dolomites, where the roads were wet and very slippery. The A50 crew had a rough time that night, for they were falling so far behind the imposed average that they looked like being excluded, so had to press on and as a result had no time for food. The car, not being suitably geared for the job, made heavy weather of the Pordoi, Pennes and Giovo passes. The Stelvio and the Gavia were worse; the latter was in fog, but John's knowledge of both stood him well and they made up a little time. Bill was on the outside of the cliff going up and could not see the landmarks because of this fog and was therefore very worried. He told me later that he would have preferred to have driven that bit even if only to sit on the 'safe' side!

Gerry had to stop to refuel on one of the tight sections and made up the lost time afterwards, but hit a rock in his hurry and had to stop again to pull the wing off the wheel. The atmosphere was not improved by the sight of the Meier and Luba DKW, which rolled down three of the lacets on the Gavia after tangling with a Porsche. Amazingly enough, the crews survived this ordeal, but the cars were a sorry sight! The Vivione was a little more suitable for the A50 and John actually overtook a Peugeot Special, whose driver was loath to let them pass, denting a few of his panels in the process. Everyone was glad to get out of the Dolomites after this. At Brescia, Gerry and Sam found that they had a defective dynamo, which proved to be serious, and the only thing to do was to buy a battery and economize in lights.

The next and last night was the worst. The A50 crew had now had nothing to eat for 25 hours, but dared not stop as they were barely maintaining the average and Gerry had to follow cars to conserve his lights although the ones he chose were usually either too fast or too slow. Finally, at Barcelonnette, John and Bill stopped for some food and hot drinks and felt much better, but they were now within 37 minutes of exclusion for lateness. They knew that they had to make up time, but on coming out of the restaurant they found it was pouring with rain. There was more difficult country ahead, the Galibier having to be crossed at 60km/h (37mph) in thick cloud and some snow. Fortunately, John knew it well and led a string of cars over at the required average. Several of the crews thanked him afterwards, but Bill Shepherd did not like it at all; he said that he was getting flung about too much to sleep, which he wanted to do to avoid thinking about the drops!

They encountered thick morning mist around Annecy and the Col de la Faucille, but at last dawn arrived with a good strong sun to dispel the moisture. Gerry bought another battery and just managed to keep going, and finally both our Austin crews arrived at Spa. They were very happy, although Gerry got penalized a further 10 points at the finish because the car would not start on the starter. Ken Richardson and Kit Heathcote finished fifth in General Classification and won their class, so we gave them a bottle of champagne, feeling they had well earned it. Gendebien and Strasse won that year in a Mercedes 300SL and the club team prize went to the RAC team. This was the subject of some unexpected publicity, being the first time that it had ever been awarded to a British team. The trophy was a fine crystal vase and we had much pleasure in handling it over to Wilfrid Andrews, the Chairman of the RAC, at a sherry party which was given at motor show time. This occurred at a time when England needed successes in the rally world.

The A50 had done better than we had thought possible. Its class was hotly contested, there being 39 starters, many of them Oscas, Ferraris, Triumphs and Porsches, for they were all grouped in the under-2-litre class. In spite of this it finished 10th in the class and would have done better with suitable gearing. The ordinary drum brakes were adjusted three times and the front ones were down to the rivets by the end. The engine ran perfectly and averaged 22mpg. Chippy Stross remarked of the Austin: "We have one and we call it the Sacred Cow for it's always bowing and scraping", but he was full of admiration for it afterwards.

We had learnt a lot; for instance that we should do more testing in the mountains to find the right ratios. We realized that to publicize the make one can run modified without any detriment in this sort of event. The Belgian distributors were pleased with the results, although the A90 was 31st and the A50 was 36th of the 56 finishers of the total of 133 starters in all classes. We decided to return the next year with sportscars, to have a try at the make team prize and also take some service cars into Italy. Those four days at the *Britannique*, with visits to the scoreboard in Liège, had been too nerve-wracking and I felt that closer contact with the rally was essential.

Whilst the 1956 event produced a great improvement on the previous year, it was not sufficiently outstanding to make any worthwhile advertising. The highlight of our performance was the winning of the novices prizes by John Milne and Dick Bensted-Smith, who finished 14th in General Classification in an MGA 1500. The story of their experiences was superbly described by Dickie in 'Blues in the Night', which appeared in *The Motor* shortly afterwards. John Gott and Chris Tooley made 13th place and Nancy Mitchell and Anne Hall were 26th, and second in the Ladies' class behind that magnificent pair Mesdames Terray and Gordine, who were 12th. We were also runners-up for the team prizes, which we would probably have won had we realized sooner that two of our crews were spending too long at a service point. We had learnt a bit more and went off to ponder on the next event.

Whilst the 1957 Liège was not a lot more successful than the year before, we did come home with the *Coupe des Dames* and provide the runners-up for it. Nancy and Joan Johns drove well to obtain 16th place in General Classification behind John Gott's 14th, both in MGA 1500s, but the highlight of the BMC effort was the drive of Pat Moss and Ann Wisdom, making their first appearance in the Liège with a Minor 1000, which obtained for them 23rd place out of 52 finishers. One of their rear shock absorbers came off before half-distance and proved impossible to refix, whilst they also lost the filler plug to their gearbox and had to improvise with a cork, so they did well to keep going. Mrs Moss was very concerned about the girls during the later stages of the rally and kept urging me to get them to retire, but Pat would have nothing of the sort and carried on undaunted. I was unable myself to attend the rally for domestic reasons and followed it by telephone with the co-operation of John Valentyne, who went to Liège, and John Williamson, who darted about Italy.

Pat was rather angry with me at this time because she felt, quite rightly, that she was ready for continental events, but that I was holding her back. I wanted to make sure that when she was launched she would come to no harm and prove herself worthy of the Moss family. I need not have worried, for she was already more than a match for most of the men. Many of them came to me after rallies and said it was a pleasure to drive behind her as she drove so beautifully.

In 1958 the Austin-Healey 100-Six seemed the right wear for the Liège. We had long felt that we needed a car with long, hairy legs to stride over the mountains and great lungs with which to rush up the hills; this seemed to be it.

The team was therefore as follows:

Austin-Healey 100-Six	Pat Moss and Ann Wisdom
Austin-Healey 100-Six	Nancy Mitchell and Anne Hall
Austin-Healey 100-Six	Joan Johns and Sam Moore
Austin-Healey 100-Six	Gerry Burgess and Sam Croft-Pearson

supported by
MGA Twin-Cam   John Gott and Ray Brookes

This was the first official entry of an MGA Twin-Cam in an International rally and we had not had much time to get the car ready. Apart from its rally equipment, such as a 20-gallon fuel tank, special seats, extra lamps and instruments, it ran absolutely standard. John had instructions to finish at all costs and keep a little in hand on the climbs. We didn't expect a great deal and John very sportingly agreed to take the car with all this understood.

As was our custom, we crossed to Belgium on Monday, August 24, staying this year at the *Hotel de Suède*. It was a good team, everyone was in high spirits, our plans were made and we thought they were good. The rally was to include a few minor changes in its character that year, notably that there were six cubic capacity classes and all Groups defined in the revisions of the 1958 Appendix J of the Sporting Code were amalgamated. The average speeds on the main roads varied in France, Italy and Yugoslavia, but the road sections, which some people thought would merely serve as easy links between the special tests, turned out to be very hard, for the penalty of lateness at any control of even a second was exclusion. The schedules for the six timed tests in France had been set at 72km/h, an impossible average, which made even the 'aces' minutes late, time which had to be regained before the next road control was reached.

There were some amusing remarks made by the French journalists about the fact that I had five ladies out of eight drivers in the Healey team. John Gott jokingly told them to wait and see what happened as '*Monsieur Chambers est specialiste avec les dames!*' As far as the opposition was concerned, there were 98 starters, of which 17 were in the Healeys' class and 23 in the Twin-Cam's!

On Tuesday the service crews set off for their allotted posts leaving one of their number, Tommy Wellman and his men, to see the cars away from Liège and then to go on to Bergamo in Italy. I had decided to go to Tarvisio, at the foot of the Predil pass on the Italian side, where the Fiat garage, which was also a Supercorte station, had promised to accommodate us. We left Liège on Wednesday morning, August 27, and stayed the night in Munich, reaching Tarvisio on Thursday afternoon, the cars being due in from 20.00 hours onwards. The garage people were full of enthusiasm and stripped the workshops of customers' cars, placed extra benches outside where we could lay out the refreshments and allotted extra mechanics to help with the rally service.

We knew that the cars would have a few minutes to spare, but would concentrate on creature comforts at the first stop. It was important that they should carry a full tank of Italian fuel into Yugoslavia, where the fuel was very poor. On the other hand, the timed section from Predil to Kransjka Gora would be best tackled with as little fuel as possible in the tank. It would have been a fairly easy matter to take 10 gallons of fuel into Yugoslavia in a service car and meet a competitor at the end of the timed section, but to take 50 gallons in would have been out of the question, so I decided to recommend full tanks and a two-gallon can. All our cars left us in good order and I set about explaining in my deficient Italian that we wished to repeat the exercise the following evening with the chance of some major repairs having to be done before departing to bed. We retired to the *Hotel Italia* for supper and a nightcap, hoping that the telephone would not ring. I had not at that time been over the Predil section, and knew only that the road was rough and dusty, with plenty of drops, and that the Moistrocca pass, which followed, was even worse!

We had picked up a little news from the crews as they came through and learnt that 14 crews had retired, including Mary Handley-Page, who had taken a wrong road on joining the *autobahn* after Kaiserslautern and had gone nearly as far as Kassel before her co-driver noticed the mistake; by that time it was too late as she could not possibly have reached the proper control on time. Some of the others, including John Gott, had made the same mistake, but had corrected it in time. The Americans, Delling and Washburn, in a Volvo, had hit a bridge when Delling fell asleep, severely damaging the car but, fortunately, not themselves. At Vipiteno the crews were told of a landslide near Misurina, which had meant a diversion of 20 kilometres via Cortina without extra time allowed. Here the Porsche and MGA crews found that they could get under closed level crossing poles by easing them up a few inches while the driver went through with the car; this gained valuable minutes, but was rather dangerous as there were some near-misses with trains.

Some time that night Joan Johns and Sam Moore returned sadly to Tarvisio. They had skidded off the road shortly after Predil and, not being certain how badly damaged the steering was, had decided to retire, coming back into Austria by the bottom road from Kransjka Gora and thence into Italy. We straightened out the steering the next day and Sam and Joan decided to follow the service cars in case any of their wheels or brake pads might be useful. They also arranged to collect food and drink and join the crews at one or two controls which we had not originally planned to cover; their superior mobility made this possible.

The following night, from 20.00 hours onwards, we listened eagerly for the slightest sound of a car coming from the direction of the pass. It was a fine warm night after a very hot day and the courtyard of the garage was floodlit, with everything in readiness. The first BMC car to arrive was the MGA Twin-Cam. John told us that three big Healeys were still running, but that the private entry of John Sprinzel and Dick Bensted-Smith was out, their Sprite having broken a left-hand stub-axle in the furthest part of the 'Jugland' section; the wheel had come off, complete with the hub and brake drum, and gone bounding down a bank into a large and swiftly flowing river where it was borne away by the current. It would probably have reached the Adriatic if a peasant had not dived in and rescued it! The adventures of the crew in their search for a new stub-axle would fill a chapter, but the palm must go to Dickie for his ride on the back of a Yugoslav scooter, clasping the broken pieces and going in the opposite direction to the rally. He and his Yugoslav friend finally located a machine shop, where the staff turned up a replacement out of an old halfshaft; this fitted so well that the nut, which had been left with the car, ran down the new thread as if it were the original. The Sprinzel Sprite thus reached Liège at about the same time as the rally ended.

Amongst the 30 casualties in Yugoslavia were Annie Spears and Madeleine Vrijman, MGA, who had an argument with a culvert while being overtaken by David MacKay in a works Sunbeam. Gunnar Andersson, the current Rally Championship leader, hit a rock outcrop, damaging his car beyond immediate repair, and the works Renault of Cordvillier was out with mechanical troubles.

In spite of the difficulties of the section, 11 cars were credited with doing the Predil section clean on the outward run; of these the Pat Moss and Ann Wisdom Healey was one. As they led the other ladies by a clear four minutes on the return to Italy, it looked as if they were in a commanding position for the *Coupe des Dames*, but Pat was to achieve greater things than that. The favourites for victory at this point were either Consten and Hébert (Alfa Romeo), Strähle and Buchet, Reiss and Wencher (Porsche Carreras) or the outsiders, Moss and Wisdom (Austin-Healey).

The second timed section, from Obravac to Saint Rok, had been up and over Mount Halanmalu, which had accounted for eight cars including one of the works Renaults. The 11 crews who had done the Col Vrsic at Predil clean, also did the Mount Halanmalu climb clean, the fastest time being made by de Lageneste and Blanchet in a Triumph TR3A. In all, 30 crews failed to make the Yugoslav section, some retiring through sheer fatigue and others because the cars could not stand the pounding. The conditions had been appalling, the heat and dust, lack of food and drink, the numerous punctures, the absence of signposts and the primitive roads all adding to the drivers' fatigue. The cars came in with loose spokes, whilst one or two had both spare wheels flat.

John and Ray were very downhearted, for the MGA Twin-Cam was not running at all well at this point. It was missing continually so that they not only had difficulty in maintaining the times, but John was rather slow in the timed climbs. He said that they were right down in the field (actually they were 26th and behind all the Healeys), but would try to press on to the finish. However, after trying everything, we found that the locking screw for the distributor had worked loose, so allowing the timing to retard itself. Once we found the trouble, we quickly put it right and John and Ray shot off much happier, with the car sounding much healthier. Everyone wanted a wash and a drink, but there was only just time for some soup at the local café while we straightened things out. Plenty of jobs had to be done and we all worked with a will; the Italian mechanics were superb and seemed instinctively to know what to do from a few signs and the odd word. Everything one touched, inside and outside the car, was covered in white dust, which fell to the floor in showers.

Pat, too, was depressed, as she usually was when doing well: she was fed up with the whole thing and wanted to retire there and then. I told her she was doing very well, and emphasized that we only had three cars left in the team and I wanted to get them all home. I therefore instructed her to take things gently on the climbs and concentrate on the road sections, making it clear that there was no such thing as taking it too gently on the road as one was liable to be excluded for lateness.

Finally, all our crews left; we helped to clear up the garage and went to bed with the horrible thought that we were due to meet them at Alessandria, about halfway between Turin and Genoa, at 4pm the following afternoon. David Hiam, accompanied by a Dunlop tyre fitter, left straight away in his Minor 1000 to see if they could fit in another control point on the way; this was typical of David's enthusiasm. In addition to Brian Moylan, I had with me Roy Brocklehurst, who had been allowed time off from the drawing office to study the product in action. He was absolutely amazed at the terrible hammering which both the cars and the crews were taking.

We left the hotel before the management was about and travelled in company with Sam and Joan in the Healey. It was as well that we did for they were troubled with a mysterious misfiring and loss of power, which we finally traced to a loose needle in the dashpot of an SU carburettor. When we had cured the trouble, we decided to let them get on ahead as we felt they could probably intercept the cars at Bergamo and again in France. In those days the *autostrada* went no further east than Brescia, so we turned south at Verona after sending a telegram to the works which, like a good many others sent from Italy, never reached its destination. We passed through Mantua, Cremona and Piacenza, finally reaching the garage at Alessandria by 16.00 hours, with time to get some refreshments ready for the crews. We had covered 545km since leaving Tarvisio.

The pattern of the rally had changed a little for, on the return climb of the Col Vrsic, Pat had dropped 16 seconds, but was now in seventh place in General Classification and still leading the ladies, the works Triumph of Annie Soisbault and Renée Wagner having retired. There had been a further sorting out of the favourites between Villa Dont and Fondo in the Dolomites, after which there were only three clean sheets, the Strähle and Buchet Porsche Carrera, the Hébert and Consten Alfa Giulietta Zagato and the Volvo of Martensson and Widell. Pat was not yet out of the running for she had only dropped 18 seconds there and this put her ahead of all the works Triumphs except the de Lageneste and Blanchet car. We had very little up-to-date news at this point, and could only urge our crews on, telling them, with what conviction we could, that the worst was over and that they had only to stay awake for another night and all would be well.

Again the MGA was our first car in, but this time John and Ray had their tails right up. The Twin-Cam was now going like a rocket and John felt that his local knowledge of the Dolomites had pulled them up several places; he was quite right, for the MGA was now up to 12th place, having overtaken all the Healeys except, of course, Pat's.

During the last night the required speed of 72km/h over some of the smaller, dusty and difficult French passes showed that the rally had a real sting in its tail. Over the Col d'Izoard, four cars made particularly brilliant times and it was evident that, barring mechanical breakdowns, the winner would be found amongst the Porsches of either Strähle or Reiss, the Alfa of Consten or the Triumph of de Lageneste. The first of these to go out was the Triumph, which broke a throttle linkage and, although a spare was carried, the crew were either unable to fit it or too tired to look for it in the spares kit.

The Col St Jean was a nightmare of loose stones, six inches deep in places. Here Buchet, driving the Strähle car, made a real effort to hold his lead and to such good effect that his privately owned car ran away from the works Porsche. Buchet had but to hold his lead to win, but on the Soubeyrand he ran out of road and lost it. The Reiss and Wencher Porsche also damaged its sump here and was forced to retire, so the Alfa of Consten and Hébert took on first place. All this automatically put Pat and Ann into fourth place, although we did not know it at the time. With two passes to come, Buchet had to decide whether to hold second place, of which he was sure, or to attack again. He decided to attack, but all was not right with his car after the Soubeyrand incident, and he dropped 20 seconds to the Alfa on the Col de la Chaudière.

The final climb over the Col de l'Echarasson was taken even slower by Buchet, who made ninth fastest time, but Pat liked the col so well that she rounded off her well-judged drive by climbing only 21 seconds slower than the

Alfa Zagato. During the last night six more cars dropped out and among these was the Ford Zephyr of King and Sproxton, due to steering trouble.

We service crews had arranged to stay that night at the *Hotel Moderne*, in Geneva, before calling at Bourg on the Sunday morning. I knew that the telephone service was good from there to Liège and planned to get the latest score that night and again in the morning. It was evident that we would have to stop for a meal as we were going to be too late reaching Geneva. We found a good restaurant in Annecy and I rang the *Moderne* from there, being very annoyed to hear that they had let our rooms as we had not been in by 6pm. As I had stayed there many times before I felt that we should have had some consideration, and said so! They finally agreed to find a room and the three of us shared it. We rang Liège and were glad to hear that all three Healeys were still in the hunt, also the Twin-Cam. Pat was then running in sixth place, as far as I remember.

It was not difficult to reach Bourg by 11am the next morning as it was a beautiful day. Buchet came in with his hard-luck tale about the Soubeyrand shunt. The Volvo was out of the running, the crew having been excluded when third for being 10 seconds late at a main control, and Pat, it appeared, was now fourth in General Classification. John Gott was confident of finishing, as were the crews of the other two Healeys. Gerry Burgess had had a minor brush with some rocks, but was all right. Pat complained of the heat in the driving seat and left the control with Ann driving and her feet sticking over the side of the car to cool off. We trailed along behind and the crews took it in turn to lead on the long, dull drag to Dole and Gray for, in accordance with the Liège tradition of no traps, the organizers had the decency to tell us where they had sited the compulsory secret controls. As we approached Belgium, the crowds began to get thicker and the news began to get about that the girls had done something extraordinary. The officials congratulated them at controls and wished them a happy journey. The other members of the team felt a bit happier now that the end was in sight. They too had done their best and we felt that we had a sporting chance of winning most of the team prizes.

We arrived at Gray with the girls and located the control, which was on the bank of the river Saone. There was a little café opposite and, having about 20 minutes in hand, the girls went in for a Coke; Ann went in first with some other driver and Pat went in with me a little later. Being Sunday afternoon the place was pretty full and the waitress was rushing about getting drinks for the crew. We got ours and were just about to take the first sip when a swarthy individual tried to trip the waitress up as she passed him. A chair fell over as well and there was an immediate tense feeling in the air. The boss came out from behind the bar and shouted, "I have warned you for the last time, I've had enough". At this, he gave the swarthy one a cut with the edge of his hand on the side of the neck which put him off balance and made him sag at the knees. The boss was not content with this, and gave him two more chops on the back of the neck while he was falling to the ground. Pat stood there with her eyes wide open and Madame from behind the bar shouted, "Now don't lose your temper, Papa, you know how you are when roused".

Papa took the swarthy one by the scruff of the neck, propped him up against the wall at the end of the bar, wiped his hands and walked back to his proper place, behind it. The tense silence was broken by the scraping of chairs, and as I felt that the storm was about to break at any moment, I seized my two most valuable possessions and hurried them out of the café without ceremony. Pat, still wide-eyed, remarked, "Well that's the most exciting thing that's happened during the whole rally!" Someone blew a police whistle and, within minutes, a car arrived and removed the still unconscious swarthy one and one of his friends. The crowd became interested in the rally once more, the Healey roared into life and the girls went off with a wave on the last 270 miles of their journey.

Finally, the 22 survivors reached Spa; thousands rightly cheered them as the cars drove at high speed over closed roads into Liège, where they were parked in the centre of the main square after the hardest postwar *Marathon* up till then. This was classic rallying at its very best; no protest from the crews, an impeccable organization and the finishing order decided solely by the performance on the road, without recourse to handicaps or the hazards of separate starting places. It was recognized that the *Marathon* was the toughest and best-organized of all the continental rallies; it was also said by two experienced drivers who had run in the East African Safari and the Australian Redex Rally, both considered very tough, that the *Marathon* was the most difficult for sheer, concentrated, arduous driving.

Every year Pat said to me after the event, "I never want to do another Liège", yet each July she would ask, "What am I going to drive in the Liège?" In the 1958 event, she went better and better as the rally ran on; as the men got more tired she seemed to improve. I kept telling her to take it easy, and on arriving in England again I received a press photograph of the girls being welcomed at Spa; it was inscribed "To 'Sir', who said 'Slower', from Faster and Faster."

I was not able to attend the 1958 prizegiving as I had promised to go to Montlhéry for the Cambridge University Automobile Club's record attempts with the Austin-Healey the next day. Before I left, however, I was delighted to hear that the team had won the manufacturer's team prize for three cars of the same make, the International club team prize for the RAC, the *Coupe des Dames* first and second places, and that Pat and Ann were fourth in General Classification (which in itself was a new record for ladies crews), and winners of the unlimited class for Grand Touring and Touring cars. I went to Paris feeling that we had at last made a breakthrough as far as the Liège was concerned, and knowing people were already saying that it would be only a matter of time before Pat and Ann won a rally outright. As four of the drivers in the successful Healey team were ladies, John Gott's comment at the start was publicly justified.

The final results of the 1958 Liège gave first place to Hébert and Consten (French), Alfa Romeo 1,290cc; second to Strähle and Buchet (German and French), Porsche 1,498cc; third to Reip and Velge (Belgian), Porsche 1,498cc, and a classic fourth to Moss and Wisdom (British), Austin-Healey 2,639cc – this incidentally was the highest place yet attained by a British crew. Ninth place went to John Gott and Ray Brookes in the MGA Twin-Cam, with Gerry Burgess and Sam Croft-Pearson in 10th position. Nancy Mitchell and Anne Hall drove a very well-judged event to finish in 15th place and consolidate the team win. There were 22 finishers.

The 1959 event was not a great success for BMC: we were only saved from complete disgrace by the achievement of Peter Riley and Rupert Jones, who won the 3-litre class for Grand Touring cars in an Austin-Healey 3000. Of the rest of the team of Healeys, John Gott and Ken James lost their way in Italy, Jack Sears and Peter Garnier lost their way in France and Gerry Burgess and Sam Croft-Pearson had a minor crash and were also eliminated. Pat and Ann, who had been doing very well in a very special A40, were finally out on time and then threw a connecting rod. It was a tougher rally than in 1958, for only 14 crews finished out of 97 starters. As a result of our navigational bloomers, I resolved that in future we would have a recce over all the tricky parts of the route. In 1960 the picture was very different.

We left England on Monday, August 29, full of confidence and determined to win the *30eme Marathon de la Route*. The Healey 3000s were beautifully prepared and in a slightly better form than when they had been so successful in the Alpine Rally only two months before. On returning to England we had gone over the weak points in the cars and had come to the conclusion that we were now getting more power than the gearboxes would stand. Whilst the overdrives had earlier given a little trouble, we had got to the bottom of it by changing the type of oil we were then using and it was obvious that the same overdrives were capable of transmitting a lot more power than we had at our disposal, for they were in regular use in the 3.8 Jaguars which ran in the Tour de France. I therefore approached Charles Griffin, the chief engineer of BMC, with our problem and he asked for the loan of one of the Alpine cars. Charles drove the car himself and then got his department to do a short instrument test on it. I think everyone was pleasantly surprised with the experience and, as a result, there was an amused twinkle in Charles' eyes when I asked for better gearboxes. He said that it would be very difficult to do this in the time, especially with the works summer holiday taking up nearly three weeks in July and August. The wheels were, however, put in motion and I could only wait and pray. To tip the scales a little in our favour I wrote a memo to Charles, with a copy to John Thornley, in which I said we would win the Liège if we had the right gear ratios. The powers-that-be said that it might be done, but that we would have to take a compromise in ratios if we wanted the gearboxes soon. We accepted this and the new boxes were fitted about three days before we went to Belgium.

We had two 'new boys' in the team, David Seigle-Morris and Vic Elford, who were without a works drive owing to the dissolution of the Triumph team. This was very bad luck on David, for he had usually been a private entrant up to then, and was about to have his second paid drive for the other factory when the blow fell. He was welcomed into the team from the start. As he was a very tough type who enjoyed exercise, we felt that we had recruited an extra bodyguard as well as a driver. I suppose the BMC team that year must have been the heaviest on record, although one must make some allowance for the ladies.

We fielded four Austin-Healey 3000s which were driven by Pat Moss and Ann Wisdom, Peter Riley and Tony Ambrose, John Gott and Rupert Jones, and David Seigle-Morris and Vic Elford.

We had not been able to induce the Morleys to come on the Liège as it was a critical time for their harvest. There had been a great deal of rain during August and they both knew that it was of real importance for them to supervise things personally. The Healeys were entered as Appendix C cars for the three-carburettor layout was not yet homologated. In addition, John Sprinzel had persuaded John Patten to buy and enter a Sprite, and they were both under our wing as regards service and spares. Owing to the fact that the *Hotel Moderne*, where we usually stayed, was booked up for some convention, we stayed at our old friend, the *Grand Hotel des Boulevards*.

The pre-rally days were uneventful, except for changing a gearbox which came too late and making some minor adjustments. The gearbox kings at Coventry had made bottom gear so indecently high that the cars were slow off the mark at the expense of the clutches. Pat, in her wisdom, had decided to use a 4.875 final-drive which was derived from the Austin taxi, but we felt that it would be too tiring, so the rest of the cars used the 4.1, which was normal with overdrive. Peter Riley and Tony Ambrose had previously gone with Barbara Ambrose to Yugoslavia for a very quick recce, both of that section and of the return route through Italy. This whole expedition was crammed into about eight days, but the recce car protested and ran out of wheel bearings, so they had a day's rest in Turin on the way home. The information that they brought back was invaluable and contributed very greatly to our results in the rally.

Erik Carlsson was not running in the event that year so decided to take his holiday following the rally and helping BMC. Bob Domei, a young American airman who had rallied a bit, joined up with him and we lent them Pat's old Liège-Rome-Liège Morris Minor 1000 as transport. This car was affectionately known as 'Grannie' and was used by Pat in many local English rallies for some time; she was to have the drive of her life in the hands of Erik!.

On Tuesday, the crews borrowed one of the tender cars and went out and practised the timed test at Montenau, which occurred just after the start. Owing to a mistake, they practised over only half the test and did a bit that was not in it, so we pulled the navigators' legs at dinner in a delightful restaurant opposite the *Moderne*, where we all congregated for mussels, trout and suchlike delicacies. This took up most of the evening, as everyone talked shop until bedtime and the waiters didn't hurry much.

The route for 1960 was very similar to those of the two previous years; it made off in an almost straight line for Karlsruhe and then joined the *autobahn* which was followed as far as Neu-Ulm, where the crews turned off to Lindau; it was here that the neutralized Austrian section began, ending at the Passo di Resia on the Italian frontier. The route then passed through Merano and circled by way of Bolzano back over the Passo di Pennes to Vipiteno and Merano and then up the main valley again to Trafoi. The Stelvio and Gavia passes were next on the route, to be followed by the Vivione, the Croce Domini and the Maniva before reaching Brescia, where the first car was due on Friday, September 2, at 01.35 hours.

On this section we had arranged to meet our team at Merano and at Trafoi and, while they were up in the clouds, we would make for Trieste, which was to be their point of entry in Yugoslavia. As there were no controls between Brescia and Kosina, in Yugoslavia, it was anticipated that they would have about an hour in hand at Trieste for some food and attention to the cars. After Kosina they were to be subjected to nearly 600 kilometres (370 miles) of very rough and narrow roads with the usual hazards of dust, rocks, bullock carts and punctures. This would be the greatest test of the whole rally, for here more than one puncture in a section would be fatal and skill in changing a wheel would make all the difference between success and failure. All our cars carried two spare wheels on this section. The Yugoslav stage terminated with

The author, wearing the inevitable headgear, and John Gott, his dedicated and hard-working leader of the BMC rally team from 1955 to 1961, about to set off on another continental foray.

Team driver Bill Shepherd, MG chief designer Syd Enever and the author find time for a personal refuelling stop at Annecy during a programme of testing in 1955.

John Williamson is sitting in front of a typical set of navigational aids for rallying in the Fifties, but John Milne seems to prefer his more traditional timepiece.

A quartet of MGAs with eight members of the Abingdon staff and the BMC transporter about to set off for the fateful 1955 Le Mans 24-Hours race.

The Le Mans pit counter being filled with essential tools and spares as start time approaches; several pairs of sharp eyes were necessary to protect them from light-fingered passers-by.

All that remained of Dick Jacobs' MGA after his crash minutes after the appalling accident opposite the pits when Levegh's Mercedes-Benz was launched into the spectator area. Jacobs survived his life-threatening injuries, but never raced again.

Bowls of soup at the ready at the BMC team's rally service point in Reims for the 1955 Monte Carlo Rally.

Apart from the rally plates, this could have been mistaken for a tourist's car. It was one of two MG Magnettes driven by the Holt brothers in the 1955 Monte Carlo Rally.

Jack Sears hard at work on the Zandvoort circuit in the Austin A90 he shared with Syd Henson and Dick Bensted-Smith on the 1956 Tulip Rally. They finished second in their class.

Ray Brookes and his father Ted displaying their trophies after becoming surprise outright winners of the 1956 Tulip Rally with their diminutive Austin A30.

Peter Scott-Russell, Tom Haig, Pat Faichney and Nancy Mitchell with the two MGAs they were to share in the 1956 Mille Miglia. By race day both cars' full screens had been replaced by tiny aeroscreens to reduce wind resistance, but the crews became drenched in the very wet conditions.

The BMC team's four MGA 1500s, complete with hardtops, about to set off for the start of the 1956 Alpine Rally in which Nancy Mitchell and Pat Faichney would win a *Coupe des Alpes* and the *Coupe des Dames*.

The MGA 1500 of John Milne and Douglas Johns receives some final service towards the end of the 1956 Alpine Rally; they finished fourth in their class.

Nancy Mitchell and Anne Hall on the 1956 Liège–Rome–Liège, their MGA dwarfed by the mountainous scenery near Zagreb.

The Cambridge University Automobile Club's endurance record attempt at Montlhéry in 1957 with an Austin A35 received the backing of BMC, who provided both financial assistance and trackside support.

The CUAC team were back at Montlhéry in 1958, this time with an Austin-Healey 100-Six, with which they bagged a further seven records despite a hairy moment when the author was at the wheel.

A small car on one of the toughest rallies. This is the Morris Minor 1000 which Pat Moss and Ann Wisdom shared on the 1957 Liège–Rome–Liège. They were runners-up amongst the ladies and finished 23rd overall.

A worrying moment during the 1958 Alpine Rally for Pat Moss and Ann Wisdom as their Austin-Healey is checked by Terry Mitchell for an oil leak, but they were able to continue and went on to win the *Coupe des Dames.*

The battle-scarred Austin-Healey of Jack Sears and Sam Moore, who finished 11th overall on the 1958 Alpine Rally, sandwiched between the similar cars of Pat Moss and Nancy Mitchell.

Both car and crew look ready for a spring clean after finishing the 1958 Liège–Rome–Liège in ninth place overall. Here are Ray Brookes and John Gott with their MGA Twin-Cam.

Most BMC badges found their way on to the International rally scene during the Fifties, including Tish Ozanne's own Riley 1.5, which was prepared at Abingdon and co-driven by Anne Hall on the 1959 Tulip Rally, when they were runners-up for the *Coupe des Dames*.

Special tests were all-important in the rallies of the Fifties, including the 1959 Sestriere, during which John Sprinzel is doing his best to avoid the oil drums and straw bales in the Austin A35 in which he and Stuart Turner finished third in their class.

Tommy Wisdom rushes through another test on the 1959 Sestriere Rally in the Austin-Healey Sprite which went on to take fifth place in the class.

Pre-rally preparations of the BMC team before the start of the 1959 Alpine. Only the John Gott and Chris Tooley Austin-Healey would survive to the finish, claiming second place in their class.

An evocative picture of the Gott/Tooley Austin-Healey 3000 at Cannes at the end of the gruelling 1959 Alpine Rally.

John Sprinzel and Dick Bensted-Smith relaxing against the backcloth of the famous Grecian ruins with their MGA Twin-Cam; their 1959 Acropolis Rally would end up in a field after a shower of rain took them off the slippery road.

The author with Willy Cave, Jack Sears and Donald and Erle Morley and their two Austin-Healey 3000s enjoying a pause during the 1959 RAC Rally. They would finish first and second in their class, the Morley brothers ahead of their team-mates.

Pat Moss and Ann Wisdom changed to a left-hand-drive Austin A40 for their assault on the 1959 Canadian Winter Rally and drove it to victory in the Ladies' class.

An immaculate line-up of Austin-Healey 3000s entered by the Donald Healey Motor Company for the 1960 Sebring 12-Hours; car No 18, driven by Peter Riley and Jack Sears, would finish third in class. Geoffrey Healey is on the extreme left and Babe Learoyd is alongside the author, who is sporting a new line in hats.

Members of the BMC team and others signing-on at Marseilles for the 1960 Alpine. Erle Morley is standing patiently behind while Ann Wisdom, John Gott and Stuart Turner hog the front row of the grid.

Pat Moss tackling the Col de Menée during her storming drive in the Austin-Healey with Ann Wisdom to a class victory and the *Coupe des Dames* on the 1960 Alpine Rally.

BMC entered a trio of Morris Mini-Minors for the 1960 Alpine Rally, the car of Tom Gold and Mike Hughes, seen here taking a tight line on the Col de la St Baune, emerging the class winner.

A prize-winning line-up after the 1960 Alpine Rally. The three Austin-Healey 3000s with their trophies and crews: Erle and Donald Morley, John Gott and Bill Shepherd, and Pat Moss and Ann Wisdom.

A coffee break for Peter Riley, Bill Bradley, John Miles and Tony Ambrose on their way towards Venice on the 1960 Acropolis Rally. The Austin-Healey crew retired, but Milne and Bradley were fourth in class with their Austin Seven (Mini).

Pat Moss with that famous handbag during the 1960 Acropolis Rally. This time she and Ann were out of luck and had to retire the Austin-Healey with steering problems.

Pat and Ann in their travel-stained Austin-Healey Sprite in which they finished second in class and runners-up for the Ladies' prize in the 1960 RAC Rally of Great Britain.

The author toes the line to provide some close-up signalling for the Parkinson/
Flaherty MGA 1600 Coupe, which won its class and finished 14th overall in the 1961
Sebring 12-Hours.

Peter Riley about to take his Austin-Healey 3000 into the half-hour Tatoi speed test
during the 1961 Acropolis Rally in which he and Tony Ambrose were third overall
and winners of the GT category.

John Gott and Bill Shepherd in amongst the rocks and the residual snow as they head for third place in their class on the 1961 Alpine Rally, the big Healey's rear tyres fighting for grip on the loose surface.

John Gott's other great joy was racing his Austin-Healey, seen here on the starting grid at Silverstone with its driver looking quietly confident.

Back together again! In 1994 there was a reunion of the staff and drivers of the BMC/British Leyland Competition Department and the staff of companies which supported the rally programme – the first for over 20 years. Seen here are, back row: Ron Crellin, Neil Wilson, Brian Culcheth, Tommy and Mrs Gold, Den Green, Willy Cave, Stuart Turner, Peter Riley, Jack Sears, Paul Easter, John Handley, Les Needham, Ted Worswick, Mike Nicholson, Bill Price, Jeremy Ferguson (Dunlop), Mike Broad, Jeff Williamson and John Smithurst (Ferodo). Centre row: John Sprinzel, Mrs Sutcliffe, Don Morley, Marcus Chambers, Anne Hall, Roy Fidler, John Hopwood and Mike Sutcliffe. Front row: Don Barrow, Val Morley, Fred Gallagher, Liz Crellin and Tony Fall.

After earlier forays with Sunbeam Alpines, Rootes returned to Le Mans in 1964 with a team of purpose-built Tigers with bodywork by Brian Lister, the first of which was photographed here at the factory by the author.

Keith Ballisat, with Rootes personnel in attendance, about to begin circuit testing of the first Le Mans Tiger at Snetterton in the hope of overcoming the handling problems revealed during the Le Mans test weekend.

One of the two Tiger prototypes being wheeled into position for the 1964 Le Mans start. The author viewed the team's appearance with considerable misgivings because it was clear that the cars were far from competitive.

At least the Tigers looked the part, but they proved fragile, this one breaking its crankshaft and causing a spectacular blow-up as Peter Procter was passing the pits nine hours into the race; the other car had retired with piston failure six hours earlier.

Rosemary Smith and Valerie Domleo rushing through the slush in their Hillman Imp on the way to outright victory in the 1965 Tulip Rally, a success which was aided by a new and complicated marking system.

Val and Rosemary with the spoils of victory. This was a highlight of Rosemary Smith's career with Rootes, which included 21 finishes from 24 starts in Internationals, nine class wins and 12 *Coupes des Dames*.

Rosemary Smith and Margaret Mackenzie about to get down to work with their Tiger, one of three which were making their competition debut on the 1964 Geneva Rally. Cooling slots were let into the front wings after overheating problems were encountered during tests.

Rosemary Smith powering the Tiger through a slippery uphill S-bend during the Geneva Rally. All three cars proved reliable and were the only survivors from their GT class.

Ian Hall and Peter Harper with the silverware which they collected after finishing first in class and fourth overall out of the 22 survivors from the 235 cars entered for the gruelling 1965 Monte Carlo Rally.

The author lent his old friend John Gott this Tiger so that he could take part in the 1965 International Police Rally in Belgium, with Sgt D E Nicholson as his navigator, and they repaid the gesture by winning the event outright.

Getting to grips with the route instructions. The author going through the small print with Ian Hall and Don Barrow, who were to share this Tiger on the 1965 Alpine Rally. Note the temporary bonnet trunking to accommodate the modified intake system.

The Peter Harper/Robin Turvey Sunbeam Tiger being put through its paces in the snow in England before setting off on the 1966 Monte Carlo Rally, from which it was retired with a damaged radiator.

Peter Harper and Ian Hall setting off on the first section of the 1966 Acropolis Rally with the familiar architectural backcloth to their Tiger.

Another personal pit stop during a Monte Carlo Rally recce. Around the table, clockwise, can be seen Brian Coyle, Rosemary Smith, Margaret Mackenzie, a smiling Andrew Cowan, Mike Wood and a pensive Tony Fall.

That successful partner-
ship again, Rosemary
Smith and Val Domleo,
this time pictured at the
end of the 1966 Acropolis
Rally with another class
win to add to their
growing collection of
awards.

Rosemary Smith and Val
Domleo seemingly head-
ing for another *Coupe des
Dames* victory in the 1966
Monte Carlo Rally until
their Hillman Imp, along
with the three Mini-
Coopers which had domi-
nated the event, were
controversially disquali-
fied because of a so-called
lighting infringement.

The London–Sydney Marathon Hunter being pounded along the dirt road between Numeralla and Braidwood on the Australian leg of the event. The Hillman moved into the lead after Roger Clark's Ford Cortina Lotus developed an engine problem and Lucien Bianchi's Citroen DS21 crashed and retired.

Night-time service in the *parc fermé* on arrival at Bombay for the Hillman Hunter with which Andrew Cowan, Brian Coyle and Colin Malkin emerged the delighted winners of the London–Sydney Marathon in 1968.

Members of the Chrysler office staff and workforce came out to welcome the Marathon-winning Hunter back to the factory, the three-man crew being perched on the roof while someone else was entrusted with the steering wheel.

Andrew Cowan left the road when his suspension collapsed, then rolled his car after clipping a bank, but the Sunbeam Imp survived, enabling him to lead the other Imps in to collect the team award at the end of the 1968 Scottish Rally.

Partnered by Brian Coyle, Andrew Cowan gave the Imp one last fling on an International when he took part in the 1969 Scottish Rally. The car finished second overall and first in class after its troublesome gearbox had been replaced with one from an old hack Imp kept on Cowan's farm.

the well-known climb up to Predil and the route then passed through Tarvisio, where the tyre people had a service point at the Fiat garage which we always used. My own service car was scheduled to join the rally again here, having come up on the main road from Trieste.

We had stationed another car at Verona, which was an important point as the rally passed through it twice. Tommy Wellman was in charge there. The section from Cibiana to Rovereto, which lay between Tarvisio and Verona, was thought by Peter and Tony to be nearly as important as the Yugoslav section. Much of it was on gravel roads and, as they put it, "There are 200 kilometres of mountain road over which you cannot afford to let up even for a moment"; this crucial stage was to be covered in the middle of the third night. The Verona party were to be supported by the brake specialists, who were of the opinion that pad changes would be about due at this point, for the rally would then have run a little over half-distance. This served to illustrate the gruelling nature of the event which, in under 2,000 miles, could wear out disc brake pads which might well last four or five times that distance under normal use.

After Tarvisio, I planned to take my party to Cuneo, where the first car was due at 16.00 hours on the Saturday; from there we would join forces with Douggie Hamblin at Barcelonnette, just over the frontier in France. After the Col d'Allos, a number of smaller French cols on mountain tracks led the competitors up to the Col de Luitel and the Col du Granier and from there to Chambéry, where they would be met by the party from Verona. From there the rally was to follow the well-known route back to Belgium via Bourg-en-Bresse, Dole, Gray and Verdun. The survivors were due to finish at Spa shortly before 17.00 hours on Sunday, September 4, after covering 4,654km (2,885 miles) in 91 hours of almost continuous driving. During the entire length of the rally the competitors were to be subject to the traffic regulations of the various countries through which they were to pass and their vehicles had to conform with the regulations as to lighting, signalling and warning devices. The entry list was somewhat smaller than usual (82 cars left Spa), but the quality was as high as ever.

Erik Carlsson had told us to expect him anywhere on the route and, knowing Erik, I was sure that he would do his best to attend the maximum number of service points and some extra controls as well. We set out for Austria on the Wednesday morning that the rally was due to start and reached Landeck in the Tyrol that evening, by way of the Füssen pass. Somewhere on this run we passed through the two villages Natter and Mutter. The *Hotel Post* at Landeck was very adequate and we spent a comfortable night, being joined there by Dunlop's David Hiam.

The following morning we crossed the Passo di Resio in beautiful weather and reached Merano in good time to do our shopping in the market. This was the first time we had brought along our new butane cooking stoves, together with all the impedimenta required to serve hot drinks and a snack to the crews. The idea arose from the magnificent service which Erik Carlsson and David Hiam had put on in an impromptu way during the previous Alpine Rally. To house all the gear I had ordered some boxes to be made with sliding trays and let-down sides which would fit into the boot of an Austin A99 or a Wolseley 6/99, together with a similar box for spares and tools. When the crews arrived at the Supercorte station which we had selected at Merano, we were ready to serve them with hot drinks, warm soup, ham rolls and tomatoes.

The snacks went down extremely well and we had nothing to do to the cars, except that of Seigle-Morris, which had broken a brake servo pipe. We blanked off the broken pipe at the manifold, took the measurements and I told David that we would make up a suitable pipe and fit it at Trieste.

As usual, we picked up a bit of news; there had been three ladies crews in the entry list and three must start in any event for the winner to qualify for Ladies' Championship points. Annie Soisbault wished to prevent either Pat Moss or Renée Wagner from getting more points, so she repeated the ruse which she had used the year before in the Portuguese Rally and refrained from starting. Renée would have none of this; aided by the officials, who were in sympathy with her, she found two Belgian ladies, Mesdames Jowett and Leboutte, obtained an entry for them and raised a rather derelict Panhard for them to start in. It mattered little whether they reached the next control as long as they got off the starting line. The Panhard started, but failed to climb the hill out of Spa and retired with a broken valve, so setting up a Liège record – for the shortest run yet!

One of the new Lancia Flaminia GTs, driven by Maglioli, burnt out its electrical system on the starting line and Rey, who had won a *Coupe des Alpes* in the 1959 Alpine, left the road before he even got to the start of the first timed test. In the Stavelot-Montenau test, Oreiller's Alfa Romeo made FTD in 11min 49sec for the 18-kilometre course. This became the 'bogey' time to which all other penalizations were related. Most of the seasoned drivers chose a middle course and refrained from trying too hard at this early stage. Pat Moss was sixth, behind the Alfa and the Porsches of Clemens, Sander, Buchet and Nokin, with a delay of 53 seconds. Walter, the 1961 Touring Champion, left the road and must have over-revved his Porsche for he retired at Stuttgart. Margulies and Turner broke a wheel on their Sprite in Germany and a Belgian Ford Anglia 105E retired with a broken propeller shaft. Peter Riley had had a sticking throttle, which put his revs up to 7,000rpm, which was to prove disastrous to him later.

We packed up and set off for Trafoi, where we met Erik Carlsson and Bob Domei. It was dark by now so we got out the butane hurricane lamps and the stoves and cooked some sausages, which were much appreciated by the crews, who arrived without trouble. We heard that the Passo di Giovo and the Pennes had eliminated the MacCartney Elite and two Alfa Giuliettas, which brought the total of retirements up to 14. It was a beautiful night and conditions seemed ideal for the climb of the Stelvio and Gavia passes. The 'bogey' time for the 30km from Trafoi to Bagni Nuovi, at the foot of the Stelvio, had been set at 36 minutes and it looked as if someone might do it; in fact only Oreiller's Alfa managed the feat. The next section was supposed to be from Santa Caterina over the Gavia to Ponte di Legno, but there had been a last-minute change owing to a landslide on the Gavia and the rally was re-routed by Edolo over the Col d'Aprica. The Passo di Croce Domini was also to have been included, but this, too, had to be cut out of the route, which was unfortunate for it took the sting out of this section.

We reached Trieste at around 5am and few people were about. We slept in the car for about an hour and then set up shop in the greasing bay of a suitable garage. The Healeys arrived early, as we had thought they would, and everyone was fed, for I had arranged for some lunch-boxes to be delivered at seven. This had been done through the Halls, who had also helped us on the Acropolis

Rally; later Mr Hall himself called to see us on his way to the office. From our crews we learnt that Pat had made a very good time on the Stelvio and was now lying equal second with the Porsche of Buchet and Bianchi, whilst the other Healeys were all in the first 20 places, headed by John Gott, who was lying 12th. At this stage in the rally, therefore, we were in a sound strategic position.

The pipe I had obtained for the Seigle-Morris car was not quite the right size, being metric, so we had to try to file the union nut to fit; unfortunately the round file we had was not the right size and the job took too long. In the end, David drove the whole rally without the brake servo working. I was rather annoyed about this, for the fitting on his car was not quite the same as on the others. Later I arranged for this part to be changed and we used a small-gauge polythene pipe to connect the servo to the inlet manifold. Amongst other retirements during the night was the Frescobaldi and Rosinsky Lancia Flaminia GT, which blew up on the Stelvio to such effect that the whole car was burnt out, the crew escaping without injury. Thus at the start of the Yugoslav section there were 64 left in the struggle.

The Yugoslav section was made up of eight stages, beginning with Pazin to Matulji, 52 kilometres over the mountains between Trieste and Rijeka, followed by a fairly easy section of 52km to Novi, where the most testing part of the route began over the dusty unmade roads to Vrbovsko. It was here that punctures were to make all the difference between success and failure, and it was noticeable that the later cars suffered less in this respect than the earlier numbers. Fortunately, Pat had chosen a late number because she liked to look at the control lists and see which of her rivals were still in the game; nearly all the times over the special stages could also be seen if there was time to look at the sheets. The rally then ran to Caber, Col and Cerkno before going over the 17-kilometre col of Cerkno-Hotavlje and back to Italy by Kranjska Gora and the climb of the Moistrocca to Predil. The average for the Moistrocca was set at 50 minutes, or 66km/h.

We were to learn later that things started to become much more dramatic in the Yugoslav section. The route from Novi Sovska onwards ran through a torrential storm which, although it laid the dust, did not improve visibility. By Caber, Trautmann had moved into the lead in his Citroen and his total penalizations were 6min 15sec against the 13min 18sec of Moss and Wisdom, who were leading another Citroen, a couple of Porsches, a Renault Alpine, another Porsche and then the Riley/Ambrose Healey. John Sprinzel was coming up the field and was 12th with 23min 32sec of penalization. The other two Healeys were falling back with a series of punctures and John Gott was having trouble with his bonnet flying up as well.

During this section it became evident that things were not right with the clutch on Pat's car for it started to slip because the oil was getting past the seal on the front end of the gearbox. It had lost the oil in the gearbox somewhere before Verona, where inspection had shown that the gearbox drain plug had fallen out or, more probably, been loosened by a rock and finally worked off. Fortunately, Syd Henson was at Verona with his Austin A90 brake and this car was robbed of the necessary plug, but the damage had been done, the gears and the shaft had got hot and as a result the oil seal had suffered. We had no suitable oil seal with us but Erik Carlsson and Bob Domei set about getting one. They telephoned Paris and located a seal, which was to be flown to Nice, where Madame Jacquin of the Sporting Garage at Monte Carlo would collect it. Her best mechanic was then to drive as fast as possible to Barcelonnette, where it was expected that the girls might have a little over an hour in hand in which it could be fitted. Meanwhile, Pat was advised to keep the oil level fairly low and watch it at every opportunity.

Yugoslavia was to shatter many hopes, particularly amongst the leaders. Oreiller retired with too many punctures and not enough spares. De Lageneste fell back to second place in his Alfa and then went out with suspension troubles. Strähle and Wencher worked up to third and blew up in the biggest possible way. Even if the cars kept going, the strain of taking them up amongst the leaders was likely to prove fatal to their chances of finishing; 64 cars went into Yugoslavia, but only 28 came out, many of those in a sad state. All of which reminded me very much of the old nautical jingle: "Beware, beware the Bight of Benin, whence few come out though many go in!"

At our Tarvisio service point, however, the Austin-Healey crews were still intact and our 'new boy', David Seigle-Morris, was doing very well despite a somewhat hard brake pedal. Peter Riley was doing even better, having moved into fourth place, just ahead of the girls, but after Cibiana one of the blades of his fan came adrift and damaged the radiator; this was almost certainly due to the vibration when his revs went 'off the clock' earlier on. It was just after Cibiana, too, that the suspension failed on the leading Citroen and Trautmann took to the countryside. Buchet and Bianchi then took over the lead in their Porsche, only to take the same wrong turning that John Gott and Ken James had taken the previous year; they suffered the same fate, too – exclusion for lateness. Coltelloni was now in first place, but it brought him no luck either, for not long after the Citroen's suspension failed and he too was out. All these misfortunes put Pat and Ann into the lead, with Sprinzel's Sprite in an unbelievable second place.

Not only amongst the leaders was trouble rife. Bill Meredith-Owen and Bill Bradley had been going well in their MGA, but had not taken the trouble to find out either how, or if, their jack worked and it was too late when they got a puncture. The girls stopped to help them, but the poor Bills were excluded for being 36 seconds late at the next control. Our service point at Tarvisio had been fully occupied, for there were several wheels to change and numerous odds and ends to attend to. We had more Italian mechanics than usual as the majority of the staff stayed on voluntarily and they worked with a will. After the last cars had gone, they brought out the wine and salami and we all toasted each other's health and the success of our cars.

We retired for a few hours' sleep at the *Hotel Italia* before setting out for the plains of Piedmont. Meanwhile, Tommy Wellman and his men were coping with the immediate needs of the cars and Syd Henson was providing a welcome cup of tea. We breakfasted in Verona in a little restaurant by the main square and, losing no time, made for Turin where we turned south towards Cuneo and managed to find a filling station with a little restaurant. We were in Cuneo in good time but it was difficult to decide where to go as there was no Supercorte station on the road into the town. After a short while a Porsche went past and we knew then we were on the route. Soon afterwards John Gott's car came in sight. Rupert Jones was driving and told us that John was not feeling well; he looked pale and I thought it was heat exhaustion so gave him a drink. I don't know if they had any salt tablets, but they are a good thing on these occasions. John gave us the marvellous news that Pat was first in the rally and that the Sprite of Sprinzel and Patten was in second place. He also told us how Erik had been trying to organize a new clutch oil seal. It was evident that Cuneo was of little importance as a service point and that we had better make haste and get to Barcelonnette to warn the others as soon as possible.

On the way to the Col de Larche, we were passed by the Austin-Healeys and finally by Erik Carlsson, who was going like a rocket in 'Grannie'. We could not keep up with him in the heavily laden A90, but we finally arrived at the outskirts of Barcelonnette and found Ann Clayton sitting forlornly at the side of the road surrounded by the catering impedimenta, tools and a welding plant which had been dumped from her car. She told us that everyone else was down in the village, so we left Ann by the side of the road for the time being and set off to locate the others. The village was very small so it did not take long to find them.

Erik Carlsson and Douggie Hamblin, aided by one of the mechanics, had commandeered the workshop where Pat's Healey was on the ramp and the gearbox was on its way out. Although we carried a spare gearbox, we had not got the oil seal which was mounted in the bellhousing. Ann Wisdom estimated that we had a little over 40 minutes left to effect the repair. The telephone rang and Madame Jacquin told me that her man had been delayed as the oil seal had not come on the first aeroplane, but that he had now left by road for Barcelonnette. It was evident that he could not arrive in time for us to use the new oil seal, and although the garage proprietor had some seals it was unlikely that they would fit. When the box came out and the bellhousing was unbolted, Douggie picked up a few likely seals and tried them, but none was any good. No-one spoke as he took the tension spring out of a slightly smaller seal and fitted it to the old one; he tried it on the shaft, it fitted and he commenced to reassemble the box. It was evident that there was little I could do now so I decided to go back and rescue Ann Clayton and her impedimenta.

The Col d'Allos out of Barcelonnette was due to be reopened to the public as soon as the last car in the rally went by, but most of the cars were now bunched together and running early. The official at the timing point at the start of the timed climb therefore assumed that Pat had retired and the official at the other end told the police that the pass could be opened. As all these assumptions were being made the gearbox was buttoned up, with a few bolts missing, and the gearbox covering fastened down with minimum number of screws. This done, the girls got away in a vicious tail slide, followed by Erik Carlsson, Bob Domei and Douggie Hamblin in one of the A90 Austins, with a bag of tools and the missing bolts. The girls made the fourth fastest climb of the Col d'Allos, passing 18 very shaken Frenchmen on the way; these same Frenchmen just had time to mutter some suitable imprecations when they in turn were passed by the Austin being driven by Eric as no Austin had ever been driven before!

We took stock of the debris, compensated the garage man for loss of trade, and looked at our watches. The whole operation had taken a little under an hour! As it was not possible to get everything into the remaining Austin and the Minor 1000, we had to leave some of the things behind. Eventually everything of importance was packed and Roy Brocklehurst was put in charge of the rather tired Minor. Shortly after midnight, we expected to catch the rally up at Le Noyer, which was reached by turning off the N85 after crossing the Col de Bayard at Les Barraques; this area seemed destined to provide drama for Pat, for it was here that she had had clutch trouble in the 1958 Alpine.

We reached Le Noyer and got the stove going as coffee would be needed by everyone. The team was still intact when the cars arrived. Pat's clutch was all right and Douggie Hamblin had been able to secure the gearbox tunnel. We exchanged Bob Domei for one of the mechanics, as Bob was quite exhausted and we felt that the freshest people should go with the flying Swede. It began to rain, but it looked almost certain that the lead would not be lost – if Pat didn't make a slip! There were 13 cars left in the rally and four of these were Austin-Healeys. Nevertheless, the BMC position was a rather dramatic one. At the beginning of the French section, Pat and Ann had a lead of nearly five minutes over the Sprite and more than six minutes in hand over Georges Sander and his son, who were then third in their Porsche Super 90, whilst David Seigle-Morris and John Gott could both climb up several places if they went fast enough in the climbs.

Over the Allos Pat dropped three-quarters of a minute to the Sanders, who in turn cut over a minute off Sprinzel's precarious lead over them. On the following St Geniez section the Sanders made FTN (fastest time of the night), stole another 44 seconds from the girls and passed into second place, now leading the Sprite by over a minute. But here the tide turned for us. At Le Noyer Pat made FTN, took back six seconds from the Sanders and David climbed into fifth place. Over the Col de Luitel Pat was only third fastest to John, who was now fighting fit again and going up fast, but she still took 17 seconds off the Sanders, whose attack was losing force. On the final climb over the Cols de Porte, Cucheron and Granier that attack faded right away; Pat was content to drive to finish, but she still took another 38 seconds back from the Sanders.

And so the Marathon was won. Apart from the girls' great drive, the other Healey crews had fought to the bitter end. Both David and John went up as far as was possible, the former finishing fifth and the latter 10th, whilst Sprinzel, although unable to hold off the Sanders' Porsche, hung grimly on to third place, which was a magnificent achievement.

Knowing little of these struggles, we arrived at Chambéry to put things in order for the long run home across France. It was pouring with rain but no-one minded. Very little needed doing to the cars, but we changed a buckled wheel on John Sprinzel's Sprite, which was about the only attention it had needed for the entire rally. Near Dole I made a small detour to Arbois and surprised my son, who was staying there, by arriving before eight. He joined us and we picked up the others at Dole. And so we reached Spa and met Peter Riley and Tony Ambrose, who had managed to get their car home. We bought a bottle of champagne and eagerly awaited the return of the victors. As usual, the team had washed their cars and finally the three big Healeys and the Sprite came into the enclosure. It was the greatest thrill of my life to see the girls welcomed as victors by Maurice Garot. This was an all-time first, in fact a triple first; it was the first time that an International Rally Championship event had been won by a ladies crew, and the first time that Great Britain had won the Inter-land Trophy, *la Trophée des Nations*. There was also the little matter of the *Coupe des Dames*, the manufacturer's team prize, the club team prize and two class wins as well. Our cups were indeed full and it was a very popular win.

That night we all sat down in the little restaurant opposite the *Moderne* for what we hoped would be an outstanding meal, but the place was too hot, everyone was too tired and one by one people had to go to bed. I felt off-colour myself and retired to bed early. Few of the rest had any real appetite and the party was not a great success. The following day, though, all was excitement. There were telegrams from George Harriman and interviews with the press. *La Meuse*, the great Belgian daily, sent its ace interviewer, Armand Bachelier, to see the girls. It was a fascinating experience to hear him questioning them, and the excellent article which appeared under his name was published in three parts during that week.

The prizegiving and the ball were held at the local casino, with all the pomp and ceremony of these occasions, but the proceedings were delayed a little by a telephone call to say that Pat had split her dress and was having to be sewn into it by Ann. At length the girls appeared, looking radiant, and so different from the couple of young amazons who had won through to this unique victory. Maurice Garot said, jokingly, in his speech, "Next year, gentlemen, we shall offer a *Coupe des Hommes!*" – a remark which was received in the spirit in which it was given.

The 1960 Liège was the highlight of my career as a Competition Manager and I was convinced that it would be a long time before another team equalled the 1960 BMC result. Even in 1961 Rene Cotton's all-conquering Citroens won neither the team prizes nor the *Coupe des Dames* and the nearest approach to 1960's clean sweep was still our own 1958 effort.

CHAPTER 10

The RAC Rally of Great Britain

"The farmer said he enjoyed rallies, for nothing happened up there, and in any case there was always the chance of getting a car cheap."

The Royal Automobile Club's rally, which was the only event run in Great Britain carrying European Rally Championship points, was as British in character as the other International events were characteristic of the nations which organized them. The very nature of motoring in this country imposed certain limitations upon the event which were inescapable. The policy of the RAC was always to organize an event which would not unduly inconvenience the normal motorist going about his or her daily task, and for this reason they always imposed a maximum average speed of 30mph between the main controls; this meant some 49km/h against the 60km/h in France, 50km/h in Italy and anything the organizers might like to fix in Yugoslavia. As long stretches of the RAC Rally route had to be over good roads, it was very easy to exceed this 30mph average and so make up enough time for meals and mechanical adjustments; however, in order to put some curb on the more enthusiastic competitors, the organizers reserved the right to impose secret controls which penalized competitors who averaged more than 40mph over a distance of 20 miles and upwards, the penalty of so doing sometimes being a loss of 300 marks.

In order to make the road section of the rally more difficult, controls were placed close together in areas such as Wales, Devonshire or the Lake District. Up to 1961, seven of the rallies were run in March, when the weather might have been expected to contribute to the difficulties of the route. If the weather was not severe, however, it was only to be expected that the winners of the event and of the various classes would be decided by a series of tests of speed and manoeuvring which took place on private roads and race tracks. In the 1958 event, for instance, there were no less than 17 of these tests.

Unlike the continental rallies, where to miss a control meant automatic exclusion, in the RAC the penalty at one time was the loss of 300 marks, so as the penalty for late arrival at a control was 10 marks per minute, it could be more prudent to avoid a control altogether if one was over half an hour late. From 1961, however, this anomaly was resolved by making the penalty for late arrival at a control a mark per minute, plus 300 marks each for missing two controls, and exclusion for doing so a third time. Another change, which helped to attract more prominent foreign drivers, was the moving of the rally to November. By becoming one of the last events it began to have a great influence on the Rally Championship, and no serious Championship contender could afford to miss it. The complexion of the event also changed for the better and it became much tougher when, from 1960, it was run through Scotland in search of more difficult sections with less traffic. The organization was put into the hands of a small sub-committee of very experienced drivers and organizers, sitting under the chairmanship of Jack Kemsley. As Jack had worked indefatigably with the organizers of the Monte and the Tulip to further the interests of British rally drivers, it was most appropriate that he should also be largely responsible for the third of the rallies which appealed most to the average British rally driver.

The revised Appendix J of the International Sporting Code was introduced in 1958. This was more realistic, but still rather ambiguous in some places and, as a result, the competitor might read it one way and the organizers another. During 1958, therefore, there were a number of test cases and *CSI* rulings, culminating in the overruling of the Monte Carlo organizers for their interpretation of the clause on planing cylinder heads in the 1959 Monte Carlo Rally regulations. I was convinced that I knew the correct meaning of this clause, and never deviated from my interpretation (which the *CSI* later approved) from the beginning of 1958. Thus, we entered our cars for the 1958 RAC Rally in the Improved Group, and prepared them by polishing the cylinder heads, planing a little off to raise the compression and fitting larger diameter exhaust pipes with a modified flange or cone at the manifold joint. At a later date, the regulations forbade any alteration to the manifold, although a larger pipe was still allowed, but all this was quite permissible at the time.

Our entries for the 1958 RAC consisted of:

Riley 1.5	Nancy Mitchell and Joan Johns
Riley 1.5	Ken Lee and Archie Sinclair
Morris Minor 1000	Pat Moss and Ann Wisdom
Austin A35	John Sprinzel and Dick Bensted-Smith
Austin-Healey 100-Six	Jack Sears and Peter Garnier

In addition to the works entries, we prepared cars for about half a dozen private entries and gave advice to many more. All our works entries started from Hastings instead of the alternative starting point, Blackpool. As the finish for the rally that year was also at Hastings, it was most convenient to leave the luggage at the same hotel where we would be staying for both the start and the finish.

I went down to Hastings the day before, taking one mechanic as a precaution, although I did not expect any real trouble. Unfortunately, John Sprinzel had some clutch trouble and had started to strip the car before we got there. Although we put this right, in the end he was not satisfied with the car, so took his own A35, which his sister Norma was to drive, and as a result she couldn't start. Similar cars were grouped together in the entry list, so that some of the works crews found themselves next to privately-owned cars which we had prepared. This bred a good team spirit between the private owners and the works drivers and I think the private owners benefited from the experience. The two Wadham brothers, for instance, were running in their Minor 1000 next to Pat and Ann, whilst the Riley 1.5 of Les Leston and Gordon

Wilkins was running between those of Ken Lee and Nancy Mitchell. Jack Sears and Peter Garnier, who were in that particularly unlucky green Healey (perhaps Healeys didn't like being painted green), had no BMC neighbours, but were running next to old team-mates Gerry Burgess and Sam Croft-Pearson, who were now back with the Ford team. The Sunbeam team were well fancied for this event, as were the modified Standard Pennants, at least three crew members of which subsequently became semi-permanent members of the BMC team.

The rally began in mild weather, but the weather forecast was not favourable, for it prophesied a cold spell with the warning that there would be snow later. There had already in fact been snow on high ground in Wales and the Lake District, and the more prudent competitors started with emergency snowchains and a pair of snow tyres. Owing to the number of speed tests which were to be included in the rally it was essential to have normal road tyres as well as snow tyres, and as the tyre companies had not then provided a rally service comparable with their racing service, the competitors and competition managers had to make the best arrangements that they could.

The Hastings and Blackpool starters joined up at Prescott, where the cars were placed in the paddock while waiting for their turn to climb the hill, which belongs to the Bugatti Owners' Club. Unfortunately, the ground was soft, and mud was taken up the hill, as a result of which the later numbers experienced more slippery conditions than the first arrivals. None of the BMC cars did outstandingly well in this test. The next port of call was at Chateau Impney, near Droitwich, where a simple manoeuvring test was held. The competitors had to accelerate up a hill for a few yards, stop astride a line, reverse into a side turning and then continue on up the hill and away over the crest, braking to a halt before a balk line. Not a very exciting test when compared with those in the continental events, but Wadham's Minor was fastest in Class 1.

After this test, the rally made its way into Wales by good roads over the Brecon Mountains to Epynt. The test here was an almost straight uphill dash on a narrow tarmac road for about 500 yards and it suited our drivers better. Pat Moss now made the best time in Class 1 and Les Leston followed suit in Class 3. The competitors then continued to Tenby and from there to Lydstep, which was another hill-climb. The weather had now turned very cold and there was a lot of ice on the approach road, which made it very slippery. There were several minor collisions here and Nancy Mitchell spun her Riley completely round. The climb itself was 350 yards long and drivers were required to stop astride a line, then reverse back clear of it and afterwards forward again to complete the test. It was Wadham's turn again to win Class 1, and Les Leston repeated his winning performance in Class 3.

The weather was now getting really nasty, with plenty of snow about, and the drivers were right in the wilds of Wales on minor roads which were every bit as slippery as anything the Monte Carlo Rally could supply. After a wintry cruise around the Pembrokeshire lanes, they were taken up north of the Cambrian mountains and thence over a hill track to the control at the *Elan Valley Hotel*, near Rhayader. There was a traffic block on the slippery hill before the control, where many cars became stuck and had to be pushed by other competitors, who had no choice but to help clear the road, although some people turned round and went back to look for another route. From

Rhayader the route went to Abbeycwmhir, where the control was on another slippery hill, in fact so slippery that the marshals begged the crews not to stop, but grabbed the route cars, stamped them and handed them back, all the while on the run.

At the Dylife control cars were going both ways and Nancy Mitchell turned back to look for another way in. It appeared that the blockage there was caused by a sudden drop over the brow of a hill, followed by a hairpin to the left about 50 yards down. There was also a cart track which went straight on, and quite a few cars took to this escape road. Other cars blocked the corner and a general melée ensued. In spite of the difficulties, three cars at least managed to get through, the Sunbeam of Peter Harper and Dr Bill Deane and two of the Standard Pennants, all fitted with chains. There were probably a few others who got through as well, but the bulk of the entry missed out the Dylife control and tried to get to Corwen by going up the old test hill of Bwlch-y-Groes. Lyndon Sims in the Aston Martin got stuck here and had to dig himself out, but in so doing he lost his route card in the snow and lost more time looking for it. Everyone who got to Corwen, therefore, was very relieved to hand in his or her route card and say "Goodbye" to Wales. From then on it was a fast run over good roads to Oulton Park, where the cars were set to cover three laps. The track itself was free of snow and a shortened circuit, taking in Esso Bend and a short-cut across Cascades, was used. Again our crews did well, Pat Moss and Les Leston making fastest times in their classes, and Jack Sears coming into the picture for the first time in Class 9.

It was not far from Oulton Park to Aintree, where the next test was run. Competitors were allowed one warming-up lap on the circuit, which was taken in the anti-clockwise direction so that none of those who had raced there before would benefit by their experience. Pat Moss continued to command her class, but Jimmy Ray's Sunbeam took over from Les Leston's Riley, although Jack Sears was still in the news in his class. It was apparent that this sort of test suited the racing boys, for Tommy Sopwith was also in the lead of Class 6 in the Jaguar. It was a straight-forward run from Aintree to Blackpool, where a manoeuvring test was held on the promenade, after which the cars were impounded in a closed park whilst the tired crews had a nine-hour rest period.

The scoreboard at the halfway stage read as follows:

1	Standard	R Gouldbourn and S Turner
2	Standard	T Gold and W Cave
3	Aston Martin	L Sims and H Walton

None of the BMC works cars were in the first 10 places, but Ken James was 10th in his privately-owned Riley 1.5. As few of the leaders had been prominent in the tests, this rally was obviously going to be won on the road.

Shortly after midnight, some 140 crews still willing to have a go headed away into the snowy darkness, with ominous reports of worse weather ahead. The first test that night was a 200-yard climb at a place called Tow Top, near Newby Bridge, where some other well-known names headed the classes, such as Anne Hall in Class 2, Edward Harrison in Class 5, both in Fords, and Paddy Hopkirk in Class 7 in one of the works Standard Pennants. As the rally headed north-west, the competitors met yet more snow and there was a control at the summit of Hard Knott Pass, which most of the crews considered too risky to visit if they were to reach the next test at Ulpha Summit, where the snow was a foot deep. As it was, only 57 cars reached this point. The results of the Ulpha test showed Pat fastest in Class 1, Anne Hall in Class 2 and Peter Harper in Class 3, while John Sprinzel was quickest in Class 7.

After a further climb over the moors, they went north to Ravenglass, Ennerdale, Loweswater and Caldbeck and then on to the plains near Carlisle. During the night there was trouble of all kinds and it was not surprising that many people were late or excluded. Cuth Harrison retired with something amiss in his steering and then heard that son Edward had hit a snow-covered heap of gravel. He took the parts which Edward needed to straighten out his car off his own and so Edward was able to continue. John Sprinzel, who had started in his own A35, that famous car 119 CMH, hit a telegraph pole near Carlisle and bent things very considerably. The same sad story continued when the rally crossed the border. Near Kelso, Paddy Hopkirk had rear axle trouble and the unpleasant noises made it all too apparent that something needed fixing without delay. He drove into the garage of a Standard agent, where the staff were sufficiently enthusiastic to remove an axle from a car in the showroom, and Paddy had another axle fitted and was away in 1 hour 4 minutes.

David Dixon, who was noted for his adventures, asked a local man the way to Otterburn. He followed the instructions to the letter, and was surprised to find himself in Otterburn, Yorks, instead of Otterburn, Northumberland. The main object of going to Scotland was the test at Charterhall, but the conditions for this were terrible as the track was covered with snow and ice. There was an unfortunate incident here involving a Jaguar which took the wrong route away from the course and met Gerry Burgess in his Ford head-on; both cars were forced to retire. Gerry, curiously enough, was involved in a similar incident at the end of the 1959 RAC Rally, fortunately without serious consequences – he was leading at the time and later won that event outright.

In spite of the weather, some good times were made by the later cars and finally Tommy Sopwith in his 3.4 Jaguar made the best time of the day. Pat, too, continued to maintain command of her class. The comic relief was supplied by John Whitmore who, having deposited his navigator in order to do the test alone, went off into the outfield and got lost for about half an hour. He finally came back and realized that the test started near where he had dropped his co-driver, but in a different direction from where he had been touring around.

The rally now returned to Otterburn where there were two more tests, one being a short sprint and the other a reversing test. The snow was even deeper here and it was now definite that the event would be won on the road, not decided by the tests. Soon after this Nancy Mitchell came to grief, overshooting a corner where a road ran downhill to cross a stream at right-angles. This was a noted local hazard, which had caught the unwary before, but would probably not have caught Nancy if it had not been icy. The Riley went through a dry-stone wall and then end-over-end down a 50-foot slope. Both of the crew were badly shaken and Nancy had a suspected cracked rib. Fortunately, Dr Penny in his Riley was one of the first on the scene, followed shortly afterwards by Dr Bill Deane, who was navigating for Peter Harper. After first aid was administered, Bill Day and Dr Penny took Nancy to the Bowes control and Les Leston followed with Joan Johns. Nancy was allowed to leave the Darlington Hospital the next day and was soon all right again, whilst Joan was able to go home that same day.

Although the results of this accident might have been more serious, I think it served to illustrate a typical rally misfortune. The modern saloon car was very strong, and if the crew were wearing good harnesses they were not likely to suffer more than bruises and shock when running out of road. Nobody had accidents on purpose and it usually took several factors to cause one; for example, lack of concentration when an emergency cropped up. Many of us have probably avoided accidents by quick thinking and many more would be avoided if only we trained ourselves to concentrate all the time so that when the emergency arose we were instinctively prepared to do the right thing. Unfortunately, the training needed to do the right thing instinctively has so often to be gained the hard way, by sad experience. It was here, I felt, that the specialized motoring schools could assist by helping to cultivate high-speed reactions on special circuits built on private ground. It was clear to me that it would be a long time before all our roads were built to minimize accidents, and I advocated that every driver should constantly endeavour to improve his own standards and get into the habit of criticizing his driving from day to day. The Highway Code by then had become a very sensible publication, yet how many of us could honestly say at the end of the day that we had not been guilty of ignoring some of its advice?

But to return to the rally. The next test was at Croft airport, near Darlington, where the drivers did two laps of a circuit, with five cars in each heat. Nothing very spectacular emerged from this test as the course was less slippery than at Charterhall. Test 14, a half-mile sprint, took place at Sherburn-in-Elmet, and by this time the competitors must have been getting a bit tired of tests which were similar enough, apart from the varied weather conditions, to make them boring. The next stop was at the Ferodo factory at Chapel-en-le-Frith, where the crews were treated to supper and were able to wash and rest.

The whole organization for this was arranged by Ferodo's Syd Henson, who must have been inspired to some degree by the excellent breakfast stop which Philips provided at Eindhoven during the Tulip Rally. A nice touch was that the loudspeakers announced the correct rally time at regular intervals, just in case anybody should oversleep. Test 15 also took place here; it was a manoeuvring test around pylons in the yard, and produced quite a different selection of class winners, with the exception of Paddy Hopkirk, who must have brought over some of his versatility from the Circuit of Ireland.

After this interlude, the rally wound its way south to better weather with speed tests at Snetterton, in Norfolk, and at Mallory Park and Silverstone in the Midlands. I attended the test at Silverstone and enjoyed seeing Pat in her Minor 1000 and Jack Sears in the Austin-Healey driving really beautifully on the Club circuit. It was the previous year that Pat had reported seeing an elephant coming down the road during the rally; she was laughed at by everyone until another competitor told the same story and it was then realized that a circus was on the move.

We drove down to the final test at Brands Hatch, which again was taken in the 'wrong' direction. Kelden, the Swede in a Saab, won the small-car class and Jack Sears repeated the performance in the big GT one. The bent cars and tired crews finally arrived at Hastings late that evening for a night in bed before their last fling the next day. This was a manoeuvring and braking test on the seafront, mainly designed to amuse the locals as it had very little bearing on the results. However, the RAC did not seem to have the same appeal as a continental event and the continentals must have thought the same thing as only one of them took the trouble to come, and he was more than a little puzzled when Paddy Hopkirk received the prize for the best 'Foreigner'.

The results were:

1	Sunbeam Rapier	657 marks	P Harper and Dr E W Deane
2	Standard Pennant	1,179 marks	R A Gouldbourn and S Turner
3	Standard Pennant	1,231 marks	T Gold and W Cave
4	Morris Minor 1000	1,474 marks	Pat Moss and Ann Wisdom
5	Morris Minor 1000	1,507 marks	W H Wadham and P C Wadham

Ladies' prize: Pat Moss and Ann Wisdom

The prizegiving took place at the *White Rock* pavilion, but the party spirit was not the same as when the crews were abroad; perhaps it was the wine, perhaps the food, but we did seem to become less inhibited as soon as we crossed the Channel. Looking back on the event, it was saved from being a dull and uninteresting rally by the weather. It turned out to be the last of the series which followed the old pattern, and I don't think anybody was sorry. The prize money was poor and the trophies were rather traditional. Furthermore, English seaside resorts are not exactly amusing in winter, with the wind whistling around the boarded-up amusement arcades and the seas dashing over the promenade.

The following year, Jack Kemsley was given a very free hand by the RAC Competitions Committee. Jack realized that the event would have to have a financial backer in the same manner as the best continental rallies, and he found a sponsor in Lombank, the finance house; from that day on the rally went from strength to strength. Each year the prizes became better, the organization improved and the route was more interesting.

The 1959 event was a great success in spite of the 'Braemar Incident', which led to a protest by Wolfgang Levy, the DKW driver from Berlin, to whom Stuart Turner was acting as navigator. The trouble arose in Scotland and I cannot do better than quote from Edward Eves' report in *Autocourse*; he wrote:

"....This year the event was run on the classic European pattern. Although there were bones of contention, notably in relation to the handling of the Tomintoul section, which landed the club with a fair sized headache, this was the best RAC Rally to date. Very courageously, bearing in mind the time of the year, the club had routed the rally as far north as Nairn and Gairloch in Scotland but had not endowed the organization in that country with sufficient flexibility to deal with the possibilities of bad weather. When it was found that the road over the Ladder Hills between Nairn and Braemar was blocked by snow, the controller at Nairn was not empowered to alter the route; thus the whole rally became a game of chance.

"The possibilities open to the competitors were either to have a go at the Tomintoul section, which meant that in the event of failure it was impossible to get to Braemar by clear roads in time; or to take clear roads from Grantown to Braemar, which meant exceeding the rally average by a big margin and still acquiring some penalties for lateness, then being faced by the Devil's Elbow, itself on the snow list and another imponderable, which meant, if closed, a huge detour to Stonehaven on the east coast, thence by the coast road to Kinross, the next control; or finally to strike west to join the A9 south of Boat of Garten, cutting out the Braemar and Blairgowrie controls absolutely. The people who took the second decision proved to be right, but in so doing laid themselves and the club open to protests about their average speed over the alternative route. Perhaps this difficulty might have been overlooked were it not for the fact that the European Touring Championship now hinged on the decision. If the protests were upheld, the outright winner of the Rally would have been Wolfgang Levy of Berlin, driving a works Auto Union 1000. When this protest had been turned down by the Royal Automobile Club, Levy's protest was to go before the *CSI* and the *FIA* in Paris. Eventually this final appeal did not take place, Levy withdrawing gracefully, and Gerry Burgess therefore became the official winner."

The lesson was taken to heart and the 1960 event improved as a result. The organization became more flexible and steps were taken to see that communication was maintained between Rally HQ and the controls. The 1960 RAC Rally was the second of the Club's new-style rallies, and it very nearly came up to the organizers' expectations. The competitors had less to criticize than ever before, so the organizers knew that the new pattern was basically right.

The rally became even more exciting than it might otherwise have been by reason of the fact that both the European Rally Championship and the *Coupe des Dames* in the same Championship could have been decided by it. The Championship was in dispute between the Germans, Schock and Moll, works drivers for Mercedes-Benz, who had 154 points, and the Frenchman, Rene Trautmann, who had collected 128 points; thus Trautmann could only win the Championship if the Germans were to be unplaced and he won the event outright.

The ladies' contest lay between the Swedish Champion, Ewy Rosqvist, who was accompanied by her sister Anita in their Volvo, and the British pair, Pat Moss and Ann Wisdom. If Ewy won the *Coupe des Dames* in the RAC, the ladies' section of the Rally Championship would be drawn, but if our girls finished ahead of Ewy, then Pat and Ann would win the title.

The BMC entries consisted of:

Austin-Healey 3000	Donald and Erle Morley
Austin-Healey 3000	Ronnie Adams and John Williamson
Austin-Healey 3000	Peter Riley and Tony Ambrose
Morris Mini-Minor	David Seigle-Morris and Vic Elford
Morris Mini-Minor	Tom Christie and Ninian Paterson
Austin-Healey Sprite	Pat Moss and Ann Wisdom
Austin-Healey Sprite	Tommy Gold and Mike Hughes

In addition to the works entries, there were several well-fancied private entries also driving BMC cars; amongst these were John Sprinzel and Dick Bensted-Smith, Sebring Sprite, and Douglas Johns and Rupert Jones in the special ex-works Wolseley 1500 which had been driven by John Gott in the 1958 Monte Carlo Rally. This car had had a busy life, starting with the 1958

Monte and running in a number of club rallies in the UK, so had done almost three years' hard work before the 1960 RAC Rally.

The rally started from Blackpool on November 21. The competitors were issued with a Tulip Rally-style road book the day before and they spent most of their spare time plotting the route on to one-inch Ordnance Survey maps. As these British maps are the most detailed in the world, plotting was not difficult for the English competitors or for the foreign competitors with British navigators. However, in spite of the excellent maps, Ewy and Anita got in a muddle and persuaded some of the Knowldale boys to help them mark their maps. I don't think much persuading was necessary, as anyone who knew Ewy and Anita might have guessed, for neither was lacking in grace and charm. I did not find out about the help which the boys had given them until later, but when I did I was very annoyed because the crews I was employing were giving aid and comfort to Pat and Ann's rivals for the ladies' crown. The offenders looked me straight in the eye and said, "I didn't think you would mind." Perhaps I wouldn't have done if I had been persuaded to mark the maps.

We made our Blackpool headquarters at the Morris agents, Brown and Mallalieu, where we dealt with several minor panics, including changing a clutch on one of the Minis. We had to send to the works for the parts and, as there was a lot of rain and fog about, I had doubts whether the car would get through on time with them, but it did and the crew stopped to help us with the work. The cars left at the usual one-minute interval from a floodlit ramp which had been erected in Middle Walk opposite the *Imperial Hotel*.

At 18.00 hours the Mayor of Blackpool lowered the Union Jack, to the accompaniment of a salvo of flashes from press cameras, and the Morley twins were the first away on a journey of over 2,000 miles. The crowd watched most of the field follow them and finally the last of the 170 starters had gone. Long before that, however, Mike Bond and I were on the road to Peebles in one of the 'Barges' (as we nicknamed the big Austin A99s) followed by three mechanics in another. We planned to get a little sleep at the Peebles *Hydro* before the first car arrived at about six the following morning. Meanwhile, the first section took the rally across Lancashire into Yorkshire, where they spent the night wandering about in the Pennines before arriving at Brough after midnight. The Morley brothers came into the control at Sayers garage without loss of points, but only five other cars arrived here without penalty. The Yorkshire section had been very foggy, and the task of keeping to a 30mph average in fog was not easy; there was evidence of this in the large number of bent front ends which had to be straightened at Brough, by which place the competitors had covered 180 miles.

It was actually before here that the final round of the European Rally Championship was decided, as the Citroen team came to grief when Trautmann went through a stone wall and was followed by his team-mate, who had been tailing him in the fog. Two of the Citroens remained in the hunt, those of Marang and Peter Bolton, but Marang's navigator, Badoche, was very car sick, the twisty British roads being too much for him. Thus Schock and Moll were unbeatable and had merely to trundle round to the finish without any risk. Unfortunately they and the other two Mercedes crews thought the rally was now a bore and the effort required for an outright win did not seem to interest them, so they decided to retire, although Schock and

Moll were only five minutes late. This unsportsmanlike action was to bring down the wrath of Mercedes-Benz on their heads, but such things were soon forgotten and before long they were back in favour again.

John Sprinzel in the Sprite was 'clean' over the first section whilst Pat and Ann dropped four minutes. The experts complained bitterly of balking by the less experienced crews. This complaint was more usual in British events run on secondary roads than in continental events where the standard of the entry in those days was certainly of a higher quality. The solution to this problem seemed to be to seed the best crews and to place them in the forepart of the entry. This was done the following year with marked success, but there were disadvantages for the service crews, who become inundated by their cars, which seemed to arrive at the same time. In some events, cars were grouped by make and cubic capacity so that those of approximately the same performance should have run in company, but the disparity in the performances of the crews usually brought the balking problem into prominence once more.

Sydney Allard had elected to run on spiked tyres, but without snow these tyres were not a great success and he left the road in his Zephyr at considerable velocity. He rejoined the rally later, but had lost a great many marks, so retired at Peebles. Amongst the more successful crews were Eric Jackson and Noel Donovan in a Ford Anglia, who were but one minute down, as also were Jack Sears and Willy Cave in the 3.8 Jaguar. Ewy and Anita had lost only three points in the Volvo and were thus leading the Ladies' class, which was a fine show for foreigners. Anne Hall and Valerie Domleo, who had had a puncture on the stage, were third with five minutes' lateness, as compared with four for our girls. It was on this rally, incidentally, that I discovered that Valerie, amongst her other accomplishments, was an officially accredited RAC timekeeper.

Peter Jopp and Les Leston had been up a 'wrong slot' and lost eight minutes in the process. Tish Ozanne and Pat Allison got stuck in a ford and were also forced off the road by another competitor and spent the night getting the car on the road again, but rejoined the rally in the morning. Gerry Burgess, too, was involved in some watery escapade and lost six minutes. Finally, Erik Carlsson and Stuart Turner, in the Saab, who were running near David Seigle-Morris and Vic Elford in the Mini-Minor, arrived without having lost any time.

The section from Brough to Peebles was not very difficult, but only 49 competitors managed to get through it without losing any marks. There was some confusion as to the exact location of a control and certain competitors eventually found their penalties annulled, so that the final number of unpenalized cars was later increased. There had been rumours before the start that farmers across the border resented the influx of cars which were to have passed through an area where there was an outbreak of foot and mouth disease. It was even said that some were about to contest the entry of 'foreign' cars with shotguns. The organizers solved the problem by avoiding the areas where the outbreaks had been reported and there was no trouble, but as a result the sprint which was to have taken place at Charterhall was cancelled.

This shortening of the route enabled the cars to arrive earlier than was anticipated at the *Hydro*, so the service crews had plenty of time for adjustments and the rally crews time for a good meal and a rest. From Peebles the cars made their way to the timed climb of Rest-and-be-Thankful, near the northern end of Loch Long, where there were two sharp turns near the top, from which it was possible to stand and observe the climb from start to finish.

Mike Bond and I had earlier left the mechanics to deal with both works and private entries at the *Hydro* and set off for the 'Rest' by a short-cut. We arrived at the summit, where the drivers parked their navigators and surplus equipment before returning to the bottom of the hill for the timed climb, and immediately we got our gas stove going, producing some very tasty sausages and buttered rolls with choice of tea or coffee; Raymond Baxter, I think, was one of our customers. Peter Riley made the fastest time of the big Healey team without meaning to do so. He had lost more road marks than the Morleys, who were still unpenalized, and had therefore been instructed to take it easy so as not to penalize them with his test points. He did so, but was still the quickest of the Healey drivers. I think this was a good example of driving in a relaxed manner and thus going faster. Several drivers did unexpected things at the second corner and had to reverse, much to the amusement of the crowd.

The next test was a two and a half mile dash over a difficult little road near Dalmally. Only one car in the entire rally did it within the correct time, and this was Erik Carlsson's Saab. One or two people suffered minor damage to the underneath of their cars as there were a couple of nasty bumps halfway up the section. There was a considerable delay here and the light must have been very poor by the time Erik Carlsson tackled the test, so his performance was all the more praiseworthy.

In order that there should be no undue haste in the outskirts of Inverness, the last control was placed at the *Drumossie Hotel*, situated a little way out of the town. The competitors came in from the direction of Inverfarigaig and were allowed half an hour to reach the closed park, which was on the other side of the town at Bught Park. Most people arrived with a few minutes in hand and our mechanics, who had come up by the direct route from Peebles, were able to take note of any requirements for servicing the next day. Cars were to be released from the closed park 90 minutes before their starting time from the *Delmore Road House* the next morning, and we were planning to make use of the excellent premises of Macrae and Dick, the Morris distributors, which were hard by the station.

Naturally, the crews did not waste much time over their evening meal at the *Station Hotel*, but I had time to check up on the various items which required attention before everyone retired to bed. One of the Healeys had a damaged sump and another car had trouble with the starter. Pat Moss as usual had already presented the mechanics with an itemized list which covered every detail. Before going to bed, I arranged to call the drivers and provide transport to the closed park. The navigators were to remain at the hotel and mark their maps while the cars were being serviced. On completion of the work, the cars would call at the *Station Hotel*, pick up the navigators and proceed to the starting control.

I took Pat down to the closed park in good time and was turning the car round to go back and fetch the next crew when I decided to stop and see that she had no trouble with starting her car. There were a few press photographers about and she spent the spare minutes with a short interview. Pat was about to enter the closed park when the official asked for her control card, as the exit gate from the enclosure was Time Control No 51. At this moment she realized that she had left the control card at the hotel and came running back to tell me. I left the area in a shower of stones and made a record run back to the hotel, having to pass two sets of traffic-lights in the process; fortunately, neither of them stayed red for long. I left the car blocking the station yard and ran into the hall. Fortunately again, I met one of our crews who knew that Ann Wisdom was correcting maps with Tony Ambrose and also remembered the room number. I ran up the stairs and burst in on the two navigators, who did not grasp the reason for my haste or lack of breath. "What card?" asked Ann; "The blue one", I gasped. Ann produced it without further comment, gave me a cold stare for having interrupted her calculations, and I got away without delay. I was back in the closed park in 11 minutes, but the delay had cost the girls five minutes and they were now down to third in the Ladies' class. A mistake like this, which had nothing to do with driving ability, was hard to stomach, but Pat and Ann set off on the next section determined to fight back.

At midday, the Morleys led the survivors away on the northern loop of a figure-of-eight which returned them to Inverness at 22.00 hours the same night. The route went round the Beauly Firth and Cromarty Firth and on to Golspie, then there was a noise control at Beauly, situated in the main street. The sound of the cars was measured accurately by means of a decibel-meter, but I don't think anybody suffered any penalties. The route then turned west and they went by way of Skiag Bridge to Stoer on the west coast. Shortly after, there was a Special Stage which began just near Inverkirkaig. This was 5.8 miles (9.28km) long and about as rough as anything to be found on any Special Stage in the Viking Rally. The road was narrow and there were plenty of rock outcrops on both sides and a high ridge covered with loose rocks in the middle. It had numerous bends and there was nowhere to run off without damage if one made a mistake. Needless to say there were plenty of holed sumps and petrol tanks and a few bent and scratched panels when competitors arrived at the other end.

Just south of this section there were considerable road repairs and road widening was in progress. It had rained a lot and the soft surface had been churned up into a sticky, creamy mudbath by the contractors' lorries. The cars arrived plastered with mud at Ullapool, where a friendly transport contractor had arranged to keep his garage open as long as we wished. Some of his staff stayed on as well and everyone was kept busy, welding sumps and straightening things out, although none of the works cars needed any attention at this point.

After this, the cars set off into the wilds again on the westerly road to Gairloch. One or two came to grief here, including John Whitmore, who went off the road through mistaking his navigator's instructions at a bend during one of the tighter sections. John was all in favour of retiring by the time they got back to Inverness, as he thought rallying far more dangerous than racing. The survivors eventually returned to the *Drumossie Hotel* at Inverness, where they were given time for a very quick meal before setting out on the second half of the figure-of-eight. It was a beautiful starlight night and the lights of cars could be seen wending their way over the moors. There were a couple of Special Stages, which were not really difficult, and the first car was back at the *Drumossie* at 05.30 hours. For want of anything better to do, Mike Bond and I went down to the *Golf View* café at Fort Augustus to see the crews through and joined the team over a welcome plate of bacon and eggs.

After everyone got away from the *Drumossie* for the last time to start the long trek down to Brands Hatch, we left for the Yorkshire section. Most of that day would be spent in reaching Bo'ness, taking the test on the hill there, and pressing on by way of Carnwath, Biggar and Broughton to the *Crook Inn*. We had been told by the navigators that there was a section near Carlisle which they had had some difficulty in interpreting from the road book. As the controls were under four miles apart, there would be no time for mistakes and it seemed prudent to check the road book on the spot and brief any of the BMC crews, private or works, who were in doubt.

Mike and I located the section in question and had some difficulty in finding our way round, for there were at least seven places where it was possible to make a mistake, although we ran over the road in daylight. There were several gates and some cattle in the fields. We contacted the local roadmender and he arranged for the gates to be left open. We asked him about the cattle and he said we should see the farmer up the road about it. The farmer said he enjoyed rallies, for nothing ever happened up there, and in any case there was always a chance of getting a car cheap. We asked him about the open gates and he said, "Well, there's not much to do up here, so maybe we'll fill in a bit of time herding them up again." Not all farmers have this point of view about rallies, and I am afraid that many rally crews are far too forgetful about gates during local events.

After we had completed our examination of this little section, Mike and I repaired to the local inn for shelter and sustenance, but there was not much comfort there. It was a small house, without electric light, with a dark bar and a poor fire. The publican was forced to work on the roads to augment his slender takings, and his wife lamented the days when they had lived nearer to Carlisle and she had been able to find someone with whom to gossip. While writing up our notes for the crews, we did at least manage to keep dry for it was pouring outside. The control was to be manned by the Army, who were using the experience as some sort of signalling exercise; they turned up in good time and set up shelter and a coke brazier as they knew that they would be there until near midnight. The local motor club officials turned up a bit later and soon the scene was set.

The Morley brothers arrived punctually and we told them that there was nothing to worry about if they kept to the right road and avoided the two or three 'wrong slots' which we indicated. I had to keep my fingers crossed because my car was fitted with a kilometre speedometer, which meant that we had to convert its readings back into miles, and to the nearest tenth of a mile at that. We waited until everyone whom we knew had gone past, and then left for Carlisle and on to Scotch Corner, where we stopped for a meal. Our own duties were now completed and we could take time off for a sleep and a meal while the rally visited such places as Lanercost, Alston, Middleton-in-Teesdale, Mickleton, Startforth, Barnard Castle and Melsonby as it swept across the North Yorkshire Moors and the Dales.

The night section in Yorkshire was the downfall of Ewy Rosqvist and her sister Anita, as they got confused at some of the junctions and arrived at a control seven minutes late; this was to lose them both the Ladies' Cup of the Rally Championship and the Ladies' Cup in this rally. Pat and Ann were now sure of winning the Championship Cup, and this achievement, in addition to their outright win in the Liège-Rome-Liège, second place in the Alpine Rally, eighth in the Tulip Rally and 17th in the Monte Carlo Rally, was to earn them the joint nomination by the Guild of Motoring Writers as Drivers of the Year for 1960. It was the first time that this highly coveted title had ever been given to two drivers jointly and the first time that it had ever been awarded to a lady. It was an award richly deserved by this magnificent crew, who had produced their very best form during 1960. What a contrast with 1959, which had started so well with a 10th General Classification and a *Coupe des Dames* in the Monte Carlo Rally and had then continued with a run of accidents or breakages, through the Tulip Rally, the Acropolis Rally, the Alpine and the Liège, before finishing, as it had begun, with a brilliant end-of-season performance as runners-up to Erik Carlsson in the German Rally. Pat had a theory that there were vintage years and non-vintage years for her in rallying and that they alternated.

It was during this night that many competitors were caught in a secret check for exceeding the top average of 40mph on one of the easy sections. This penalized about 20 crews, but as the clocks could only be read to the nearest minute there were protests, and the penalties were 'scrubbed'. It was most unfortunate that the Club chose this particular place and time to impose this type of control, as the road was very good and there was no traffic about so that in fact it was difficult to average less than 40mph.

Mike Bond and I spent the night at Doncaster and left fairly early on the next day for the Wolvey Anti-Skid School, where there was to be a test. During that night and early morning, the crews had visited Elvington Airfield and Mallory Park for speed tests. We did not get to Wolvey in time to see the larger cars perform, but managed to see the Austin-Healey Sprites and the Mini-Minors on the skidpan. The surface had been liberally dosed with what looked like soft soap, but this had been rather overdone and the course was so slippery that the test was rather a farce. However, David Dixon showed that he could skate on thin ice as well as anybody and made the best time for a big Healey, whilst Mike Sutcliffe in a Mini made FTD. Another excellent run was done by Marang in the Citroen, whose navigator pointed out to him the correct way to go by reading out instructions which John Gott had translated into French.

The rally was supposed to circumnavigate London by way of High Wycombe, Marlow, Maidenhead and Guildford and then through Reigate and Redhill to Brands Hatch. As the journey from Guildford to Brands Hatch had to be undertaken in the height of the evening rush-hour, it soon became evident that to average 30mph on what was then an antiquated apology for a main road was an impossibility and those who drove with reasonable caution failed to make the last control on time. As a result, the organizers rightly decided to cancel the time penalties incurred on this last run-in. We saw the cars parked in pouring rain for the night at Brands Hatch while the competitors were taken to London in motor coaches and dropped at their various hotels.

Tommy Gold turned up at the finish after spending most of the rally at Brough where he had run into gearbox trouble and had sought the help of the 'Allison' garage. Father Allison, whose son Cliff and daughter Pat had made names for themselves in motorsport, provided and fitted a service box. Tommy and Mike had retired from the rally, for they would have served no useful purpose by finishing at the end of the entries, which they would have done, even supposing they could have missed only two controls by the time the new gearbox was fitted. As it happened, the exchange gearbox was not available until the next day, so they filled in the time while the rally went to Scotland by seeing the sights of Brough when the pubs were shut and by serving behind the bar in one of the 'locals' during opening time. As Tommy had got into training while up there, he demanded large quantities of draught beer from our hotel and was somewhat put out to be told that they didn't serve draught beer. I don't think Tommy approved of my choice of London hotels, but I thought it very comfortable.

The following morning we all returned to Brands Hatch for the races, which were to be run by classes over the new long GP circuit. Unfortunately they had lost some of their importance as some classes were so small, and the position was further complicated by the fact that competitors who had failed to finish the road section within the time allowances, and who were therefore not really finishers at all, were allowed to compete. This was done to give the private owners full value for their entry fees, but it was a little hard on drivers in search of test points.

The track was wet and slippery and the first race promised to be as exciting as any. The front row of the grid comprised John Rhodes in an Aston Martin and the three works Austin-Healey 3000s driven by Donald Morley, Peter Riley and Ronnie Adams. As John Sprinzel was placed equal second with the Morleys in General Classification, with two road marks lost, the other members of the team had instructions to let Donald Morley finish in front of them, and we hoped that Donald would beat the Aston Martin. This would make it imperative for John Sprinzel to win his race if he wished to hang on to his second place. Naturally this was not of vital importance for they were both in Austin-Healeys and both were British-entered and driven.

The flag fell and the four cars surged forward in line abreast to Paddock Bend. It looked as if no-one was going to give an inch, and no-one did until Peter Riley slid off on the outside and took to the grass; he straightened it up and got back on the track about 200 yards further on. This exploit was copied by the Aston Martin, which was right on Peter's tail. The resulting scramble put Donald Morley off his line and he spun down the hill into a convenient bay on the right-hand side of the track, where he had to wait until the rest of the field had gone past. Donald put on his pass lights and set to work to make up the lost time. Driving like a master, he was soon through the ruck of the field and back in fourth place. His two team-mates noticed that he was missing and slowed down on the back part of the course, letting the Aston Martin through to win. Donald eventually caught them up and a well-disciplined team finished with Donald in second place and the two other Healeys in line astern just behind him. The Aston was well driven, but I wish Donald had been up with Rhodes during the first lap and then we should have seen an even better race. As it was, Donald and the team got the applause of the crowd for a fine display of team driving and a good recovery from what might have been a disastrous situation. The fact that all our cars finished the race clinched the award of the manufacturer's team prize to the Austin-Healeys, making the third that season.

The race for Touring cars up to 850cc was almost as exciting. The front row of the grid comprised our friend Erik Carlsson in the Saab, who was now the outright winner of the rally, David Seigle-Morris in a Mini-Minor and John Whitmore, who technically was not in the rally at all, also in a Mini. Much to everyone's surprise, David reached Paddock Bend before Erik and established a comfortable lead by the end of the first lap. By means of some very furious driving John Whitmore eventually also caught Erik, who must have been taking things fairly quietly. They both entered Paddock Bend together and John took Carlsson on the inside, forcing him onto the grass, but he took this all in his stride and was soon back on the road to finish third. Erik's comment afterwards was, "David's Mini, she go very well I think." After some more calculations were made, it was evident that John Sprinzel was firmly entrenched in second place whether he won his race or not, so he was content to finish at his own pace, as his back springs and shock absorbers were not quite right. Anne Hall was flagged in a lap too early in her race, but she still won the Ladies' Cup with a loss of only five points on the road section.

I put in a mild protest about the marks lost by our girls at Inverness, but was reminded by the Stewards that the exit control was a time control, so that if they did not penalize us for the lateness they could penalize us much more for not obeying an instruction in the Red Book. I did not protest with a view to depriving Anne Hall of her laurels, but because I felt that there should be no penalty for removing a car late when in practice it only deprived the crew in question of the use of the car and had no bearing on their performance in the rally. For example, suppose a crew felt that rest was more important than service to the car, why should they have to remove the car from the closed park before they needed it to drive to the Starting Control? Still, rules are written to be obeyed and we should all have read them more carefully. As a result Pat and Ann were second in the Ladies' Cup and second in their class.

After all this, there was a rush back to London and from our hotel to the 'Talk of the Town' at the *London Hippodrome*. The winning Saab and its crew arose from below the stage in front of the organizing committee, who sat behind the impressive array of prizes. The floor show was dazzling and Eartha Kitt was her usual exotic and seductive self. This was just the type of show to blend with the prizegiving and the speeches were short and to the point. The dinner was adequate for the occasion and a very good time was had by all. There was no doubt that Jack Kemsley and his hundreds of unseen helpers had done a good job of work.

We came away with a fine collection of prizes, including the coveted manufacturer's team prize. The class places BMC gained added up to one-third of the total, and were as given below. Particularly meritorious amongst the BMC results were those of David Seigle-Morris and Vic Elford in the Mini-Minor, second in their class and sixth in General Classification, and of Douglas Johns and Rupert Jones, who won the 1,301 to 2,000cc class for Grand Touring cars in their modified Wolseley 1500 against some strong opposition.

Touring cars up to 850cc

1	Saab	E Carlsson and S Turner (and outright winner)
2	Morris Mini-Minor	D Seigle-Morris and V Elford
3	Morris Mini-Minor	T Clark and K Coombs

851 to 1,000cc

1	Triumph	I Lewis and G Sheppard
2	Ford	G Crabtree and S Woolley
3	Ford	Mrs A Hall and Miss V Domleo

1,001 to 1,600cc

1	Volvo	J Wallwork and H Brooks
2	Volkswagen	A Bengry and D Skeffington
3	Sunbeam	J Ray and P Dingley

1,601 to 2,500cc

1	Citroen	M Marang and M Badoche
2	Citroen	P Bolton and G Shanley

Over 2,500cc

1	Jaguar	P Berry and J Sears
2	Ford	G Burgess and S Croft-Pearson
3	Ford	I Walker and J Uren

Grand Touring cars up to 1,300cc

1	Austin-Healey Sprite	J Sprinzel and R Bensted-Smith
2	Austin-Healey Sprite	Miss P Moss and Miss A Wisdom
3	Austin-Healey Sprite	J Kirkham and J Baldam

1,301 to 2,000cc

1	Wolseley	D Johns and R Jones
2	Sunbeam	J Melvin and W Bennett
3	Wolseley	C Bent Marshall, D Pratt and R Gahan

Over 2,000cc

1	Austin-Healey 3000	D Morley and E Morley
2	Austin-Healey 3000	P Riley and J Ambrose
3	Triumph	G Grimshaw and B Melia

Manufacturer's team award

BMC Austin-Healey 3000 D and E Morley, P Riley and J Ambrose, R Adams and J Williamson

Ladies' Cup

Ford Anglia   Mrs A Hall and Miss V Domleo

CHAPTER 11

The Portuguese and other rallies

"I felt sure the Customs officials would arrest me at any moment for my four crossings of the International Bridge in 15 minutes."

During my time with BMC there were other International rallies besides the famous six to which I have devoted separate chapters, but most of the others had varying fortunes and few were run to the same pattern each year. An exception was the Midnight Sun, this Swedish event really being the preserve of the Scandinavians, for other European rally drivers had never made much of an impression there. The road section was easy, but the Special Stages were so specialized that a great deal of local knowledge and technique was necessary if fast times were to be made.

The Viking Rally, which became the Norwegian National Rally and no longer a Rally Championship event was again the preserve of the locals and was similar in character to the Midnight Sun. The Rally of a Thousand Lakes, the Championship event for Finland, was also likely only to be won by Scandinavians; the few British crews who had competed had crashed, but at least they had had a real try.

The Geneva Rally, organized by the Automobile Club of Switzerland, was not held regularly and ranged from a promenade sprinkled with regularity tests to a very sporting event of considerable toughness. Owing to the Swiss attitude to competitive motoring, it was run in France and Italy, with a token crossing of the Swiss frontier for the start and finish. The 1960 event was well-organized and proved a good test for both car and crew. The German Rally also took place in the French Alps and was well run, but there had been a sad bias in favour of some of the German crews on occasions. The Yugoslav event was another rally which had an intermittent career and the results sometimes took so long to obtain that one wondered what they were at.

The Polish Rally had the making of a great event once the organizers overcame the difficulties allied to state control of all transport there. It was impossible to bring any prizemoney out of Poland and petrol was very expensive, as well as being of poor quality. The Poles were enthusiastic spectators at the speed events and turned up in their thousands, as was to be expected of a nation starved of entertainment.

The Spanish and Portuguese National Clubs took it in turn to run the Iberian Rally but, due to the fact that motorsport was then non-existent in Spain, the Portuguese eventually took over the event completely. As a courtesy, the rally started from various cities in Spain and Portugal, but a common route was used after the necessary mileage had been accumulated. The 1959 Portuguese Rally was of some importance to us because it took place at the end of the season and we hoped that Pat and Ann would obtain some Ladies' Touring Championship points and catch up with Annie Soisbault. In order that there should be at least three feminine crews at the start, we ran two of these ourselves, but Annie had other ideas. I also decided to use the event as a try-out for the Mini-Minors before starting them in the 1960 Monte Carlo. We therefore started with Pat and Ann in an Austin-Healey 3000 and two Mini crews made up by Nancy Mitchell and Pat Allison, and Peter Riley and Tony Ambrose. For fun, I entered myself with Den Green as my navigator in the Wolseley 6/99, which carried the crews' baggage and spare parts. The team's adventures in the rally make such a contrast with one of the great 'classics' that I cannot forbear to relate some of the more hectic moments.

We crossed over to Dunkirk on the night boat on Monday, November 30, that is to say, we all crossed except Pat Allison, for she had left her passport in London and had to go back for it! This was not exactly the right way to start as co-driver to Nancy Mitchell, who liked efficiency in all departments and especially in her co-drivers. Pat was told to catch a 'plane to Barcelona and we set off for Limoges. I felt in my bones that the expedition was not going to be a success, and this was the first setback. We reached Limoges without further incident, but the hotel was being redecorated and looked terrible.

The following morning was foggy and depressing, but everyone was ready to start on time and we were soon on our way, making good time as far as Brive, where Ann Wisdom discovered that she had left her tartan holdall complete with her passport in the hotel garage. The girls were sent back to fetch it and the rest of the party arranged to meet them in Toulouse, if they did not catch us up before. We went on through Cahors and Montauban and finally reached Toulouse for lunch without worrying too much, for we thought the girls must have stopped for a meal further back. We selected one of the best eating places in the city and started lunch. I think it was the *Richelieu-Michel* and, judging by the locals who patronized it, we had picked well. It was an excellent meal and we kept two spare chairs at the table as we thought Pat and Ann might come in after all. Of course, the fatal 'phone rang and my lunch was abruptly terminated by the news that Miss Moss had been involved in an accident with a cyclist and a stationary Citroen in Cahors.

I sent others on to Barcelona and Dennis and I made good time back to Cahors. On reaching the girls, it was evident that things could have been better but, on the other hand, they could have been a great deal worse. Pat and Ann, having found the missing bag at the hotel in Limoges, were returning by the same route as they had taken and had got as far as Cahors. They were through the town and nearly out of the suburbs when a cyclist, who was on the right-hand side of the road, decided to turn left into a factory without a signal of any sort. Pat's amazingly quick reaction undoubtedly saved the youth's life, for he was knocked off his bike by the action of running into the right-hand side of the Healey, as Pat swerved to the left. There was an imprint of the cyclist's posterior on the right-hand rear wing of the Healey to prove the point. Unfortunately, Pat was now on the left of the road and forced to a quick stop by the fact that the road was blocked by a stationary ID Citroen belonging to the local taxi-driver. He had stopped at a coachbuilder's to see about a minor repair and now needed a front valance and repairs to the bonnet as well.

The Healey had broken both the foglights, damaged one headlight and some of the radiator surround and there was a minor derangement to the steering. Den Green and I, assisted by the local panel-beater, set to work on the car but, after I had acted as interpreter and got the job going, I took the girls off to find a pair of French foglights and to get something for them to eat. All the hotels were closed for the afternoon and none of them was prepared to do anything about it; the town seemed to be the most inhospitable I had ever encountered in all of France. After we had tried no less than six restaurants, we found the *Eskaulduna* in the Place Thiers where they were extremely helpful and put on an impromptu meal without further delay. When we finally returned to the garage, the job was well advanced and after about an hour we were able to leave.

As the Healey steered all right and the lamps were working, there seemed to be a good chance that we would reach Spain that night, but it was dark by the time we had passed through Toulouse and darker still after we had stopped for a coffee and a cake at some café near Carcassonne. I had not had time to look up the opening and closing times of the frontier posts, but it was evident that we would have to hurry if we were to get to the frontier by midnight. We stopped again at Perpignan to fill up with petrol and I asked when the frontier closed, for it was about 11pm. The man said "They close at nine in the winter, Monsieur." So that was that, until nine the next morning when they would open again. We found a hotel with some spare rooms and a built-in garage and retired without delay. It seemed to have been a long while since we left Limoges.

The next day we crossed over the frontier, after the usual long-winded Customs formalities which were a feature of some countries in those days. We were in Barcelona for a late lunch, scrutineering and the start of the rally, and I was relieved to see that Fanny Allison had turned up. John Sprinzel said he knew the way to the scrutineering and volunteered to lead us to it, but after taking us five times round the middle of the city in the evening rush-hour he lost us and departed. At this moment it became apparent that the front wheel of my car was about to fall off. Investigation showed that all the wheel nuts had come loose, which was curious as they had been tightened that day. I can only suppose that someone bore me a grudge and made the wheel loose, hoping it would come off during the rally. We picked up a taxi-driver who knew where we were to go and all was well; Sprinzel arrived afterwards. The cars were passed and nobody said that they thought there was anything wrong with our numbers.

That night we set off for Madrid and I was sorry to have seen so little of Barcelona for it was, I discovered later in the rally, the most exciting city we were to see in the whole Iberian peninsula. The hotel we stayed at was wonderful and the service was superb, but unfortunately our stay was too brief. The road to Madrid was varied in both surface and traffic; there were few private cars in Spain, but plenty of buses and lorries, and they all drove in the middle of the road until the last moment. There was no welcome from the Automobile Club in Madrid and, as far as I know, nothing was arranged in the way of refreshments. Nancy excelled herself by arriving slightly late at the control and reversing backwards downhill into it and was thus unpenalized.

Leaving Madrid, we ran north across the windy plains which were swept by rain shed from the low grey clouds. I had always thought of Spain as sunny in winter, but all we saw was rain and muddy side roads. We reached San Sebastian that evening, where we had time for a meal before returning to Burgos and then on to Valladolid. I think it was at Salamanca that we ran into Annie Soisbault in her Triumph who, by a complete coincidence, had turned up to watch the rally with some trivial excuse for not having started. The Portuguese Rally was therefore a non-scorer for Ladies' Championship points, for only our two ladies' teams had started. We crossed the frontier into Portugal, but found that we had two hours to wait, for the organizers had allowed one hour for Customs formalities and seemed to have forgotten that there was a difference of an hour between Spanish and Portuguese times.

After we reached Portugal, there was a test of total regularity with several secret checks. We were doing quite well when Dennis told me that he had stopped the watch by mistake; I told him not to worry as I had started the spare one that I had round my neck on a lanyard. We made all the controls on time and went on to Aveiro for a couple of tests, which took all day. The first was a very long manoeuvring test which the local entrants must have known by heart, for the Mercedes 300SL driver was doing power turns round the pylons with great skill. I lost myself near the far end and wasted about 15 seconds, so losing a place in the class as a result. The afternoon test was run in rain and consisted of two laps round a block of houses, of which each side was about 200 yards long. The object of the operation was to go as fast as possible, but at equal speeds. Pat drove absolutely superbly and managed to set the Healey up in a powerslide of nearly 45 degrees, coming out of the last corner on each occasion. This appealed to the Portuguese, who must never have seen a woman drive like this before. The safety arrangements were sketchy, as there were a number of unpadded lamp-posts and a local school situated on the course, but nothing unpleasant happened.

The last test was at Estoril, but before that we lost the way through following that great navigator – shall I dare say it – Miss Ann Wisdom! Luckily Dennis spotted the mistake and we got to the control with a few seconds to spare. Dennis jumped out with the card and ran towards the clock, but failed to notice a low stone wall which caught him on the shins, so that he landed at the appropriate place on his face. A very gallant navigator indeed! The last test was a farce as a difference of a hundredth of a second could fatally affect the result. I think two-hundredths actually dropped one man 30 places! As it was timed by a piece of cotton which the cars had to break to stop the watch, and not by a photoelectric eye, there was plenty of room for error.

When the results were published they showed that nearly all the foreign crews had been penalized for using numbers which were not black on a white circle. We all pointed out that our own numbers were readable and that there could not have been anything much wrong with them as we had all been observed to have done the regularity test correctly by night. I also added a clause to the effect that we felt that such a penalty was not within the spirit of the International Sporting Code, and not likely to foster friendly relations. The officials sent one of their lesser office staff to deal with us and never even condescended to see any of the protesting crews in person. The sequel to our protest was a further penalty of 10 points for incorrect numbers on the other side of the car.

We left Portugal the next day without any regrets and scraped through the

Spanish Customs at one minute to nine, much to the annoyance of the Spaniards who had already put the chain in place across the road. We spent the night at one of the national guest houses, known as *paradores*, at Cuidad Rodrigo, a great castle with enormously thick walls and great polished floors. The housekeeper was beautiful and severe and looked as if she might have come out of a novel by Daphne Du Maurier. The food, although not up to the standards of Estoril, was adequate for the surroundings, but perhaps this impression was due to the champagne being less than 10 shillings (50p) a bottle.

The next day we lunched at Burgos and looked forward to sleeping the night in France. These calculations were nearly brought to nothing by a landslide, which made a diversion a necessity. The more obstinate members of the party pressed on and waited until the road was cleared, whilst those who were travelling behind took the diversion. The result of splitting up the party was that Fanny and I found ourselves at Hendaye, armed with Nancy Mitchell's passport. After waiting at the French Customs for nearly an hour it dawned upon us that the bridge over which we had come was not the International Bridge and we went off to find it. Our suspicions were confirmed, for there were the others sitting in a café at the other end of the International Bridge. I walked back to the Mini, collected Nancy's passport and then crossed the bridge for the third time with the vital document. The others did not give us a hearty welcome, as most people were thinking about food and beds. I felt sure that Customs officials would arrest me at any moment for my four crossings of the International Bridge in 15 minutes. Peter Riley, with his infallible skill for choosing a good restaurant, piloted us to a very excellent Basque house a couple of miles away and we all felt much better after we had eaten. We stayed that night in Biarritz, and the next day the team went off to practise for the Monte Carlo Rally, whilst I took Pat's Healey back to England. The run up to Paris was one of the most enjoyable I have ever had, for the roads were almost empty and the car was going well. I did the 747 kilometres in a little under seven and a half hours, which must be an average of around 62mph.

The sequel to this Portuguese Rally took place in Monte Carlo in 1960, when the *CSI* heard the protest which the Germans, French and British had submitted to them through their own National automobile clubs, who supported them to the hilt. The result was that the protests were upheld; my own, concerning the numbers and the way in which we were treated in Portugal, was withdrawn when I was told that the French and Germans had won the day. The principle had been established, so there was no point in taking the matter any further. The Portuguese decided after this that they did not wish to run a Rally Championship event again and so the rally was not held in either 1960 or 1961. To be fair to the younger Portuguese drivers, who were good sportsmen, they came to us after the event and explained that the organizing club did not represent the wishes of the majority of the competition drivers, but that there was another club which did, and this organized a first-class sporting event of national status. There seemed to me to be a similarity here to Portuguese politics.

Another event, which used to follow soon after the Monte Carlo Rally, was the Sestriere Rally. The 1960 rally was to have taken place in February, and the BMC team arrived in Turin a couple of days before the start. Several of the passes over which the route lay were snowed up, but a thaw was setting in.

The Minister for the Interior, however, decided that the road conditions were too bad, bearing in mind the number of police who would have had to be out on the roads before and during the event, so refused the permit. The organizers returned the entrance fees and divided the prizemoney equally between the entrants.

We returned to the *Hotel Ligure* feeling in need of a drink and a meal before planning to return to England the next day. There was a telegram waiting for me and, on opening it, I learned that Margaret Hall, my assistant, had been killed in a car accident. This was a terrible shock and, assisted by Tony Ambrose, I drove back across France that night, reaching Abingdon the following afternoon. During the previous two years, Margaret had lived for two things, her two boys and her work. She was loved and admired by everyone who met her, and through her work the department went from strength to strength. It has always been a source of deep regret to me that she never lived to see the great successes which followed in the years of 1960 and 1961. Fortunately, the Royal Air Force Benevolent Fund looked after the education of her two boys, John and Bobby, and her many admirers contributed quite a sizeable sum which was placed in trust for the boys.

In 1959 there was a small team of enthusiasts who raced an MGA and an Austin-Healey while they were up at Balliol College. They often came to visit me in my office, and whenever I wanted a file or a telephone number I used to yell at Margaret around the corner of the dividing doorway. When the leader of the team was due to return to Canada, there was a little celebration at which I was presented with a silver hand-bell, suitably inscribed, so that Margaret might be summoned in a more dignified manner. The bell has long been silent.

CHAPTER 12

Long-distance records

"I thought that I must be quite mad rushing round a concrete saucer in the middle of the night while my wife and children were at home depending upon me."

The *Federation Internationale de l'Automobile* supervised the observance of long-distance record attempts which could be undertaken by cars running under various cubic capacity classes known as Class A, B or C, and so on. The records began at the one-kilometre standing start and went as far as the aspirant had the time and money to attempt them, separate records being recorded at regular intervals for time and distance. The recognized distances were measured in both kilometres and miles. Naturally, the shortest records, such as the flying-kilometre and flying-mile, usually stood at the highest speeds. The World's Land Speed Record, being the average speed for two runs in opposite directions, could be held by a car of any engine capacity. For the long-distance records, all the tools and spares had to be carried in the car attacking them.

Some of the long-distance records had not changed hands for many years because so few people had had the time and money to attempt them. Records could be attempted with any type of car having an internal combustion engine to propel it, but bodywork had to be either of a normal touring type or of a single-seater racing type. Obviously, if the record was captured with a comparatively standard type of car it was very good publicity for the factory concerned.

At the end of 1956, the secretary of the Cambridge University Automobile Club, Gyde Horrocks, called to see me about long-distance records. He wanted to know if BMC would be interested in lending a car to his club for an attempt on the seven-days record for Class G, 750 to 1,100cc. If we prepared the car, the Club undertook to provide the drivers, man the pit and keep account of the laps run. This seemed to me to be a well-founded suggestion, for Gyde had made a considerable study of motor race management and, in particular, of record-breaking. The existing record from four to six days inclusive stood at 67mph, and the targets Gyde suggested were those for four, five, six and seven days, 10,000 miles, 15,000 kilometres and 20,000 kilometres. The record for under four days stood at 86mph, which we did not consider to be within the scope of the car selected. The car chosen for the attempt was to be an Austin A35, with suitable modifications to the standard specification.

I felt that it would be very good publicity to use as many standard parts as possible and to keep the modifications within the Appendix J regulations of the International Sporting Code, with the engine tuned as that of a Group 2 rally car would have been. Much of the preliminary organization was carried out by Gyde Horrocks. He booked the track at Montlhéry, made the arrangements with the *FIA*, who were to provide the scrutineer and timekeepers, and visited the track to fix up accommodation for the drivers and pit personnel. The attempt was scheduled to take place during the first week in July 1957, as this would be the most convenient time to gather together 15 undergraduates for a week before they dispersed to various parts of the world for their long vacation. Five drivers were to be supported by 10 pit crew, who were to handle pit signalling, unofficial timing and lap scoring and servicing of the car. A permit had to be obtained for the fuel for, owing to the Suez crisis, France was still rationing fuel. The de Vries organization came to the rescue here as they had the right contacts to secure the permits we required.

We had hoped that the restrictions concerning petrol would be lifted in time for the Alpine Rally, so continued with our plans to run a team in it. I therefore made arrangements for our mobile workshop to call in at Montlhéry on its way to the South of France, in order to leave the spare parts and wheels required for the record attempt and later to pick up the same gear from Montlhéry after the rally was over. I also promised that I would drop in at Montlhéry on my way to the start of the Alpine to see that everything was going all right. I consulted our chief designer at MG's, Syd Enever, on the horsepower required for the attempt and the most suitable axle ratio for the car, bearing in mind that the body was to be the same as the production cars' (with the exception of the bumpers, which were to be removed). The front apron was extended and contoured a little to make the car look neater after the removal of the front bumper. Syd's reply was characteristic of him, simply reading: "Ordinary 950 in good order should be OK without tune. I will order 3.5, 70mph at 4,000. 30bhp reqd." We carried out some preliminary tests using various axle ratios at the Motor Industry Research Association test track near Nuneaton, and these in fact showed that a 3.9 axle ratio gave better results and that a top speed of 80mph was easily maintained and held.

We used the standard sump, but fitted an oil cooler with flexible pipes to the engine; this added 1 pint to the oil capacity of the engine. The carburettor was a 30mm VIG downdraught Zenith, without air cleaner, the jets being: main 95, compensator 90, pump 5.0, choke 27mm. This was fitted to the production inlet manifold using a Zenith petrol filter of the commercial multi-ring type. 'Brightray' exhaust valves and Vandervell thin-wall main bearings were fitted to a carefully selected production cylinder block. A 50-litre fuel tank was made up from the standard tank by extending it upwards into the boot, from which twin fuel lines led to an SU petrol pump. The tyres used were Dunlop D2/103, with standard treads made of special material. The Lucas dynamo was fitted with ball-bearings at both ends of the armature as we had to rely on our own headlights for the entire seven days.

We carried a spare coil and used the standard battery. The propeller shaft was carefully balanced and the shock absorbers were set up by 20 per cent. We also increased the diameter of the downpipe from the exhaust manifold to silencer to 1¾in, and used Ferodo VG95 brake linings, a hard racing-type lining, as we intended to lose as little time as possible when making a pit-stop. The instruments included a rev-counter, oil pressure gauge, water thermometer and ammeter. It was evident that it would be very difficult to hold the accelerator at precisely the right level for the three-hour spell that the drivers would be required to serve, so I arranged to have an adjustable stop made up for the accelerator pedal, which one could manipulate from the driving seat.

The high-speed circuit at Montlhéry measured 2.548 kilometres and had a reputation for roughness. The quality of the track's surface varied a great deal at different points on the banking, both as to height up the banking and location along it. For instance, it was easier to find a smooth passage about a third of the way up than higher, where the faster cars travelled. A car must, however, be allowed to find its natural height on the banking, this line being dictated by the speed and weight of the individual car. It should be quite possible to release the steering wheel completely on the smoother parts of the banked track if the steering was in good condition, with castor acting, and if the right line had been chosen.

The BMC party crossed over on June 29 and arrived at the track the following morning, when some of the Cambridge boys came in from various places such as the Loire valley, Le Mans and England. It was evident on arrival at the track that something unusual was afoot, for there was a VW camping van under the trees, parked near a pre-DB Aston Martin and a 3-litre Bentley.

I contacted my old friends, M Colibert and M Peix. The former was the track manager and the latter the manager of the whole autodrome, which was the French equivalent of the Motor Industry Research Association track in England. I had met both of these gentlemen in 1955 when BMC took six production cars to Montlhéry in an attempt to cover at least 100 miles in the hour on each one. Our drivers on that occasion were Ken Wharton, Ron Flockhart and John Gott, who stayed with us at the track, and Bob Porter, who stayed in Paris, but came down to drive the Riley Pathfinder, which did just over 108 miles in the hour, with his wife and two friends as passengers. John Gott was very unlucky in these runs, for he burst a tyre on the Austin A90 when his run was almost finished and had to start all over again, eventually doing 101 miles in the hour. As he later did the same in a Wolseley 6/99 and then 112 miles in the hour in an MGA in speed trim, he covered more than 400 miles at over 100mph in three different cars on that day. All this ultra-fast motoring, however, did not deter him from leading the mechanics in one of the best rags in which I have ever assisted.

We were all staying in a single-storey wooden hut opposite *La Potinière* restaurant. It was very pleasant to be back at the track amongst my old friends and to stroll over to *La Potinière* to be greeted by Madame as if we had been there yesterday. Gyde Horrocks introduced me to the members of his team, all of whom were great enthusiasts attending entirely at their own expense. Most of them knew a great deal about the sport and I felt that I would have to be very careful not to display my ignorance on some aspects of it.

Gyde had divided the crews up into five teams, consisting of one driver and two helpers, who were either to keep the lap score, do the signalling or help with the pit-stops. In practice, the BMC mechanics, aided by two of the CUAC boys, looked after the pit-stops, whilst two more of the team looked after the lap scoring, so that with the stand-by driver there were always two CUAC teams on duty. In theory this gave everyone 18 hours off duty, but many people stayed for more than their duty period during the first part of the attempt. By the time meals and sleep were taken away from the off-duty period, only six hours in the day were left for recreation. The scrutineer appointed by the *FIA* was my old friend M Massonet, who had done the same job for us in 1955. He measured the engine to see that it complied with the class for the record we were to attempt, and checked over the spares to see that those used were actually carried on the car. The timekeepers were advised of our starting time and we were all set for July 1. The teams of drivers are shown in full at the end of this chapter, so I will only refer to them now as they turn up in the story.

We had decided to have two sorts of pit-stop, apart, of course, from any involuntary halts which might occur. A normal stop was to take place every three hours for the purpose of changing the driver, refuelling and checking the level of the oil and water, and the windscreen and headlamps were to be cleaned at the same time. These stops became the subject of very healthy rivalry between the teams, who were always trying to get the completion of this operation down to under a minute. The weather was warm and there were signs that it would get warmer, but the night before the attempt some of the more energetic members of the team set off to run round the track, for Gyde had said in his instructions that everyone must take plenty of exercise. As a precaution against the chances of either the heat or the food having an adverse effect on anyone, Gyde had put me down as a reserve driver, for drivers had to be nominated and had to hold an International Competition Licence before the attempt was started.

The track was being used during the day for experimental testing by the French motor industry and we were therefore often accompanied by a number of Citroens and Renaults circulating at a moderate pace to test such things as oil consumption or cylinder-bore wear. The drivers of these vehicles regarded the whole attempt as a bit of a joke, but waved good-naturedly whenever we passed them. It soon became evident that we would have to find a suitable swimming pool for the off-duty crews, so various people went off to spy out the land. After a day or so, we found a good swimming pool at La Ferté Alais which became very popular with everyone. The mechanics, however, were loyal to a man and decided to stay in the pit area for the entire seven days, except for their meals across the track. They slept in the mobile workshop, and the only relaxation they had was chatting with the visitors who came to the track.

We started the attempt on July 1 without any marked ceremony. Nobody really expected a troublefree run of such duration, for it seemed to be asking too much of the little car to cover a distance which most private owners only achieved in a year in just seven days. Gyde had arranged with Schweppes to provide a large quantity of their now famous 'Bitter Lemon', and this was placed at eveyone's disposal. The thermometer ranged around the nineties and showed no sign of dipping. At night it never fell below 80deg F, although it seemed to be a lot cooler than in the daytime. In order to augment our precious stocks of imported drink, we went into Linas-Montlhéry to see what we could buy. We did very well for about four days, but then it became apparent that there was a shortage of mineral waters everywhere. Such was the heat in Paris that the mineral water manufacturers could not keep pace with the demand.

Meanwhile, the gallant little car had settled down to a regular cruising speed which produced an average speed of 75.20mph for the first day, 75.16 for the second and 75.03 for the third. The routine was the same each day and every 12 hours the car was checked over with great care. The gearbox level was checked, as was the rear axle level. The steering was greased and tyres changed around on the advice of the Dunlop tyre representative. Flies were blown from the radiator core with compressed air and the battery level was checked. In addition to all this, the sump was drained each morning at the 9am stop and the oil filter element changed every third day. We removed the plugs and re-gapped them at one stop. Some of these attentions were not really necessary, but were done as a precaution.

On the second day, Gyde Horrocks was suffering from the heat and nearly fainted when he got out of the car. It was more a case of overwork than heat-stroke and he decided to call in my services as a driver. Records which run into days are a mixture of boredom and excitement, boredom when everything is going to plan and excitement when it is not. All sorts of pastimes were devised to keep the driver amused. We had a large board and a couple of alphabets in card which could be hung up. There was also a blackboard for messages and some numbers to signal the number of minutes and seconds for the last lap, the number of laps completed and the lap on which to come in. The CUAC boys soon invented a system for playing noughts and crosses between the pit signaller and the driver. The moves were made in some mysterious manner by using the indicators in conjunction with the sidelights, and a game could take up to 12 laps. The driver was also asked questions on the blackboard and replied by using a scribbling pad and throwing the note out of the window.

The windows had to be kept almost completely shut; if opened too far the throttle had to be opened as well to combat the extra drag. Any drink carried in the car became very hot and, if not consumed within the first half-hour, it reached a temperature of something above blood heat. I found that glucose tablets were good in so far as they made me feel more alert when I got too bored. I was always very glad when my tour was over, although there was a great sense of accomplishment at having put another 227 miles on to the clock. No doubt the comfort-lovers will want to know why we didn't have a radio and carry our drink in insulated containers. The answer to the first query is that we did have a radio, but the wind noise at 75mph made it impossible to hear it when wearing a crash hat. The answer to the second is that we never expected it to be so hot, otherwise we might have come better prepared for the heat. The astonishing thing was the low consumption of water by the car, which only needed a little once a day.

Another occupation which kept everyone on his toes was lunch-time debating, if it could be called that. A great deal of my time was spent in a mildly heated argument with Peter Riviere. Peter had at that time a very acid wit, which he used with marked effect. I think the discussions amused everyone, but I am glad for Peter's sake that his tongue became less barbed or he would have made fewer friends as a motoring correspondent on the staff of *The Autocar*; I suppose we all become a little less angry as we get absorbed into an establishment. Another subject for discussion was the fact that the official timekeepers seemed to gain about one lap per day over our own lap scorers. Whether this was a correction which they applied automatically I never found out. We began to think that we would average over 75mph for the entire distance, when we had a slight setback on the fifth day with an unexpected stop of 12 minutes due to a broken rear spring shackle. This was repaired with a bolt and was the only breakage in the entire run.

The four-day record was taken at 74.9mph, the five-day record at 74.95mph and the 15,000-kilometre record at 74.82mph, whilst the 10,000 miles and the six-days fell to us at 74.79mph. All these records were raised by over 13 per cent except the four-days, which was raised by 12.4 per cent. Completely new records were established for the 20,000 kilometres at 74.89mph and for seven days at 74.9mph.

On the last day the heavens opened and flooded the track for about six hours, when maximum throttle had to be used to keep up the lap speeds. Those last two days were rather an anticlimax, and when the final lap was run at 3pm on July 8 most of the crews had gone for a swim. Our friends the works testers and M Colibert were really more enthusiastic than we were ourselves.

John Thornley sent us a very nice telegram before we were halfway through in which he expressed his entire confidence in the successful conclusion of the attempt. It was interesting to note that years afterwards no less than six of the team were still connected with motorsport in some way or another. John Aley, who was our very efficient pit manager, made a name for himself in saloon car racing; the Rev Rupert Jones became well-known in the International rally field; Peter Riviere drove with distinction in the Algiers to Cape Rally and wrote for *The Autocar*; Tom Threlfall owned a garage and had raced on the Continent; Ray Simpson joined the competition department of Castrol and specialized in rally service; and John Taylor raced an Austin-Healey and got it into reserve place at Le Mans in 1961.

The experiment was a success, and when all the bonus was collected I don't think any of the boys were out of pocket. That autumn they were all invited to a little celebration by C C Wakefield, the makers of Castrol, and the party was presided over by George Eyston, who knew more about record-breaking than any man alive. It was therefore not too long before Gyde Horrocks rang me to ask about the Class D 2,000 to 3,000cc records which he thought were ripe for the picking with an Austin-Healey 100-Six. We decided to try for the two-to-seven-days records inclusive, but were determined to make the attempt at a time when the thermometer would be less likely to run up above the 90deg mark!

The next CUAC project was a much more ambitious affair and required more research and preparation on our part as the existing records for the two to seven days stood at between 90 and 86mph and were held by a Citroen, which took them in 1935. The attempt had two objects, firstly to break the existing records and secondly to put the speeds up to over 100mph for the whole week. Many of the same people who worked so well together were available for the second year, and the new ones soon got the idea and the whole team worked very well together.

After the success of the previous record attempt, it was much easier to enlist the help of the boffins at Coventry and Abingdon. There were, however, a lot more problems: we now had to use road racing tyres, and Dunlop wanted us to use larger tyres than standard because of the higher wear that was expected. The larger tyres, which were run at higher pressures than were used on the road, brought about shock absorber and spring problems. The cruising speed which had been selected would have meant operating the engine at a steady

4,000rpm, but Eddie Maher, who was going to prepare the two engines we required, thought that there would be a vibration at those revolutions which might be harmful to the engine. We were advised to use a direct top gear, as opposed to the overdrive normally used, as this would have saved a few horsepower, but finally we settled for a 3.9 final-drive and overdrive. The Laycock overdrive was made by Birfield Industries Ltd and they kindly agreed to let their technical representative, Harry Winter, attend for the entire record attempt; we had seen Harry on a few rallies and were to see him on many more. Generally he hadn't much to do as his overdrives gave very little trouble, but when they did he got to the bottom of the trouble very quickly.

The engine was fitted with two large carburettors and the specification was basically the same as for the 1958 Sebring 12-Hours race cars. There had been some trouble with oil in the clutches, but it was proposed that a better seal be fitted to the gearbox primary shaft. It was also suggested that we used an oil cooler, but I disliked external oil pipes and settled that we would run on Castrol R instead. In view of the fact that the engines were being prepared in Coventry, it was felt that one of the fitters from Eddie Maher's department should attend. As during the previous attempt, the mobile workshop was to be placed off the track, which had the advantage of providing facilities for sleeping, cooking, eating and repairing cars. The body of this vehicle had been built by Appleyard of Leeds on a Morris Commercial chassis for the MG racing team and was first used at Le Mans in 1955. It was to prove a very useful vehicle and went on to perform with distinction in all parts of Europe.

The main party crossed over to France on September 3, and were scheduled to have daylight and after-dark practice sessions on the following day, the record attempt itself being due to begin at midday on the Friday. I had just assisted in the Liège-Rome-Liège Rally and after the prizegiving was over I drove to Paris, where I left my car and flew back to London. The Healey was ready and everyone was raring to go, so I saw them off and then was able to deal with a few things before flying back to Paris on September 4. Everyone had arrived safely, the practice sessions were underway and the publicity department had sent over our old friend 'Goody' Goodchild to get some pictures, just in case.

The drivers complained bitterly about the lights during the evening session, and with good reason because the headlights illuminated a portion of the banking which seemed to be much more to the right and higher up than the point which we wanted lit up. Of course, this was a feature of the banked track and the high position upon the banking, so the lights were given a set to the left and everyone was happier. A few dim red lanterns were placed at the edge of the inside of the track, but they served little purpose, and by the end of the attempt I think we could have driven round with one headlight without any trouble at all.

As usual the de Vries organization came into the picture. We had decided to use a Pye two-way radio and there was a little trouble in getting the necessary permits. M de Vries soon had this in hand and his local representative obtained the necessary licence. This set was a great asset and functioned perfectly during the entire week, even continuing to do so after the mounting brackets had come unbolted and the whole set had fallen onto the floor, where the vibration must have been excessive. The great advantage of wireless communication was that drivers could warn the pit if they intended to call in for an emergency stop, and in the event of a breakdown they could tell the pit where they were and what was wrong. This time I had arranged to stay at the *Deux Lions de Bel Air*, which was a few kilometres down the main road to Étampes.

The record attempt started on time and the car circulated with regularity at over 100mph until the evening, when I decided to retire for the night. Gyde was acting as pit manager for that night and therefore I was not required until the next morning. The mechanics in charge were Douggie Watts, Douggie Hamblin, Gerald Wiffin and Derek Lowe. They had imported some bacon and eggs and other comforts and set up home on the track, where they stayed for the whole week.

It had been thundering when I left the track and by the time I reached the main road large drops of rain were falling and the long straight just past Aparjon was awash. This was the section of the N20 where at one time the World Land Speed Records had been attempted. I reached the *Deux Lions* and turned in early. The telephone was silent during the night and I assumed that all was well when I returned to the track next morning. I drove into the gate and, upon stopping my car, I was soon aware that there was no sign of activity. The track was quiet and upon reaching the pit I saw that the Healey was in the shed.

There had been plenty of excitement during the night, and I soon heard the story. Bill Summers had been driving when the thunderstorm hit the track, reducing visibility to something less than 100 yards. The car was travelling at about 110mph and was coming off the east banking just past the pits, and Bill had probably never driven at over 100mph with a really thick layer of water between his tyres and the concrete. The front wheels planed, the steering went light and he lost control. The car spun at least once and probably did another half-turn before he hit the grass on the inside of the track, while still going backwards. On the way he must have missed the safety wall on the outside of the track, where the road circuit branched off to the right, by a small margin. Both car and driver were badly shaken when they came to rest after a skid of about 400 yards, which must be one of the longest skids on record outside of Bonneville Salt Flats.

Examination showed that the car had a couple of buckled wheels but nothing serious. They continued the run, but clutch slip started after 10 hours and the attempt was abandoned for the time being. Unfortunately the clutch was changed before anybody thought of trying to bed it in with a little vigorous work on the clutch pedal. This remedy is of no use when a normally well-used clutch gets oil on the face, but is successful if the lining has not been ground dead flat and is therefore only presenting about two-thirds of its face to the pressure plate. In this case the lining chosen was very hard and took a long time to bed in, for there were practically no gearchanges up or down to assist the process.

The next attempt lasted for 30 hours and the car covered over 3,000 miles in that time, but it soon became apparent that the rear springs just could not take the punishment handed out by the patched concrete and the expansion joints between the track sections. Both rear springs had to be replaced, and as this left us with no spares, we had two more flown out very promptly thanks to the good offices of my friend John Suter of Mory and Co, who specialized in the air freight business. John was on the committee of the London Motor Club and had done a fair amount of rallying. The springs came just in time and we carried one of them in the Healey for the next attempt. I knew that the replacement springs were not going to last any longer than the previous pair, so suggested that we bound them with whipcord after greasing the spring leaves and wrapping them in tape. Douggie Watts had no suitable grease handy, so he lubricated the spring with cooking fat, bound it in tape and then corded it up. I suggested that they used the type of spring binding that Bentley mechanics used at Le Mans. This was taught me by Joe Grant, who used to work with Bentley's at Cricklewood. The cord is centred at the beginning of the binding in two equal lengths, the two cords are crossed over and pulled back to the other side of the spring where they are crossed over each other again and so on. This makes it possible to pull the cord very tight without it slipping and a rather pleasant pattern is made in the process. The spring is made much stiffer and the binding holds the leaves together even after a breakage.

We changed the cylinder head as an added precaution, as Douggie Hamblin thought the plugs looked as though the mixture was too weak for French fuel. This was a common fault when changing from British to French fuel and was very hard to detect in time unless the fuel tank was drained or run dry on arrival on the Continent and the carburettors retuned on undiluted French fuel. In view of the very stiff suspension we decided to cut the driving spells to two hours and to reduce the average speed to just under 100mph although the other extreme might have been to raise the speed and try the higher and smoother part of the track near the top of the banking. We could not afford to delay our preparations any more as the track was booked for the following Sunday and was reserved for a French club for practice on the Saturday. It was thought that we might be able to use a bit of their time if really necessary, but Sunday was out of the question. We took the two-day record at 98.73mph at 8am on September 11 and followed it very soon after with 5,000 miles at 98.28mph. Clutch slip became apparent as light oil mist crept into the depressions in the woven fabric and was flung on to the friction surfaces. I suggested that we left the pit in second gear and that the first lap of each spell was used to warm the clutch up with a few gearchanges. This had the desired effect and the clutch got better.

The radio was very useful and it was possible to collect some quite useful information in both directions. On Friday night I was driving and looking forward to the end of the attempt, which had not gone so well as I would have wished for we would have to forego the five, six and seven-day records. It was a beautiful night and most of the drivers and helpers were sitting in the control tower. I was coming round the western banking which leads to the pits when I saw a large triangular lump of concrete in the headlights. This lump was a piece which I must have loosened on the previous lap and had tilted up like a piece of broken pack-ice. I hit it just in line with the right-hand side of the chassis at a little over a hundred. The impact sounded like a small bomb exploding and bits flew everywhere. I don't think I could have avoided it and my main concern was to spare the sump and the stub-axle. There was no time to pull into the pit as I was looking at the oil pressure as I came off the banking. I told control on the radio that the track was breaking up on the west side and that they had better go and have a look at it. They thought I was joking, for we had all knocked small pieces out of the concrete both that year and the year before. I went round once again passing through a few more lumps and missing the hole by passing below it. I then thought that I must be quite mad rushing round a concrete saucer in the middle of the night while my wife and children were at home depending upon me.

Meanwhile, the boys had leapt into the duty car and set off round the track to inspect the damage. I decided to visit the pit and see if the sump was leaking. I arrived at the floodlit pit area to find it bereft of mechanics, but occupied by a French soldier and his girl, who had been visiting the tanker crew. They were as surprised to see me as I was to see them, for the Frenchman was embracing his lady in a very Gallic fashion right in the middle of the shed! I looked under the car, found that all was well and departed. On the next lap I found the helpers were in position but, owing to the steepness of the banking, they were having difficulty in reaching the crater. There was also the delicate question as to whether I should pass below, across or above the hole. After a time they took one of the red lamps from inside of the track and perched it in the hole. The next day some wit climbed up from under the banking and inserted an umbrella in the hole.

We finally captured the 15,000-kilometre and 10,000-mile records and the attempt ended around lunchtime on Saturday, when the team departed to see the bright lights of Paris. When we got the car back to England we found that the front engine bearers had fractured and one of the spring leaves was broken, but the Austin-Healey was in fine fettle as one of the final laps was run at over 124mph. I would still like to have picked up the records for those extra three days!

I never went to Bonneville Salt Flats with any of the MG or Austin-Healey record-breaking cars; they were the products of the development departments of the MG Car Company and the Donald Healey Motor Company. George Eyston was the moving force behind the very exact science of long-distance records on the Salt Flats and without a doubt he knew more about the organization required to set up either a long or a short record attempt on the Salt Flats than anybody else. I always thought of him as the Squire of Salt Lake. A German motorcycle manufacturer once went all the way to Salt Lake City to make the necessary preparations for a record attempt. They visited the local civic dignitaries and were directed to Bonneville, from there to Wendover and thence back to Salt Lake City. When they were getting nowhere and were a bit tired of the whole thing, someone told them that they had wasted their time in coming at all, for the man they really should have seen in the first place was Captain George Eyston in London – and so it proved to be!

I think I enjoyed long-distance record attempts more than any other aspect of the sport; it was a very restful way of spending your time at somebody else's expense.

Records established at Montlhéry by the CUAC team

      Class G   Date: July 1-8, 1957
      Car   Austin A35 saloon

Drivers: G Horrocks, T Threlfall, P Riviere, R Simpson, J Taylor and M Chambers

		mph	Record raised (%)
4 days	11,572.965km	74.91	12.4
5 days	14,475.451km	74.95	13.7
15,000 kilometres		74.82	13.4
10,000 miles		74.79	13.2
6 days	17,341.537km	74.79	13.3
20,000 kilometres		74.89	New record established
7 days	20,250.512km	74.90	New record established

      Class D   Date: September, 9-13, 1958
      Car   Austin-Healey 100-Six hardtop

Drivers: G Horrocks, J Clarke, R Jones, R Simpson, W Summers,
         J Taylor, T Threlfall and M Chambers

	mph
5,000 miles	98.5
10,000 kilometres	97.31
2 days	98.73
3 days	97.33
4 days	97.04
15,000 kilometres	97.04
10,000 miles	97.13

CHAPTER 13

The Sebring races

"I will admit that it was not easy to time three cars on one split-second stopwatch, but Stan did it for nearly 12 hours and between us we never missed a car."

Sebring is in south central Florida. It is not a great scenic district, being covered with pine trees and scrubland on sandy soil. Much of the land has been cleared to provide space for citrus growing, but the small town became internationally known on account of the airfield which was built as a base for B-17 bombers during World War Two. This became the site of the race track where the Automobile Racing Club of Florida held its 12-Hours race, which counted towards the World Sports Car Manufacturers' Championship.

Being part of a perfectly flat aerodrome which had seen better days, the venue offered conditions which tested even the best suspension systems. The lack of landmarks made the judgment of correct lines and cut-off points difficult, and portions of the course which were on the edge of the main runway were simply marked off with cones. Elsewhere there were some difficult corners to catch out the unwary, a hairpin and seven right-angled corners making up a lap of 5.2 miles. The event put a considerable strain on both the car and its drivers.

The 12-Hours race traditionally started at 10am so that the finish took place after dark. March was supposed to have good weather, but on occasion it might rain for several days. In spite of these disadvantages many of the most famous factories sent in entries as they could not afford to neglect the opportunity of winning World Championship points.

On the credit side was the incredible reception which the visitors received from Alec Uhlmann, the man who started it all, and the ARCF officials, stewards and marshals, as well as the locals. Going to Sebring for the 12-Hours was like attending a well-run club meeting on this side of the Atlantic during the immediate postwar years.

MG participation started in 1956 with three MGAs, one prepared by Inskip Motors of New York, one by Manhattan Auto of Washington, and the third in Warren, Pennsylvania. The cars were stripped down and rebuilt to standard specification, then fitted with safety equipment, aeroscreens and straight-through exhausts. They were driven in a disciplined manner and won the team prize, finishing fourth, fifth and sixth in class behind three Porsche Spyders, the two quickest MGs averaging 65.43mph. In 1957 the same sponsors entered three more MGAs and achieved an even better result, taking the team prize and first and second in the class.

That year the Donald Healey Motor Company of Warwick entered three special-bodied Healeys fitted with 2,639cc six-cylinder engines built by Morris Engines of Coventry. These incorporated six-port cylinder heads, three dual-choke Weber carburettors and nitrided crankshafts, which gave an output of 150bhp at 5,500rpm. Hambro Automotive of New York, who were the Morris importers at that time and handled all BMC products, looked after the entry of the cars for the race and the organization of the teams at Sebring. They also took care of the shipping and forwarding of the spare wheels and parts for both the Healeys and, later, the MGs with great efficiency. The drivers were chosen by Hambro from American sources. The race was run in good conditions at very high speeds, being won overall by Fangio and Behra in a 4,451cc Maserati. Two of the Healeys went out with a thus-far undisclosed mechanical problem and the third, which had been driven at a reduced speed, finished down in 26th place.

When the cars were returned to England the engines were sent back to be stripped down for the *post mortem*, and Eddie Maher, the chief engineer at the engine development department at Coventry, soon got to the root of the trouble. There was a weakness in the connecting rods at the point where the rod had been machined to take the head of the big-end bolt. Several rods were cracked at the same point, so there was no reason to doubt the cause of the failures. Morris Motors redesigned the rod and the result was one of the most beautiful connecting rods fitted to any engine at that period. As Laurence Pomeroy said to me so often: "If it looks right it is usually right." That incident produced the connecting rods for the famous Austin-Healey 3000 and they never let us down, even when running at much higher revolutions than those Sebring specials. The six-port cylinder head was soon fitted to the production 100-Six Healeys and it was then possible to produce a 160bhp competition car.

In 1958 there were no MGs at Sebring, but the BMC flag was kept flying with the entry of three 100-Six cars with specially prepared engines from Eddie Maher; they were fitted with twin SU HD6 carburettors as they were derived from the standard production models as homologated in the GT class. Several of the drivers from the 1957 race were used again, and Gus Ehrman, who had been in the MG team in 1956 and 1957, joined the Healey team.

There was no shortage of people to help in the organization, and Geoffrey Healey later set the scene very well in his book *Austin Healey: The Story of the Big Healeys*:

"Old Austin men like Peter Millard from Austin of Canada attended to general administration. Peter put in a tremendous amount of effort that made life at Sebring very enjoyable. Various BMC distributors attended in force; Fred Royston, a fiery character from Philadelphia, arranged a train to carry friends and dealers to the circuit. He organized a party before the race which was widely attended by drivers of competing teams and was the social event of the race. Ed Bussey and Frank Wilson of Ship and Shore Motors, BMC distributors in Florida and adjoining States, flew in and after the race gave a party for the team at the Sailfish Club in Palm Beach. The food was the best I have ever had in America, and the sea food probably had not any equal on earth. All the dealers were delighted at the efforts being made at Sebring. If they had any grumbles, they were generally about the number of Austin-Healey and MG cars they were limited to for the year. They could see the Japanese infiltrating the gaps left by poor delivery."

The race went well apart from some oil getting into the clutches as a result of high revolutions and hard braking, which proved to be too much for the conventional type of oil retainers used on the input shafts of the gearboxes. These were subsequently changed to moulded rubber lip seals on the production line.

The Austin-Healeys won the team prize, finishing 14th, 17th and 22nd overall. Geoffrey Healey remarked that the Sebring 12-Hours race could produce wear in the gearboxes equivalent to 60,000 miles of normal road use; racing does improve the breed when production models are used and the factory takes notice of the evidence.

My first visit to Sebring took place in 1959, when it was decided that the factory would enter three MGA Twin-Cam Coupes. A practice car and three race cars were prepared to the standard specification and shipped out through the Hambro organization, together with the spare parts, wheels and tyres. Fifteen Canadian mechanics were to attend along with 14 Canadian and American drivers. This situation was brought about by the entry of three Austin-Healey Sprites. I was glad that John Thornley was there to supervise the entire operation as he knew all the key personnel very well and had had some influence as to the choice of drivers. Gus Ehrman was back with the MG team for what must have been his fourth drive at Sebring.

The Sprites were prepared at Warwick, and Geoffrey Healey was to go over and manage the team as usual. I had known Geoffrey since the end of the war, and we had both been on the race management side of things for a long while. It was therefore very pleasant to travel out with him and hear how things were arranged at Sebring.

Geoffrey Healey, Douggie Watts, Stan Nicholls and myself were to go by the Britannia night flight to New York. Due to a mistake, the departure time written on our tickets was 23.59; fortunately we were early, but we only just made the call for our flight as the real departure time was 23.00, and luckily for Stan they delayed the flight for him and he just managed to catch the plane. Owing to strong headwinds over the Atlantic, the Captain decided to land at Keklivic, in Iceland, an inhospitable place where they refused to take sterling in the duty-free shop. We touched down at Idlewild just before 9 o'clock the next morning. We were met there by Babe Learoyd, who was catching the same plane as us to Tampa, Florida. Eventually we got our baggage, mine having been temporarily mislaid, and had it loaded onto the Central Airlines plane, which was staffed by some lethargic air hostesses of Hispanic extraction, who treated the passengers with disdain. The first two hours of the journey were rough, and some of the passengers looked equally rough and a child was not at all well. We touched down 45 minutes late and expressed the hope that we would not fly by Central Airlines again.

We were met by Jack Flaherty, one of our drivers, who chewed cigars with a wooden mouthpiece and wore a Texan-style hat... He drove us to Avon Park in a new ZB Magnette, one of the first to reach the States, but it only just made it to Avon Park as it had a cracked distributor cap.

It seemed that I had been booked in at Sebring by someone who should have known better. I felt that it would be difficult to manage the team which was based at Avon Park as it was seven miles away. There was a bit of a fracas when Frank Harrison, the service manager of Hambro, arrived and found that Douggie Watts and Geoffrey Healey were in the room he had picked for himself. But all went well in the end and Frank, who was very tired from his drive down from New York, was all charm the next day. Peter Millard, service manager of BMC Ontario, was the diplomat who sorted out all our troubles and always took a cheerful view of the situation. I shared a room with Stan Nicholls, and any meetings we had with the team personnel took place there. The next day we prepared a programme for the week and Mrs Harrison, one of our many lady helpers, typed it all out in as many copies as were needed.

Whenever we went to the track or to the race office in Sebring we found the officials were really keen to make us feel welcome and they always went out of their way to sort out any queries that we might have for them. It was such a contrast with some events run on our side of the Atlantic that I could not let it pass, so I wrote an appreciation in one of the issues of *Safety Fast* in which I said: "Never have I felt under such an obligation to do the right thing by the officials; their charm is compelling, and one's pit marshals immediately identify with the cars that they are supervising." Southern hospitality personified.

Unfortunately, the weather was not as hospitable and one practice session was washed out. When practice was permitted the Twin-Cams gave twice as much trouble as the Sprites and we had to limit them to 5,000rpm. Our cars were No 28 for Gus Ehrman and Ray Saidel, No 29 for Jim Parkinson and John Dalton, and No 30 for Ray Pickering and Jack Flaherty, with Sherman Decker as reserve driver. Sherm was not happy as reserve as his times were better than the others, but as the drivers had been selected on a regional and dealer-volume basis I had to leave matters as they stood.

We had another problem which caused me considerable anxiety. Gus Ehrman and his friend Hal Wallace had invented a system which was supposed to supply fuel to the race cars at one gallon per second. In practice a considerable amount of that gallonage deposited itself on the track and, even worse, onto the pit counter and floor. I gave them an ultimatum: one more trial, and if it leaked we went back to the gravity system. By some miracle it came good on the day.

We had trouble with heat in the cockpit of the MGAs and drilled extra holes to let the air in, but when it rained on the race day it let the water in as well!.

The day of the race had dawned fine, and we were all ready to go by 8.30am with everyone in the right place and knowing what he had to do. There was plenty of time for me to walk along and look at the opposition and inspect the facilities in the shape of hot-dog stands and orange juice dispensers. Someone gave Stan and me day passes to the ARCF marquee, which had everything in the shape of refreshment and fabulous food served by Southern Belles under the blue-and-white striped awning... I sat next to Señora Rodriguez at lunch, the mother of the two brilliant drivers Pedro and Ricardo, both of whom sadly were subsequently to be killed whilst racing.

The bands paraded up and down in front of the pits and the drum majorettes went through their routines accompanying the various beauty queens such as 'Miss Citrus Grove', 'Miss Sebring Sports Car Race' and others. Stan had his watches at the ready and I sat next to him to act as his stand-in when he needed a break. I will admit that it was not easy to time three cars on one split-second watch, but Stan did it for nearly 12 hours and between us we never missed a car. He let me practice on some of his spare watches, all of which held the A-CU certificates from his timekeeping of the Isle of Man Tourist Trophy races.

The Sebring race story has been covered in detail by those better suited to do so than myself, so I will just relate some of the adventures that came to my notice at the time. Ed Leavens, in Sprite No 53, found some of the rubber course markers obstructing his chosen line and arrived in the pits with two of them jammed in his left rear wheelarch. We had to take off the wheel to get them out, but there was no damage to the car. John Christy, in Sprite No 55, broke a throttle spring and went off the course, damaging his exhaust system. He called in the pits where it was all put right, although inevitably he lost some time.

The Sprites went well and all finished with creditable average speeds: No 53, 141 laps at 61.65mph; No 54, 148 laps at 64.16mph; and No 55, 140 laps at 60.77mph. They thus gained the first three places in the 750cc to 1,000cc class. They also won the manufacturers' team prize, a matter of some mystery as the nominated teams were not published before the event started.

The Twin-Cams started well and were purposely held back to see how the race would develop. Unfortunately, heavy rain coincided with our orders to speed up, so we did not do as well as we had hoped as the course became very slippery. Car No 28, with Ray Saidel and Gus Ehrman, had a good run apart from a slight entanglement with a straw bale; No 29, with John Dalton and Jim Parkinson, had an obscure fault in the starter motor after one hour – this refused to disengage and the car ran for some distance with it stuck in. They lost about an hour by this and Douggie Watts sustained minor burns from hot oil as he had to remove the oil filter from the engine to get at the starter. After 10 hours No 30 was stopped with some expensive noises in the engine, but Sherm Decker waited until the race was run and pushed the car over the line to count as a finisher.

A Porsche won the class and the two other MGs finished with second and third places in the class. In spite of the weather, everyone remained astonishingly cheerful and Gus Ehrman made us all laugh when he removed his pants in the pit and wrung them out, much to his wife's embarrassment.

John Thornley expressed his satisfaction concerning our participation and we went back knowing that we could do a lot better next time. When John got back to Abingdon he received a letter which I think shows how things can be run if people have the right attitude. It read as follows:

Dear Sirs,

It was my pleasure to have been assigned to the MG and Austin-Healey Sprite pits as a Steward.

I want to commend the entire group and especially 'Doug', your technician, on their efficient and courteous manner in carrying out their duties.

'Doug' is a wonderful representative of true sportsmanship. I trust I can look forward to working with your staff again next year.

Yours truly,

Frank Sheffield.
3020 Oxford Street,
Orlando, Florida, USA.

Sebring in 1960 was to be a more professional affair so far as Abingdon was concerned; whilst the Healey organization had plenty of experience in running their own teams at Sebring, it was only the second year in which the new Abingdon competition department would be participating. Before that the whole operation had been in the hands of the American importers and their dealers, and it was good to know that we still had their organization upon which we could count to process the paperwork entailed with the shipping of the cars and their equipment, as well as booking the accommodation. This arrangement would leave us free to prepare and test the cars with some of our own drivers.

BMC entered three MGA Twin-Cams and three Austin-Healey 3000s, while The Donald Healey Motor Company entered two Austin-Healey Sprites, one in the 1,100cc Sports category and another specially tuned for the 4-Hours Grand Touring Car race, which was to be held on Friday, March 25.

The Twin-Cams were fitted with aluminium hardtops and ran without bumpers, and their headlights were augmented by two extra driving lights. There was a cold-air intake to the carburettors and an extra vent in the right-hand front wing to reduce under-bonnet temperature. There was an oil cooler in front of the radiator and a quick-release oil filler cap was fitted to the engine. A 17-gallon fuel tank was mounted in the boot, the fuel being fed by a twin SU electric pump, and there were improvements to the run of fuel lines. The headlights were to be covered during daylight with Perspex covers to prevent damage by stone chips, these to be removed at the last pit-stop before dark set in. Two-speed windscreen wipers were fitted as a result of the previous year's experience, and there were extensive changes in the drivers' area, including better seats, isolated electrical circuits and instruments which were more easily read. In fact many of the items were derived from the 1955 Le Mans cars.

The drivers were an international mixture. Car No 38 was to be driven by Ted Lund and Colin Escott, both from England; Car No 39 by Ed Leavens and Fred Hayes, from Canada; and No 40 by Jim Parkinson and Jack Flaherty, of the United States.

The three Austin-Healey 3000s were prepared at Warwick to the 1960 Grand Touring regulations, which permitted us to fit a Sports camshaft, 2in SU HD8 carburettors, a competition clutch, a competition exhaust system and a higher-output Lucas dynamo. Chassis changes included Girling 16-3 brakes at the front and 12 Hs at the rear, a 3.54:1 axle, 600 x 15 tyres and a 25-gallon fuel tank. All these alterations were homologated by the competition department. Two extra cars were prepared to the same specification, one as a practice car and the other for Austin's to race during the coming season in Canada.

Of the two Sprites entered by The Donald Healey Motor Company, one was to be driven by Stirling Moss in the 4-Hours race, and the other shared by John Sprinzel and J Lumkin in the 12-Hours race on the Saturday.

There was a variation in the travel arrangements that year and we arrived in New York in the afternoon and were booked in at a very splendid hotel near Central Park. We were met by representatives of the Hambro organization, who looked after us until we left the next day. I took the opportunity of visiting the *Chanteclair* restaurant, which was run by the famous French racing driver Rene Dreyfus, whom I had not seen since prewar days. He remembered me from the time when I drove an HRG at Le Mans and we had a most agreeable evening.

The next day we flew down to West Palm Beach, arriving very late as the Captain of the airliner had received a signal telling him to reduce speed by about 100 knots as there had been a serious failure in the structure of a similar plane that day! After landing we picked up three hire cars and drove to Sebring, and this time everything went very smoothly. The race cars had been sent down on transporters and were waiting for us at Avon Park. I enjoyed having some of my own drivers with me and we found time to visit some of the local sights such as the water ballet at the Cypress Gardens, where the drivers had an opportunity to chat up the beautiful girls who strolled round the gardens dressed in traditional Southern-style costumes of the mid-19th century. One of the ladies turned out to be the daughter of a parson and came from a village in Norfolk not far from where Jack Sears – one of the Big Healey drivers – lived. Of course, the publicity men visited us at Avon Park and we got photographs of the drivers gazing into the eyes of 'Miss Orange Grove' or 'Miss Sebring'.

Neither the Twin-Cams nor the Austin-Healey 3000s gave us much cause to worry during practice, but Geoffrey had some problems with the quickest Sprite, which had been tuned by Harry Weslake, the gentleman from Rye, in Sussex, who designed the combustion chambers on most of the BMC engines at that time. A hole was found in one of the inlet ports, and Geoffrey had to decide whether to use a standard cylinder head and lose performance or chance it and have the head welded up. He decided to risk the latter and found a local man, who did a good job on it, but could not avoid a small restriction in the port. The car ran very well in the race and only lost a little of its performance at the top end.

I was only concerned with the three Twin-Cams during the race, and things began badly when we lost No 38 (Lund and Escott) after two laps with a broken valve spring. However, the other two cars went well until they came in with brake trouble of a type which we had never encountered before. The brake pipes fixed to the chassis had cracked, either because they had been fastened too securely to the crossmember and suffered from vibration due to the rough track, or perhaps because the material was incorrectly annealed and too brittle. This cost us a lot of time, and the two cars could only finish third and fourth in their class at 69.11mph and 64.08mph, respectively.

The big Healeys circulated very easily at their scheduled speed until Spross crashed in No 19, fortunately without injury. Then all went well and at six hours No 18 was one lap ahead of No 20. There was a routine stop for front brake pads to be changed, then shortly afterwards Peter Riley came in to report that he had only top gear. The Austin Canada mechanics changed the box in under an hour, but the trouble returned and Peter had to drive with only top gear for the last hour or so of the race. He was told to finish at all costs and to keep out of the way of faster cars. The greatly improved torque of the 3000 enabled him to pull out of corners at only 1,000rpm, and he continued to lap only 25 seconds slower than his best times. The other car also lost some gears, but managed to keep going and finish second in class and 15th overall at an average of 72.2mph, followed by Peter and Jack in third place.

The gearbox problem was soon solved by Healey's; it was found that the boxes had been fitted with plain bronze bushes on the layshafts, so they were promptly fitted with improved bearings.

The Sprites did well, Stirling winning his class and finishing second overall in the 4-Hours race at 72mph behind a very fast Abarth. The other Sprite won its class in the 12-Hours race despite having to be pushed to the pits by John Sprinzel to have the head gasket changed.

After the race some of the drivers went on to the Florida coast for a couple of days and we were taken out fishing by the local dealer, and of course they went to the Sailfish Club, which lived up to expectations. Palm Beach was most impressive, with the millionaires' homes situated on broad lawns which led down to the backwaters where their yachts were moored. The de luxe shops in the town were all branches of the most famous names from New York, and the avenues seemed to be lined with Rolls-Royces, Cadillacs, Lincolns and Jaguars.

We had a night in New York on the way back and were taken to see one of the big floor shows; I was not very impressed. The next day we were booked on a Constellation with an airline which boasted that it served a gourmet dinner with specially selected French wines. The menu card was imaginative and the meal was something above the ordinary airline fare, but it was certainly not as promised in the publicity handouts. We were invited to send in our comments to the airline concerned. I addressed mine to the President and in due course got a very courteous letter from the gentleman saying that he regretted that our meal had not come up to expectations and that due to problems the idea would have to be revised somewhat. I felt they were trying a bit harder than Central Airlines!

The trouble with the gearboxes in the 3000s enabled us to improve the boxes in the rally cars at a time when we needed some success with the new cars. It was still early in the year and the matter was put right in time for us to achieve some spectacular results from then on.

The following year there were two entries for Sebring from BMC in the shape of MGA 1600 Coupes to be driven by that experienced pair Jim Parkinson and Jack Flaherty (car No 44) and Peter Riley and John Whitmore (car No 43), with Bob Olthoff as reserve driver and mechanic. In addition to the MGAs there were three Austin-Healey Sprites for the 12-Hours race and six in the 4-Hours race. As I was supposed to keep an eye on all of these I felt that there was rather a surplus of Sprites, but all went well as Geoffrey Healey took care of the Donald Healey entries. The Sprite driven by John Sprinzel and Paul Hawkins was a Speedwell Performance Conversions entry from the company of which they were both directors, and their entry was sponsored by Castrol.

The three Sprites for the 12-Hours race were No 2, for Sprinzel and Hawkins, No 4 for Bozetta and Carlson and No 65 for Colgate and Leavens. The 4-Hours race, which took place before the main event, needed only one nominated driver for each entry, but Donald Healey had managed to get a string of big names to drive his cars: Pat Moss for No 1, Stirling Moss for No 2, Walter Hansgen for No 3, Ed Leavens for No 4, Bruce McLaren for No 5 and Briggs Cunningham for No 6.

Long before the Sebring races, and even before the two MGA 1600s were built at Abingdon, the pending struggle for supremacy in the 1,600cc Grand Touring class had received a lot of publicity in the British motoring press. Our main rivals, the Sunbeam Alpines, had put up some good times at Silverstone during tests and had not been slow to exploit this on television and in the journals. However, this policy proved to be a boomerang so far as they were concerned, because it put Abingdon on its mettle and encouraged the greatest co-operation between the departments concerned in preparing the engines and chassis of the MGs.

The cars were only just ready in time and, as a result, had to be shipped on the *Queen Elizabeth*. The two 1600 Coupes were lightened to within the 5 per cent allowance for Grand Touring cars, the engines were tuned in accordance with the recommendations laid down in the *MG Tuning Manual*, and the chassis were fitted with the optional Dunlop disc brakes with knock-off wheels. Seventeen-gallon tanks were fitted, giving a capacity of 20.41 US gallons. On arrival at New York the MGs, together with John Sprinzel's Sprites, were sent down to Avon Park by road transporter.

Douggie Watts was to be in charge of all the mechanics, and the inscrutable Stan Nicholls was to be our timekeeper. We were joined by Babe Learoyd, the head man from the BMC New York office, and Peter Millard brought his mechanics down from the Canadian competition department. The Sprite team joined us at Avon Park and it was good to have Geoffrey Healey there as the manager, knowing that he would do everything possible to keep things running smoothly.

On stepping out of the plane at West Palm Beach, the British contingent were immediately struck by the local temperature, which was a shade over 80 degrees F, and by the number of expensive British cars around. Ed Bussey, of Ship and Shore, the local distributors, was there to meet us in an Austin-Healey 3000. We got into our various hire cars, and without much trouble reached Avon Park in time for our evening meal and a swim in the adjoining pool.

The next few days were spent in dealing with the various formalities such as scrutineering, allocation of passes and drivers' medicals. This period also served to get the British contingent acclimatized. The local food was widely appreciated and one or two people put on weight quite noticably, whilst others appeared in rather exotic colours and excited the comment: "You British look more Texan than Texans!" Perhaps we did rather overdo it; the climate probably had something to do with it.

Pat Moss and her fiancee Erik Carlsson arrived in a Ford Thunderbird convertible, which was just right for the weather we were experiencing, and the swimming pool became the centre for social gatherings when anybody was off duty.

Practice revealed that the MGs were at least as fast as the Sunbeams, and knowing how we stood we felt confident. Tyre wear was reasonable and suggested that we would have to change wheels only once, and the brake pads were likely to do the whole race. The pressure-fuelling system of Hal Wallace seemed to have been completely tamed, and we estimated that fuel stops would take under a minute. We had some stiffer anti-roll bars flown down from Canada and we were ready.

Stan Nicholls and I decided that we would use the 4-Hours race as a tryout for our lap chart and timing for the big race, assisted by Gil Geitner, Fred Hayes and Grant Clark. This was one of the most exciting small-car races I ever saw, the Fiat Abarths and Austin-Healey Sprites changing places all the time. Pat Moss swopped cars with Stirling on the startline because the clutch release was suspect on his car, but in spite of this she lost only 75 seconds to

Stirling in the first 75 minutes. Pat then came in and handed the car over to Paul Hawkins, John Sprinzel's partner, because she felt that she might wreck the gearbox with no clutch release at all. Meanwhile, the race was being led by Harry Washburn in an Abarth, hotly pursued by four Sprites of Hansgen, McLaren, Moss and Leavens, who thrilled the crowd on almost every lap. Stirling's clutch started to slip and he fell back a little, then a duel developed between Robert Leiss in an Abarth and Hansgen. The fight for second place became so acute at the finish that few people knew who had crossed the line first. The organizers gave the Sprite as second in the press handout, but changed their minds before the prizegiving. So the amended result was Sprites third, fourth, fifth, sixth, seventh and eighth; a fine demonstration of reliability.

The day of the 12-Hours event dawned fine and warm. Our cars looked very smart in their British Racing Green, and the American-driven MG was distinguished by a white-painted front valance below the foglamps. We had no intention of being hurried at the start, for 12 hours is a long time, and the first few laps of a race of this sort were likely to be full of unexpected incidents. Unfortunately, Peter got behind four much slower cars whose drivers would not let him through, and this cost him nearly half a minute in the first half-hour of the race. Jim Parkinson drove strictly to orders and let the Sunbeams go; they were lapping about four seconds a lap quicker than we were. At the end of two hours the class order was Hopkirk/Jopp (Alpine), Procter/Harper (Alpine), Parkinson/Flaherty (MG) and Riley/Whitmore (MG), all with 29 laps completed, and the leading Sunbeam with 1min 42sec in hand.

During the third hour, all four cars made pit-stops for fuel, and the Sunbeams had to change tyres and adjust brakes. The first pit-stops were noteworthy as they showed us the pattern of the race and how slowly we could afford to run. Peter came in at 38 laps and handed over No 43 to John, stopping for 69 seconds, against the time taken by the Alpine of Procter and Harper of 2min 9sec on its 42nd lap. Jim came in to hand over No 44 to Jack and stopped for 54 seconds against the stop of the Hopkirk/Jopp Sunbeam of 4min 11sec. At three hours the order was Parkinson/Flaherty (MG), Procter/Harper (Alpine), Riley/Whitmore (MG) and Hopkirk/Jopp (Alpine), with the MG leading by 46 seconds.

This was very satisfactory as we knew from Dunlop that we would have to change only one set of tyres during the race on each of our cars. Very soon after this the Wilson/Tamburo Alpine retired with bearing trouble, which tidied things up as we now had the two faster Sunbeams running against the two MGs; the two Elvas in the race were never in the picture.

At four hours Jack Flaherty had increased the lead over the nearest Alpine to 1min 28sec and John Whitmore had come up to second place in the class. At five hours the lead had been increased to two minutes without a stop having been made by our rivals, which showed that we were lapping faster. Soon after this both MGs stopped for fuel and tyre changes, the Parkinson/Flaherty car taking 2min 25sec and the Riley/Whitmore car only 2min 8sec against the 4min 44sec for the Hopkirk/Jopp Alpine.

At half-distance the order was the same, but with the track being clearer due to retirements the lap speeds had improved, the MGs settling down to a lap time of 4min 5sec. The Hopkirk/Jopp Alpine was in trouble with overheating caused by a broken dynamo bracket, which allowed the fan belt to slacken off, and lost a further 70 minutes at the pits. At this time we had a lead of one lap and 55 seconds over the Procter/Harper Alpine. Two more short pit-stops were made, but it was evident that we should have to come in for fuel near the end of the race. This was done at the 11th hour (literally), but the drivers were not changed. And so the two MGs took the chequered flag for first and second places in the class, Parkinson/Flaherty also managing fourth overall in the Grand Touring category.

We all felt very happy, and not as tired as some people, for when things go smoothly no-one wears himself out. We had a good team of drivers and mechanics, and an excellent timekeeper in Stan Nicholls, who provided all the information needed to run an accurately controlled race. Our task had been made a great deal more pleasant by the friendly and efficient pit marshals, who had volunteered to supervise our pits because they were MG owners or fans. The Club encouraged this system, and it was a pleasure to see some of the familiar faces each year at Sebring.

There was also an excellent result for the Donald Healey Sprite, which finished between the two MGs in General Classification. Driven by Joe Buzzetta and Glen Carlson, it was only one lap behind the leading MG and one ahead of the other one at 175, 174 and 173 laps, respectively, which meant 14th, 15th and 16th in General Classification. This car was ably managed by Lou Comito, who handled all the Sprites in both races.

A test on the Parkinson/Flaherty MG after the race showed that it was actually 10mph faster than when it had started. Racing obviously improves some cars as well as the breed.

We had two days' holiday on the coast and we were all taken out fishing and entertained most lavishly by Ed Bussey and his partner. Returning to the chill winds of Oxfordshire was a bit of an anti-climax, but we were compensated for that by the warmth of the welcome we experienced when we got there. It was the most successful Sebring sortie to date, and just what the North American agents had wanted.

CHAPTER 14

Interlude

"...there was little doubt that I would miss the camaraderie of the many fine people with whom I had worked and whose company I had enjoyed during my seven years of competition management."

One of the joys of working at the heart of motorsport is that you meet a lot of interesting people, and another is that from time to time, if you are seen to be doing your job with a certain amount of efficiency, you tend to get the occasional career opportunity.

One day – it was during an Alpine Rally – Ian Appleyard sounded me out as to whether I would be interested in changing direction and joining his expanding retail motor business in Yorkshire. I thought about it for a while, and then, when he repeated the offer during 1961, I decided that perhaps it was time to move on, especially as it would mean a considerable increase in income. So I tendered my resignation from BMC and became the Service Manager of Appleyard's of Bradford.

There was a certain attraction in the prospect of being able to spend more time at home instead of having to rush around Europe and further afield so much, but equally there was little doubt that I would miss the camaraderie of the many fine people with whom I had worked and whose company I had enjoyed during my seven years of competition management. It would be the end of an important part of my life, one which had given me a lot of vivid memories, and I was encouraged by the number of people who urged me to set these recollections down in a book; the result was *Seven Year Twitch*, which was published in 1962 and now forms the basis of much of this current volume.

I ended my earlier book with a short chapter in which I set out the duties and responsibilities of the Competition Manager as I saw them during an era when it was still possible for a private entrant to compete against and occasionally beat the works teams. I then added some thoughts about the way in which the sport was being covered by the press, and went on to add a few somewhat pessimistic forecasts for the future of rallying in its then current form. I think some of the words bear repeating here, if only to remind ourselves of the less intense, in some respects less complicated and most certainly financially more frugal environment in which motorsport was conducted more than 30 years ago. This is the gist of what I wrote:

A Competition Manager must always expect to find himself under fire from several sides: from the drivers who want better cars with more rides and more money; from the directors who want a series of outright wins; and from the private owners who want assistance in the shape of free preparation and advice.

The Competition Manager must not neglect the private owners and should foster their enthusiasm without jeopardizing the preparation of his own cars, for each private owner is a potential salesman for the marque because in their own locality he (or she) is often regarded as the motoring expert and can therefore exert considerable influence on local sales. I have known satisfied private owners who not only ran BMC cars themselves, but changed the whole of their business' commercial vehicle fleet to BMC products because they were satisfied, through their own competition experience, that the products were sound. If they are neglected and their inquiries ignored they may well transfer their allegiance to another factory.

The Competition Manager is also the target for demands for help in the organization and financing of stunts, which may vary from trips round the world to driving around the coastline of this small island at some illegal average speed. Most of such stunts are of little or no value because even if the objective is achieved it is soon forgotten; it is far better to spend the available funds on International rallies or record-breaking.

It is debatable whether the title of European Rally Champion makes much impression on a public who knows more about the champions of golf, tennis or football. If the aspirant had to nominate his or her car at the beginning of the season and run it in catalogue trim I think the Championship would have much more interest to the ordinary motorist.

I have often been asked by private owners if it were possible for them to win an International rally with their own machine. If they take enough trouble to see that it is well-prepared and choose the right event they can expect a class win, and in fact several genuine amateur crews do have them to their credit. The chances of an outright win, however, are slight.

I would also like to mention the fine work done by members of the technical press who follow the sport. They drive great distances to report on rallies and visit as many of the timed climbs as they can, so their transport is put to a real test. It is usual to lend works demonstrators on these occasions and they are not spared; I have seen cars leave us with a good set of tyres and return with them bald after a fortnight.

These knowledgeable gentlemen write good, honest reports about events and the cars they drive, and many of them have engineering qualifications which enable them to write with authority. I am sorry I cannot say the same of some reporters of the non-technical press, who are incapable of distinguishing between a disc and a drum-braked car and whose driving ability is such that they never extend a vehicle under test, except in a straight line. Editors should realize that there are some intelligent motorists amongst their millions of readers!

Members of a works team should always remember that they represent their country, the marque and themselves, in that order, and that when on public view they should behave accordingly. This sense of responsibility is well imprinted in the Moss family, for both Stirling and Pat will never refuse a request for a photograph or an interview, or even an autograph, however tired they may be. For example, I saw Pat and Ann sign nearly a hundred autographs at the end of the Liège-Rome-Liège Rally in 1960, and that after four days on the road.

As I see it, the future for rallying is not good. Rallies are being crowded off the road and as a result their planning will have to undergo a change if they are to continue. The 1961 Tulip Rally provided a possible pattern, with easy road sections which linked the special tests used to decide the outright winner and class victors. Competitors could choose their own time to clock in at the tests provided they reached the road controls, which were few and far apart, at the proper times and showed that they had not exceeded the ceiling average speed before or after the test. This system will, I think, be followed by other organizers in western Europe, but tougher events will have to go further east, where there are fewer tourists and the roads are rougher. Events held over the east European roads are of great value in developing suspensions and brakes capable of standing up to the thousands of miles of dirt roads which exist in other parts of the world.

Motorsport will endure in one form or another for as long as the automobile exists, but when a new generation of young men and women come to compete and organize, I hope they will bear in mind that their sport will only live on if they do not inconvenience people who have other interests and pastimes...

And with that I turned my back on motorport...at least for a while. Little did I think when I moved north to begin a new stage in my career that within three years another offer would come my way, one which would take me back into another spell of competition management, not this time with BMC, but with a member of the opposition.

CHAPTER 15

My return to motorsport

"There were several contenders for the appointment of Competition Manager, not least because there were a number of factions within the company, each with a particular axe to grind."

During the three years between the time I left BMC and when I first became involved with Rootes and Chrysler there were dramatic changes both within the industry and in the wider world of motorsport. Gone for good, it seemed, was the halcyon period of which I have already written.

Whilst working at Appleyard's of Bradford from 1961 to 1963 there was ample evidence to remind me that the co-driver whom I had recommended to John Thornley at MG as my successor had been the right person for the job of Competition Manager of the British Motor Corporation.

Stuart Turner, who never stood still for very long, had approached the question of "Where do we go from here?" by taking a new look at the International rally scene from a different point of view to my own. He now had a brilliant new rally car in the Mini-Cooper, as well as the Austin-Healey 3000, which was at the zenith of its performance. He could forget the badge-engineered models which I had sometimes been obliged to use as fill-in for a likely class win. In Pat Moss he had the best lady rally driver in the world, who was showing that she could beat the male opposition in a succession of events; and when Pat and Ann Wisdom left Abingdon he found another pair of ladies in Pauline Mayman and Valerie Domleo, who were in the same class as their predecessors, but armed with a car which was easier to drive than a Healey 3000. Ann, who had married Peter Riley, left Abingdon after she and Pat had won the Tulip Rally in May 1962. After that, Pat had her most successful year in competitions with Pauline Mayman as her co-driver, but she was made an offer she could not refuse by Ford and left BMC at the end of 1962. Pat married Erik Carlsson, the most famous of all the Scandinavian drivers, on February 11, 1963.

Stuart had become convinced that the Scandinavian drivers were quite exceptional, and he abandoned the 'British only' driver policy which I had kept from the beginning for patriotic reasons. He also had a team of dedicated mechanics and office staff who could be relied upon to work until they dropped to get the job done properly.

So there we have the BMC picture, which was the most successful anywhere in Europe from 1961 to 1967, when Stuart left to join Castrol for a while before he moved on again to achieve further distinction as Ford of Europe's Director of Motorsport.

Late in 1963, my old friend Peter Wilson, who was now the engineer in charge of development at Rootes, in Humber Road, Coventry, rang me to ask if I was interested in going back into competition management. Peter had been one of the drivers selected by John Thornley to drive a Le Mans MG in the 1955 Ulster TT, and he had been my co-driver in an experimental sortie with some modified Austins in the Geneva Rally in 1956, and again in a trial run with a Mini in the 1959 Viking Rally. He told me that the famous Norman Garrad was retiring and that Timothy Rootes wanted to find a replacement who would take a new look at competitions policy and try to take Rootes back into the forefront again. When I visited Peter at his home on January 1 I discovered that the company had entered two Sunbeam Tiger prototypes for Le Mans because they wanted to get as much publicity for the production model as possible. The Hillman Imp was also mentioned, but I will discuss that project separately.

There were several contenders for the appointment of Competition Manager, not least because there were a number of factions within the company, each with a particular axe to grind. Some people had been told that they were in the running for the job, and other directors seemed to think that they had a better right than Timothy Rootes to appoint the next Competition Manager. Broadly, the factions were split into engineering, who could benefit from accelerated testing derived from rallies; advertising, who felt that they should control the type of event entered in order to gain the best publicity; and the followers of Norman Garrad, who felt that he might put in a good word for them even if they were not well fitted for the appointment.

Peter took me out in one of the development Tigers and I was suitably impressed, even if it was a rather dark night. Timothy Rootes saw me the next morning and he offered me the job. There were to be competition department meetings in his office at Ryton at 9.30am every Monday to report progress. I told him that I would have to give Appleyard's a months notice and would have to take a bit of time to find a new home. He was generous in that he laid on a car for me to go home to Shipley at weekends until I moved south. Unfortunately, we did not manage to sell our house for some time, so I moved into a private house near Weedon, where they catered for my wants very well until the time came to move my family in July.

I started at Humber Road on February 17 and was not unduly surprised at the sad state of affairs which I found in the competition department. I had talked things over with Peter Procter, a Rootes racing and rally driver of considerable experience, who lived near me in Yorkshire, so I had been well briefed as to the state of things as he saw them.

The staff were demoralized, having had no leadership or well-defined programme for some time except for the Le Mans 24-Hours race and a proposal to enter three Sunbeam Tigers in the Geneva Rally in October. Two people who really belonged to other departments were 'residents' in my department. One of these was John Rowe, of publicity, who was installed as team manager and, it transpired, had been promised the job of Competition Manager by Brian Rootes. He lived at Croydon, which could not have been very convenient or efficient as a base for him. There was also a very abrasive young man called John Goff, who later stressed that he was the competition department's resident engineer, and not my technical assistant.

Now if you have people who have a foot in each camp during a very stressful period they often return to their base with only half of a story, which in turn can lead to further misunderstandings. I soon found that I had made an enemy in Brian Rootes for a number of reasons, the principal one being that I did not intend to allow Norman Garrad to be part of my party at Le Mans.

Of course, I could see no good reason why we should be going to Le Mans anyhow. It had all come about because the Sunbeam Alpines, with nicely profiled Harrington hardtops, had performed modestly and reliably at Le Mans in 1961 and, much to everyone's surprise, had won the coveted Index of Thermal Efficiency, beating Porsche by a very small amount. Peter Wilson had traded on Rootes success there and talked the Board into running two of the new Sunbeam Tigers in the 1964 race, But the specification and performance of the Le Mans car had not been thought through. The Board insisted that the cars should resemble the production model as closely as possible, but Brian Lister, who was to build the prototype, wanted to build a spaceframe car with an aluminium shell; he was overruled.

A golden opportunity had been missed from the sales point of view in planning the appearance of the new model. Harrington of Brighton was building a very attractive Alpine coupé, which might have commanded a much higher price and a certain exclusive quality even at a reduced output. There was also the Venezia coupe, created and designed in Italy by Touring of Milan as an alternative for the Humber Sceptre, which might have provided further inspiration. It could easily have been ascertained that of the 25,000 or so Corvettes which were sold per annum in the States, 35 per cent were fixed-head models. The Americans seemed more likely to pay a few more dollars for a Corvette with its home-grown characteristics. The name Sunbeam did not cut much ice compared with other European manufacturers such as Jaguar, Bentley and Porsche.

Rootes had no experience of building race versions of Ford V8 engines. The 260cu in (4.2-litre) engine had been chosen for its ability to fit into the production model, which was after all only a Sunbeam Alpine which had started life with a 1,494cc engine in 1960. Carroll Shelby had built the prototype which Ian Garrad had brought over to England in order to sell the whole scheme to the directors. Shelby therefore agreed to build the race engines and some spares, which could be used for the rally cars. As the cars had to resemble the production Tigers in specification as closely as possible we were precluded from using the much better and more reliable 289cu in (4.7-litre) engines which Shelby would race himself in the Le Mans Cobra.

On February 19 I went to see Brian Lister at Cambridge with John Goff, who was in charge of the project for Peter Wilson. We went in what must have been the last of the works Sunbeam Rapiers, which I had asked Jim Ashworth to prepare for me. He was the competition department's so-called chief engineer, with Gerry Spencer as chief mechanic. At BMC I would have ranked them as foreman and deputy foreman, but perhaps Rootes preferred to give people more prestigious titles.

I had always regarded the Rapier as being something special as it had been the main weapon of my opposition for so long. The power was there, but the suspension might not have existed; they could have bolted the axles to the chassis and I would not have noticed the difference. My ride to Cambridge increased my admiration for the works drivers, such as Peter Harper, 'Tiny' Lewis, Andrew Cowan, Keith Ballisat, Peter Procter and Rosemary Smith (Paddy Hopkirk had gone to BMC in 1962). The time would come when I would meet these drivers and see if we could fit them into a proper rally programme. But meanwhile, the mystery remained as to why the technicians had not been allowed to develop a car with a working suspension which would have been less tiring to drive.

Brian Lister, who was well-known for building a string of successful sports-racing cars such as the Lister-Jaguars, showed me the car and told me of his problems. The main worry was the late arrival of the principal assemblies, such as the engine from Shelby and the rear axle from Salisbury, as this was holding up the panel-beaters, who wanted to check the wheelarch dimensions. The Dunlop competition manager had told Peter Wilson that we would need 15in wheels as our estimated speed on the straight would be in excess of 150mph. They had a suitable alloy wheel, but it was not yet available in the numbers we wanted. I went back to Coventry with a long list of problems and the knowledge that the Le Mans test weekend was fixed for April 18 and 19.

I met Alec Caine of engineering the next day, and he was most helpful; he knew about all the problems as he had been the engineer in charge of the Sunbeam Tiger project from the start and was working closely with Kevin Beattie of Jensen Motors, who had built the 12 AF (Alpine-Ford) prototype test cars. It was confirmed on February 28 that we had two cars entered for the 24-Hours race. Oliver Speight of Dunlop called and took the order for the wheels; I needed 32 at £38 each, but the red tape for the order indicated that Rootes paperwork was still in the quill pen era.

Wednesday, March 11, and still there were no Salisbury axles, so I rang them and was told "Monday". Monday came and still no axles, but I put one of my terriers onto the job and I think Brian Lister received the first one that week, only to find that the track was wrong.

Meanwhile, I was not making much progress at Timothy Rootes' Monday morning meetings; anything of a controversial nature was brushed aside and I had much difficulty in getting answers to matters which needed to be settled urgently. For example, there was the replacement for John Rowe as my assistant and team leader; I had chosen Ian Hall, who had been a works co-driver, and eventually I did get him appointed. He joined us on April 1. I also needed to know if I would take the place of Norman Garrad on the Sporting sub-committee of the Society of Motor Manufacturers and Traders, which was a non-executive committee composed of the competition managers and trade representatives of specialist equipment suppliers, as well as a member of the RAC Motor Sports Department. The minutes of that committee went up to the main SMMT committees, and this kept them in touch with the feelings of the racing and rally fraternity.

By this time our department's budget had been severely eroded by overspending on the Le Mans cars, and that sum would inevitably be deducted from the money allocated for rallies in 1964. The 1964 Alpine Rally had been omitted as it started on the same weekend as Le Mans.

Finally, on April 14, the first Le Mans Tiger was collected from Cambridge, carrying the registration number 7734 KV. There were many minor faults in the car, but there was no time to go to Silverstone for some handling tests. Instead, we set off for Hurn Airport on Friday, April 17, leaving the works at

6am. The Rootes personnel were John Goff, Jim Ashworth, George Coles, Tom Cobley (engineering) and myself, with Ken Hazlewood of Listers. The race car was driven on the road in convoy with our van. Laurence Pomeroy, the Technical Editor of *The Motor*, who was due to travel in the plane ahead of us, wanted to know where we were staying, but I was not keen to have him with us as we did not welcome the press in any form at that moment.

Apart from some brake adjustments, the race car behaved quite well as far as Loué, some 28 kilometres west of Le Mans, where we were to stay at the *Hotel Ricordeau*. This had been booked for the team by Norman Garrad, and it turned out to be a very expensive establishment where the presentation of meals took no account of time that might be needed for urgent work. I had considerable disagreement with the management concerning the size of the bill before we left for England and made them fully aware that we could neither afford their prices nor their old world attitude to more pressing affairs. The hotel was later sold and renamed the *Laurent*, and subsequently it was awarded a Michelin rosette.

The next day we arrived at the pits in good time to start testing at 10am with two of our chosen drivers, Peter Procter and Keith Ballisat. When the car was brought in for us to hear the drivers' comments, Mike Parkes, who had left Rootes to join Ferrari, came over to the pit and very kindly offered to take the car out for a couple of laps. He came back on the third lap having timed himself on the flying lap and through some of the sections for which he had a yardstick. He was polite, but inferred that we had a lot more to do to become even slightly competitive. We were no longer in the Alpine class, something that the management failed to grasp even when the race was over.

Tests showed that the only engine which we had so far received from America ran hot with low oil pressure, caused, it was thought, by oil surge in the sump. We had the opinions of both Mike Parkes and Keith Ballisat to confirm that the roadholding was poor and the brakes were worse. The maestro had lapped in 4min 26.4sec against his Ferrari time of 3min 47.1sec. We returned the next day having reduced the oil level in the sump a little, and Peter Procter turned in a lap of 4min 33sec and saw 6,000rpm on the straight, which was over 150mph. We were using a bigger radiator, which helped things a bit, but the real handicap was the poor roadholding, even with different rollbars. We did not continue for long as we knew that we could investigate the problems which had arisen at Silverstone, on the banked track at the Motor Industry Research Establishment at Nuneaton, or at Snetterton, which was more convenient for Listers. So the whole party broke up and went their respective ways on the Monday morning.

We arranged a test session at Snetterton on April 29, the driver being Keith Ballisat, and all the specialists were present from both engineering and Listers. The rear springs had been changed by building them out of Hillman Husky and other pieces to give a rate of 180lb, and Koni shock absorbers were fitted to a setting recommended by Ferrari! After lunch the Konis were readjusted and the Panhard rod location was lowered 3in from what it had been at Le Mans. These alterations cured the axle tramp and Ballisat put in a lap at 1min 50sec without extending things, saying that he had about 5sec in hand. Mike Parkes had lapped Snetterton in 1m 39sec. We tried a sandbag in the tail, which improved matters, and decided to lower and reposition the fuel tank. It was felt that at the front the car should run with 6in tyres, a stiffer rollbar and higher-rate springs. We went home feeling more optimistic, but my nagging fear was that the engines would let us down.

I had been told that our old friend Stan Nicholls, who had been our timekeeper at Sebring several times, was now working for Rootes. He had been made redundant by the GEC export department when they closed it in May 1963 and had got a job in the parts department of Rootes at the old Singer factory in Birmingham at a sadly reduced salary. There would be no problem in getting his services without his pay being docked this time, and I invited him to come and see me, knowing that I had one of the best timekeepers to be found anywhere.

By the middle of May we had the fourth Shelby engine and some parts. We took the test car to Silverstone, with Bernard Unett as the driver, and he lapped in 1min 52sec with the high axle ratio, which was quite good. Bernard, who was renowned for calling a spade a spade, thought very little of the roadholding, but being a master of throttle control, he was probably doing better than our drivers would do when it came to the race.

At the end of May we had completed some high-speed tests at MIRA and were satisfied with the engine cooling, but not the oil temperature or the low oil pressure as a result of it; some work on sump baffles helped, but low oil pressure was to be our problem on all the Shelby engines.

On June 5 it was announced that Chrysler had taken 30 per cent of the Rootes shares for £12 million. Most of us thought that it would be a good thing, but I knew that the Tiger with a Ford engine would not last long. The question which occupied the engineering department from that moment concerned the availability of a suitable Chrysler engine.

On Sunday, June 14, I went to my office to check that all was ready for an early start the next day. Everything seemed to be in order, and I told Jim Ashworth to see that the race numbers were covered up on two of the cars; the prototype was going as well as it might be needed for practice and in any case would be useful for spare parts. The next morning we set off for Hurn with the service cars (the race cars went down by transporter via Cherbourg), and by evening the Tigers were safely stowed away at a garage we had reserved at Arnage. I had also booked accomodation near the garage for the mechanics.

The drivers, technicians and engineering department personnel were all staying at the *Hotel de Paris*, in Le Mans. We had arranged to have a caravan in the paddock. Scrutineering took place on the Tuesday at the track after lunch. We had furnished the organizers, the *ACO*, with certificates signed by the RAC, which quoted the engine number and cubic capacity of each engine after it had been inspected by the Royal Automobile Club at our works: car No 8 had the wrong engine number, but the representative of our club vouched for it; car No 9 was in order. I was not impressed by Jim Ashworth, who had had to borrow a spanner in order to drain the fuel tanks in order that their capacity could be measured; they proved to be 137 and 135 litres, respectively. Both cars weighed 1,187kg.

The drivers pairings were as follows:

> No 8: Claude Dubois and Keith Ballisat   ADU 179B
> No 9: Jimmy Blumer and Peter Procter   ADU 180B

When the cars practised the next day No 8 ran a big-end after only one and a half laps, while No 9 was not performing as well as we would have liked when compared with the prototype, in which we had had a reasonable amount of confidence. We left that to the engineers to sort out as it might have been caused by a number of things, beginning with a suspected low-reading tachometer. The engine in No 8 was changed and I went back to the hotel and rang Coventry to discuss with Peter Wilson the possibility of having to withdraw both cars before the race. John Rowe, who was with me, decided that we had better start, even if we didn't manage to finish, but I was against that policy. Of course, we were in this sorry state of affairs because the whole programme had been started six months too late. The other handicap was the weight penalty; the cars were 160lb heavier than the Shelby Cobras, which had the bigger Ford engine in any case, as well as 66lb heavier than the production Tigers which they were meant to represent, a matter of which Brian Lister had warned us repeatedly, but which the management had chosen to ignore.

I went back to the garage at Arnage that night and waited until the engine change was finished, then I took the car out with Jim Ashworth as a riding mechanic; I selected the road to La Fleche as being the best on which to do a running-in test; we went down to the end a couple of times and managed an indicated 150mph, which at any rate proved that the headlights were adequate.

Race day arrived, and the best thing that could be said of our cars was that they looked well turned out. Car No 8 retired with piston failure after three hours, prior to which it had been timed at 161.6mph on the Mulsanne straight, although it was never placed better than 26th. Car No 9 ran for nine hours before it retired with a broken crankshaft, probably caused by too much clearance in the main bearings. It had completed 123 laps at an average speed of 107mph, been timed on the Mulsanne straight at 162.2mph and had climbed to 18th position in the last hour.

Peter Procter was driving when the end came and, years later, he recalled the episode in graphic detail:

"It was quite funny when it happened, funny when I got over the shock of it, that is! It was dark, of course, and I was bombing past the pits; we had been doing 164 or 165mph on the Mulsanne straight and it was nearly as quick down through White House and past the pits in those days – and there was no barrier between the track and the pit lane. Just as I got level with the beginning of the pits the engine blew. I just remember a flash of fire coming out from under the bonnet. The steering locked absolutely solid – it was full of knuckle joints, and the engine had blown up in such a big way that it jammed all these, and I just couldn't move it a fraction of an inch.

"I hit the brakes very hard and drifted over the demarcation line between the track and the pit lane. I gradually crept nearer to the pits, still going at quite a rate. Eventually I rubbed the car against the pit counter and stopped. When I got out, Marcel Becquart, I think it was, who was the pit marshal, rushed up to me and said: 'Ah, Pierre, you are in trouble, you have crossed the line, you are not allowed to do this', and so on. I was still trying to get over the shock, so when he said: 'We must move the car', I said: 'All right, you steer, I'll push'. So he climbed in and after a while he said: 'It will not steer', and I said: 'That's why I parked it up against the ******* counter!'

"It was very lucky that there was no car refuelling at that point, otherwise there would have been another disaster."

Some people thought that the handling was poor, but Keith Ballisat thought that it was adequate for the Le Mans circuit. Of course, spoilers were in their infancy, and sportscars with fastbacks must have been pretty light at the back when doing 160mph. John Wyer with the GT40 had worked this out during the practice weekend at Le Mans in April as his drivers had complained about funny roadholding. When they came back they made some spoilers and created a downforce of over 300lb at the back end, then ran the cars with spoilers during the 24-Hours race... That was why our bag of sand seemed to make things better, but our engineers drew the wrong conclusion.

A Shelby Cobra finished fourth and proved that the Ford V8 could last for 24 hours. We were told by someone whom we could trust that he had heard that the Shelby testbed had been out of action for a fortnight at about the time when our engines were being prepared. Eventually we obtained a refund from Shelby and no doubt it was used to buy engines for the rally Tigers.

We returned and took stock of the situation. The improved Hillman Imp was not ready, but the production Tiger was not only available but it had been homologated and could therefore start in International rallies.

The two race cars were sold off at knockout prices, but I was able to keep the mule, 7734 KV, which with the connivance of engineering was lent to Bernard Unett. Bernard takes up the story in his own inimitable style:

"I was working in the Rootes experimental department at the time, and I'd won the Freddie Dixon Trophy the year before – 1964 – in an Alpine. Marcus Chambers lent me the practice car, the mule, to run in the *Autosport* Championship in 1965; it was never actually my property, even though I kept it at home in my chicken shed. Rootes didn't provide any cash, and as for spares – well, I worked there...

"We modified it extensively from how it ran at Le Mans. We worked on both the front and rear suspension (pick-up points and so on), fitted larger rims with much bigger tyres, and halfway through the season we installed a 4.7-litre engine, complete with Weber carbs, Shelby heads, hot cam and so on. It was close to GT40 spec, and I reckon we were getting about 360bhp. There was also a lightweight gearbox, from memory, but we didn't do much to the brakes – they were pretty impressive with massive discs all round.

"Even so it was a pretty horrible car, with horrible handling. It was awful, very twitchy. The wheelbase was far too short – I reckon that with the fat tyres on the back there was more width than wheelbase. It was really a point and squirt car: the front end wasn't too bad, even though it was heavy up there, but the rear end was very, very light. You had to be gentle with the gas, as they used to say, otherwise you'd be round on yourself. I remember at Crystal Palace, going out for practice, first lap, ahead of everyone, and spinning at the Glades! It was close... On the straight, of course, it was phenomenal.

"I had some good races at Brands, Oulton, Silverstone, all over. The opposition came from John Miles in a Ginetta, Martin Hone in a Porsche and Ron Fry in a Ferrari 250LM. The best race, though, was at the back end of the season, at an AMOC meeting, it wasn't even a round of the Championship. There was a scratch race, and I was up against Astons and Cobras and things – and I won, much to the horror of the AMOC – I've still got the candelabra from that.

"Stronger opposition came from Brian Redman in the Red Rose lightweight E-type. He didn't do the Championship, he'd just appear at Oulton and blow me into the weeds. Until Croft, the first race with the 4.7-engine – then I blew him into the weeds.

"I enjoyed it, though it was all so different, you could have a good weekend's racing for £25, so you didn't need to bother with all that sponsorship rubbish. It was a wonderful season, especially winning the Championship.

"The next year I raced Alan Fraser's Tiger in marque races. The authorities put a clamp on the LM Tiger, saying it wasn't eligible, so we took the bits out of it and put them in the standard car... I remember the LM body sitting in a field behind Fraser's for a long time afterwards."

The two Le Mans cars have since been well restored and are now worth more than we spent on the whole adventure.

CHAPTER 16

Rallying with the Tigers

"For Des O'Dell it was a strange change from the smell and noise of GT cars in the pits, but he took it all in his stride..."

With the Le Mans problems out of the way and the first of the scheduled rallies, the Geneva, to be planned for, drivers to be selected and homologation papers checked, there was plenty to do. The Hillman Imp had run in a number of rallies in 1964, but without any success, and I decided that we would at least show what the Tigers could do before turning our attention to the complex problem of converting the Imp into a competition car.

The first of the production cars which were being prepared for rallies was ready early in July, but owing to minor faults it was not ready for an appraisal trip which I had laid on to start on July 12. Instead, the development department lent us one of their cars, and I set out with Gerry Spencer in an estate car and Peter Riley in the Tiger to pick up Tiny Lewis at Halkin Street, in Knightsbridge, and John Goff at The Oval tube station and we reached the *White Cliffs Hotel* at Dover in good time for an evening meal. It was the first time in six months that I felt I was back on the right track and getting paid to do something I really liked. I think Tiny and Gerry both felt the same way about things, and although the trip was to have its unfair share of misfortunes, we managed to enjoy every bit of it. This was not to be a recce trip in the BMC and Rootes tradition; it was an appraisal to see what would fall off, if the cooling was adequate, whether the brakes would stand up to mountain driving, and if the roadholding was adequate. Of the available power I had no doubt.

We were due on the boat at the West Dock at 11pm. This was the ferry that used to take the night train to Brussels and Paris, which came on board at about the same time. Cars were very few and were put in a garage on the upper deck; their drivers and passengers had cabins on the same level, with a small breakfast room and bar adjacent. I had often used this crossing as one had the advantage of a very early start from Dunkirk.

It took a long while to get the cars stowed because one of the stevadores who were supervising the job had a difference of opinion with his mate, who took the tickets from the drivers, because he hadn't written down the registered number of the cars each time he collected them. Finally, the other one took his clipboad and the tickets, threw them onto the ground and walked off. After some delay he came back and we were allowed to drive on board. We had some warm beer and a very hot cabin, the latter because the steam heating on those ships all too often could not be turned off because the taps were seized solid.

We started to disembark at Dunkirk at 4.30am and were away from Customs half an hour later, which was about right. The Tiger was to go on ahead on an agreed route; we breakfasted at Reims and reached Val Suzon, just short of Dijon, for lunch.

The weather was perfect, and the luncheon was served in the garden: melon with port, crab avocado, then guinea fowl followed by cheese and then raspberries. The *Hostellerie Val Suzon* was one of those unique establishments which either John Gott or John Williamson must have introduced me to 10 years before. It is still in the Michelin, but one should consult the opening hours with care.

Our post-prandial contentment was marred by the failure of the Tiger's starter, then, after a short delay, we went by one of Tommy Wisdom's 'quiet roads' to Bourg-en-Bresse and Bourgoin across country, passing the holidaymakers bathing in the river Ain, to reach the *Parc Hotel*, Grenoble, which I suspect must have come from one of Norman Garrad's lists, for it was much too upmarket for me. However, the restaurant was closed, so we had a good meal in the 'place' nearby, and retired feeling that we had covered a reasonable distance.

We were away at 04.15 the next morning to attack the Col de Menee, reaching the Col de Rousset at about 6.30am, when we found that the tyres were fouling the wings, so a bit of panel-beating was needed. Also, the Panhard rod retaining bracket had become unwelded, so the rod was removed temporarily. The car was sent off and the two-way radios were tested out. Of course, there was very little chance of meeting any traffic, and some good runs were made. I noted that the gearing seemed about right for the gradients. We had finished that section by about 09.00 and drove down to Die for breakfast.

There was not a lot that we could do except make for our night stop, which was the *Hotel Cour* at Carpentras, which was a favourite of the HRG drivers and, later, the BMC crews. It will not be found in the guides, if it still exists, being very unpretentious, with lace curtains hiding the view through the ground floor windows. It had a very useful garage at the back, which was large enough to take half a dozen cars and enable one to unpack all one's gear and restow it in a more accessible manner. The food was traditional French cuisine, and the welcome from the two aged proprietors made me feel that I was picking up where I had left off three years before.

We were lucky to find a local garage after lunch which was open on July 14, being the *fête nationale*. Fortunately they had a lift, and the Panhard rod bracket was soon fixed. We had a walk around to look at the decorations and sample the local beer, and after an early evening meal retired for a call at 04.15 with Mont Ventoux in mind.

This was to be a test with two fans fitted, one standard and one electric in front of the radiator. A number of climbs were made, starting from Bedoin, and to begin with the temperature continued to rise until the summit was reached, where the control was placed for the Alpine Rally. We removed the foglight and the bar and dropped the temperature by 8 degrees C, which was reasonable. A number of climbs were made, and the radio, when used with an observer nearly halfway up the climb, proved very effective. However, the shock absorbers were not standing up to the work, but Tiny Lewis said that they would suffice for the tests.

It is known that the exposed position of Mont Ventoux, at 1,909m, affects its climate to a marked degree and there is nearly always an average difference of 11 degrees C between the top and the foot of the mountain. Until 1973, the road was used as a speed hill-climb and featured in the European Mountain Championship; that year, Mieusset, driving a March, took 9min 3.6sec for an average of 142.278km/h – about 90mph.

We left the Ventoux area after lunch and reached the *Ferme Napoleon*, at Le Logis-de-Pin, on the N75, by late afternoon. It was a luxurious one-night stopping place, and the guests were a rather gilded collection comprising all sections of the moneyed classes. However, it was completely lacking in anything like that which the French call *accueil* as there appeared to be no host. We amused ourselves at dinner in speculating on the relationships between the ladies and their escorts, and decided that none of them were married couples. I think it is the hotel which figured in *The Day of the Jackal*. Needless to say, the food was excellent.

The following morning the Tiger was away at 04.30, with Gerry Spencer and myself making our way to Sigale by soon after 7am and the Tiger, which had gone by way of Entrevaux, arriving half an hour later. We had breakfast in the tatty little cafe in the square by the church. Afterwards we went back via the Col de Bleine, and I thought of the last time I had driven along that road in a BMC 'Barge' with Douggie Hamblin when we had followed the Morley brothers to victory in the *Coupe des Alpes*. Now, here we were, a rather inefficient unit, testing a car with great potential; the whole thing had to be built up all over again, and how exasperating it was not to be able to get even the most normal things done quickly and efficiently.

Meanwhile, it was back to the *Ferme Napoleon* and then off to Nice, lunch by the harbour and then along to the airport to put John on a plane to London at 3pm. We went to Juan for a swim on the way back as it was so hot that even an ice cold beer failed to cool us down. We were glad to get back to the *Ferme Napoleon*, which was much cooler, but there was no swimming pool there.

We left before 5am the next morning, got to the Col d'Allos (2,240m) at about 7am, and found that the Tiger had had a fire in the main battery cable, which the crew had insulated quite effectively. They had made a number of climbs and decided that the axle ratio was too high. We could not use the two-way radio, and that led to an accident, about which Peter Riley filled in some of the details not long ago. Tiny was driving and Peter told him that he was going too fast as there might be local traffic. On a blind hairpin they hit a Renault Dauphine head-on. The luggage in a Dauphine, being a rear-engined car, was, of course, carried at the front, and in this case the lid popped up and out shot madame's suitcase, which opened and spread her interesting lingerie all over the Tiger's bonnet. Quite rightly, both Monsieur and Madame were extremely annoyed and Peter and Tiny did their best to help by finding a telephone and getting the garage at St Andre-les-Alpes to send out their crash wagon. Some weeks later Peter was in my office when the insurance claim for the Renault arrived. The car was a write-off, but Peter pointed out that monsieur was claiming for a Renault 8, a more expensive car than the model that he had lost. However, the difference was not all that much, so we both signed the form and hoped that he was suitably compensated.

The Tiger was sorted out, and on a day which the local papers would claim was the hottest for 60 years, we drove on to Barcelonnette for a lunch stop and thence to Briançon to stay at the Vauban, where that evening we enjoyed a leisurely dinner as we had no early start the next day.

The following morning we climbed the Col de Lautaret (2,058m), the Galibier (2,640m) and the Col du Telegraphe (1,570m), which is a great scenic drive, with plenty of snow on the mountain peaks even in July; then we lunched at St Jean-de-Maurienne and continued on past Lac d'Annecy, Frangy and Bellegarde to St Claude, a useful test for the Tiger. We stayed at an auberge that night and left early for Pontarlier and Belfort to test on the Ballon d'Alsace, going via the Col de Bussang and the Col de Bramont – a very easy climb, which was probably used in the Tulip Rally as it would be easy to get it closed to traffic for timed tests. After that we found a nice little roadhouse between Remiremont and Epinal, just by Pouxeux, which was being run by a couple of very pretty young ladies; after consuming a well-cooked and moderately priced meal we unfortunately had to press on, in spite of being asked why we couldn't stay longer! I expect the establishment has long gone as these days a trunk road passes the front door. We reached Bar-le-Duc, on the Marne, that evening and crossed the Channel the next day.

It had been proposed that we ran a Tiger in the *Tour de France*, but Peter Riley, who had been on that event previously, was concerned about the cooling as the circuits were fast and there would be a lot of full-throttle driving. However, the scheme was dropped because we could not use the right wheel sizes for racing tyres, and Dunlop would not agree to us using our 13in wheels with a gross weight of 23cwt (2,576lb).

Meanwhile, by July 25, I had finally found somewhere to live, and we moved to the *Old Forge* at Braunston, near Rugby, which was located most conveniently just opposite an old inn called *The Fox*.

I expected that we would encounter car problems of a different type from those we had suffered at Le Mans, and I wanted to see John Wyer, whom I had first met when he was a young salesman for Solex Carburettors at their Marylebone service depot in 1933. I had gone there to have a new carburettor fitted to my 2-litre RM Alfa Romeo.

John was beginning to run his very successful team of GT40 racing cars from his works at Slough. We had discussed the prospects of joining up in a tuning and race preparation business during the last year of the war, but the project fell through and he joined Peter Monkhouse and Ian Connell at Monaco Motors to make a name for himself in race preparation which was to lead, by way of HRG and Aston Martin, to Ford and Porsche.

In 1963, John had set up the new premises at Slough where Eric Broadley, of Lola Cars, was to join him, coming from his overcrowded premises in Bromley. Owing to personality clashes and the fact that neither Broadley's key personnel nor John Wyer's had had their terms of reference set out clearly enough by the Ford Motor Company, there was still friction even after the move. This did not make for the happiest of working conditions at a time when there was so much to get done in a limited time.

In 1964, those terms of reference were tidied up after Le Mans, and I was amused to read them some years later in Wyer's book *That Certain Sound* and to see that as a minor matter it included, "Liaison with Rootes, who were using a Ford engine in the Sunbeam Tiger", along with liaison with two other racing car builders in the UK who were also using Ford engines. The Ford

Motor Company's Special Vehicle Activity became Ford Advanced Vehicles in July 1964, shortly after their own *post mortem* into the results of their first entry into Le Mans.

No-one had told me anything about this liaison, but it didn't matter as I knew that I would get some sound advice from John Wyer, as I had always kept in touch with him and his wife through Peter Clark and Eric Thompson and had a great respect for him as a team manager and engineer. We had a chat on the phone and John said that he might be able to find me a good man who knew about Ford V8 engines and had enough initiative to find and cure troubles without too much delay. At about the same time Peter Wilson must have been talking to John Wyer as well, and told him of my problems, because shortly afterwards I had a telephone call from John to say that he had someone who would suit my requirements. However, he did point out that the man whom he recommended was in a bit of a predicament. Although he was reluctant to leave FAV, which was going through some stress and confusion at this time, his wife Jean was about to produce her first child, and he was anxious to have a job with a more stable environment.

He was Desmond O'Dell, who had been doing a lot of overtime during the last few months and no doubt was feeling the stress. However, he was still very loyal to John, having come over with him from Aston Martin. After an interview with Peter Wilson, Desmond took his wife to look at likely places in which to buy a house, and the charm of Leamington Spa finally tipped the scales. It was decided that I should have Des with me as my technical assistant, and John Goff should return from whence he came; Des joined us at the end of October, and I was to wish that he had been available sooner.

During the latter half of July and all of August, when not interrupted by annual works holidays, I had been able to improve the first of the rally Tigers using the data which we had obtained in the July tests in France. Helped by the remarkable Leo Kuzmicki, I gradually obtained more power from a Group 2 Hillman Imp and started on plans for a 1,000cc Group 3 car.

Alan Fraser was a well-to-do gentleman who lived at Hildenborough, in Kent. He was a personal friend of Norman Garrad and Brian Rootes and had been quite successful as a private entrant in rallies. I was told by Timothy Rootes to give him as much help as I could and that he was going to switch from Sunbeam Rapiers to Imps and Tigers. Alan Fraser came to see me and told me that he had entered a Rapier and a Humber Super Snipe in the forthcoming *Marathon de la Route*, the Spa-Sofia-Liège Rally. I couldn't imagine why he had entered the Snipe. He wanted to know if I would take a mechanic and give them some service on the route because, I assumed, I knew Yugoslavia better than his people... The event was to take place from August 25 to 29 so would not interfere with our preparations for the Geneva Rally in the middle of October.

I took two mechanics and a Hillman Minx Estate loaded with spare wheels for the Rapier and the Snipe. We went straight to Novi, in Yugoslavia, where there was a control at the end of a fairly easy section. We saw the cars through there and then went down the coast road to try to get to Perast, on the Gulf of Kotor. The coast road petered out about 30 miles after Split and we wasted a lot of time on back roads before getting to Dubrovnik and then reached the Gulf of Kotor, one of the most impressive places to be found anywhere on the Adriatic coast. We eventually set up our service point on the Thursday night to wait for the cars coming from Sofia.

We were woken up at 2.30am by the familiar roar of an Austin-Healey, driven in this case by Aaltonen and Ambrose, who arrived exactly on time and were soon away towards the rough roads over the hills to Trebinje. The Sunbeam Rapier (Bill Bengry and Ian Hall) and the Humber Snipe (John La Trobe and his co-driver Skeffington) arrived at 5am and had their tyres changed. We followed by the same route and tried to telephone both Liège and the Novi Viladonski control during the day, but gave up as it wasted so much time. We had been dogged by punctures in our Hillman and ended the day crawling into Split with Snipe wheels fitted at the back and Sunbeam ones at the front after having suffered no fewer than five punctures on the way and been left with no tread on the tyres we now had on the road. We gave up and stayed at the Split motel.

Most of the next day was spent visiting the tyre specialist, next to the *Excelsior Hotel*, getting the overloaded roof rack welded and sorting out the ignition and other defects on a Sunbeam Rapier which belonged to a Dutch lady who was touring those parts with her mother. In return for our help she acted as an interpreter as she spoke fluent Serbo-Croat, and we rounded off the day with a well-deserved swim in the Adriatic.

The next day we reached Bad Gastein, after going through the Felbertauern tunnel, and the following day we drove into Liège at 21.00, had a meal in the *Moderne* and went to the Club, where we were surprised to find that the Snipe had finished 13th and won its class, and that the Sunbeam was 14th and also with a class win, both cars being in Group 2. Bill Bengry had won a Gold Cup for three consecutive finishes in a *Marathon*, so everyone was happy.

We met Fraser somewhere on the way back, but he declined to suggest that we might have contributed to his success, and as a result of his offhand attitude I never managed to get on very good terms with him or his stable while I was with Rootes/Chrysler. I had driven 3,500 miles in eight days.

The Geneva Rally took place towards the end of October and the cars and crews were as follows:

Sunbeam Tiger	AHP 294B	Ian Lewis and Barry Hughes
Sunbeam Tiger	AHP 295B	Peter Riley and Robin Turvey
Sunbeam Tiger	ADU 312B	Rosemary Smith and Margaret Mackenzie

On October 12 the three rally cars and two service cars were shipped by air from Baginton airport, Coventry, to Calais. The plane, a Carvair, was late arriving from Calais, and Gerry Spencer had overfilled his fuel tank, thus causing the Captain's displeasure and resulting in a prohibition against smoking while we were airborne.

The cars were to run in pairs, with myself in the fifth car bringing up the rear. The main party took the wrong turning somewhere owing to the fact that Ian Hall had not given them a general map of France, Michelin 989. However, having avoided further misfortune, we all arrived safely to the *Grand Hotel* at Troyes by 20.30 and had an excellent if expensive dinner before retiring.

The next morning we managed to get everyone ready by 09.00, the rendezvous for lunch being *Le Paris*, Arbois, one of my old haunts, which I had discovered 10 years earlier on a Monte Carlo recce. Unhappily it was shut on Tuesdays, so we ate at the *Balance*, which was not in the same class. *Le*

Paris is now named *Jean-Paul Jeunet*, to perpetuate the name of its famous founder Andre Jeunet, and his son has subsequently been awarded a rosette in the *Guide Michelin*. That evening we reached the *Hotel Angleterre* in Geneva, having been delayed for a while sorting out ignition and other minor problems in AHP 295B. Pat and Erik Carlsson came down to the hotel later and some of us went to the restaurant next to the *Hotel Moderne*.

Fortunately, we had a first-class agent with a well-equipped garage in Geneva, run by Monsieur and Madame Henri Ziegler, who could not have done more if we had wanted them to. Tiny Lewis took his car out next day and managed to get the clutch lining detached from the plate. The gearbox had to come out and the clutch was rebuilt; the foglamp brackets were not quite right, and so on, but all the cars were ready for scrutineering at 14.00 on Thursday, complete with plates and numbers. Our rally numbers were 1, 2 and 3, as they were the biggest cars in the GT class. The start time was 17.00, and Henri Ziegler had arranged to meet them at St Claude and Chambéry. We went down the road to Grenoble, then Jerry went on to Recorbeau and we went to St Jean-en-Royans with SAAB service, no doubt Erik's idea. The cars came through OK, but there was some fan belt trouble which I thought might affect the alternator output, so I decided to tell the crews to keep 10 per cent of their revs in hand. The distance between the pullies on those engines was rather long and the alternator pulley seemed to be small. We should have had no problem in finishing first, second and third in the class as the rest of the class were out of the rally! Rosemary Smith was annoyed with Margaret because she had made a mistake in the route, which put them six minutes late at a control and dropped them from 16th to 20th in General Classification.

On Friday morning we went round by Crest to Die and then on to Guillestre, where we got a snack and found that Dunlop Service was missing. We had to rob service cars of tyres, but we managed to get everyone away. Then we went over the Lauteret pass to Grenoble, finally got through to the Garage Geneve (Zieglers) on the phone and asked them to bring some fan belts to the *Hotel Croix Blanc*, Chamonix. Dunlop were there, so we could put on fresh tyres as well as refuel the cars before they went into the *parc fermé*. Tiny thought he knew what was wrong with the fan belts. The crews had enjoyed about five and a half hours' rest when I called them at 2.15am, saw them off, then went back to bed.

We were away the next morning soon after 10am, met Ziegler just over the Swiss frontier and went to the control there. Peter Riley's mother and father had come over from Montreux in a nice 2+2 Ferrari. Rosemary was 22 minutes late at the control due to another mistake by Margaret, so there was a tearful situation, which ended well, however, because the organizers cancelled the last two controls – due, I seem to recall, to the density of the traffic. So we had a nice looking result for the advertising people after all.

Des O'Dell joined us at the end of October and was given a free hand to sort out the list of faults which we felt were still handicapping the Tigers. His remarks on how he dealt with the situation after he had been put fully in the picture illustrate his practical outlook on rally preparation.

He said: "I just employed my GT40 experience to make the Tiger more reliable, using 289 crankshafts and rods because they were so much stronger, and which I was able to buy direct from Ford at Slough.

"But initially, cooling was a problem. When I first came I had several discussions with the sliderule boffins, chaps who had never sat inside a (competition) car in their lives. They told me that I should raise the engine by an inch and move it back in the frame by an inch and use a larger fan. Well, I would have preferred not to use a fan at all, and as for raising the centre of gravity....!

"The problem was that the car overheated even on early morning runs down the motorway, so it was certainly going to overheat on something like the Acropolis Rally. Using one of the development cars, I would go for a run down the motorway and open it up to 120mph, but within about six miles it would boil!

Anyway, I did some checks and found that the air was passing through everywhere but the radiator, so I instructed the engineers to put in more air ducts. Then I remembered that Aston Martin and Mercedes had suffered from similar problems, and they had cured them by altering the header tank arrangement, so I repiped the Tiger to match the Mercedes layout. I took a pipe from the header tank to the bottom hose, a modification which the boffins said would never work, and tried again. I took it onto the motorway, tucking in behind a lorry until it boiled, and then broke free and went like hell, and the temperature went down. I had cured the problem in three weeks. We lowered the suspension using Koni dampers and introduced dual-circuit braking... On tarmac it was impressive, but it was never any good in forest rallies!"

What Desmond did not say was that dual-circuit braking became compulsory in the GT class, and we fitted electric fans, displacing the large plastic fans which wasted power and obstructed the airflow; this in turn reduced the load on the alternator drive belt. We also changed the make of carburettor to another which had a different float chamber position, which cured our fuel starvation when accelerating and braking on twisty roads.

There was another snag in that the Sunbeam Tiger's wheelbase was too short in relation to its track, being 7ft 2in, with front and rear tracks of 4ft 3in and 4ft ½in, respectively. This compared unfavourably with the MGB wheelbase of 7ft 7in and the MGA's at 7ft 10in, both with similar track measurements to the Tiger's. The Austin-Healey 3000 wheelbase was 7ft 8in, with 4ft 1in at the front and 4ft 2in at the back. The centre of gravity of the Tiger was probably further forward than the Healey's and the car would therefore tend to understeer rather more than its competitors. It was also about 150lb heavier than a A-H 3000, depending on the rally specification in use.

With the arrival of 1965 we approached the Monte Carlo Rally, for which we entered two Tigers and three Hillman Imps, and for convenience's sake, I will include the performances of the Imps in this chapter. Our entries were as follows:

Sunbeam Tigers   London starters

No 107   ADU 312B   Peter Harper and Ian Hall
No 103   AHP 295B   Andrew Cowan and Robin Turvey

Hillman Imps   London starters

No 113   7674 VC   Rosemary Smith and Margaret Mackenzie

No 95   4525 KV   David Pollard and Barry Hughes
No 124   Ian Lewis and Brian Culcheth

I have already explained how weather can play an important part in the fortunes of competitors in the Monte Carlo Rally because competitors on the various routes which eventually join up some distance before the final control at Monte Carlo may have experienced entirely different weather conditions. This factor was to have a marked effect on the final placings in the 1965 event. As an example of this, we have the experiences of two Minis which started from Athens. There is always the risk of heavy snow in the Balkans, and this time there was nothing to worry about until the Franco-Italian frontier except a little snow between Ljubljana and Trieste. They arrived at the Sestriere control to find blizzard conditions, but fortunately the Mini-Coopers were carrying a couple of spiked spares, so they got through to St Claude in the Jura on time.

This was where the common route began, and they joined the London starters and began to compare notes with them concerning the weather so far. But the weather had worsened, and whereas from Bourg-en-Bresse to St Claude there had been snow, after that point it became really thick and visibility was down to 10 metres before the next section to Chambéry. The early numbers, up to about 95 or 100, had better conditions from St Claude and some passed through that part in daylight, but the London and Frankfurt starters had heavy snow, and all the works Fords had lost time by the time they reached Chambéry. The Renault team was eliminated, and only one Lancia got through within the maximum time allowance of an hour.

Road signs were obliterated, and many crews got lost due to the fresh falls, which in one case drifted across the correct route so that many cars took the wrong turning and lost even more time. Ian Hall told me that sometimes there was only a hole in the snow and one simply hoped that it was the right one. Fortunately, he didn't make any mistakes and they got through without losing their way. From Chambéry conditions were still difficult as the route went over the Col du Granier.

There were 276 entries that year and 237 started, but there were only 35 finishers at Monte Carlo. Of those, 32 came from between the starting numbers 1 and 150 and just three from 151 to 276. The elimination test the next day was almost a formality. Timo Makinen and Paul Easter (Mini-Cooper S No 52) won with about twice the number of penalty marks as Paddy Hopkirk had dropped the previous year. Bohringer and Wuthrich (Porsche 904 GTS No 150) were second, and third were Pat Moss-Carlsson and Liz Nystrom (SAAB No 49). There were few mechanical failures, most of the retirements being due to driver fatigue, as there is nothing worse than driving through a snowstorm. Erik Carlsson and Gunnar Palm suffered from an unusual problem: snow thrown up from cars they were trying to pass blocked the air intake to their air filters and froze so hard that they lost a lot of time clearing the stoppage, but they made the next control with a minute to spare. They arrived at Monte Carlo in last place, but ended up 20th after the 380-mile mountain test in which 35 started and 22 finished within the 30-minute time allowance.

We had reason to be happy because we had entered two Sunbeam Tigers and Peter Harper and Ian Hall had finished fourth in General Classification and first in the GT class, with Andrew Cowan and Robin Turvey second in the GT class and 11th overall, which must have been due to the most amazing skill, as sheer power had little to do with performance in those conditions and the Tiger not being exactly the easiest car to drive in snow. David Pollard and Barry Hughes (car No 95) finished 15th and second in their class for GT cars up to 1,000cc, while Rosemary Smith and Margaret Mackenzie (car No 113) were 22nd overall, fourth in their class and second to Pat in the *Coupe des Dames*. This was the first time the Imps had run with 998cc engines, which put them in the Grand Touring category.

The morning after the cars arrived at Monte Carlo a driving test was held down beside the harbour in which Andrew Cowan made the fastest time of the day in the Tiger.

Eight of the first 20 cars had front-wheel drive and three were rear-engined and rear wheel-driven, the rest being front-engined with rear-wheel drive! *Motor Sport* summed it up as follows: "This was without doubt one of the best Monte Carlo Rallies for several years for although no rally driver positively enjoys driving for hours on end through heavy falling snow, it does make the event one for the men (this said despite the fact that Pat Moss finished third!) and finishing in a year like this is an achievement that will outweigh any number of finishers' bars from other years. This rally was also won on the road and it was road marks that decided the winner rather than marks computed in seconds taken over special stages."

Our service crews did a very good job under difficult conditions as getting to their next rendezvous was often a very hazardous undertaking in itself. For Des O'Dell it was a strange change from the smell and noise of GT cars at the pits, but he took it all in his stride and I was glad to have someone who could take care of the service crews in such an efficient manner. I returned to England feeling that we might be getting our act together at last.

John Gott had asked me if we would lend him a Sunbeam Tiger for the International Police Rally to be held in Belgium in May, when he would have to take a member of the Force as his navigator. I think he had won it the previous year, he also knew a lot of the roads that would be used and he thought that he had a good chance of winning. I agreed, and said I would accompany him with a service car and take one mechanic. There were 92 entries from seven countries, and the start and finish were at Liège. His navigator was Sergeant D E Nicholson. They had a troublefree run over 690 miles in 24 hours (in AHP 295B), lost no points on the road and made the fastest time in two of the speed hill-climbs. John duly won the event by a handsome margin.

The Alpine Rally, in which we fielded three Tigers, should also have been a great victory. We had overcome the overheating problems and the cars had been tested in the Alps; we now had Techdel Minilite alloy wheels, which should have allowed more air to reach the brakes. We were going to use Dunlop racing tyres on some sections and there had been some improvement in the handling. Desmond had put in a lot of work since the Monte and it should have paid off. Rosemary Smith and Sheila Taylor were entered in a 998cc Imp, which ran in the up to 1,000cc class of the Grand Touring category.

The Alpine, organized by the *Automobile Club de Marseilles et Provence*, was true to its tradition and ran over all the famous Alpine passes in July, just before the tourist season. The entries that year were as follows:

ADU 312B   Peter Harper and Mike Hughes
AHP 294B   Tiny Lewis and Barry Hughes
ADU 311B   Ian Hall and Don Barrow

The rally lasted for five and a half days, starting in Marseilles and after 2,250 miles finishing in Monte Carlo, where I was to have yet another encounter with the scrutineer of the *ACMP*, with whom I had frequently fallen out in my days with BMC. An entry of 93 cars left Marseilles for the first stage to Grenoble, and Peter Harper had to have a starter motor changed on the first day. Ian Hall, meanwhile, had been doing very well until he reached the Col d'Allos, but after the timed test for the climb, which started at la Foux d'Allos and went to the top of the pass, he set off down towards Barcelonnette, which was 20 kilometres, downhill all the way. The brakes were in good shape and in any case were not likely to overheat for the first part of the descent. There was a little bit of straight after you passed the *table d'orientation*, with good visibility, which one could use to gain a little time before the lacets started on the steeper part. This straight led into a deceptively sharp left-hander just by a whitewashed roadmender's hut and an Armco barrier. Ian had been working very hard before the start of the rally in marking maps and routes for some of the service crews, and he thinks that he was not as sharp as he should have been when listening to his navigator; anyway, he went into the corner too fast and the dreaded Tiger understeer took the matter out of his hands. He grazed the Armco sufficiently hard to put the steering temporarily out of action and the time lost in getting things straightened put him out of the rally.

He was having a chat with Simo Lampinen a little later, and Simo said: "Oh, we have that one in our notes as dangerous, we call it 'White Shed' corner and treat it with respect," and that must be really important when it comes from a Scandinavian driver!

Tiny Lewis had brake trouble of a major nature, a small fire caused by brake fluid leaking into the hot brake drum was extinguished, but the rebuilt brakes were soon in trouble again and the car crashed. This enabled the three service crews to keep Harper and Smith in good condition until the end of the rally.

When he finished it seemed likely that Peter Harper had won the Grand Touring category, having lost just one minute on the road. However, the scrutineer disqualified Harper's car on the grounds that the exhaust valves were smaller than the size given in the homologation form. Their argument was that the smaller valves had made the car more reliable!

It will be remembered that the first two engines that were fitted in the competition department at Coventry had been supplied by Carroll Shelby as replacements for the faulty Le Mans engines. Those engines, I suspect, were used by us to obtain the measurements for the homologation of the cars. I also knew that there had been a apaper issued by the *FIA* which indicated that the engine specification should always be for the model having the highest state of tune for the series being homologated, provided that the qualifying production run had been made. We gained a lot of publicity from this unfortunate error, and issued this official statement through our publicity department:

"By fitting smaller valves to the Tiger, we certainly did not gain any advantage in performance, and this was only done to bring the rally car specification into line with that of the current models. The discrepency arose because the initial production Tigers registered with the *FIA* were produced for the US market and employed larger valves than those currently fitted to production models. Negotiations are in progress with the *FIA* to register the latest specification, but in any case we believe that it was not vital to notify a modification which detunes engine performance."

I felt sorry for Peter Harper and even more so for Des O'Dell and his mechanics who had worked so hard. We were compensated to some extent by a brilliant drive by Rosemary Smith and Sheila Taylor, who came fifth in the Grand Touring category, first in the up-to-1,000cc class and won the *Coupe des Dames*. They could not have done better.

The following year Peter Harper and Robin Turvey won their class in the Tulip Rally with FRW 668C, and with Ian Hall as co-driver he went off to Greece a month later and won his class again. That was the last time we entered Sunbeam Tigers in rallies.

CHAPTER 17

The Imp's struggle to success

"When the final results of the 1966 'Monte' were posted that evening, the cars which had been in the first four places had been disqualified and Rosemary Smith's Imp had been eliminated from the Coupe des Dames.*"*

By 1962 the sales staff of Appleyard's of Bradford already had a 997cc Mini-Cooper in the showroom. Ian Appleyard had previously let me have a run in the first example of the model which had been delivered to Appleyard's of Leeds. Although its 55bhp did not seem to me to be enough, and the ground clearance, which I had criticized in the Mini which I had driven in the 1959 *Rallye Viking*, was still inadequate for rougher stages, it seemed to me to have distinct possibilities. However, the Cooper S, with its 1,071cc engine giving 70bhp, and improved handling, arrived in May of the following year and was a much better rally car.

I remember clearly, and with some misgivings, the launch of the Rootes Group's new small car in May 1963. I just could not see the Imp designer's reasoning in having taken what seemed to us, as front-wheel-drive enthusiasts, to be such a retrograde step. Putting the engine in the back and the fuel tank in the front, where it was more vulnerable in an accident, coupled with the disadvantage of a small luggage locker, seemed to me all wrong. But at that stage I had not driven an Imp.

The Imp plan had started in 1955 when two young engineers in the design department talked over the idea that Rootes needed a very basic small car to fill a gap in the model range. Thus it came about that Mike Parkes and Tim Fry went along to see Bernard Winter, who was then Director of Engineering, with only the skeleton of a plan for such a vehicle. It was a surprise to them when he said: "All right, get on with it then". They were unaware that the Board of Directors had been toying with the idea for some time, but had yet to form a firm idea as to the size or shape that such a car should take.

The young engineers were lucky in that there was an empty space at the South Works, in Ryton-on-Dunsmore, where the main assembly line was situated. This was in a very solid brick-built building at the west end of the complex, which had been built as an aero engine test shop in the days when it had been a World War Two shadow factory. They were able to hide themselves away there and develop the prototypes which eventually became the Imp.

During the evolutionary period the performance and general utilitarian appearance of their creations did not receive the slightest approval of the Board. Rootes had always made cars which had a little more quality than their rivals, which was something their dealers liked to stress. The thought of a Rootes car propelled by an air-cooled two-cylinder engine must have put the the directors off their lunch on a couple of occasions!

It was inevitable that the Imp would require a four-cylinder engine, but it was also clear that none of the available small cast-iron lumps would be suitable. Mike Parkes thought that Coventry Climax, whose factory was quite close, might have a suitable engine.

For many years Coventry Climax had supplied reliable little 20hp engines to the Government to drive fire-pumps. At the time of the Korean war, the Ministry of Defence suddenly changed its requirement and insisted on a pump which would give double the output and weigh half as much as the equipment they had been buying. Walter (Wally) Hassan, one of the greatest engine designers that this country has ever produced, was their chief engineer at the time.

They found the solution to Rootes' problem in a highly efficient light-alloy engine, the prototype of which they evolved in just seven months. The engine, which gave 38bhp from 1,020cc, was known as the FWA and was exhibited as a marine engine on the Coventry Climax stand at the Earls Court motor show. Its cubic capacity was inconvenient for a competition engine, so subsequently, when it was decided that motor racing might be good publicity for the company's more staid products, they elected to build two sizes of engine, the first having a capacity of 1,098cc. It soon became available with an increased compression ratio and many uprated working parts, and in this form it produced 72bhp at 6,100rpm. This type of engine was later to be made in several different capacities and Coventry Climax became suppliers of pure racing engines to a number of British racing car builders.

In 1958 Tim Fry managed to get hold of one of their 750cc engines and spent many hours trying to fit it into the space where previously he had installed a two-cylinder air-cooled Villiers engine, but it would only go in at an angle. There were also to be other problems, including the transmission, which had been adequate for the air-cooled engine, but would not be robust enough for the new engine. Meanwhile, BMC were well ahead in the race with their Mini design.

After three weeks Tim Fry eventually succeeded in getting the 750cc Coventry Climax into the engine compartment at an angle of 45 degrees, but suitable inlet and exhaust manifolds had to be made and fitted in time for the next appraisal by the Board. This time the directors gave the go-ahead, and Tim had to think about refinements to the transmission.

It is interesting to note that the Mini had also been considered with an alternative twin-cylinder air-cooled engine. It is also amusing to note that Tim Fry and Mike Parkes were in the habit of occasionally having supper with Alex Moulton and Alec Issigonis, Moulton being the designer of rubber suspension units used by Issigonis for his Mini. Inevitably, their talks did not go into details concerning their respective prototypes, but whenever automobile engineers discuss cars in general they are bound to generate similar trains of thought from time to time.

Peter Ware had now taken over from Bernard Winter as Technical Director, and his influence over Imp development was to have a marked effect from that moment. The rear suspension became more sophisticated by fitting trailing arms, which were refined by Harry White and his chassis engineers. This neutralized the adverse effect of the rear engine and, coupled with the original swing-arm front suspension, produced a small car which handled in a quite outstanding manner.

The gearbox and differential had to be incorporated in a single transaxle unit, and this was new country as far as any British manufacturer was concerned. Fortunately there was a young man called Adrian West, who had won a travelling scholarship to Europe to study gearbox design, and he had just returned with a wealth of knowledge about continental transmissions. In November 1960 'Bill' West was appointed senior transmission engineer, over a team of six engineers, to design and develop the Imp transaxle. The code word for the whole project, Apex, was used until a suitable name could be found for the car.

The inevitable problems involved in producing a satisfactory transaxle, which had to be of an unorthodox design, were overcome as far as the production cars were concerned, but competition driving, involving the use of higher rpm and horsepower with larger-capacity engines, was to produce an entirely new set of problems a year or two after the announcement of the Imp.

The gearbox in the standard Imp had been an instant success in the opinion of the motoring press, who praised the quick, light and precise gearchange. They liked the synchromesh on all four gears, and the ratios, which had been chosen for economical and quiet cruising on motorways and included quite high third and fourth ratios.

I will deal with the mechanical problems that arose in the competition cars more or less as they occurred. Leo Kuzmicki, who had worked with Joe Craig on Norton engines and, later, on the Vanwall Grand Prix engine before joining Rootes, was given the job of designing the engine. It was to be manufactured by Rootes, but would be based on the Coventry Climax unit which had been fitted in the prototype. It was to be die-cast in aluminium, like the gearbox casing, and for a variety of reasons it went into production with a capacity of 875cc. This was a grave handicap as far as I was concerned as it placed us halfway between the rarely used 750cc class and the 1,000cc class. The engine developed 39bhp and I knew it needed another 31bhp in order to be competitive, but the Board had decided that the Hillman Imp would be unnecessarily powerful with a 998cc engine.

The die-cast cylinder block meant that very expensive replacement dies would be required if any significant change was to be made to the capacity by substantially altering the bore or stroke dimensions, so this was obviously ruled out for an engine that would only be required in limited numbers for competition purposes. However, there were obvious ways in which the single-carburettor engine might be improved, and we were much helped in this respect by Leo Kuzmicki. As a short-term solution to the shortage of power, we decided to homologate the Imp in the Grand Touring category as we would be able to use a 998cc engine which was derived from a production model in that category. This was done by using wet liners in a way which I will explain later.

The Apex was tested extensively from 1961 to 1963 and many of its initial faults were eliminated. The cars were run under extremes of heat and cold weather, and although the development engineers would have liked more time and money to improve matters, there was no chance of postponing the announcement date.

The car would be assembled at the new Linwood factory on Clydeside, which HRH the Duke of Edinburgh was to open on May 2, 1963. The choice of Linwood had been forced upon the company. It was one of the three development areas in which the Government insisted that new industries should be located if they were to be granted substantial government loans. Rootes badly needed the money to launch the new model, but they underestimated the disadvantages in having a major plant situated so far away from the traditional heart of the British motor industry, which had always been in the Midlands. The established skills of several generations of light engineering workers was absent at Linwood, and the workforce had to be drawn mainly from the unemployed of heavy industry, who in turn had to be recruited, trained and disciplined. The makers of major components, such as brakes, electrical equipment, instruments, tyres and wheels, were all situated in the Midlands. If there was any difficulty with either the reliability or the supply of anything in those areas there was to be an inevitable delay in getting a representative to visit the works. If the Imp had been built in Coventry, none of those problems would have arisen. There was, however, one advantage in that the Pressed Steel works was adjacent and would produce the body pressings.

Some time after the Imp went into production, Tim Fry built a very nice little two-seater sports edition of the car named the Asp, which caused very few problems in bringing to the prototype stage. It had the radiator at the front and was fitted with an experimental alloy 998cc engine which allowed the pistons to run directly on aluminium bores. This low-friction engine performed very well, and the excellent handling of the Asp and the fact that it could exceed 100mph made it a pleasure to drive. Tim told me that he could average higher speeds across country than he could manage in much more exotic machinery. All the running gear was essentially the same as on the production Imp, but the chassis was made of steel and the bodyshell of glassfibre. It would have been an outstanding small sportscar, but by that time money was very short and Chrysler, who were now in charge, was allowing the Imp to wither on the vine.

With hindsight, Rootes might have done better if they had built an Asp to run in the prototype class at Le Mans in 1965 instead of wasting half a year's rally budget on the deplorable Le Mans Tigers. An average speed of over 100mph would have been possible and the publicity would have done the Imp a great deal of good, just when it was needed; such a programme could have been put into action before the charcoal-suited bean-counters arrived from Chrysler in 1967.

Rootes had either entered or sponsored eight perfectly standard 875cc Imps in the 1964 Monte Carlo Rally, seven of which finished, one of them winning a prize for the best British private entry, although perhaps inevitably they all finished very low down in the list of finishers. In the Scottish Rally, which was held in June, the Imps fared badly and Rosemary Smith, who was later to make quite a name for herself when driving Imps, failed to finish. The RAC Rally in November that year was another disaster due to a combination of mechanical failures and driver errors.

The 1965 Monte Carlo Rally was the first event in which we expected the

Imps to make a showing. We were using 998cc engines this time and running the cars in Group 3. We bored out the dry liners, which had the cylinder block cast around them in the production Imp. We then inserted a thin shrunk-in liner into the bored-out block and brought the bore up 72.5mm. This was to be only a temporary solution to the problem and later we fitted proper wet liners, but the cylinder blocks were not rigid enough to hold the wet liners accurately for very long, and the dimensions had to be checked at each engine overhaul.

The Hillman Imps all started from London with the Sunbeam Tigers, the drivers being as listed in the previous chapter. The weather after Bourg-en-Bresse was to prove very bad, but the handling of the Imps was so good that, as mentioned previously, David Pollard and Barry Hughes finished 15th in General Classification and second in class and Rosemary Smith and Margaret Mackenzie 22nd overall, second in the *Coupe des Dames* behind Pat Moss (SAAB) and fourth in class. Only 22 cars completed the Mountain Test.

At Easter, Rosemary Smith and Sheila O'Clery were entered in the Circuit of Ireland Rally, accompanied by Colin Malkin, both in 998cc Imps. Colin won the class and Rosemary was second, also winning the *Coupe des Dames*.

At this point I had to consider which drivers I wished to retain as I already had five good drivers and a brilliant private owner in Colin Malkin waiting for a works drive; it seemed unlikely that I could afford to keep all of them. If we were to continue to run the Tigers I expected to use Peter Harper, Andrew Cowan and Tiny Lewis, all of whom had some Tiger experience. However, it seemed unlikely that we would be able to field two three-car teams in the four International rallies which we had planned for the rest of the year. It was also going to be too costly to pay retainers to six drivers, so I had to do the best I could for those I wished to encourage. I had 'inherited' all of them from the Norman Garrad period and there was no question as to their ability, and in the case of Peter Harper there was a long list of successes to prove it.

Andrew Cowan came from the Border country, where his father owned Blackadder Farm, in Duns, and he had grown up only two miles away from Erdington Mains, the home of young Jim Clark. They both became members of the Ednam and District Young Farmers Club and so joined a fraternity of young men who drove anything on wheels that would go anywhere, in any weather conditions, in snow and ice, flood and mud, or heat and dust. Later, they both joined the Berwick and District Motor Club, which at that time was an extremely successful and well-run club, and was later to produce a number of famous race and rally drivers, although Clark and Cowan seem to have been the only pair who were to excel in their age group.

They were lucky to be growing up in countryside where there were roads of every sort, some narrow and twisting, others open and sweeping across moors, where the driver could exercise his skill swooping down the sides of valleys, then climbing up through balking corners and shifting gears with increasing skill and precision. There were few towns or villages to the west of their homes, and the Border police must have been very thin on the ground. It is surely no coincidence that Louise Aitken-Walker also comes from the Border country.

Tiny Lewis was a motor engineer, who had a car business near Bristol, had taken up competition motoring as a young man and found he couldn't let his work interfere with his love of the sport. His record was excellent, and he had all the qualities that go to make a good team driver and test driver. He was also blessed with a good sense of humour, even in adversity.

Rosemary Smith, whose name became a byword for excellence in the two spheres in which she chose to cultivate her talents, was a bit of an enigma when I met her in 1964. Most of the information that I had been given about her was untrue. She was known in the motoring press as 'the dress designer from Dublin' who drove for Rootes. She had come into the International rally scene during the time I was working for Appleyard's. Peter Procter, who drove for Rootes at that time, lived near us in Shipley, but I do not remember that he ever mentioned her.

Rosemary came from a motoring family, her father having raced a Chrysler at Brooklands before the war and raced at Phoenix Park from time to time. Rosemary could drive at the age of 11 and her first car was a Triumph Herald, in which she did a few club rallies and driving tests, but she did not like the car and graduated to a Mini shortly after its introduction. She progressed to more club rallies and then drove in the Circuit of Ireland Rally. Her father and her brother helped her with the upkeep of the car, and she had Frank Bigger's wife, Delcine, as her co-driver. They generally did well, usually getting a class place or the Ladies' prize. Then, when, as Rosemary describes it, "I was really too young to go into serious driving", she caught the eye of Norman Garrad, who offered her a works drive. This was a great opportunity for Rosemary as she was running out of money having just done another Circuit of Ireland with Delcine Bigger.

So when did the dress designing come into her life? During the Mini period she had finished her course of art at the Academy of Arts and Design at Dublin and was now earning a living as a dress designer, which she continued to do until she became a full-time rally driver and motoring journalist. There is no need to wonder whether she was successful as a dress designer as she always dressed with remarkably good taste.

I recently asked her if she still carried on that business and she told me that there are a number of ladies in Eire who do not wish to be seen at some of the more select gatherings dressed in anything that might be duplicated on the same occasion. She therefore does, occasionally, design and make with her own fair hands some exclusive models.

She is the only lady rally driver I have ever known who could arrive at the end of a very tough rally section and step out of the car looking neat, tidy and well-dressed.

But one should not be lulled into feeling that there was a pliant young lady who would take orders without questioning them. The Irish sense of humour and charm, sprinkled with a great deal of commonsense, could be banished to produce a withering riposte.

Rosemary drove for me for nearly four and a half years and during that time she drove Imps in 24 Internationals, finished in 21 of them, won one outright, and collected 12 *Coupes des Dames*, nine class wins and was placed in her class at least six times. She was unlucky to get caught in the lighting dispute in the 1966 Monte Carlo Rally when she was the moral winner of the *Coupe des Dames* with Val Domleo.

David Pollard, who was also an excellent driver, came from Bradford and had an engineering business. He had done well in the Imp in the 1965 Monte Carlo Rally to finish 15th in General Classification and second in his class with Barry Hughes as his navigator. That was the Monte which sorted out the men from the boys and proved that the ladies could cope with the really bad weather equally well. David, who had also driven for Norman Garrad with some success, was a very determined character, but I felt that he was the driver whom I might have to drop if the budget became any slimmer.

By this time Des O'Dell had become accustomed to the requirements of a works rally team, both at home and away, and his priority was to develop a reliable 998cc Imp. The main weaknesses were in the transmission and cooling, with minor troubles with the fuel system and brakes. The rubber couplings which were placed between the transaxle and the driveshafts to the rear hubs were very unreliable and could fail between 500 and 1,000 miles of rally driving. The gearboxes became very hot and the lubricant was not getting to the right places. This caused either complete failure of the gearbox or locking up of the gearchange, so that the driver only had one gear to use. The water pump seals leaked, and if too much coolant was lost the head gasket blew. The fuel in the carburettor was overheating and the vibration of the engine was causing fuel to fail to reach the jets when it should have done. This in turn led to a weak mixture, which was suspected of causing the exhaust valves to burn out. The pneumatic throttle system had to be replaced by a cable, and there were other problems of a not so urgent nature which had to be solved quickly.

The 1965 Tulip Rally was about to be run with a new set of rules. Being held in mid-April, there was hardly any risk of meeting snow-covered roads in the foothills of the Alps and Jura. The organizers always tried to think up a formula which might equalize the chances of a private owner when competing against the works cars. Marks could be incurred either by losing time on the road sections, at a rate of 60 marks per minute, or on the speed tests, where each second taken to perform the test counted as one mark.

At the end of the rally, each crew would have their penalty points totalled, the finishers in each class being arranged in order of ascending penalty marks in the usual way. But to arrive at a General Classification, each class was given a mark, calculated as the average of the best marks in that class, the class above and the class below. Each of the marks in the class was then expressed as a percentage of the average mark, and the car possessing the lowest percentage was declared the overall winner.

A complicated process, but one that was reasonably fair and did not have to rely on preconceived formulae in order to equate the performances of such widely differing cars as an Austin-Healey 3000 and a Hillman Imp. However, trouble could be caused when a leading car had lost time on the road. Normally, such a thing was unlikely to happen because cars which were quick enough to win their class tended not to lose any points on the road. But when road marks were lost (as they were that year by virtue of the severe weather conditions) and then had to be counted in with the performances on the speed tests, the whole result of the rally could become distorted. The purpose of the average mark and the percentage calculation was to reduce the advantage that a powerful car might have had on the uphill speed tests, so if the road marks had been considered separately and the percentage calculated on the results of the speed tests alone, the system might have achieved its objective more easily.

As it was the result was not unfair as the two Hillman Imps driven by Rosemary Smith with Valerie Domleo, and Tiny Lewis with David Pollard, which finished first and second overall, had performed very well to get round the road section 'clean' and then record creditable times in the speed tests. Their team-mates from Rootes, Peter Harper with Ian Hall and Peter Riley with Robin Turvey in the two Tigers, had been involved in incidents on the snow-covered sections which eliminated them.

However, the pre-eminence of the Imps in this rally was not simply the result of their excellent performance, but rather because the cars in the class above them (the Mini-Cooper of Julian Vernaeve and the Cortina GT of Eric Jackson) and the cars in the class below them (the works DAFs) were all quite heavily penalized on the road, being late by having to trudge through the snow. Nearly all the competitors were on normal road tyres and some were on Dunlop racers.

The testing section after the Col de Faucille, which itself eliminated many cars, was from Champagnole to Mont Saleve and back to Champagnole via the Faucille. Many got stuck, some were late, a few were clean, but whatever the organizers might have done to alter things at the last moment would have led to protests from those who got through and so as far as we were concerned it was a marvellous result, coming at the right time. It was a case of "He (or she) who dares, wins". There had been 157 starters, but only 47 finished.

Of course, there were enough tall stories to fill an evening in the bar after it was over. One of the Minis was seen going up the Faucille in reverse with Paul Easter sitting on the bonnet, and Valerie helped Rosemary to get going at some point by standing on the Imp's rear bumper and hanging on to the sill of the opening rear window. The DAFs went up the Faucille in line ahead and tooted their horns as they went by, but they came to grief later. Back at Noordwijk, they were filming *The Spy Who Came In From The Cold* with Elizabeth Taylor and Richard Burton, and they asked Rosemary about the rally as we sat at the bar the next night. Rosemary was sent a bouquet of flowers by Elizabeth Taylor. The rest of the season went well, good results being secured in the Scottish Rally in June, then a class win in the Alpine Rally.

The regulations were available for the 1966 Monte Carlo Rally at the end of November and we knew that it was to favour Group 1 Series Production Touring cars, of which 5,000 examples had to have been manufactured. There was to be a penalty of 18 per cent if you ran in any other Group, such as GT Group 3.

At the time when the entries should have been sent to the *Automobile Club de Monaco*, through the Royal Automobile Club's Competition Department, the competition managers of the British car manufacturers had still not seen a copy of the *FIA*'s 1966 Appendix J of the Sporting Code. We held a meeting to discuss the matter, and Stuart Turner (BMC) and Henry Taylor (Ford Motor Co) arranged to see the *FIA* officials in Paris to obtain answers to about 100 questions needing clarification. These questions arose because the RAC had circulated an unofficial translation of the French text, which was still in draft form.

In the past, when there was to be a change in the regulations, it had been the custom of the *FIA* to issue translations into English from the French text simultaneously with the publication of the French text; both languages could then be taken as being part of the official text. Even then there were sometimes words which needed clarification as the translations were never perfect. Under the preamble which led up to the Sporting Code it stated that the French text took precedence over the English text in the event of a dispute arising from the rules.

Later in December we received an English translation of the draft copy of the 1966 Appendix J and we had a copy of the questionaire that had been taken to Paris for clarification. There was still no copy of the final text in its approved form in either French or English. There was a feeling on our side of the Channel that the French were holding this up and that the RAC were not being firm enough in demanding that copies should be made available without delay.

There was no mention, in either the RAC's draft copy or in the list of answers, of any change in the lighting regulations except for a clause which limited the number of driving lights that might be fitted (mention was made that the matter could be left to the discretion of the organizers of the event, who might amend the restriction as to the numbers if they felt it necessary).

In previous years, it had been the custom to dip the lights by using another externally mounted pair, so that the main beam would come from either a single-filament bulb (lately of the new quartz-iodine type), mounted in the headlights or in the other externally mounted pair. Yet another pair of lights mounted lower down might give a wider and shorter beam, which would illuminate the edge of the road. A three-way dipswitch could give the driver a choice as to the most suitable arrangements for the conditions he was experiencing. This arrangement would give a much better light in the dipped position, and it complied with the Geneva Convention of 1949 in the matter of automobile lights.

I had also looked at the French road code regulations, and found nothing in them to make it obligatory to incorporate the dipping system in the same headlight as that which was being used for the main beam. The French police had pointed out to me a couple of times that when driving in fog with a pair of foglights, the headlights had to be extinguished.

It was implied elsewhere that if lamps were of the type which were fitted to the vehicle in the country of its origin they could be used. As UK lights have to dip to the left, this might have been an excuse for British competitors to fit separate pass lights.

By the beginning of January nobody seemed to be bothering about lights, and the lighting regulation was the only one which had not been queried during the visit to Paris. It must have been more than coincidence that the three leading British works teams all came up with the same answer on their Group 1 cars. Ian Hall remembers drawing up a specification for a Group 1 Imp in December 1965 with the 'as-used' Monte lighting system, and it was based on the RAC draft. In mitigation, it might have been said that the matter was unambiguous. The factory entries were also backed up in their interpretation of the regulations by Ray Wood, of Lucas, who supervised the electrical installation on all the British rally cars.

Rosemary Smith told me that when she was on a recce for the Monte at the end of 1965, or perhaps a week later, she was up in the mountains having a look at the roads where the final tests are usually held. She stopped for some reason and met a local farmer, who asked her if she was practising for the Monte Carlo Rally. When she told him that she was, he said: "You are wasting your time, everyone knows that Citroen are going to win this one". When Bill Price got to Monte before the Monaco-Chambéry-Monaco test was started, he went up to the *Bec Rouge* restaurant, which was just above where the *Hotel du Helder* used to be. One of the two owners told him that it would be impossible for a Mini to win that year. In addition there was another reliable account from Paul Easter, who was with Timo Makinen (Morris Mini-Cooper S) when they were practising at about the same time as Rosemary, and who spoke to a girl on the road near Bollene, nearly 200 miles from Monte Carlo, and from whom they had the same story. Perhaps there was a feeling that the rally was going to be rigged even before it was run. There were no SAAB or Volvo entries because their cars were not homologated in Group 1 in time, and in any case they still had no copy of the new regulations. There were to be the smallest number of private entries since 1939.

The rally was not run during bad weather conditions, so there was no argument about favoured starting points. There were 192 starters of which 164 reached Monte Carlo, and of these 157 had lost no marks on the road, so had qualified to take part in the Monaco-Chambéry-Monaco test, which was run overnight and went through Bollene into the Ardeche before returning via Chambéry. Of the 83 cars which returned, 60 were to be allowed to start in the final test, among them the Hillman Imp of Rosemary Smith and Val Domleo; no mean achievement for a Group 1 875cc car.

Before the 60 cars were allowed to start the Mountain Test, held in the foothills of the Alps behind Monte Carlo, the crews were summoned to attend by their cars in the *parc fermé* to have the dipping arrangements of their headlights tested. This was done by placing a shoe-box in front of the headlight and operating the dipswitch. No comments were made as to the legality of any particular system. To be on the safe side we changed the headlight bulbs on Rosemary's Imp at our final service point between Sospel and Menton on the last leg of the test.

The provisional results were posted that evening and the three Mini-Coopers of Timo Makinen, Rauno Aaltonen and Paddy Hopkirk were in the first three places. Roger Clark in the Lotus Cortina was fourth in General Classification, and Smith and Domleo were winners of the *Coupe des Dames*.

The Mini-Coopers were taken up to the Auto Riviera garage, which was usually used for scrutineering. The BMC mechanics were in attendance to remove the cylinder heads, but this time it was not just the cylinder heads which were to be removed. The mechanics were instructed to strip down the engines and the transmissions to the last nut and bolt. Every part which was declared in the homologation papers was weighed, a pair of kitchen scales being used to do this. The scrutineers were not very able and some of the weights and measurements had to be interpreted for them. After a whole day they could find nothing wrong and the *verification technique* had been passed.

When the final results of the 1966 'Monte' were posted that evening, the cars which had been in the first four places had been disqualified and Rosemary Smith's Imp had been eliminated from the *Coupe des Dames*. The reason given was that the disqualified cars did not comply with the 1966 Appendix J in respect of the lighting regulations. The world's press lost no time in making it headline news.

The French press accused the British manufacturers of cheating and the British press accused the organizers of changing the rules to effect a French win, and much else. BMC obtained a standard Mini-Cooper from a local agent's showroom and put on a convincing test for the press which proved that the showroom car was actually quicker than the rally car. Stuart Turner, who is a master when it comes to publicity, soon had a Carvair available at Nice airport, and the three Minis, the Ford and the Imp were soon on their way to England with their crews to meet the press in strength, and the fact that Toivonen and Mikander, a couple of Finns, had won the Monte Carlo Rally with a Citroen paled into insignificance. Mabbs and Porter in a Rover were the best British pair, finishing 10th in General Classification. Toivonen, being a sportsman, refused to go to the *ACM* dinner, as did most of the British entrants.

It seems that the organizers would have liked to get the Minis excluded for failing to run standard machinery, but failing that had to resort to the lighting irregularities, and in so doing caught out a bigger number of entrants than were necessary to get a French win, as a result of which both Ford and Rootes were caught in the net.

Of course, we protested to the Club and had our protest turned down; we then protested through the RAC to the *FIA*, but without success; they appealed on our behalf but finally lost. That took until April, and the final judgment was given in May. The official copy of the Appendix J in its final form did not reach us until the end of March. During the intervening period the Italian Rally of the Flowers had been run and two BMC cars were disqualified for Group 1 infringements from that event, too. I feel that the RAC and the *FIA* were to blame for not making the latest rules available in plenty of time before the events and for not having Stewards who were firm enough to deal with matters of importance before the start of the events. After all, the lights could have been checked at the starting points if anybody had been in possession of the new rules at the time. It is perhaps significant that the 1967 edition of the Appendix J Group 1 had the paragraph relating to the lighting regulations picked out in italics. I wonder why?

It is worth noting that Volume 14 of *Automobile Year*, covering the 1966 season, made a point of listing, below the final placings, all the drivers and their cars who were disqualified from the *35eme Rallye de Monte Carlo*, which remains the most controversial event ever held in the Rally Championship.

In contrast, the Circuit of Ireland went well, the 998cc Imps being placed second, third and fourth in General Classification and Rosemary winning the Ladies' Cup, a fairly regular achievement for her in that event.

The Acropolis Rally also went very well for us; the Sunbeam Tiger driven by Peter Harper and Ian Hall won their class and finished eighth in General Classification, with Rosemary Smith and Valerie Domleo also winning their class and finishing 11th overall, both excellent performances in such a difficult event.

The Imps did very well again in the Scottish Rally, which followed so closely upon the Acropolis that the crews were given rides in police cars from the final test to the airport to get home in time. It was worth it as we had a very good result; Imps were third in General Classification, and first to fourth in their class as well as winning the Ladies' Cup.

I had been thinking about the Shell 4000 as it represented new territory for us and received good publicity in Canada and possibly in the States. It took place early in May, starting from Vancouver, and took just over a week to reach Montreal, making it the longest event in the world to be run under *FIA* regulations at that time. No servicing was allowed *en route*, except for a bit of tinkering, which I suspect went on at the few rest stops; there was no time to do very much anyway. The competitors were followed by service crews, who no doubt were allowed to provide refreshments as well as encouragement.

I decided to get approval from Timothy Rootes, although Brian Rootes would have been a better supporter as he knew that market very well. So Rosemary, who I think had a Canadian navigator, was to take part in a 998cc Imp which incorporated as many of Desmond's improvements as possible.

The pattern of the rally was a nominal 4,000 miles which incorporated some rough special stages, some fairly difficult route-finding and some rather boring driving to get across from one side of Canada to the other. The first two days were spent in the Rocky Mountains, followed by three days crossing the Prairies, then there were three days on rural roads around Quebec and Ontario, where the spring rainstorms caused some very muddy conditions on the dirt roads. Heavy cars did not do well as they were too difficult to push when they got stuck in the mud. I decided to send Des O'Dell as he could advise Rosemary in a very clear manner if there was anything that she needed to do to the car; Des was not allowed to touch the car himself. Rosemary got the bit between her teeth and kept going to the bitter end, still contriving to be nice to the press at the same time. The result was first in class, first in the Ladies' class and eighth in General Classification.

In October, the Imp Sport was introduced in time for the Earls Court motor show; it was a step in the right direction if enough examples were to be made to enable it to comply with the Group 1 figure of 5,000. It developed 52bhp at 6,100rpm as a result of the improved breathing due to twin Stromberg carburettors and a more efficient four-branch exhaust manifold. There were a lot of other improvements and the car was well received by the press, but production never reached the magic 5,000, so the model remained in Group 2, for which only 1,000 examples were necessary.

Chrysler took complete control of Rootes on January 10, 1967. There were many rumours as to which members of the Rootes family would go and whether we would benefit or not. We had arranged to enter the Monte, so we got on with the job to the best of our ability. We were running three Imps, starting from Monte Carlo, the crews being Peter Harper and Robin Turvey, Andrew Cowan and Brian Coyle, and Rosemary Smith and Valerie Morley. They had done recces and we had also been able to find solutions for some minor faults and make some improvments to the crews' comfort. The entire route would be in France, a matter which made the job of the service cars reasonably easy.

This was the year when there was to be a limited choice of tyres, which were to be marked after being chosen before the start. This arrangement was supposed to cut costs, but the choice was still sufficient to make it necessary to have all varieties available in case the weather changed. In fact Stuart Turner had obtained a set of every sort of tyre and stud configuration for each of his cars. BMC was reputed to have spent £15,000 on tyres before the rally started and to have the best weather reporting system of any team. We spent a great deal less, but did not deprive our drivers of any type which they wanted.

We had some good luck and some bad, but the results were better than I had expected. Cowan and Coyle won the Group 2 1,000cc class with one of the new 875cc Imp Sports, and a privately entered 998cc Imp won the 1,300cc GT class. Rosemary had a minor accident, which put her out during the final test, and Harper and Tovey were halted 20 miles from the finish of the final test due to a dropped carburettor needle, but they still managed second in the 1,300cc GT class. So with two class wins we had something to advertise. BMC were the outright winners, with Rauno Aaltonen and Henry Liddon, so were able to prove that the BMC-Cooper was still the best rally car.

I was not happy in that I had to ferry John Panks, Cyril Weighell and George Hartwell around the mountains on the last night. They had come to Monte to see what we were doing, and it was obvious that the time had come for them to look at our activites more closely as there was always a chance that a different part of the company might be asked to take over the competition department.

John Panks had been in charge of Rootes' New York office since 1953 and had recently returned to England to run the overseas operations and home distributing companies from Ryton. As Timothy Rootes seemed to have lost interest in our activities I was now answerable to John, an arrangement which suited me well as John was keen on motorsport and vintage cars. He read the current reports in the motoring press with interest, and so could listen to our problems and discuss them in a pragmatic manner.

Cyril Weighell had become Technical Director (Product Planning and Development) after Peter Ware left to go to Dunlop in 1966. He inherited a very much more efficient engineering department than that which Peter Ware had joined in 1958. He did not seem to me to be very interested in rallies.

George Hartwell was Home Sales Director and owned the Rootes main dealership at Bournemouth. He had been very successful in racing, rallies and hill-climbs at home and on the Continent a few years earlier. He had a very efficient development department attached to his workshops at Bournemouth where they had recently developed some excellent stages of tune for the Imp, which were designed to suit every type of customer. With hindsight I feel that we ought to have been allowed to co-operate much more closely with Hartwell Motors during that period.

The Shell 4000 came to my rescue again. This time I sent both Des O'Dell and Ian Hall out to help Rosemary, who had a Miss A Coombe as her navigator. Des felt he needed some help as it was a bit much for him to follow on his own, although he had Gerry Spencer with him. Unfortunately Ian was taken ill soon after the start and had to fly home suffering from some rare bug which affected his vision.

There was some drama near the end of the event; a number of cars got stuck in a long muddy, flooded track, the Citroen DS21 which had been leading the rally for five days getting stuck in a deep water hole, as did the Imp, although it was soon extracted by willing helpers and went on its way. However, when trying to get back onto a proper road, they went off the top of a high bank and crash-landed the front end onto a hard surface. This resulted in excessive negative camber for both front wheels and bad wheel misalignment, making the car very unstable. Des managed to smuggle the car into a barn and do some first-aid repairs, but it was never right after that and could not keep up with the motorcycle police escorting them to the finish in Quebec. However, they did make it on time and were 13th overall and won the *Coupe des Dames* again and, I think, the class. Roger Clark and Jim Peters won the event in a Ford Cortina Lotus. A press report said, "In the Ladies Cup, Rosemary Smith performed impeccably as usual, and had taken the Coventry prepared Imp as high as eighth overall when she too got stuck in the 100yd waterhole by

Georgia Bay. Luckily the Imp was more easily extractable than the Citroen, and she only dropped to 17th and eventually recovered to 13th." The area round Georgia Bay, incidentally, was the scene of the Canadian Winter Rally, by reputation a very tough all-snow event.

The Scottish and the Alpine rallies went well, with a class win and fourth in General Classification for Rosemary Smith and Susan Seigle-Morris in the former. Whilst an Imp did not win its class in the GT category in the Alpine, they finished ninth and 10th in General Classification and second and third in their class. The rally was won by Hopkirk and Crellin in a Mini-Cooper with a couple of Alfa Romeos behind them.

The RAC Rally of Great Britain, which should have started on November 18, was cancelled the night before, due to a foot and mouth disease scare, but it was agreed that the Camberley Special Stage, which would have been the first to be used in the rally, should be televised to show the cars in action. Competitors were to be allowed two runs, although there was no obligation to participate.

The stage was long, flatish and wet, and favoured the fast cars. Andrew Cowan was nervous on his first run and took a slow corner too fast, got the car sideways and handbraked, but the car didn't come round and so he went wide and lost time. Further on he spun and as a result he was only fifth fastest. On the second run he was much smoother and made second fastest time of the day and finished third on aggregate.

From the end of 1967, one could say that serious works competition in Imps started to decline. The whole of that year I had spent too much time in trying to get Chrysler to make up their mind as to whether they wanted to rally or race, whether they wanted to have their own competition department to carry out a planned programme for either sort of event, or if they were going along another road, to subsidize private entrants in National and International events. There was another matter which muddied the waters; there were two or three departments keen to enjoy the advantages of securing the competition department under their wing, but none of them wanted to pay for it out of their own budget.

In spite of these problems, we managed to get both Rosemary Smith and Andrew Cowan signed up as contracted drivers with a retainer, and we managed not only to stay in business the following year, but also to get ourselves a budget and make a considerable name for ourselves in doing so.

CHAPTER 18

Politics and problems

"The feuding and the fighting had started, and rumours were flying about as to which director or departmental manager would go next."

In 1966 I had been elected to the post of Chairman of the Sporting sub-committee of the Society of Motor Manufacturers and Traders. It was a committee which was supposed to act in an advisory capacity to the car section committee. It had no executive power, but being composed of representatives of car, accessory and component and tyre manufacturers, it was very much in-the-know when it came to every aspect of motorsport.

This was the beginning of an evolutionary period, when it was becoming evident that some of the rules governing the sport were being outdated by modern technology and new media methods. Urgent consideration was needed to examine such things as sponsorship, advertising on cars and defined areas for trade support. Television brought new problems, one of which was the provisions of the Television Act 1964 and the BBC's limits in advertising, together with the RAC's rules and the SMMT's own outlook in that area. Thus we found that there were at least five interested parties who had to thrash out an advertising policy, without even going into the problems which we would find on the Continent. A framework was needed to support and advise the many small sports and kit car builders, so that they might air their opinions and get advice as to the latest Road Traffic Act regulations. It was also to be the beginning of a multi-million pound drive in the export of British Formula cars and race engines.

The Royal Automobile Club had direct contact with the *Commission Sportive Internationale (CSI)*, which was the part of the *Fédération Internationale de l'Automobile (FIA)* which dealt with motorsport. It was now evident that there were too many interested parties for their views to be channelled through one or two spokesmen.

The Grand Prix car builders needed their own governing body which would be directly answerable to the *CSI*. They had the sponsors and the financial clout and could be and were, as far as the SMMT was concerned, left to fight it out with the circuit owners, the drivers and the National clubs (who each governed the running of the sport in their own country).

I met Stuart Turner at Monte Carlo in the January and he told me that he was leaving Abingdon and that Peter Browning was to take over the competition department there. As Peter was known to be interested in motor racing management, I could see that there might be a change of policy in that area.

In March I was appointed to the Sporting committee of the *Bureau Permanent Internationale des Constructeurs d'Automobiles* (*BPICA*), later to be known as the *Organisation Internationale des Constructeurs d'Automobiles* (*OICA*), with headquarters in Paris. Brian Rootes had resigned as the British representative of that committee, and as I was already the Chairman of the SMMT's Sporting sub-committee in the UK it was felt that I would be the most useful candidate for the post. This was an interesting and rewarding appointment as it enabled me to find out the views of the continental manufacturers and their competition policies. I hoped that we might come to think along similar lines and thus be able to exert more influence on the *CSI* whenever they were about to change anything in the International Sporting Code, with particular reference to Appendix J.

Let it not be thought that these two committees were mere talking shops; it should be stressed that both of them had contacts with the *CSI*. The British line was through the RAC via Dean Delamont, who was Director of the Motor Sports Division. He had to put his problems to the British representative on the *CSI* at that time. It was strongly resented that we had only one member (and so only one vote) to represent us when we had more works teams and makers of sporting equipment than any other nation.

The Sporting committee of the *BPICA* met two or three times a year, the meetings often taking place at the same time as one of the International motor shows, a most convenient arrangement as the members of the main *BPICA* committee were all associated with well-known car companies.

I was thus able to renew my acquaintance with my old friend of previous race and rally years Huschke von Hanstein (Porsche). I also got to know Jacques Rousseau (Simca) and Alberto Bersani (*ANFIA*), who were in similar positions to myself and were to became friends over the time when I served on the committee.

The *BPICA* had more influence over the *CSI* than the National automobile clubs, and its members sometimes attended *CSI* meetings and were thus able to look at drafts of new regulations and bring them back to our own committees for critical examination; looking over the minutes of meetings which took place between 1966 and 1970 I feel that we made a contribution to the administration of the rules governing motorsport, and I think we helped to avoid the sort of misunderstandings which had led to the unfortunate 1966 Monte Carlo Rally disqualifications.

I was the Chairman of the SMMT Sporting sub-committee for four-and-a-half years, and for part of that time on the RAC Competition Committee as well, so I suppose I might have been considered as a suitable consultant on those matters by our new American masters. Alas, that was not to be the case as, with one exception, none of their executives or directors took the slightest notice of my many reports until it was too late.

The feuding and the fighting had started, and rumours were flying about as to which director or departmental head would go next. We were told by our accounts department at Humber Road to make up a budget for 1967-68, which was not really possible as we had been given no idea as to what the total available funds would be, neither had we been given a policy document which might have indicated the models which we were to support in competitions.

We were soon to be visited from time to time by Chrysler accountants with separate demands for budgets, and one got the impression that there were different interests operating within the company. This happened whenever the management decided to graft us onto another department, and of course the budget had to be supported by a plan.

The trouble was that nobody wanted us on their budget as they were finding it hard enough to make ends meet without unnecessary additions. I wrote several reports to give our new bosses some idea as to where the emphasis should be placed, but by the time they had got to the right desk, we had been eliminated from that section and had to find another sponsor, who in turn wanted it all explained once again. I did that three times before the year was out and still had no proper niche by the beginning of the following year. My workshop staff had been reduced to the minimum and my office staff were getting very disillusioned.

I knew that we should terminate the contracts of all our works drivers except the two I wanted to keep, and hire any others on an event to event basis. We did eventually do this, but some of the old hands went up to Devonshire House and started to do their own lobbying with the new bosses. I eventually put an end to that and managed to pay them off. We had another running sore in the shape of some of the private racing stables, who had persuaded the Rootes family that they could do a better job than the factory; they had been given unlimited quantities of parts and enough money, which had been taken out of my budget and would have enabled me to enter two cars in major rallies in any year.

We were not helped by the fact that the Rootes family were having a fight between themselves and some of the shareholders of the retail distributors, so we had less support than we should have had if things had been more tranquil. George Hartwell had been deposed in an overnight coup. I was told by Peter Wilson that 40 per cent of the Robbins and Day shares were owned by the Rootes family; Robbins and Day was the holding company for their retail dealerships, and George Hartwell held 15 per cent of the shares. The family wanted to keep half the depots and that these should be the best ones, leaving Chrysler to have what remained. Apparently George said that this was not an honest way to do things and that it should be done in an above-board manner. George received his notice the next morning.

It was said that the object was to dispose of as many of the retail dealers as possible and keep control of the main dealers who handled more sales. As Robbins and Day owned most of the distributors, that would keep the majority of sales in the hands of the family, but only if they had won George Hartwell over to their point of view. Meanwhile, we were still answerable to John Panks administratively, and he gave me the impression that he was going to stay with Chrysler.

I never managed to get Alan Fraser to keep to the arrangements under which he obtained financial and material help from the department. Alan Fraser Racing had its good points, and Alan spent a lot of his own money on development of the Imps which his team raced in the British Touring Car Championship and various other events. We had agreed that he would furnish us with detailed reports concerning the specification of his cars, the horsepower and so on. He was not to approach anyone in the company except through myself. It became intolerable when he started to approach directors for more money over my head and I told him that he could not expect my co-operation if he did not stick to his part of the bargain. His cars and drivers did very well, but a lot of the success was due to Des O'Dell's help and the money from my budget. Things came to a head in April when Alan Fraser went to Devonshire House, which was the head office at that time, and complained about the lack of help from us. John Panks had received complaints from a director to the effect that I did not trust either Fraser or Nathan, another race tuner; I told him it was not so much a lack of trust, but their seeming inability to stick to any previous arrangements.

By this time I was disillusioned with the Rootes set-up and went up to London to see Larry Rice, a Chrysler Marketing Director who had been appointed in May. After a friendly meeting with him, at which I told him the history of the affair as I saw it, and finding at last a director who was willing to support competitions, even if it was in a limited manner due to lack of finance, I came back a lot happier.

At the end of June we handed back the 1926 Sunbeam V12 'The Tiger' to its owner, Sir Ralph Millais. It had been in our workshop for about six weeks having the Lockheed braking system completely rebuilt by Automotive Products and then had been to our test track at Wellesbourne for final tests.

On June 30 all managers were summoned to the *Hilton Hotel*, in Park Lane, to hear our Managing Director Gilbert Hunt explain the Company's position. We were £8 million in the red, and it would take two years to recover from that situation. He went on to try to instill some confidence into the senior staff, so that they might take back a cheerful report to their juniors. I came away wondering why Gilbert Hunt was there anyway; he had a good reputation, and I would have expected him to find something better to do than shore up an ailing branch of Chrysler. Still, I suppose I might have examined my own predicament in much the same light.

We all knew what was needed; we wanted a management that would stop putting things off, take some painful decisions, and take a firm line with the trades unions, who had done their successful best to sabotage the workings of the company at every turn.

Even the test drivers in the development department of engineering had refused to average more than 30mph on endurance runs. Their excuse was that the RAC laid down an average speed of 30mph for the road sections of rallies and that was what they were going to produce. We knew that they drove flat-out down the M1 motorway and then spent the night in the cafés playing cards, or probably went home to bed. Tachographs, if fitted, would have brought the whole factory to a standstill.

By December I heard that the new sales and marketing manager was very opposed to competitions in any form. I also found out that the worthy gentleman had been a submariner, but as he never surfaced to express his opinion personally I suppose he must have been uncharacteristic of the Silent Service. Bill Elsey, the Sales Director, told me that we were off his budget and would be part of engineering, so I sat down to write my fifth programme and budget for the year.

Things took a new turn in the New Year of 1968; we had just two Imps in the Monte, there was not much snow, and my service car broke a halfshaft climbing the long hill to the south of Millau. I left it there and hired a rather tired Citroen DS estate, which I hated. It did take all our spare wheels and tools, but its performance even when driven flat-out left a lot to be desired. The heater just could not cope with the internal capacity of the body and we sat and shivvered for the next week wherever we went. The result was that Andrew Cowan and Brian Coyle won their class and finished 22nd in General Classification, something happened to Rosemary and Margaret Lowrey and so they were second in the *Coupe des Dames* and 42nd in General Classification.

But what was much more interesting was the announcement that the regulations were available for the forthcoming *Daily Express* London-Sydney Marathon.

I was back at Coventry by January 30 and soon had a message from Peter Wilson and Harry Sheron, the Technical Director, to the effect that we should expect a visit by Chrysler's chief planning engineer, Mr Gibson, and his number-two in charge of Europe, Mr Scales, on the Monday afternoon; they wanted an estimate on 'Stock Racing, European Championship' (*sic*), which I interpreted as meaning the European Touring Car Race Championship, and the London-Sydney Marathon. I knew that we would have to get a new set of crystal balls pretty quickly and I went off to find Des O'Dell at his house at Leamington first thing in the morning. The news cheered Desmond up considerably. The Touring Car race business was one of Larry Rice's pet ideas, and I thought there would be scope for the Frasers and Nathans to deal with that while we made a real attempt to win the Marathon. February passed by with the usual inter-departmental skirmishes.

On March 5 I was at the offices of the *Daily Express*, in Fleet Street, to meet Jack Sears, who was on the organizing committee. I was told that the first part of the route would be London, Paris, Turin, Trieste, Lubliana, Zagreb, Belgrade, Istanbul, Sivas, Erzincan, Tehran, Kabul, Delhi and Bombay. Some were unfamiliar places, some we knew from the past and some conjured up visions of Omar Khayyám. I rushed off to 'The Map Shop' in Long Acre, where I failed to find what I wanted, but warned the salesperson that there might be a rush for Turkish, Iranian and Afghan maps shortly. When I got home I found I had quite a good set which had come to me over the previous few years by courtesy of the American *National Geographical Magazine*.

Hurdles to be leapt were numerous; for example, we had no official budget to prepare a car, to build a recce car or to carry out a recce as far as Bombay. The management was in a dither as to how to dispense with Rosemary Smith. Gilbert Hunt refused to see her, neither would Larry Rice; I was landed with the job because the so-called executives were afraid of her. The result is that she went back to Dublin without a contract and I had to tell her that we couldn't keep her on any longer. It actually released her to make other arrangements for the Marathon and she was to drive a Ford Lotus Cortina entered by the Irish Ford factory, Henry Ford and Son.

We now had an estimate for the Marathon which was between £18,000 and £20,000, and the money would be provided by just keeping the Circuit of Ireland, the Scottish and the London rallies in the 1968 programme, and leaving out the Tulip, the Acropolis, the Alpine and the RAC; with any luck we could balance to books.

In June John Panks showed me a letter from Larry Rice to confirm that the competition department would stay in business. The situation, however, was not improved by the departure of John Panks to become Managing Director of British Automotive Products, at Leamington. Harry Sheron had his budget cut and suggested that we applied to Marketing to be put on their's. This had been brought about by poor sales of the Imp and the Minx and presumably the Hillman Hunter. Production and testing programmes were being constantly sabotaged by restrictive working practices and strikes.

In August, Russia sent tanks into Czechoslovakia, which worried the organizers of the Marathon, but in five days the Russians had an iron grip on Prague. In September we were finally given permission to go on with our programme and enter the Marathon; the cheque reached the *Daily Express* on the day before entries closed, but only after Tommy Sopwith had persuaded Gilbert Hunt that Chrysler must enter a Hillman Hunter as all the other principal European factories had entered their best teams.

The next day the Dunlop alloy wheels which were on fatigue test at Camberley test track all failed, so we knew we had to run on Techdel wheels like everyone else, but it was going to cost us a lot more than it might have done on Dunlops. From then on it was up to Desmond to produce an indestructible Hunter and the crew to find out all they could about the route and conditions, which were likely to produce an adverse effect on both car and crew during the event.

We had decided to build a second car for the RAF Motor Sport Team; there seemed to be some surprising benefits in so doing, as the information which became available from their transport and medical departments would help us to minimize some of the risks which our crews were about to experience...

CHAPTER 19

A Marathon finale

"...the nearest run thing you ever saw in your life."
The Duke of Wellington

About the middle of March 1968 I had to go to a meeting of the sporting committee of the *Bureau Permanent Internationale des Constructeurs d'Automobiles* in Geneva, where the annual motor show was being held. I ran into Erik Carlsson of Saab in the foyer of the hotel after the meeting ended, and he told me that he had just been to Belgrade where he had met Michael Borislovjevic, whom we used to know as one of the Yugoslav officials on the Liège-Sofia-Liège Rally. He said that Boris wanted to help us during the forthcoming Marathon and would like me to get in touch with him, which came as a pleasant surprise as I needed help in Yugoslavia. Erik told me that Boris was the director of the mechanical engineering faculty at the University of Belgrade.

I soon got in touch with him and we arranged to meet at Orebic, on the Dalmatian coast, where I had planned to take my family camping in July. Boris said he would be there at the same time, but he only arrived on the day we were leaving for England. However, we did have enough time to devise a plan for our cars to use his workshops when they arrived in Belgrade, the details being completed by post.

We started testing a prototype rally car at the military test track at Bagshot early in the summer. I had already selected Andrew Cowan and Brian Coyle as the crew. We had two oldish Hillman Hunters which could be used to carry out the proving runs; one car was to be used for the recce as far as Bombay. We were going to use Australian-built cars for the second part of the recce. The Bagshot car was to be tested to destruction.

When Andrew had got as far as Bombay he told us that he wanted a third crew member, so I contacted Colin Malkin, who lived near Coventry and who was available to help with the development work. I think the original pair would have liked another Scotsman, but I knew we had picked the right man for the job. Colin had a great sense of humour and was incredibly tough as well as being a good driver.

We had been approached by the Royal Air Force Motor Sports Association earlier for the loan of a car, but were doubtful if we would have time to build it, but after we had gone into the advantages of helping them we decided to go ahead.

We were also in contact with Henri Rousseau, the competition manager of

Simca, which was also then a Chrysler-owned company, to see if we could help each other in the matter of service support. A meeting was arranged for August 7 at a point about halfway between our respective offices. Flt Lt David Carrington was to meet me at Ferryfield, in Kent, where we would leave our cars, fly to Le Touquet in one of the car ferries, to be met and taken to Montreuil for the conference.

However, things did not turn out quite as expected; I left Abingdon very early on slippery roads and was nearly killed by a large tipper which did a pirouette coming towards me at Nuffield. I met David as arranged, but our flight was delayed for an hour, and then we were given the option of going to Calais or waiting for the fog to clear at Le Touquet. We went to Calais airport, where we were given a strict search by the Customs before catching the bus to Calais station; we found out later that Calais was one of the places where they trained the newly joined *douaniers*. After three train changes we got to Etaples and took a taxi to Montreuil, arriving at about five o'clock.

The *Hotel de France* was still in the stage-coach era and we had to prise the serving wench from the arms of the waiter as there was nobody in reception; the evidence was there in the shape of a depression on one of our beds. The waitress agreed to show us a short-cut across the fields to the *Auberge La Grenouilliere*, where Messieurs Rousseau and Heu were ensconced with their wives. We were led down an alleyway opposite the hotel and through devious paths over the ramparts, and then down into the dry moat and across a couple of fields. There she stopped and, pointing through the fog, told us to go straight on; we arrived seven hours adrift, feeling that the air of mystery and intrigue had all the elements of a wartime escape story.

We were well-received, but the French team could do little to help us except provide a copy of their road notes which our own drivers later deemed to be inaccurate and not as good as the Castrol notes which Henry Liddon had prepared for the event. By a curious chance, one of the Simcas was to be No 46 and the RAF Hillman Hunter was drawn No 45; both cars were to be classed as finishers. We had a most excellent meal that evening with our French friends and there was a surprise for me as they had found out that my birthday was August 8 and had persuaded the management to concoct a Siberian omelette with a suitable inscription especially for me at lunchtime the next day before taking us to Le Touquet to fly back to Ferryfield.

David Carrington arranged that he would lay on two lectures to be given by specialists on hygiene, tropical survival and diet, which were to be attended by as many of the drivers and support crews as possible. The advice that was given kept everyone fit for the entire event and would have added considerably to the wellbeing of anybody who broke down in the more arid portions of the route.

Andrew and Brian went off to survey the route at the end of August. The car that they were using was really pretty standard except for the suspension and general strengthening of the bodyshell. They were delayed by a broken halfshaft in Bulgaria and had to hire a lorry to get the car to Istanbul, where Chrysler had the right organization to get the parts out of Customs – a little matter which would have taken a normal citizen weeks to do.

We didn't hear any more of Andrew until he rang up from London to say he was back and the car was in Bombay, and that Brian was on his way to Australia, where Brian Corey of Chrysler Australia was to take him over as much of the route as they could cover in the available time.

Tests were going on at Bagshot, and by October we had received the new Dunlop alloy wheels which they had offered us on very advantageous terms. Des O'Dell had very wisely included them in the 200-mile rough test programme which had been set up to see if the car could survive without any terminal trouble in its rally form; that was to be run at maximum speed with a full load. The wheels broke up after 25 miles and there was no time for Dunlop to retool in order that we could retest the modified wheels and ship them out to the service points. We had to go cap-in-hand to Minilite, who had been ruled out on account of cost, and ask them for wheels. They told us that they had insufficient for us as so many of the entrants were using them. In the end Minilite just managed to give us enough wheels in time for Jeremy Ferguson of Dunlop to get them out to the vital points in time. We also flew a few steel wheels to places in Asia just in case they were needed.

Air Atlas had taken over the entire freighting operation for us and managed to get two crates to Kabul, Afghanistan, as well as two more to Bombay. High-octane fuel was being delivered to some very remote places through the good offices of Castrol, and I was able to do a deal with their competition manager, Ray Simpson. I had shipped a very efficient drum pump out to Kabul, and Ray realized that he needed it more than we did, but we were still contracted to run on Shell oil.

The final days of preparation were fraught with more drama, and we only just managed to get our entry sanctioned by the management on the last day. I suspect that Tommy Sopwith, who was organizing the event on behalf of the *Daily Express*, must have told our Managing Director that our entry had not been received and that something had to be done pretty promptly.

Then the shop stewards at Humber Road said "Everybody out!" and on November 8 we were told that there would be no exception for the competition department. By the 16th we were allowed back again, but no overtime was permitted, yet on the 22nd, by a miracle, both cars were finished and taken down to London for the start. I kept out of the workshop for the whole of that week and left Desmond to sort it out.

My part in the event was to take the grossly overloaded Minx Estate to Belgrade. My co-driver was Derek Hughes, one of our best mechanics. We left for Dover on Friday, November 22 and arrived to find that the ferry to Dunkirk was to be delayed by four hours; there was trouble with the lock which kept the vessel at the right level for the night train to be shunted on board.

We had bunks and so got some sleep and a good traditional breakfast. We got away from the docks at 5.30am and had a good run on the motorways to Frankfurt, where we had a quick lunch at the international airport. Munich was reached in the rush-hour, which put me in a bad humour by the time we got to the frontier at Kufstein, where the Austrians told us that we would not be permitted to drive on their roads with 14 wheels and some spares and a jack. We started a debate on the matter which proceeded intermittently because the official concerned liked to walk away to deal with other vehicles whenever we wanted to press a point. A compromise was reached, we unloaded half the wheels and drove the car through Customs. We then got a baggage trolley and took the rest of the load through the barrier and reloaded it onto our car in the car park, where the Customs man could not see it. All this took nearly two hours, so we were glad to spend the night at the *Andreas Hofer*, a lovely old inn not too far away.

We called Des at his hotel and he was happy to tell me that the cars looked the smartest at scrutineering, and that everyone was ready for the start on Sunday, November 24. We had travelled 645 miles that day and had overcome two lots of officialdom – the Germans had been difficult as well – so we slept like logs.

Next morning we went through that neat and tidy town, Kitzbuhl and through the Tauern tunnel to Villach in good weather. We lunched at one of my old Liège-Sofia-Liège haunts, the *Hotel Post*. I expected some trouble at the Yugoslav frontier, even though we had Rally Service plates on the car, but all was well and we gave the official a couple of packets of cigarettes. Derek put in a Scottish Rally badge for good measure and we were away to Zagreb to stay at the *International*.

Monday morning saw us on the road by 6am, weaving past the wrecks on the dreaded *autoput* in thick fog and bound for Belgrade. Luckily the fog cleared after about 100 miles and we reached Belgrade unscathed. The technical engineering department turned out to be very close to the *Metropole Hotel*, where the main control was to be. There was nobody about when we got there as it was lunchtime, so we were able to look around. The walls were lined with white tiles, the painted floors were polished, the lifts – of which there were several – were lit from above and below. The architecture was like something out of the film *Metropolis* and there was a faint suggestion of *1984* about the place; I expected the loudspeakers to suddenly burst into life with some propaganda.

The local agent soon turned up from Unikomerc, our dealers, so we were able to leave all our gear safely locked up and sign in at the hotel. The rest of the day was spent briefing everyone, shopping for last-minute items, such as mugs, meeting some of the students that I had made friends with at Orebic in July and trying to get to bed early as the workshop was to open at 4am.

The next morning we were ready in the workshops for any emergency. Our first car, No 45 (RAF Motor Sports Association), came in at 04.45 and No 75 (Cowan, Coyle and Malkin) soon afterwards. The crews went off to bed and Derek was able to spend three hours checking everything. The other private entry, No 5, a Chrysler Valiant Estate (Lumsden, Sargent, Lewis and Fenton), came in with a tachometer fault, which was rectified, and the car was also checked over. They were very unlucky to have drawn such an early number as at the time they arrived in Turkey the notorious local truckers had not woken up to the fact that there was a rally in progress, and theirs was one of the first cars to be written-off. Fortunately, the crew were not injured in the accident, which apparently was quite a common occurence, especially on the road from Istanbul to Teheran.

We were due to leave for Athens after lunch and lightened the service car by leaving quite a few useful spares with the agent. We were provided with a pilot car to take us out onto the road to Nis and Skopje; there was no need for us to see the cars away to Istanbul, where they would be met by our foreman Gerry Spencer, who was covering Turkey before flying on to Bombay. Desmond and Dick Guy were on their way by air to Teheran, and we reached the Greek frontier at midnight.

On arrival we drove straight to our agents, EFTA, getting there as they opened. It had been a longer journey than I had expected; I must have miscalculated somewhere, but there were 744 miles on the odometer to show that it had been a long hard night.

I was looking forward to a nice lunch and a bit of a rest before we would catch the plane to Teheran that evening, but I had not counted on the extraordinary pantomime which was caused by the fact that we would have to leave our Hillman Estate and a few bits and pieces in the care of the Customs before we would be permitted to leave Greece. Fortunately, the Customs office was near our agent and we could call upon his help if needed. The official forms had to be inspected and stamped by no less than five separate officials, some of whom did not appear to be on speaking terms with the others, even though they were seated in the same room. Nobody could sell us the fiscal stamps which were needed to complete the authorization, so we had to go down into the street and buy them from a little office situated in a fish shop opposite.

Finally we seemed to have got everything right; we had to take an official who would show us the way to the bonded garage, then the Rootes dealer brought them back while I drank Turkish coffee in his office for what seemed like hours, but then the traffic in Athens is terrible. Dick had managed to get his toolkit down to manageable proportions and we finally took off for Iran about an hour late due to the delayed arrival of our plane.

We reached Teheran too late to get anything to eat, the hotel was cold and the hot water system was out of action. Our plane for Kabul was due out at 5am and by a miracle our taxi arrived on time.

Fortunately, dawn was fine and we had some superb views over the Hindu Kush with a snow-capped panorama, which comprised some of the highest peaks in the world, stretching away for hundreds of miles. The BL mechanics were on the same plane and it was good to see my part-time navigator in the shape of Den Green amongst them. We were met by Mr Irwin, of Afghan Insurance, a contact made by Andrew on his recce, who made things much easier for us. He introduced us to Abdul Amami, who was to be our guide and interpreter for the next three days. He had hired two Russian-built jeeps with their drivers who were to be on call for the next 72 hours.

There was an ominous atmosphere in the street and we soon found out that it was due to the holy festival of Ramadan, when it is forbidden for Muslims to partake of food and drink between sunrise and sunset during the ninth month of their year. The religious fervour makes the locals a bit touchy and one came across large crowds of Afghans who were listening to their holy preachers and standing about armed to the teeth.

The next morning I passed a shop which sold ex-Indian Army Lee Enfield .303 rifles and Webley and Scott revolvers, which must have been captured in one of the frontier skirmishes many years before. We managed to get our crates of spare parts out of the care of the Customs just five minutes before everything closed for the weekend. We also got the loan of a welding outfit, which was so old that the acetylene was generated with carbide and water in a miniature gasometer.

Des and his crew came in on the lunchtime plane from Teheran with the news that our cars had been serviced at the Pekan works, which was the Iranian assembly plant for the Hillman Hunter, and all was well. Des loaded up the spare parts and welding gear and went down to the service point, which was at the entrance to the city. We stayed behind to meet the crews at the *parc ferme*. It was very cold and the service crews lit fires to keep warm while waiting. Andrew was on time, but the RAF car had bent a track rod crossing the desert after Teheran and was going back there when they met one of the Iranian national service cars, whose crew had the right parts with them. They were only three hours late, but the incident led to another matter, caused by a missing wheel spacer which had been overlooked in the dark.

The *parc ferme* was in the centre of Kabul and consisted of a roped-off car park guarded by some armed police. Some of the local VIPs' cars were parked in it and the Afghan public were milling around, dressed like the traditional Khyber Pass tribesmen, on the other side of the ropes. I found myself standing next to Stuart Turner, who was officiating on the event, in the cold evening sun. We had been told that the first cars had arrived at the service stop, but the crowd was getting restless and the police didn't look too happy, even after using their belts as flails, as was their custom. Just as Stuart and myself were debating as to whether it would be safer to get onto the top of one of the larger limousines or hide underneath one, the wife of one of the government officials, dressed in an impressive shaggy coat which reached down to her magnificent embroidered leather boots, and her head crowned by a fur hat, strode forward and proceeded to lash the unruly peasants with her tongue. This seemed to be something that even the wildest tribesmen resented and they retreated to a safe distance and stayed there.

His Majesty the King of Afghanistan drove up and the first rally car arrived in the floodlights at 8.49pm on November 29. All was well, and the drivers were ferried to their hotels, fed and bedded, except for the unfortunate ones who were wandering around looking for bits or specialists in mending broken parts and offering much gold to anybody who could solve their problems. The RAF crew had lost or broken their jack, so one of our lads was sent out after dark in the strange city to find one. Much to our surprise he soon came back with a suitable screw-jack of unknown vintage which he had bought from a local taxi driver.

Our service point was to be at Sarobi, at the end of the Special Stage, which was 46 miles long and had to be covered in one hour. I had tried to go over it in one of the Russian jeeps two days before, but decided that it would take us at least two hours, and even if we came back by the alternate route on the main road it would have been too dark to see much, so I had abandoned the project.

The stage was reputed to be very difficult and Colin Malkin was said later to have gone to earth under a rug on the back seat of the Hunter when our car went over it. We did not know until the start at 4.42am that the government had graded the earth road the day before, and it was now much faster. Des and his men joined the Ford and BMC service crews at Sarobi and I stayed at the hotel so as to be near a telephone if there was an accident.

Andrew Cowan dropped six minutes against Roger Clark's five minutes in his Ford. Andrew reported that the RAF car had lost a wheel due to broken wheel studs halfway through the stage. After trying to get a vehicle through to them with the bits, Derek got a ride on a police motorcycle and was able to rig things up sufficiently to get them to the end of the stage. A complete repair was then made, but they had lost 179 marks on the section, although they remained in the event. The trouble was caused by the wheel spacer being left off at the Kabul service point when the wheels were changed.

After braving the Khyber Pass and the suicidal crowds of spectators in India, most of the crews reached Bombay without further incident. Cowan's Hunter was placed sixth at that point.

We flew to Bombay via Delhi the next day and reached there in time to see the service crew which had flown in from Turkey working on the Hunters in the service area. All the work had to be carried out in a limited time under artificial light and in great heat and high humidity. The cylinder head was changed on No 75 as the fuel in Australia would be of a higher octane rating. All the shock absorbers were changed, and brakes and steering checked. Any unused or replaced parts had to be handed back to the Customs for return to the UK.

This was the last chance to prepare the cars for the 3,000-miles run from Perth to Sydney. Most of the spares could now be dumped as there was very little that could be done in the running time if one was to stand a chance of winning. It would be flat-out all the way except for quick stops for fuel and refreshments. One of the advantages of being in sixth place was that the cars would now leave Perth in their General Classification order and there would be fewer cars to pass in the very dusty conditions.

The cars were steam-cleaned in Bombay and shipped with their crews on the cruise liner *Chusan*. The crews would have nine days to relax before reaching Fremantle, the port for Perth, Western Australia. The Aussies would also have nine days to make the Poms frightened with tales of deep holes, great drops and gigantic kangeroos. Our service crews would fly to Perth on the day the *Chusan* sailed, except for Derek, who was to go back to Athens to collect my car and drive it back to the UK.

I left Des and his merry men, who would stay in Perth until the rally left and then try to set up a service point on one of the loops in Western Australia. The service cars were too slow to catch the rally after that so he would have to set up an alternative plan. I went to Adelaide, where Chrysler had a large assembly plant for Valiants and Hunters. I was to be lent a car and would supervise the loading of a Valiant Estate equipped with automatic transmission with a few useful standard Hunter parts. We had lost the privately entered Valiant Estate in Turkey, when it was written-off by the truck.

Apart from our own cars, I was interested in the MG Midget No 52, driven and prepared by my old friend John Sprinzel, with Roy Fidler as his navigator. He had discussed the preparation of the car with me and the fact that he would have no help from the factory. John had driven Austin-Healey Sprites in most of the great continental rallies with considerable success, and although he had never been a member of the works team, I had always given him every assistance before and during the events. He knew that he could not afford the space or the weight penalty of taking much in the way of spares. The passenger seat was made to recline fully in order to become a bed, and the extra fuel tank took up most of the remaining space.

I reminded John that he had broken a Sprite stub-axle in the Liège-Sofia-Liège and how the complete wheel and hub had gone floating down a river and he had had to dive in to retrieve it! John was 24th at Bombay and looking forward to winning the prize for the best private entrant.

Seventy-two cars left Gloucester Park, Perth, in a blaze of publicity watched by 10,000 spectators, who were entertained by girl pipers and marching bands.

The Australian media was doing the event proud, with the hundreds of local radio stations, which gave half-hourly reports, and the national TV, which gave an hour to the departure of the contestants. People were driving hundreds of miles to settlements through which the rally passed and often swelled the population to four or five times the normal figure, to the delight of the local bar-keepers. The locals sometimes put out trestle tables with spreads of food and drink for the competitors. The temperature began to soar in more ways than one; it was December 14, the start time was 4pm and officially it was Australian mid-summer.

The Adelaide staff had been very helpful and had been in touch with the New South Wales Motor Club, who had produced a volunteer in the shape of young Andrew Chapman, who was to accompany me when we joined the rally in the Flinders Mountains, north of Fort Augusta. He joined me in Adelaide the day before we were due away and helped me to stock up with some rations and, more importantly, a large ice box. I was soon initiated into the workings of the Australian ice machine; the procedure was to put the box under the chute, insert the appropriate coin, press the button and Bingo!, you got a jackpot full of egg-sized ice pellets. The beer and Coke took up the rest of the room.

As I had been driving around the local roads and was already used to driving on dirt roads in East Africa, I was familiar with corrugations and knew that the faster you went the better was usually the ride. Corrugations usually formed on main roads as the slower traffic did not go fast enough to form them on more minor roads. Our Valiant was comparatively dust-proof, but the luggage compartment was a real dust trap. When we got onto main road portions of the rally route the next day, we cruised as fast as road conditions permitted, and in fact we covered 1,200 miles in 36 hours. I drove all the way as I had always enjoyed driving fast on dirt roads and felt that I would probably be prepared to risk a little more than Andrew Chapman.

The Western Australian section was run over a great zig-zag. The first stage was 350 miles, north-east from Perth at an average speed set at 50mph, with a good bitumen road for the first 200 miles and a good dirt road to Youanmi. Drivers who had to finish repairs as a result of Asian problems missed out the Youanmi control and headed down to the end of the next section at Marvel Loch and so lost 1,440 points, but stayed in the event. Youanmi to Marvel Loch was 243 miles at 60mph and was the first bit of real nastiness. It was very dusty and unsurfaced; the first car was due at 11pm and the last at 3.03am. Thirty-eight lost time on the stage and one entrant put a rod through the block of his Volvo and sold it for $3,000 on the spot. Three cars hit 'roos during the night. The population of Marvel Loch was normally 170, but there were plenty more that night.

The next section to Lake King was said to be impossible at the set average of 60mph for the 119 miles. The track was just a car's width and went through impenetrable bush for 70 miles. Roger Clark was still ahead in his Cortina and had lost no more marks at Lake King, which was where the rally turned east again. The second part of the section was rough and rocky with large potholes, some 2ft deep. Three cars did this clean, the Cortina of Clark, Lampinen's Ford Taunus and Lucien Bianchi's Citroen. Andrew Cowan dropped five minutes. Forrest and Tubman, in Volvo No 12, had done a good recce, being Aussies and sponsored by TVW Channel 7 Daily News Perth, and had found a detour along a fast road which, although 23 miles longer, should have saved them 15 minutes, or so they calculated. But unfortunately for them it joined up with the route at a point where 2,000 campers and spectators had chosen to roost. Forrest had a minor accident in getting out of the car to guide it through the camp and suffered a minor abrasion, which handicapped him for the rest of the event, and to make matters worse they dropped 16 minutes. Evan Green, co-driving with 'Gelignite' Jack Murray in BMC 1800 No 31, dropped two minutes due to a puncture. The dust was terrible.

The next section from Lake King to Ceduna was 892 miles in 14hr 52min. Arrival time was set for 8.24pm on December 15, with the clocks put forward one hour for Central time. This crossed the notorious Nullabor Plain of varied surfaces, of which 400 miles were the worst. This was a real bogey for the drivers as it was virtually desert and the temperature might be as high as 130 degrees F. It was possible to get stuck in the deep powdery dust or have one's suspension destroyed by hitting one of the enormous holes, which, although marked on some pace notes, were not easy to locate as there were few landmarks, and mileposts were also few and far between. Furthermore, continuous wheelspin made dead reckoning impossible. It was fortunate that on the day the temperature was only between 70 and 80 degrees.

There was an airstrip at Norseman, by Lake Cowan, which was the last place for a service crew to operate and then fly on to the other end of the section at Ceduna or Port Augusta; about 15 light aircraft and a Martinair DC3 for the DAF team were there. The DC3 was too heavy for the tarmac and had sunk in and needed to be pushed onto firmer ground by willing helpers before it could take off. Cars turned up with bits missing or hanging off, and there were plenty of broken suspensions. The Denton and Boyce MGB, No 47, sponsored by *Nova Magazine*, had a holed radiator, but thanks to some MG Car Club members who borrowed a radiator from a generous member, they got going again five hours late; they had to average 82mph to Ceduna to avoid exclusion. Yorkshire grit ensured that they did so, but they dropped another 195 marks, making their total 457 at Ceduna, but they kept on and finished in 42nd place. This was the spirit in which the event was run, finish at all costs; to be in the finishers list was an honour even if you were not in the money.

The Mercedes all had radiator trouble, which in turn caused overheating and cylinder head gasket trouble. Clark was still leading at Ceduna, and the next section came as a relief, only 314 miles in 6hr 18min to Quorn. There was to be a Dunlop service point at Ceduna, also one by AMOCO. Here there was a fruit-fly control where the cars were sprayed with chemical as they were entering South Australia, an important agricultural area. Although it was possible to get telex messages in the most unlikely places, I had lost contact with my Western Australia service crews. We intended to provide major service at Port Augusta as it was only 26 miles from Quorn on a good road. We went down to the airstrip and found the Dunlop service crew were just arriving and that Des and his two mechanics had been able to hitch a lift with them and would now be able to take over the Chrysler Estate and follow the rally from here on.

It was at this point that Roger Clark's Cortina gave trouble, arriving on three cylinders. The other works Cortina of Ken Chambers and Eric Jackson arrived with the news that Roger was 50 miles away but still motoring. The cylinder head was removed from Ken's car and fitted to Roger's when he arrived and he left two minutes before he was due at Quorn, where he dropped 14 minutes.

The leaders at that point were Simo Lampinen and Gilbert Staepelaere in a Ford 20 RMS, with 20 points. Andrew Cowan was sixth equal with Green and Murray (BMC 1800) with 32 points, so there were seven cars in the running for a win.

I rejoined the rally route the next morning at Branchina after we had slept in the car. There had been two sections, Quorn to Moralana Creek, 64 miles in 1hr 17min, described by the organizers as a back road not marked on many maps. It was more like a Special Stage designed for FWD vehicles; and it was there that Evan Green very sportingly stopped and helped the Hunter crew out of a 6ft deep ditch which Brian Coyle had got it into. The classic remark made by Green at that time must go down in motoring history. "Hell, this is motorsport, not war!" Unfortunately, Green got a crack in the ribs during this incident and felt bad for the rest of the rally.

Various cars were late here or badly damaged, but had to get out of the gorge by tackling the next stage to Branchina of 75 miles in 1hr 30min with a wet creek which had to be crossed 20 times without bridges. Des put his service crew right alongside the control, which was lucky because Andrew Cowan arrived with a broken brake pipe soon after another incident, when spectators got him out of some sand. He had not lost any marks since Lake King.

I had stationed myself about a quarter of a mile further up on the very wide dirt road that ran alongside the railway that went up to Alice Springs. We were to take care of the RAF Hunter and were placed alongside several of the Aussie service crews, some of whom had rigged up boiler plates over gas rings and were having eggs and bacon. The smell soon drove us across the road to an enterprising hot-dog stall to have our own breakfast. I had a short-wave radio and was able to monitor the arrival times of the cars at the Branchina control and hear if they had any time penalties. The RAF car soon arrived, but without brakes, having had one of the bleed nipples knocked off by a stone. Andrew Chapman was familiar with the Hunter as he owned one which he had rallied in New South Wales, but he made a mistake in adjusting the rear shoes as we had changed the backplates, and he was not given enough time to bleed the brakes properly. The car ran off the road later, but Des was following it and soon put things to rights.

At this point Evan Green and Cowan were equal fifth and Lucien Bianchi was leading in his DS21, being the only car to lose no marks in Australia. Lampinen was having steering trouble and Evan Green was stopped with a seized-up hub. Andrew took a message to the BMC service crew, but it was four and a half hours before they were rescued from the next stage of 208 miles. We followed, but hardly knew which day it was or how far it was to the next place; maps for that area were not very helpful. We just kept going and hoped we would not come across any of our cars. By taking a short-cut which we knew had been covered by the Valiant Estate we caught up with some of the stragglers and were able to get to Menindee by afternoon; the first cars were due there at 13.21 and clocks were advanced by one and a half hours. After Broken Hill, a famous mining town, we came across John Sprinzel with his MG Midget jacked up, waiting for a stub-axle which someone had located by radio. The only Midget for hundreds of miles was being stripped and he hoped to get the part by light plane within the hour. We had to press on, but heard later that they had stripped the wrong side and poor John was excluded by the time he had fixed the car. This was a great shame as he would almost certainly have won the private entrant's prize if he had been sent the right part.

We hoped to get to Braidwood, our next service point, by 6am on December 17. Braidwood was about 50 miles east of Canberra and about 576 from Menindee, near where we had seen John Sprinzel, by the short route. The rally leaders, who were about an hour ahead of us, had 918 miles to go before we would see them again. Desmond knew he would never catch them up, so he did what he could at the last turn-off point and arranged to meet us at Braidwood where we were to have some support from the local Chrysler garage. The rally route went over the Snowy Mountain where there would be no time for service anyway. It was easy to get to Dunbar, 246 miles over a fast level road, and for the crews to have a meal, courtesy of the locals, in a cow shed with a large sign above reading "Dunbar Hilton". The next 222 miles were easy as well in 4hr 26min, but the next bit – 48 miles from Edi to Brookside in the dark in an hour – was more difficult as it climbed the slopes of Mount Buffalo and was full of ups and downs with apparently bottomless drops. Roger Clark, in his usual dry manner, remarked afterwards "If you'd gone over the edge there, your clothes would have been out of fashion before you hit the bottom." The score was Bianchi 27, Clark 29, Lampinen 36, Cowan 38 and Hopkirk (BMC 1800) 39, after putting in a late spurt.

From Brookside to Omeo, over much the same sort of country, was 92 miles in 1hr 55min, very dark through tall forests, followed by 101 miles from Omeo to Murrindal by 04.06. Halfway there was a town called Bruthen, where Roger's back axle went out with a crunch, but he negotiated with a local fisherman at three in the morning for the axle off the private car and arrived only 97 minutes late at the control. Bruthen is derived from the aboriginal word meaning 'evil spirit'. The Murrindal-Ingebyra section was 74 miles, and Bianchi dropped two minutes with a puncture here. The New South Wales police got themselves a lot a bad publicity by having six police patrol cars out in a town called Cooma to see that competitors did not exceed 35mph; Paddy gave them a real going over when he got to the television cameras at the finish. The last difficult section was Numerella to Hindmarsh, 34 miles in 42 minutes over a loose surface of winding forest track through hilly country at an average of 48mph. Hopkirk lost one minute, Cowan two, Bianchi three and Clark two. Lampinen took a cattle grid too fast and got it sideways, hitting both sides on gateposts, and in spite of getting some help lost two hours, but still finished 16th at Sydney.

We reached our rendezvous near Braidwood on the Hindmarsh to Nowra section and met the locals. I was worried about Desmond as I had not seen him since the Flinders Mountains, although I had heard of him *en route*, but he turned up on time.

It was here that we met a young man who was watching his first rally; he seemed to be the Australian equivalent of a country bumpkin. He asked me who we wanted to win and, of course, I said "Cowan in the Hillman". He then asked me who was winning, and I said "The Citroen". Then he said "Don't worry, I'll fix it, just tell me when the Citroen comes round the corner." We waited a bit, then Bianchi's Citroen appeared and I said "That's the Citroen." He put his hands up and pointed with both forefingers at the car, said nothing and then walked away.

Hopkirk and Cowan soon came along. Andrew was very angry about the

Cooma police and said he would have to be very careful from now on as he had been warned that the police were even stopping cars to check brake lights and dip switches. Desmond said he would stay to see the RAF car through if we would follow Andrew to the finish. We followed, knowing that our car was now in second place. After a few miles we caught up with Andrew, who had stopped and was talking to the crew of a police car, but he waved me on and so we went on slowly until he passed us and gave a thumbs-up sign.

It was only a few miles later when we came round a bend in a forest and found Bianchi's Citroen blocking half the road, with the wreckage of a Mini which had been coming the other way. Ogier, who had been driving at the time of the accident, said that the Mini seemed to be out of control. There were plenty of people helping as Paddy Hopkirk had raised the alarm and help came from nearby. The radio soon announced that the Citroen had crashed and we knew that Andrew had only to keep going carefully to be the winner.

At Warwick Farm there were thousands of spectators, but as we had rally plates and Chrysler decals on the doors we managed to get right up to the *parc fermé*, which was enclosed by a high wire fence to keep the public out. There were plenty of old friends there and it was good to have a beer and watch our crews sitting on the top of their cars and enjoying the limelight. The official arrival time for Warwick Farm was 13.19 on December 17, 1968, and it took me a long time to realize that we had just won the longest rally that had ever been staged up to then.

London-Sydney Marathon Results

General Classification to 10th place

1st: £10,000 and the Daily Express Trophy.
      Car No 75, Hillman Hunter.
      A Cowan, B Coyle, C Malkin (Rootes Motors).

2nd: £3,000 and Sydney Telegraph prize.
      Car No 51, BMC 1800.
      P Hopkirk, T Nash, A Poole (British Leyland).

3rd: £2,000 and Sydney Telegraph prize.
      Car No 24, Ford Falcon GT.
      I Vaughan, R Forsyth, J Ellis (Ford Motor Co, Australia).

4th: £1,000.
      Car No 58, Porsche 911S.
      S Zasada, M Wachowski (S Zasada).

5th: £500.
      Car No 61, BMC 1800.
      R Aaltonen, H Liddon, P Easter (British Leyland).
6th: £250.
      Car No 29, Ford Falcon GT.
      B Hodgson, D Rutherford (Ford Motor Co, Australia).

7th: £150.
Car No 92, Ford 20MRS.
H Kleint, G Klapproth (Ford Deutschland).

8th: £100.
Car No 2, Ford Falcon GT.
H Firth, G Hoinville, G Chapman (Ford Motor Co, Australia).

9th: £100.
Car No 74, Citroen DS21.
R Neyret, J Terramorsi (R Neyret).

10th: £100.
Car No 48, Ford Cortina Lotus.
R Clark, O Andersson (Ford Motor Company).

Other Rootes/Chrysler cars placed:

32nd: Car No 45, Hillman Hunter. Flt Lt D Carrington,
Sqdn Ldr A King, Flt Lt J Jones (RAF Motor Sports Association).

40th: Car No 46, Simca. B Heu, J Syde (Simca Motors).

Started: 98
Arrived: 56

We managed to get the Hunter flown home on the same plane as the BMC cars as soon as the prizegiving was over. It would have been futile to have done otherwise and I didn't care where the £500 freight fee was coming from, I just sent a telex telling London to expect the winner. By 'chance', there was a Hercules waiting to take the RAF car and its crew back to the UK. We set out three days later, suffering from every form of fatigue, and it took over 24 hours to get to Heathrow where we went through the VIP lounge and on to a press party at a local hotel. It was nearly Christmas day by the time this was all over.

There was a real VIP reception at Heathrow, where we were all taken through the special lounge, past a very informal Customs inspection and outside where we found the cavalcade ready to take us to the press conference at the *Heathrow Hotel*, followed by a dinner at *Quaglinos*, in London, which was attended by Andrew Cowan's parents and his sister, as well as my wife and several friends and public relations people, who had all been brought up to London specially for the event. I was really too tired by then to appreciate the evening's entertainment and had great difficulty in staying awake.

The Rootes management was in a state of complete shock when we arrived back. Their publicity department hadn't expected a win and had no press handouts ready. Chrysler Australia were ready to capitalize on the win and had a nice car called the Hillman Hunter GT ready for production, and announced it two days before the rally finished. It was a twin-carburetter Hunter finished in a de Luxe style and offered in a range of distinctive colours. I had driven it when at Adelaide and liked it, but had made some minor criticism about the spring rates, which were promptly changed in production. It was a nice car to drive on the average Australian road.

Rootes had nothing to offer the public and never cashed in on the win. The Sales Director said that he had no confidence in competitions and we felt the same about him. I did however manage to get a substantial payment made to the drivers and persuaded the management to give them each a car.

Of course we had spent too much money and would not be able to plan for a new rally programme until we had a proper budget. Unfortunately, the management saw it another way and decided to put the competition department into suspended animation; no decisions were to be made about anything for the time being. Des O'Dell and myself made several visits to Bowater House, the new head offices at the top of Sloane Street, where we saw Gilbert Hunt, Bill Elsey and others, but nothing came of it. By February I had been transferred to the road proving department, charged with the job of investigating the design and construction of test tracks, with particular emphasis on the Air Ministry's surplus aerodromes. At the end of that year I had compiled a large file, which gave information on just about all of the world's motor industry proving grounds, together with a plan for converting the Air Ministry aerodrome at Bruntingthorpe, Leicestershire, which was under consideration as a Chrysler proving ground for both Rootes and Simca.

Whilst I had enough to keep me occupied and was still able to attend SMMT and *Bureau Permanent* meetings, Des had very little to look forward to. Andrew was sent round the world on a public relations mission and had enough time to take a look at things from the point of view of the shrewd Scottish businessman, which he was later to become. In May, the competition department was closed, but key personnel were kept on to build special engines and supply rally parts to private owners, and no doubt hand over the special parts to the Alan Fraser Racing team. Andrew came back from his world tour and felt that he was honour-bound to enter the Scottish Rally, which he had so nearly won the year before.

This was to be a private entry, but the entrant had no car for the event. Andrew found that Derek Hughes was still at Humber Road, building engines. They arranged to smuggle a works 998cc Imp up to Blackaddar Farm, Duns, at the right time, and Derek went as well, presumably on holiday. All went very well until about the middle of the rally, when Andrew had gearbox trouble. He arranged for the only Imp gearbox he could get hold of in a hurry to be fetched. It came from his old and battered green Imp, which lived on his farm. At the end of the day, with some time in hand, they took out the gearbox and put it on the back seat of the Rally Imp. The car was then pushed into *parc fermé* by the crew. Next morning it was pushed out again, the gearbox from Duns was bolted in and they finished the rally by winning the class and finishing second in General Classification to Roger Clark. Andrew says that was the last appearance of a works Imp in an International rally, and he should know!

Meanwhile, my compilation of data on all the significant proving grounds and test tracks in the world had been quite an interesting exercise, and I was quite pleased with the large dossier I had been able to provide for the possible conversion of Bruntingthorpe. So, it seemed, was one of Chrysler's directors who flew over from America to take a close look at the project. When he suggested that the person who had compiled it ought to be the one to take the project a stage further he was told that this might be rather difficult: I had just been made redundant! An effort was made to woo me back, but by then I had

had enough of the organization, which in any case seemed about to be off-loaded by Chrysler on to Peugeot-Talbot.

For a while there was a possibility of Des O'Dell and myself setting up a small independent competitions facility, the idea being that we would take on this work on behalf of the factory, but nothing came of it in the end. Then John Surtees approached me and asked whether I would be interested in running his Formula 1 team for him. Although I was grateful for the offer, I declined because not only did I know precious little about Formula 1, but I realized that both John and I were people with very fixed ideas about the way things should be done, and I couldn't see us working together satisfactorily for any length of time.

So instead I spent the next five years helping John Sprinzel to run his string of garage businesses, after which, in 1975, it seemed to be as good a time as any to retire. Not that retirement has meant a life of idleness. Instead, it has been a time for doing all the things for which there had never seemed to be sufficient time or opportunity in the past.

My wife and I still take great enjoyment from water-colour painting and sketching whilst travelling the Continent – at a somewhat more leisurely pace than I set myself 40 years ago – and these days one of my greatest pleasures is in maintaining the many contacts from my years in motorsport and enjoying new friendships amongst people who are active in it today. In recent years this has taken on a new impetus with the seemingly ever-increasing fascination with historic rallying and racing, and I am most heartened by the thirst for knowledge about 'my' era amongst so many of the younger motorsport enthusiasts, who perhaps have grown just a little tired of seeing a sport dominated by hard-nosed professionalism, bewildering computerized technology and unbelievable sponsor-supported budgets.

We didn't have any of these things, but although we tried as hard as we knew how, we did still find time for the occasional laugh. Yes, it was hard work, but a lot of fun, going racing and rallying with my *Works Wonders*!

APPENDIX A

BMC successes in International rallies and races, 1955–1961

This Appendix lists the major successes achieved by BMC cars when driven either by the works team drivers or by works-assisted private owners from January 1, 1955 to September 30, 1961, when Marcus Chambers retired from management of the BMC Competition Department. The numbers shown in brackets after the rally titles refer to the number of starters and finishers in each event.

1955

March   *RAC Rally of Great Britain* (238/145)
        MG TF   C Shove/J Shove   1st in class
        MG Magnette G Holt/J Brooks   1st in class

June   *Scottish Rally* (67/55)
        MG TF   N Patterson/A Craig   1st in class
        MG TF   E Herrald/J Murray   2nd in class
        MG TF   R Kay/D Mickel   3rd in class
                     Team prize: MG TFs
        Austin A90   Mrs J Johns/Mrs M Inglis   Ladies' Cup

August *Liège-Rome-Liège Rally* (126/56)
        Austin A90   G Burgess/S Croft-Pearson   RAC team prize
        Austin A90   J Gott/W Shepherd   RAC team prize
                     Team prize: RAC (third car was a Jaguar)

1956

January *Monte Carlo Rally* (308/233)
        Austin A90   M Couper/P Fillingham 1st *Concours de Confort*

March   *RAC Rally of Great Britain* (213/165)
        Austin A90   Mrs J Johns/D Johns   6th overall
                                  2nd in class
        Austin A50   J Sears/K Best   3rd in class
                     Team prize: Austins

        Lyons-Charbonnières Rally (113/54)
        MG Magnette Mrs N Mitchell/Mrs D Reece   *Coupe des Dames*

May   *Tulip Rally* (220/189)
              Austin A30   R Brookes/E Brookes   1st overall
              Austin A90   J Sears/S Henson/R Bensted-Smith   2nd in class

      Geneva Rally (58/49)
              Austin A50   J Sears/K Best   1st in class
              Austin A90   J Gott/W Shepherd   2nd in class
              Austin A90   P Wilson/M Chambers   3rd in class

July   *Alpine Rally* (79/34)
              MGA hardtop   Mrs N Mitchell/Miss P Fraichney   *Coupe des Alpes, Coupe des Dames*

September *Liège-Rome-Liège Rally* (86/35)
              MGA hardtop   J Gott/C Tooley   13th overall
              MGA hardtop   J Milne/R Bensted-Smith   14th overall
              MGA hardtop   Mrs N Mitchell/Mrs A Hall   26th overall
              Team prizes (3): runners-up MGAs

1957
February *Sestriere Rally* (125/110)
              Morris Minor 1000   R Brookes/E Brookes   3rd in class

March   *Lyon-Charbonnières Rally* (96/35)
              MGA hardtop   Mrs N Mitchell/Mrs D Reece   *Coupe des Dames*

August   *Liège-Rome-Liège Rally* (102/52)
              MGA hardtop   Mrs N Mitchell/Mrs J Johns   *Coupe des Dames*

1958
March   *RAC Rally of Great Britain* (196/130)
              Morris Minor 1000   Miss P Moss/Miss A Wisdom   4th overall, Ladies' Cup, 1st in class

April   *Circuit of Ireland* (99/88)
              Riley 1.5   Miss P Moss/Miss A Wisdom   Ladies' Cup, 3rd in class

July   *Alpine Rally* (56/25)
               Austin-Healey 100-Six W Shepherd/J Williamson *Coupe des Alpes*, 7th overall, 2nd in class
              Austin-Healey 100-Six Miss P Moss/Mrs A Riley *Coupe des Dames*
              Austin-Healey Sprite J Sprinzel/W Cave   1st in class
              Austin-Healey Sprite T Wisdom/J Hay   2nd in class
               Austin-Healey Sprite R Brookes/R Wells-West   3rd in class

August   *Liège-Rome-Liège Rally* (98/22)
              Austin-Healey 100-Six Miss P Moss/Mrs A Riley   4th overall, 1st in class, *Coupe des Dames*
              Austin-Healey 100-Six G Burgess/S Croft-Pearson 10th overall, 2nd in class

Austin-Healey 100-Six Mrs N Mitchell/Mrs J Johns   15th overall
 Manufacturer's team prize: Austin-Healeys
MGA Twin-Cam   J Gott/R Brookes   9th overall, *Prix Triennial*
 Club team prize: RAC (2 Austin-Healeys and MGA)

1959

January	*Monte Carlo Rally* (322/184)		
	Austin A40	Miss P Moss/Mrs A Riley	10th overall, 2nd in class, *Coupe des Dames*
	Austin-Healey Sprite	J Sprinzel/W Cave	3rd in class

February	*Sestriere Rally* (68/42)		
	Riley 1.5	Miss P Moss/Mrs A Riley	*Coupe des Dames*
	Austin-Healey Sprite	T Wisdom/J Lucas	1st in class

	Canadian Winter Rally (162/125)		
	Austin A40	Miss P Moss/Mrs A Riley	Ladies' Cup

March	*Sebring 12-Hours*		
	MGA Twin-Cam	G Ehrman/R Saidel	2nd in class
	MGA Twin-Cam	J Parkinson/J Dalton	3rd in class
	Austin-Healey Sprite	P Stiles/H Sutherland	1st in class
	Austin-Healey Sprite	E Leavens/H Kunz	2nd in class
	Austin-Healey Sprite	J Christy/J Colgate	3rd in class

 Manufacturer's team prize: Austin-Healey Sprites*
 (*Donald Healey Motor Company entry)

	Lyon-Charbonnières Rally		
	Austin A40	Miss P Moss/Mrs A Riley	*Coupe des Dames*

	Circuit of Ireland		
	Morris Minor 1000	Miss P Moss/Mrs A Riley	Ladies' Cup, 2nd in class

May	*Tulip Rally* (169/99)		
	Austin-Healey 100-Six	J Sears/P Garnier	8th overall, 1st in class

June	*Alpine Rally* (59/27)		
	Austin-Healey Sprite	T Wisdom/J Hay	2nd in class
	Austin-Healey 3000	J Gott/C Tooley	2nd in class

September	*Liège-Rome-Liège Rally* (97/14)		
	Austin-Healey 3000	P Riley/Rev R Jones	1st in class

October	*German Rally* (64/36)		
	Austin-Healey 3000	Miss P Moss/Mrs A Riley	2nd overall, 1st in class, *Coupe des Dames*

November *RAC Rally of Great Britain* (131/53)
Austin-Healey Sprite T Gold/M Hughes 2nd overall, 1st in class
Austin-Healey 3000 D Morley/E Morley 4th overall, 1st in class
Austin-Healey 3000 J Sears/W Cave 2nd in class

December *Portuguese Rally* (86/67)
Austin-Healey 3000 Miss P Moss/Mrs A Riley *Coupe des Dames*

1960
January *Monte Carlo Rally* (307/149)
Austin A40 Miss P Moss/Mrs A Riley *Coupe des Dames*

March *Sebring 4-Hours*
Austin-Healey Sprite* S Moss 2nd overall, 1st in class
(*Donald Healey Motor Company entry)

Sebring 12-Hours
MGA Twin-Cam F Hayes/E Leavens 3rd in class
MGA Twin-Cam J Parkinson/J Flaherty 4th in class
Austin-Healey 3000* Gietner/Spencer 2nd in class
Austin-Healey 3000* P Riley/J Sears 3rd in class
Austin-Healey Sprite* J Sprinzel/J Lumkin 1st in class
(*Donald Healey Motor Company entry)

April *Geneva Rally* (77/38)
Austin-Healey 3000 Miss P Moss/Mrs A Riley 7th overall,
1st in class, *Coupe des Dames*
Austin Seven D Morley/E Morley 1st in class
Austin Seven Miss P Ozanne/Mrs P Wright 2nd in class

May *Tulip Rally* (165/114)
Austin-Healey 3000 Miss P Moss/Mrs A Riley 8th overall,
1st in class, *Coupe des Dames*
Austin-Healey 3000 D Morley/E Morley 3rd in class
Austin A105 P Riley/A Ambrose 2nd in class
Morris Mini-Minor J Sprinzel/M Hughes 2nd in class
Austin-Healey Sprite T Gold/M Wood 3rd in class

June *Alpine Rally* (66/42)
Austin-Healey 3000 Miss P Moss/Mrs A Riley *Coupe des
Alpes*, 1st in class
Austin-Healey 3000 J Gott/W Shepherd 2nd in class
Austin-Healey 3000 D Morley/E Morley 3rd in class
Team prizes (5): Austin-Healeys
Morris Mini-Minor T Gold/M Hughes 1st in class

September *Liège-Rome-Liège Rally* (82/13)
Austin-Healey 3000 Miss P Moss/Mrs A Riley 1st overall,
1st in class, *Coupe des Dames*

Austin-Healey 3000	D Seigle-Morris/V Elford	5th overall, 2nd in class
Austin-Healey 3000	J Gott/Rev R Jones	10th overall, 3rd in class

Team prizes (3): Austin-Healeys

Austin-Healey Sprite	J Patten/J Sprinzel	3rd overall, 1st in class

September *Viking Rally (64/59)*

Austin A40	Miss P Moss/Mrs A Riley	*Coupe des Dames*

October *German Rally (69/45)*

Austin-Healey 3000	D Seigle-Morris/S Turner	1st in class
Austin-Healey 3000	D Morley/B Hercock	2nd in class
Austin-Healey 3000	Miss P Moss/Mrs A Riley	3rd in class
MGA 1600	P Riley/A Ambrose	2nd in class
Austin-Healey Sprite	J Sprinzel/N Sprinzel	2nd in class

November *RAC Rally of Great Britain* (172/138)

Austin-Healey 3000	D Morley/E Morley	3rd overall, 1st in class
Austin-Healey 3000	P Riley/A Ambrose	2nd in class
Austin-Healey 3000	R Adams/J Williamson	4th in class

Manufacturer's team prize: Austin-Healeys

Morris Minor 1000	Miss P Moss/Mrs A Riley	2nd in class
Morris Mini-Minor	D Seigle-Morris/V Elford	2nd in class
Wolseley 1500	D Johns/Rev R Jones	2nd in class

1961

January *Monte Carlo Rally* (305/156)

Austin A40	Miss P Moss/Mrs A Riley	3rd in class

March *Sebring 4-Hours*

Austin-Healey Sprite*	W Hansgen	3rd overall
Austin-Healey Sprite*	B McLaren	4th overall
Austin-Healey Sprite*	S Moss	5th overall
Austin-Healey Sprite*	E Leavens	6th overall
Austin-Healey Sprite*	Miss P Moss/P Hawkins	7th overall
Austin-Healey Sprite*	B Cunningham	8th overall

(*Donald Healey Motor Company entry)

Sebring 12-Hours

MGA 1600 Coupe	J Parkinson/J Flaherty	1st in class
MGA 1600 Coupe	P Riley/J Whitmore	2nd in class
Austin-Healey Sprite*	J Buzetta/G Carlson	2nd in class
Austin-Healey Sprite*	J Colgate/E Leavens	3rd in class
Austin-Healey Sprite*	J Sprinzel/P Hawkins	4th in class

(*Donald Healey Motor Company entry)

May	*Tulip Rally* (132/113)		
	Austin-Healey 3000	Miss P Moss/Mrs A Riley	1st in class, *Coupe des Dames*
	Austin-Healey 3000	D Morley/E Morley	2nd in class
	Austin-Healey Sprite	T Gold/M Hughes	8th overall, 1st in class

Manufacturer's team prize: Austin-Healeys

Austin-Healey Sprite	J Sprinzel/M Wood	2nd in class
Morris Mini-Minor	P Riley/A Ambrose	1st in class
Morris Mini-Minor	D Seigle-Morris/V Elford	3rd in class

Acropolis Rally (76/45)

Austin-Healey 3000	P Riley/A Ambrose	3rd overall, 1st in class
Morris Mini-Minor	D Hiam/M Hughes	2nd in class

June *Midnight Sun Rally* (201/108)

Austin-Healey 3000	P Riley/A Ambrose	12th overall, 2nd in class

Alpine Rally (64/27)

Austin-Healey 3000	D Morley/E Morley*	1st overall, *Coupe des Alpes*, 1st in class
Austin-Healey 3000	J Gott/W Shepherd	3rd in class
Austin-Healey Sprite	J Sprinzel/W Cave	2nd in class

Team prizes for speed tests (2): Austin-Healeys

September *Liège-Sofia-Liège Rally* (82/8)

Austin-Healey 3000	D Seigle-Morris/A Ambrose	6th overall, 1st in class

* The Morley brothers again won the Alpine Rally in an Austin-Healey 3000 in 1962.

APPENDIX B

BMC Competition Department policy

The following is an extract from a document which each works driver received from Marcus Chambers at the end of the year, together with a covering letter indicating the events for which they were being invited to drive during the following season.

Notes to rally drivers
It is not our intention to ask you to commit yourself to a formal agreement for the season. An agreement of a formal sort will, in my opinion, produce the wrong sort of relationship between the driver and the factory. If either side should have to take steps to enforce the terms of the agreement, the relationship between the two parties will have deteriorated to the extent that it would be better severed.

What we have done is to set out a form of reasonable behaviour to which we expect works drivers to conform and in return we also set out the obligations of the factory to you.

We feel that it should be borne in mind that the policy of the factory dictates the programme of competitions for the ensuing year and as a result we cannot vary the programme to suit individuals.

At the time of writing, our competitions record has been mostly concerned with two makes, namely Austin and MG. As time goes on, it may be necessary to introduce other makes and types into the programme. Drivers should therefore be prepared to identify themselves with BMC rather than an individual make.

It is not the policy of the Competition Department to prepare cars for any event of less than International status for first grade drivers. We cannot afford to labour for National and Closed events.

We shall have a number of ex-competition cars which will be replaced by more modern vehicles and those drivers who have driven regularly for the BMC will be considered as purchasers, if genuinely willing to run a BMC car of their own.

Publicity and the press
It is the duty of a works driver to protect the good name of the factory for whom he drives. If he is not satisfied with the car any statement made to the press must be as guarded as possible. Opinions should not be aired in public. The team can get together and a friendly discussion be held, culminating in a

statement if required. If the competitor is satisfied with his performance, he is automatically satisfied with the car, and naturally says so.

We realize that most of our drivers are asked to speak at luncheons, dinners and motoring clubs about their experiences with us. We also realize that a great deal of goodwill is built up in this manner. We hope that they will be able to show suitable cars to their audiences as time goes on, either by owning an ex-Competition Department car or by having the loan of one for specific occasions.

Drivers' reports
Whilst it is not our intention to vary the specification of the vehicles to suit individuals, we do appreciate a detailed report of the car's performance in an event. If a case is made out for an alteration which can be made without infringing the rules, this alteration will be made to all the cars simultaneously. We have, for example, now standardized the rally timekeeping equipment in the Austins, and the layout seems to have met with complete approval.

Contact with the factory
This should always be through the Competition Department.

APPENDIX C

Liège-Sofia-Liège briefing notes

<u>LIÈGE—SOFIA—LIÈGE — Team Leaders' Appreciation</u>

1. <u>DOCUMENTATION</u>

The Yugoslavs and the Bulgars are both pretty 'hot' and you must have —

(i) <u>Two</u> Transit Visas for Yugoslavia.
(ii) <u>One</u> Visa for Bulgaria.
    The Visa stamped in the Passport <u>must</u> show entrance at KALOTINA and exit <u>via</u> GJUESHEVO.
    If this is not so, get it changed at once, or you will be held up at Customs and the time loss may put you out of the rally.
(iii) International Driving Licence, (grey book).

2. <u>HOW THE TIMING WORKS</u>

I hope that you have fully appreciated the implications of Article 4(a). If not, try this exercise!

Take Table II on page 39, and assume your starting time from SPA is 10.42 p.m. (as it may be for some of us). Add the times allowed for the stages cumulatively to 10.42 p.m. which, if you are not late, (and make up the time you will inevitably lose over the MOISTROCCA!), gives you an E.T.A. at ZAGREB of 03.02 a.m. — by which time reference to Table 1 on page 38 will show you that the control has been shut for over $2\frac{1}{2}$ hours, and you've had it!

In other words, if you do not consistently average a lot more than the set average and continue to build up your time in hand, you will not be penalised for being late on the road, you will just be excluded because the control will be shut when you arrive!

In addition there is the neat trick of 'neutralisation'.

Austria is 'neutralised' and that is good, because we can then have enough time to eat. However, Garot proposes to 'neutralise' the fast road between the Vivione and the Gavia, so turning them into timed climbs without letting it so appear in the Regulations.

These are the neatest stratagems ever devised for 'hoodwinking' the authorities "on paper", yet ensuring that the Liège remains the greatest road-race ever!

As in France last year, you fix your own time of booking-in, (and simultaneously booking-out), between the times that the controls are shown as being open in your road-books, but with this important difference — holding the schedule only, won't keep you in the rally.

For instance, on the run to SOFIA, starting at 10.42 p.m. you would have to make up 2 hrs. 32 mins. on schedule to arrive in time to be booked in.

In fact, we want to aim at making up around 6½ hours.

Not all drivers have appreciated this point, so don't chat about it outside the team.

3. STRATEGY

Quite clearly early numbers have an advantage as the 'control open time' is longer for them. Equally clearly later numbers must move up through the field to arrive when the controls first open, particularly at the Yugoslav and Bulgarian frontiers.

This 'go-as-you-please' system will also help us to close up the team and take it in turns to lead on the easy sections and so rest the crews.

Quite clearly, time in hand is not going only to be useful, it is going to be vital if you want to stay in the rally, and it cannot be used for meals, service, etc., unless it is absolutely essential.

4. ROUTE PATTERN

I have had a chat on the telephone with Tony Ambrose and a long talk with Jim Cardwell, (the Safari expert), who have just got back from recces. Both agree broadly, so it is quite safe to make the following prediction.

As in 1960, the rally will be won or lost between SOFIA and ROVERETO, and my guess is that a time loss of around 20 minutes would be a winning lead.

Tony will be letting us have detailed notes, but SKOPJE to SPLIT and NOVI to COL will be vital. Treat as RED.

The latter we know from last year, but the former is new and Tony says in parts it is worse than anything on the Acropolis and Jim says it is much worse than anything on the Safari — so you are warned!

There are also a lot of tourists, (mostly French 2 C.V.s), but we go up the Adriatic coast by night, so they may not be quite such a hazard as they were on the recces.

The run to SOFIA is not unduly difficult, the only sections where you are bound to lose marks being STAVELOT to MONTENAU and PREDIL to KRANJSKA GORA.

The former is as last year, but the surface is better, but the latter is 1.5 km further, as the section finishes in K.G. instead of by the Hotel Erka.

Bianchi (Porsche) and Trautman (Citroen) alone did the section 'clean' last year, and some may do it 'clean' this year.

However, losses on these two sections are not going to mean a great deal and you shouldn't strain either yourself or your car in trying to take a terrific lead so early on.

You must husband your strength and save your car for SOFIA to ROVERETO and put in a 10/10ths., (and winning) effort there.

Finally, unless the pattern is so firmly fixed by Yugoslavia that positions can only be changed by 'shunts' or mechanical failures, you might have to call on your last reserves for a final supreme effort on BAGOLINO to TRAFOI.

5. SUPPORT

Final details will come from Marcus and Oliver, but this will be on a very generous scale with penetration into Yugoslavia, for the first time.

Probable bases are—

TARVISIO, ZAGREB, NOVI, GORIZIA (but there may be others), and the cars will follow us up.

6. FINALLY THIS —

We have the toughest rally cars in the business, and the best support and preparation. We know what we are up against and how to cope. We have the firmest determination to repeat our 1960 showing — and we will!

The best of luck,

See you at Southend,

John GOTT.

P.S. Copies have been sent to all the crews and David Hiam.

21st August, 1961

M. Chambers, Esq.,
Competitions Department,
British Motor Corporation,
ABINGDON-ON-THAMES,
Berks.

APPENDIX D

Liège-Sofia-Liège spares listing

Austin Healey 3000

LIÈGE—SOFIA—LIÈGE 1961
Spares to be carried in Tender Car

1 Reverse Lamp
1 Fan Belt Healey
1 R/Counter Healey
1 Complete 3000 gasket set
1 Set front hub shims
1 Accel. Cable Healey
2 Front Hub Seals Healey
2 Rear Hub Seals Healey
1 Qt. Tin Amber Brake Fluid
1 Soldering Iron & solder
1 Hand Drill Tools
1 Front Hub R/H & L/H complete
1 Rear Hub complete 576 Fog Lamps
1 SLR   "   "
1 Coil Electric Wire
1 Squirt Gun
1 Kit Mec. Tools
1 Hand Soap Nuts, Bolts, Washers, Split Pins
1 Roll insulating tape
1 Roll masking tape
2 off every type bulb in each car
1 Yellow jack
1 Tow Rope
1 Tow Bar complete
1 Roll mutton cloth
1 Foot pump

1 Coil Locking wire
1 First Aid Kit
1 Healey King Pin
2 Headlamps 700 LHD
2 Track Rods — Healey
1 Petrol Can
1 Set brake pads 421
1 Set water hoses — Healey
1 Healey rocker
1 Push rod
1 Distributor Top Plate — Healey
1 Set brake flex pipes — Healey
1 Triangle sign
1 Speedo cable 5'/6" MGA
1 Speedo dual drive
1 R/Counter Cable 1B9140
1 Safety Gauge
1 Trip Recorder
1 Fuse Box
1 Relay
1 Control Box
1 Dynamo brkt.
1 Oil gauge pipe
1   "   "   flex pipe
1 Tapered dolly
1 Water pump
2 Wiper motors
1 Welding Kit
1 1lb. Tin BNS Grease
1 Special G/Box Oil Seal
1 Sponge

2 Eolopresses
6 N9Y Plugs
1 5.50 x 15 Inner
   Tubes
   Assorted Petrol
   Flexes
   Carb. return springs
2 Stop & tail lamps —
   Healey
1 Clutch flex hose —
   Healey
1 Overdrive solenoid —
   Healey
1 Overdrive switch
   Healey G/Box
12 Rear Hub nuts — Healey
1 Dynamo 22724A
3 Galls. XL
   Grease Gun filled
1 Clutch oil seals
   Tools (special)
   Box selected switches
   etc.
1 HT 12 coil
2 7lb. Rad. caps

1 Leather
1 Tyre Gauge
1 Brake Master Cylinder
1 Clutch   "   "
1   "   Slave cylinder
2 U bolts
1 Clutch plate
1 Marchal Lead Lamp

APPENDIX E

Stelvio Pass timing notes

KM.	Points for check and comments.	Ideal TIME.
—	TRAFOI.	
	Cars may well be started three abreast, — or however many of group are left — and it is most important that you take the lead into the first fairly sharp RIGHT hand corner about 100 yards after the start; this is tarmacadam.	
.3	Hairpin No. 4 — No 48 is the top one!!	00.30"
	Almost immediately you are onto dust surface, but is fast up amongst trees.	
	All the hairpins are concreted, and an MGA will go round in one swing. If wet, you may get spin. In any case you will probably want bottom gear round the hairpins.	
	The hairpins are numbered on the outside of the corner, i.e. on the side facing you, and your co-driver should check them.	
	Nos. 8 to 13 hairpins are in a tight group, and you may want bottom gear the whole way over this group.	
4.2	Red building on right of road — Magazino	7' 10"
7.5	Hairpin No. 27 — check by road coming in on left of apex.	10' 25"
	From now onto the summit you may have cloud, but it is easy to pick up the hairpins. After hairpin No. 48 there is approx 250 yards to the summit,	

	where there may be lights in the big hotel on the left.	
14.2	Summit.	19' 15"
	Straight over small plateau and downhill about 100 yards for LEFT hand hairpin — loose surface.	
17.5	CUSTOMS HOUSE, on right — you don't have to stop!!	22' 30"
	HAIRPIN LEFT, (loose and probably banked-up dirt), into Italy.	
	There are now some long straights downhill where you can really get cracking — do so!	
22.5	Watch for Kilometre stone on left, reading Bormio 14.5 Km.	28' 00"
	Almost immediately you will come on a series of SIX hairpins on loose dirt.	
26.7	Hairpin LEFT, (yellow building on right).	33' 30"
	Very soon FIVE rock tunnels, (marked Galleria!), will be coming up. Treat with caution — they are very slippery, (wet cobbles), and I have known of cars sliding sideways and blocking the road. The last tunnel comes just after a large red building, (road repair depot) marked SS 98, on your left.	
30.2	Hairpin LEFT and you are onto tarmacadam surface once more. 6.5 km to go — pull out all stops.	36' 00"
32.3	Rock archway — may be loose gravel surface for about 200 yards. 3.5 km to go, to commencement of town, another .5 km. to control.	38' 30"
	Very fast now.	
	Watch for Elongated 'S' bend, Right hand and then LEFT hand semi hairpin, downhill, but partly banked.	

36.3   Control will probably be centre
        of town, on your Right, out-
        side station.   42' 00"

Notes. 1. Distances are for your guidance only,
           and you should not rely 100% on
           them, as they may be upset by
           wheelspin.
        2. In any case, I have always made the
           run more than the 35 km. given in
           the Road-Book. Michelin makes it
           36.5 km: T.C.I. 36.8 km., and I
           reckon it is well over 35 km.
           However, the under-estimate is the
           same for all!
        3. The ideal times are for guidance
           only, if you hold them you should
           be O.K., but don't worry if you
           don't. Last year the fastest MGA
           did 43' 44" and the slowest 44' 32",
           but you should beat these!

Bibliography

Maintaining the Breed John W Thornley, 4th Ed 1990 (Motor Racing Publications)
Marathon Nick Brittan, 1969 (Motor Racing Publications)
Why Finish Last? Andrew Cowan, 1969 (Queen Anne Press)
Tiger: The Making of a Sports Car Mike Taylor, 1979 (Gentry Books)
Tiger, Alpine, Rapier Richard Langworth, 1982 (Osprey Publishing)
Hillman Imps T C Millington, 1969 (Foulis/Haynes)
Apex: The Inside Story of the Hillman Imp David & Peter Henshaw, 1988 (Bookmarque Publishing)
The Works Minis Peter Browning, 1971 (Haynes)
The BMC/BL Competitions Department Bill Price, 1989 (Foulis/Haynes)
Austin-Healey: The Story of the Big Healeys Geoffrey Healey, 1977 (Wilton House Gentry/Haynes)